T0334344

SOCIAL MEDIA AND CRISIS COMMUNICATION

The second edition of this vital text integrates theory, research, and application to orient readers to the latest thinking about the role of social media in crisis communication.

Specific crisis arenas such as health, corporate, nonprofit, religious, political, and disaster are examined in depth, along with social media platforms and newer technology. *Social Media and Crisis Communication, Second Edition* provides a fresh look at the role of visual communication in social media and a more global review of social media and crisis communication literature. With an enhanced focus on the ethics section, a short communication overview piece, and case studies for each area of application, it is practical for use in a variety of learning settings.

A must-read for scholars, advanced students, and practitioners who wish to stay on the leading edge of research, this book will appeal to those in public relations, strategic communications, corporate communications, government and NGO communications, and emergency and disaster response.

Yan Jin (PhD, University of Missouri) is a Professor of Public Relations and the Georgia Athletic Association Professor at Grady College of Journalism and Mass Communication, University of Georgia. She has authored more than 90 peer-reviewed journal articles and over 20 book chapters. She is the lead editor of *Advancing Crisis Communication Effectiveness: Integrating Public Relations Scholarship with Practice* (2021) and co-editor of the first edition of *Social Media and Crisis Communication* (2017), both published by Routledge. She received the 2019 Kitty O. Locker Outstanding Researcher Award from the Association for Business Communication and is an elected member of the Arthur W. Page Society.

Lucinda Austin (PhD, University of Maryland) is an Associate Professor and PhD Program Director in the Hussman School of Journalism and Media, the University of North Carolina at Chapel Hill. She is co-editor of *Social Media and Crisis Communication* (First Edition) and has published in *Communication Research,*

Journal of Applied Communication Research, Journal of Public Relations Research, Public Relations Review, etc. She received the Association for Education in Journalism and Mass Communication's (AEJMC's) Promising Professors Award, AEJMC Public Relations Division's (PRD's) SuPRstar Award, the Page Center's Legacy Educator and Scholar Awards, and NCA's PRIDE Award. She is AEJMC PRD head (2021–2022).

SOCIAL MEDIA AND CRISIS COMMUNICATION

Second Edition

Edited by Yan Jin and Lucinda Austin

Routledge
Taylor & Francis Group

NEW YORK AND LONDON

Cover image: © koyu / Getty Images

Second edition published 2022
by Routledge
605 Third Avenue, New York, NY 10158

and by Routledge
2 Park Square, Milton Park, Abingdon, Oxon, OX14 4RN

Routledge is an imprint of the Taylor & Francis Group, an informa business

First edition published by Routledge 2017

Library of Congress Cataloging-in-Publication Data
Names: Austin, Lucinda L., editor. | Jin, Yan (Sociologist), editor.
Title: Social media and crisis communication / edited by Lucinda Austin
and Yan Jin.
Description: Second edition. | New York, NY : Routledge, 2022. | Includes
bibliographical references and index. |
Identifiers: LCCN 2021041528 (print) | LCCN 2021041529 (ebook) |
ISBN 9780367488994 (hardback) | ISBN 9780367489007 (paperback) |
ISBN 9781003043409 (ebook)
Subjects: LCSH: Communication in crisis management. | Social media.
Classification: LCC HD49.3 .S629 2022 (print) | LCC HD49.3
(ebook) | DDC 658.4/5--dc23/eng/20211019
LC record available at https://lccn.loc.gov/2021041528
LC ebook record available at https://lccn.loc.gov/2021041529

ISBN: 9780367488994 (hbk)
ISBN: 9780367489007 (pbk)
ISBN: 9781003043409 (ebk)

DOI: 10.4324/9781003043409

Typeset in Bembo
by KnowledgeWorks Global Ltd.

CONTENTS

FIGURES

TABLES

CONTRIBUTORS

Editors

Yan Jin (PhD, University of Missouri) is a Professor of Public Relations and the Georgia Athletic Association Professor at Grady College of Journalism and Mass Communication, University of Georgia. She has authored more than 90 peer-reviewed journal articles and over 20 book chapters. She is the lead editor of *Advancing Crisis Communication Effectiveness: Integrating Public Relations Scholarship with Practice* (2021) and co-editor of the first edition of *Social Media and Crisis Communication* (2017), both published by Routledge. She received the 2019 Kitty O. Locker Outstanding Researcher Award from the Association for Business Communication and is an elected member of the Arthur W. Page Society.

Lucinda Austin (PhD, University of Maryland) is an Associate Professor and PhD Program Director in the Hussman School of Journalism and Media, University of North Carolina at Chapel Hill. She is co-editor of *Social Media and Crisis Communication* (First Edition) and has published in *Communication Research, Journal of Applied Communication Research, Journal of Public Relations Research, Public Relations Review*, etc. She received the Association for Education in Journalism and Mass Communication's (AEJMC's) Promising Professors Award, AEJMC Public Relations Division's (PRD's) SuPRstar Award, the Page Center's Legacy Educator and Scholar Awards, and NCA's PRIDE Award. She is AEJMC PRD head (2021–2022).

Chapter Authors

Lucinda Austin (PhD, University of Maryland) is an Associate Professor and PhD Program Director in the Hussman School of Journalism and Media, University of North Carolina at Chapel Hill. Austin's research focuses on social media's influence on strategic communication initiatives and explores publics' perspectives in corporate social responsibility and organization–public relationship building.

Mark Badham (PhD) is a Senior Lecturer in Corporate Communication at Jyväskylä University School of Business & Economics, Finland. His research is focused on news media roles in mass communication processes, as well as crisis communication in digital arenas, social media engagement, relationship management, and organizational legitimacy.

Hamilton Bean (PhD) is an Associate Professor in the Department of Communication at the University of Colorado Denver. His most recent book, *Mobile Technology and the Transformation of Public Alert and Warning* (2019), provides a comprehensive account of how mobile-smartphone systems are transforming the practice of public alert and warning in the United States and internationally. The book earned the 2021 Sue DeWine Distinguished Scholarly Book Award from the Applied Communication Division of the National Communication Association. His research also appears in journals including the *Journal of Applied Communication Research*, *Journal of Contingencies and Crisis Management*, and *Natural Hazard Review*.

Rebecca Fuller Beeler (PhD) is a communications professional with expertise in crisis communication, issues management, and internal communication. She has worked with a national disaster relief organization, in higher education and in healthcare, in each setting focusing on meeting audience needs using a variety of communication tools and strategic leader communication. Her research interests include leadership communication in global and changing organizations.

Vince Benigni (PhD) is a Professor of Communication at the College of Charleston. His research focuses on the impact of mediated communication on sport, primarily from a fandom and social perception standpoint. In addition, he regularly contributes to the study of public relations pedagogy. He has nearly four decades of experience in the fields of sport communication and public relations.

Marilyn Broggi (MA, University of Georgia) is a doctoral candidate in the Department of Advertising and Public Relations, Grady College of Journalism and Mass Communication, University of Georgia. Her research examines consumers' information processing and subsequent behavioral outcomes associated with exposure to native advertising.

Natalie Brown-Devlin (PhD) is an Assistant Professor in the Stan Richards School of Advertising & Public Relations and the Associate Director for Research in the Center for Sports Communication & Media at the University of Texas at Austin. Her research interests examine sports media, crisis communication, and digital media.

Feifei Chen (PhD, Texas A&M University) is an Assistant Professor in the Department of Communication at the College of Charleston. Her research interests focus on social-mediated public relations, including risk and crisis communication, issues management, corporate social responsibility, and nonprofit communication.

Yang Cheng (PhD) is an Assistant Professor at North Carolina State University. Her research interests include corporate artificial intelligence, relationship management, and crisis communication. Dr Cheng has rich experience with marketing and social science research and has published numerous articles in top journals such as *New Media & Society, American Behavioral Scientist, International Journal of Communication, Telematics and Informatics, Journal of Contingencies and Crisis Management*, and *Public Relations Review*. She has also received many awards and honors from global institutions.

Minhee Choi (PhD, University of South Carolina) is an Assistant Professor in the Robertson School of Media and Culture at Virginia Commonwealth University. Her research interests center on strategic communication with a particular focus on advocacy and activism by examining the effects of communication strategies related to various controversial social issues. Before academia, she worked with international nonprofit organizations.

An-Sofie Claeys (PhD, Ghent University & Royal Military Academy) is an Assistant Professor of Corporate Communication at the Department of Translation, Interpreting and Communication of Ghent University in Belgium. Her research interests include verbal and non-verbal crisis communication, stealing thunder, and emotions in crisis communication. Her work has been published in the *Journal of Communication, Communication Theory, Public Relations Review*, and *Journal of Public Relations Research*.

W. Timothy Coombs (PhD, Purdue University in Public Affairs and Issues Management) is the George T and Glady H Abell Professor in Liberal Arts in the Department of Communication at Texas A&M University. His primary areas of research are crisis communication and corporate social responsibility (CSR), including the award-winning book *Ongoing Crisis Communication*. His research has appeared in *Management Communication Quarterly, Public Relations Review, Corporate Reputation Review, Journal of Public Relations Research, Journal of Communication Management, Business Horizons*, and the *Journal of Business Communication*.

Cheyenne Dalton graduated from North Carolina State University with her master of science degree in communication. Her research interests include public relations and crisis communication. Currently, she is a communications specialist located in North Carolina.

Aurélie De Waele (PhD, KU Leuven) is a part-time professor and post-doctoral researcher at the University of Antwerp (Belgium) and a lecturer at KU Leuven (Belgium) in the field of corporate communication. Her research mainly focuses on crisis communication. Her work has been published in *Communication Research, Public Relations Review, Journal of Nonverbal Behavior,* and *Journal of Applied Communication Research.*

Audra Diers-Lawson (PhD, University of Texas at Austin) is an Associate Professor and Senior Researcher in Strategic Communication in the Department of Communication, Leadership, and Marketing at Kristiania University College in Norway. She is presently the Crisis Section Chair for the European Communication Research and Education Association and editor of the *Journal of International Crisis and Risk Communication Research.* Her research focuses on the relationships between organizations, stakeholders, and the issues affecting them.

Melissa D. Dodd (PhD, APR) is an Associate Professor, Advertising-Public Relations, at the Nicholson School of Communication and Media, University of Central Florida. Dodd has presented her award-winning research about activism/advocacy, CSA, CSR, and social capital around the world and has published in discipline-leading journals. She was named Arthur W. Page Center Legacy Scholar for her corporate social advocacy research, a term she coined, and has since studied hundreds of instances of corporate controversial issues engagement.

Silvia Dumitrescu is the Vice President, Communications, for the International Food Information Council, working with subject-matter experts and the communications team to raise awareness and improve understanding of food science from farm to fork. She leads internal and external communications, including digital strategy and media relations, as well as strategic engagement initiatives. Silvia holds an MBA from American University and an executive certification from Columbia Business School.

LaShonda L. Eaddy (PhD, APR) is an Assistant Professor of Public Relations at Penn State University. Dr. Eaddy is a crisis history expert and investigates ways that crisis history can inform crisis communications scholarship and crisis communication strategy. The self-proclaimed "practitioner scholar" is passionate about public relations research as well as practice. She is accredited in public relations (APR) and has spent time as a public relations professional, primarily in the healthcare industry.

Heather Davis Epkins (PhD, University of Maryland) is the Communications Director for Maryland Governor Larry Hogan's Coordinating Offices. For over

20 years, she has served as strategic communications lead for local, state, and federal government on Capitol Hill, corporations, associations, and nonprofits. She has experience as a journalist and has taught for Maryland, Johns Hopkins, Towson, and other local institutions. Her research on national security reporters and terrorism has international reach and has appeared in several publications including the *Journal of Media, War, & Conflict*. She is a former START Fellow (UMCP), and serves as a board member for PRSA Chesapeake Chapter.

James D. Firth (MBA, University of New Hampshire) is a strategic communications and public affairs executive. He served as a senior vice president at Exelon Corporation, a Fortune 100 energy company based in Chicago. Firth led the company's communications organization, where he oversaw corporate communications, internal communications, public advocacy, and corporate giving. Firth serves on the boards of WTTW/WFMT, Chicago's public television and radio stations, and Chicago's Boys and Girls Clubs. He is also an Arthur W. Page Society member.

Finn Frandsen (PhD) is a Professor of Corporate Communication in the Department of Management at Aarhus BSS, Aarhus University and currently also serving as Professor II in the Department of Communication and Culture at BI Norwegian Business School, Oslo. His primary research interests include crisis management and crisis communication, internal crisis communication, visual crisis communication, crisis consulting, and organizational legitimacy. He is the co-editor of *Organizational Crisis Communication: A Multivocal Approach* (2017), and *Crisis Communication, Handbooks of Communication Science* (2020).

Karla K. Gower (PhD) is the Behringer Distinguished Professor and Director of the Plank Center for Leadership in Public Relations in the College of Communication and Information Sciences at the University of Alabama. She holds a PhD from the University of North Carolina at Chapel Hill. Dr Gower has published more than 45 journal articles, book chapters, and encyclopedia entries. She is the author of *Public Relations and the Press: The Troubled Embrace* and a supplemental textbook on legal and ethical considerations for public relations practice.

W. Scott Guthrie is a doctoral student in the Grady College of Journalism and Mass Communication at the University of Georgia. He has previously served as a research assistant for the Virtual Fitness Buddy project with the National Institutes of Health. Scott investigates virtual reality communication and explores how virtual experiences affect and influence real world behaviors and attitudes.

Jennifer L. Harker (PhD, University of North Carolina at Chapel Hill) is an Assistant Professor of Strategic Communication in the Reed College of Media at West Virginia University. Dr Harker researches sport communication, stakeholder perceptions, and networks.

Amy A. Hasinoff is an Associate Professor in the Department of Communication at the University of Colorado Denver. Her book *Sexting Panic* (2015) is about the well-intentioned but problematic responses to sexting in mass media, law, and education and won the National Communication Association Diamond Anniversary book award in 2016. Her research also appears in journals such as *New Media & Society, Critical Studies in Media Communication*, and *Feminist Media Studies.*

Eve R. Heffron (MA) is a doctoral student at the University of Florida's Department of Public Relations. Her research interests include relationship management, corporate social advocacy, and corporate purpose communication. She currently serves as Teaching Chair, AEJMC Graduate Student Interest Group. Heffron earned her BA in International and Global Studies and MA in Communication from the University of Central Florida with certificates in Corporate Communication and Intelligence and National Security. In 2019, Heffron was awarded UCF's Outstanding Master's Thesis Award.

Sherry J. Holladay (PhD, Purdue University) is a Professor of Communication at Texas A&M University in College Station, Texas. Her research interests include crisis communication, issues management, corporate social responsibility and irresponsibility, and activism. Her work has appeared in *Public Relations Review, Management Communication Quarterly, Journal of Public Relations Research*, and *International Journal of Strategic Communication.* She is co-editor of the *Handbook of Crisis Communication* and co-author of *It's Not Just PR: Public Relations in Society* and *Managing Corporate Social Responsibility.*

Valerie Hum is an Associate at a leading global consumer internet company founded in Singapore, focusing on corporate communications. Prior to this, she was an Executive at a strategic communications consultancy that specializes in corporate and financial communications and was a Public Affairs intern at a global investment firm headquartered in Singapore. Valerie graduated from Singapore Management University with a Bachelor of Social Sciences in Political Science and Communication Management.

Yan Jin (PhD, University of Missouri) is the Georgia Athletic Association Professor and a Professor of Public Relations at Grady College of Journalism and Mass Communication, University of Georgia. She is also the Associate

Director of Center for Health & Risk Communication and Co-Founder of the Crisis Communication Think Tank at the University of Georgia. Her work serves as a framework for crisis management and risk communication in a rapidly evolving media landscape and amidst emotionally charged conflict situations.

Winni Johansen (PhD) is a Professor of Corporate Communication in the Department of Management at Aarhus BSS, Aarhus University, and currently also serves as Professor II in the Department of Communication and Culture at BI Norwegian Business School, Oslo. Her primary research interests include crisis management and crisis communication, internal crisis communication, and crisis consulting. She is the co-editor of *Organizational Crisis Communication: A Multivocal, Approach* (2017), *International Encyclopedia of Strategic Communication* (2018), and *Crisis Communication, Handbooks of Communication Science* (2020).

Seoyeon Kim (PhD, University of North Carolina at Chapel Hill) is an Assistant Professor of Advertising and Public Relations at the University of Alabama. Kim's research focuses on public relations functions of corporate social responsibility and health/crisis communication.

Debbie Lee is an Associate at a leading consumer internet company founded in Singapore, focusing on talent engagement. Debbie most recently held the role of executive at a strategic communications consultancy with operations in Singapore, New York, and Dublin, where she played a pivotal role in providing public relations counsel to emerging technology firms in sectors such as blockchain and insurtech. Debbie graduated from Lee Kong Chian School of Business at Singapore Management University (SMU), specializing in Communications Management and Marketing.

Yen-I Lee (PhD, University of Georgia) is an Assistant Professor of Strategic Communication in the Edward R. Murrow College of Communication at Washington State University. Her primary research is in the areas of health communication and strategic communication, focusing on the role of messaging content, technology use, visual attention, and emotions in the context of health crisis and risk communication.

Weihui Leow received her Bachelor of Arts in English Language from the National University of Singapore and her Master of Mass Communication from the Nanyang Technological University, Singapore. She is currently working in corporate communications, with a focus on branding, marketing communications, and public relations.

Richard Levick (Esq.) is Chairman and CEO of LEVICK, representing countries and companies in the highest-stakes global communications matters.

He was honored multiple times on the prestigious list of "The 100 Most Influential People in the Boardroom" and has been named to multiple professional Halls of Fame for lifetime achievement. He is the co-author of four books and is a regular commentator on television and in print.

Hayoung Sally Lim is a doctoral candidate in the Stan Richards School of Advertising & Public Relations at the University of Texas at Austin. Her research examines brand crisis communication, brand identification, and consumer brand relationship management on social media.

Jason Shi-yang Lim is an Assistant Manager at the Agency for Integrated Care Singapore, currently supporting the Electronic Financial Assistance Schemes System (eFASS) which is a nation-wide system for application of financial assistance schemes. He was previously a public relations manager in town councils managing feedback from residents and the media. He graduated from RMIT University with a Bachelor of Communication (Mass Communication) with distinction and completed his Master of Mass Communication from the Nanyang Technological University, Singapore.

Matias Lievonen (DSc, Econ.) is a Postdoctoral Researcher in Corporate Communication at the Jyvaskyla University School of Business and Economics, Finland. His prior research has focused on stakeholder and consumer engagement behaviors in online brand communities and social media.

Wenlin Liu (PhD, University of Southern California) is an Assistant Professor of Strategic Communication in the Jack J. Valenti School of Communication, University of Houston. Liu's research focuses on social media-mediated disaster communication, interorganizational alliance building, and multiethnic community building using a social network approach.

Gindelin Low is a Senior Executive at an independent communications consultancy in Singapore that focuses on delivering analysis-driven integrated communications strategies. Her experience in running communications and media relations campaigns extends across a wide array of industries and verticals, including pharmaceutical, energy, logistics, and consumer/lifestyle clients. In her prior capacity, she served as a consultant with a strategic communications agency and played a crucial role in providing counsel to an extensive portfolio of clients including healthcare, retail and nonprofit organizations. Gindelin graduated from Lee Kong Chian School of Business at Singapore Management University (SMU), specializing in Communications Management and Marketing.

Xuerong Lu (MS, The Ohio State University) is a doctoral candidate at the Grady College of Journalism and Mass Communication, University of Georgia.

Her primary research areas focus on how publics respond to competing and conflicting information (e.g., misinformation vs. corrective information) spread on social media in times of public health crisis or risk situations.

Vilma Luoma-aho (PhD) is a Professor of Corporate Communication and Vice Dean at the School of Business and Economics (JSBE), University of Jyvaskyla, Finland. She has published many articles and books related to arenas, stakeholders, and intangible assets, and her research currently focuses on disinformation, brands, influencers, and young people in social media.

Carmen Daniela Maier (PhD) is an Associate Professor at the School of Communication and Culture, Aarhus University, Denmark. Her research interests revolve around corporate communication issues and include, among others, crisis communication, corporate social responsibility (CSR) communication, environmental communication, social semiotics, and multimodal communication.

Itsaso Manias-Muñoz (PhD, University of the Basque Country UPV/ EHU) is an Assistant Professor of Journalism at the University of the Basque Country, Spain. Her research interests pivot on organizational communication, crisis communication, crisis management, strategic communication, (slow) journalism, and mass media. She is a member of the research group Media, Society & Education (HGH) of the same institution, where she collaborates in different research projects. Prior to her academic career, she worked as a communication manager for various companies and projects.

Alessandra Mazzei is an Associate Professor of Corporate Communication at Università IULM, where she is also Coordinator of the bachelor program in Corporate Communication and Public Relations, Deputy Director of the Department of Business LECB "Carlo A. Ricciardi", and Director of the Centre for Employee Relations and Communication. Her main research interests are corporate communication, employee communication and engagement, organizational voice, silence and dissent, diversity and inclusion, and internal crisis communication.

Jordan Morehouse (PhD, University of North Carolina at Chapel Hill) is an Assistant Professor of Strategic Communication in the Department of Communication at Clemson University. Her major research areas include engagement, relationship management, religious communication, and nonprofit organizations. Her work has been published in the *Journal of Public Relations Research*, *Public Relations Review*, *American Behavioral Scientist*, and *Journal of International Crisis and Risk Communication Research*. Jordan is a 2021–2022 Page/Johnson Legacy Scholar of the Arthur W. Page Center for Integrity in Public Communication.

Brooke W. McKeever (PhD) is an Associate Professor in the School of Journalism and Mass Communications at the University of South Carolina. Her research focuses on nonprofit and health communication. She has published numerous articles and received awards for research and teaching. Before earning a PhD and an Interdisciplinary Health Communication Certificate from the University of North Carolina-Chapel Hill, McKeever worked for a public relations agency in Chicago and for nonprofit organizations such as St. Jude Children's Research Hospital.

Dean Mundy (PhD) is an Associate Professor, Public Relations at the University of Oregon's School of Journalism and Communication. His research focuses on the role public relations plays in fostering diverse and inclusive organizations and how organizations convey those values to key internal and external stakeholders. He also explores advocacy communication, specifically through the lens of LGBTQ organizations at the local and state levels. Mundy has presented his research at premier conferences and has published in leading PR journals.

Xian Hui Ng has been a journalist, public relations practitioner, and now a full-time fundraiser. She received her Bachelor of Science (BSc) in Banking and Finance from the Singapore Institute of Management and a Master of Mass Communication from the Nanyang Technological University.

Lan Ni (PhD, University of Maryland) is a Professor in the Valenti School of Communication at the University of Houston. Her research focuses on intercultural public relations, understanding publics, relationship management, and community engagement. She has received research grants from agencies including the National Science Foundation and Urban Communication Foundation. She is the lead author of *Intercultural Public Relations: Theories for Managing Relationships and Conflicts with Strategic Publics* (Routledge, 2018).

Augustine Pang (Ph.D.) is a Professor of Communication Management (Practice) at the Lee Kong Chian School of Business, Singapore Management University (SMU). He is a Lee Kong Chian Fellow at SMU and is appointed as Academic Director, MSc in Communication Management. His research interests include crisis management and communication, image/reputation management and repair, media management, and communication management. He is an Honorary Fellow at Hong Kong Polytechnic University and a Fellow of SMU Academy.

Jonathan Peters (JD, PhD) is a Media Law Professor at the University of Georgia, where he has faculty appointments in the College of Journalism and Mass Communication and the School of Law. He is the press freedom correspondent for Columbia Journalism Review and a co-author of the book *The Law of Public Communication*. He has written for *Esquire*, *The Atlantic*, *Sports*

Illustrated, *Slate*, *Wired*, and *CNN* and blogged about the First Amendment for Harvard Law Review and Harvard Law and Policy Review.

Lance Porter (PhD) is the Class of 1941 Alumni Professor at Louisiana State University. He directs the Social Media Analysis and Creation (SMAC) Lab in the Manship School of Mass Communication. He holds a joint appointment with LSU's interdisciplinary Center for Computation and Technology (CCT), where he is the area lead in the cultural computing focus area. With over 25 years of experience in digital media, his research focuses on emerging media and cultural studies.

Silvia Ravazzani (PhD) is an Associate Professor in Management at the Department of Business LECB "Carlo A. Ricciardi", Università IULM, Italy. Her research interests revolve around corporate communication issues and include, among others, CSR/business ethics, digital/social media, crisis and employee communication.

Bryan H. Reber (PhD) is a C. Richard Yarbrough Professor in Crisis Communication Leadership and Head of the Department of Advertising and Public Relations at the College of Journalism and Mass Communication, University of Georgia. He holds a PhD in Journalism from the University of Missouri. Dr Reber has published over 50 journal articles, book chapters, and encyclopedia entries. He is co-author of the book *Gaining Influence in Public Relations: The Role of Resistance in Practice* and three top-selling public relations textbooks.

John Rich is an expert on exponentially advancing technologies (from machine intelligence to genetic editing) that are upending our behavior, businesses, governments, and lives. As a futurist using the framework of the Law of Accelerating Returns, Rich consults with and speaks to individuals and organizations to identify the trends and actions that create the greatest opportunities for a preferred future. His specialties include speaking and presentations, technology forecasting, technology conference development, exponential thinking workshops, and innovation lab design.

Brett W. Robertson (PhD, University of Texas at Austin) is an Assistant Professor in the School of Journalism and Mass Communications at the University of South Carolina. He studies communication technology use in organizational, risk, and mass communication contexts. His research projects explore how individuals use social media and mobile devices in the workplace and disaster-related contexts. Much of his recent focus has been on disaster preparedness and prevention communication.

Matthew W. Seeger (PhD) is a Professor of Communication at Wayne State. His work on crisis communication includes *Effective Crisis Communication* (2007), *Theorizing Crisis Communication* (2014, 2020), *Crisis and Emergency Risk Communication* (Second Edition, 2015), *Narratives of Crisis: Stories of Ruin and Renewal* (2016), and the *International Handbook of Crisis Communication* (2016). He was the founding editor of the *Journal of International Crisis and Risk Communication Research* (JICRCR). He has been quoted in the *Washington Post*, *New York Times*, *Atlanta Journal-Constitution*, and *Rolling Stone*.

Deanna D. Sellnow (PhD) is a Luminary Professor of Strategic Communication and Assistant Director in the Nicholson School of Communication and Media at the University of Central Florida. Her research focuses on strategic instructional communication in health, risk, and crisis contexts. She has conducted funded research for a variety of government agencies and collaborates regularly with colleagues across the globe to conduct and present research, which appears in numerous national and international journals, communication encyclopedias, edited books, and textbooks.

Timothy L. Sellnow (PhD) is a Professor of Strategic Communication at the University of Central Florida. His research focuses on risk and crisis communication. He has published many articles and six books on risk and crisis communication, and he has conducted funded research for the Department of Homeland Security, the United States Department of Agriculture, the Centers for Disease Control and Prevention, the Environmental Protection Agency, the United States Geological Survey, and the World Health Organization.

Tamika Sims (PhD) is the Senior Director of Food Technology Communications for the International Food Information Council. Dr. Sims leads science communication efforts focused on food safety, biotechnology, agricultural sustainability, and other related food production areas. Sims holds a BS in Biology from Spelman College, MS in Biomedical Science (with an emphasis in Microbiology) from Georgia State University, and a PhD in Virology and Immunology from Morehouse School of Medicine.

Rodrigo Soares has more than 15 years of experience as a practitioner in the communication field, holding leadership positions in multinational companies such as Shell and Vale. He is currently completing his doctoral degree at the University of Central Florida. His research focuses on risk and crisis communication in health and organizational settings. He holds an MA in Communication from UCF, an MBA from IBMEC-Brazil, and executive certification from MIT Sloan School of Management and Stanford Graduate School of Business.

Cylor Spaulding (PhD, University of Miami) is an Assistant Professor in the Department of Communications at California State University, Fullerton. Prior to this, he held academic and administrative positions at Georgetown University and Towson University and spent a decade working in public relations agencies. His research focuses on public relations and its intersections with history, religion, and the LGBTQ community.

Tomeeka Spruill graduated from North Carolina State University with her master of science degree in communication. Her research interests include public relations and crisis communication. Currently, she is a social media community manager located in North Carolina.

Keri K. Stephens (PhD) is a Professor of Organizational Communication Technology and Co-Director of Technology & Information Policy Institute (TIPI), and she manages the OPTICLab in the Moody College of Communication at the University of Texas at Austin. She examines the role of technology in organizational practices and organizing processes, especially in contexts of crisis, disaster, and health. She has authored over 85 articles, and her most recent books are *New Media in Times of Crisis* (Routledge, 2019) and *Negotiating Control: Organizations and Mobile Communication* (Oxford, 2018).

Toni G. L. A. van der Meer (PhD) is an Associate Professor in Corporate Communication at the Amsterdam School of Communication Research (ASCoR), University of Amsterdam, Netherlands. His research interests include crisis communication, news framing, processes of mediatization, misinformation, and (negativity) bias in the supply and demand side of news.

Taylor S. Voges (MS, Texas Christian University) is a doctoral candidate at the Grady College of Journalism and Mass Communication, University of Georgia. She studies public relations and ethics with interest in conflicts, decision-making, and legal issues. She has been published in *Public Relations Review* and the *Journal of International Crisis and Risk Communication Research*. She has worked on a Page Center–funded project. In 2020, she received an AEJMC Top Student Paper Award and an NCA Top Paper Panel Participant Award.

Joseph Watson, Jr. (JD, Harvard University) is the Carolyn Caudell Tieger Professor of Public Affairs Communications at the University of Georgia and directs the first-in-the-nation Public Affairs Communications Program there. Watson has over 20 years of experience in campaigns and communications. He served as an appointee in the Administration of President George W. Bush, served as a senior aide to former US Senator Peter G. Fitzgerald, and established and led the public advocacy group for Fortune 100 company, Exelon Corporation.

Logan White has had a lifelong passion for both writing and communications. She graduated magna cum laude from the University of Georgia with a Master's in Integrated Advertising and Public Relations in 2021, in addition to receiving a Bachelor of Arts in Public Relations and a Minor in Studio Art in 2020. *PETA'S Crisis History* is an excerpt of her graduate crisis communication research. Logan is currently working in the digital communications space for a well-respected marketing agency writing for Fortune 200 and Fortune 500 companies.

Claresta Si Ya Yeo is currently working in marketing communication functions for global corporations and has a passion for content creation. She is a graduate of Master of Mass Communication from the Nanyang Technological University, Singapore, with a Bachelor of Arts, Double Major in Communication and Psychology from the University at Buffalo, The State University of New York.

Xinyan Zhao (PhD, University of Maryland) is an Assistant Professor at the University of North Carolina at Chapel Hill. Her research focuses on social media and crisis communication, health communication, and computational methods to communication. She has published in journals including *Communication Monographs, Telematics and Informatics, Public Relations Review,* and *Journal of Health Communication.* She is a winner of multiple awards and grants, such as ICA Top Papers in 2017, 2018, and 2020.

INTRODUCTION

Yan Jin and Lucinda Austin

Over a half decade ago, we started the conceptualization of *Social Media and Crisis Communication* with Routledge as the first scholarly book on this topic. The first edition was then published about half decade ago (Austin & Jin, 2017). With the continued support of Routledge and the overwhelmingly positive feedback from our readers and book reviewers, we have worked on the second edition since early 2020 and wrap it up now with excitement and gratitude.

The first public relations theory focusing on social media and crisis communication, the social mediated crisis communication (SMCC) model (Jin & Liu, 2010; Liu et al., 2012), was published over a decade ago. Since then, social media and crisis communication has become not only an emerging research agenda in communication science but also one of the predominant public relations research areas, featured in recent seminal volumes such as *Crisis Communication* edited by Frandsen and Johansen (2020) and *Advancing Crisis Communication Effectiveness: Integrating Public Relations Scholarship with Practice* edited by Jin et al. (2021). As the landscape of social media and digital communication continues to evolve, severely threatened by the COVID-19 pandemic, we need to reflect and rejuvenate our research agenda, collaborating in more innovative ways to make new discoveries and provide insights that are meaningful and translational to practice.

As a scholarly book representing an updated look into the influence of social media on crisis communication across industry sectors and countries (Jin & Austin, 2017), our *Social Media and Crisis Communication (Second Edition)* continues to (1) showcase updated theories that describe, explain, and predict current and emerging crisis phenomena, (2) gauge next-generation research questions with empirical foundations, and (3) provide evidence-based insights for effective

DOI: 10.4324/9781003043409-1

and ethical crisis communication practice that protects public health and safety as well as helps organizations manage complex crisis issues.

As Manias-Muñoz et al. (2019) revealed from an international Delphi study on crisis communication, bridging the academia-industry gap and advancing crisis theory development cross-culturally are among the main challenges scholars agreed upon. Scholars further advocated the need to expand our "horizons with a more global perspective that better recognizes the work, theories, and differences around the world" such as "crises that span boundaries, including public health outbreaks" (Liu & Viens, 2020, p. 10). The COVID-19 pandemic illustrates such challenges and the urgent need for advancing crisis knowledge in order to protect community health, business continuity, and even save lives. *Social Media and Crisis Communication (Second Edition)* responds to these calls by incorporating more global and international perspectives and inviting more chapters authored by crisis scholars outside the United States.

As a reminder or wake-up call to scholars, Claeys and Opgenhaffen's (2016) article asked a fundamental "so what" question: "Why practitioners do (not) apply crisis communication theory in practice" (the very title of their *Journal of Public Relations Research* article). This "scholar-practitioner divide" (p. 233) (e.g., crisis communicators often do not apply scholarship to inform their crisis response) is caused by practitioners' perception that "theories are too abstract and …are not readily applicable by professionals in times of crisis" (p. 238). Since the publication of the first edition of our book, the world has experienced ongoing technological disruptions and increasingly intense social unrest triggered by historical, political, and social-economic issues. Organizations are urged, often pressured on social media, to make tough calls and sound decisions on how to communicate with publics online and offline with speed, accuracy, and purpose. This is the time when the "so what" question (Claeys & Opgenhaffen, 2016) and the call for more scholar-practitioner collaboration (Manias-Muñoz et al., 2019) become more pressing than ever. Ongoing and emerging crisis and/or crisis issues of high uncertainty, complexity and severity have presented unprecedented "sticky crisis" challenges to us all (Jin et al., 2021), the management of which requires advanced crisis communication knowledge and insights generated and shared by both scholars and practitioners. *Social Media and Crisis Communication (Second Edition)* responds to such urgent needs by adding short case chapters to Areas of Application section, bringing in case illustrations and practical takeaways shared by leading practitioners and emerging scholars in these crisis arenas.

Furthermore, "Sticky crisis," a new crisis concept developed by the University of Georgia's Crisis Communication Think Tank since 2018, serves as the foundation of the 2021 Routledge book *Advancing Crisis Communication Effectiveness: Integrating Public Relations Theory with Practice* (2021) (edited by Jin, Reber, & Nowak). By definition, a "sticky crisis" is caused by industry-wide, complex, and challenging crisis issues that are often intertwined and likely to reoccur in the future (Coombs et al., 2021; Reber et al., 2021). A sticky crisis issue impacts organizations and publics alike. As Reber and colleagues (2021) articulated, sticky crises demand not only a near-instant response, but they may require crisis communicators to see possibilities, understand the potential breadth and scope of an emerging crisis, which can bring "additional complexities and communication demands" (p. 7). Given that social media platforms often function as forms of main disruptors that trigger and/or aggravate sticky crisis situations (Coombs et al., 2021), *Social Media and Crisis Communication (Second Edition)* further illustrates current theoretical and practical efforts in tackling challenges posed by complex and challenging crisis issues as they exhibit varied different patterns and exert challenges to organizations and publics in different countries and cultures via various social media platforms. Keeping these emerging challenges in sight, we have built *Social Media and Crisis Communication (Second Edition)* upon the successful book structure of the first edition, continuing to comprehensively cover essential topics and complex phenomena of social media and crisis communication, from current issues, theoretical frameworks and directions, to areas of application in different crisis arenas contributed by established scholars and thought leaders from public and private sectors.

To reflect the increasingly more complex and demanding crisis landscape, *Social Media and Crisis Communication (Second Edition)* examines specific crisis arenas (i.e., health, corporate, nonprofit, sport, political, and disaster) in further depth and investigates the role of emerging social media platforms and newer technology in crisis communication management. New areas of discussion include corporate social responsibility (CSR) and crisis, religious crises, and internal/employee communication crises. It also provides an enhanced focus on the ethics section and a fresh look at the role of visual communication in social media and a more global review of social media and crisis communication literature.

As the field constantly rethinks and reinvents itself, we add a new subsection to this volume (i.e., *Characteristics and Types of Social Media*), examining new types of social media platforms and merging technologies such as artificial intelligence (AI), virtual reality (VR), and mixed reality (XR) and discussing possibilities and new research directions regarding how to prepare the future of effective and ethical crisis communication via AI and human intelligence (HI). We also extend global discussions on measurement advancements and emerging directions for building social media and crisis-specific theories and frameworks contributed by crisis communication theorists and methodological experts. Scholars, advanced students, and practitioners, who wish to stay on the leading edge of research, might find the insights from this volume relevant to their work in public relations, strategic communications, corporate communications, government and non-government organization (NGO) communications, and emergency and disaster responses.

To close, we thank our publisher and contributors for their tremendous support. We hope that *Social Media and Crisis Communication (Second Edition)* will serve as another seminal scholarly collection, a useful reference for practice, and a helpful teaching tool as we manage changes and conflicts for our organizations and communities with courage and resilience.

As author Anton Chekhov once wrote, "Don't tell me the moon is shining; show me the glint of light on broken glass." In a time of complex crises and challenges of all sorts, let us share the lamp of hope and pass on the light of endurance, compassionately and undauntedly.

References

Austin, L., & Jin, Y. (Eds.). (2017). *Social media and crisis communication* (1st ed.). Routledge.

Claeys, A., & Opgenhaffen, M. (2016). Why practitioners do (not) apply crisis communication theory in practice. *Journal of Public Relations Research, 28*(5–6), 232–247. https://doi.org/10.1080/1062726X.2016.1261703

Coombs, W. T., Holladay, S. J., & White, R. (2021). Sticky crises and corporations. In Y. Jin, B. H. Reber, & G. J. Nowak (Eds.), *Advancing crisis communication effectiveness: Integration of public relations scholarship and practice* (pp. 35–51). Routledge.

Frandsen, F., & Johansen, W. (2020). *Crisis communication (Handbook of communication science)*. Mouton de Gruyter.

Jin, Y., & Austin, L. (2017). Conclusion. In L. Austin and Y. Jin (Eds.), *Social media and crisis communication* (1st ed., pp. 449–452). Routledge.

Jin, Y., & Liu, B. F. (2010). The blog-mediated crisis communication model: Recommendations for responding to influential external blogs. *Journal of Public Relations Research, 22,* 429–455. https://doi.org/10.1080/10627261003801420

Jin, Y., Reber, B. H., & Nowak, G. J. (Eds.). (2021). *Advancing crisis communication effectiveness: Integration of public relations scholarship and practice*. Routledge.

Liu, B. F., Jin, Y., Briones, R., & Kuch, B. (2012). Managing turbulence in the blogosphere: Evaluating the blog-mediated crisis communication model with the American Red Cross. *Journal of Public Relations Research, 24,* 353–370. https://doi.org/10.1080/1062726X.2012.689901

Liu, B. F., & Viens, J. I. (2020). Crisis and risk communication scholarship of the future: Reflections on research gaps. *Journal of International Crisis and Risk Communication Research, 3*(1), 7–13. https://doi.org/10.30658/jicrcr.3.1.1

Manias-Muñoz, I., Jin, Y., & Reber, B. H. (2019). The state of crisis communication research and education through the lens of crisis scholars: An international Delphi study. *Public Relations Review, 45*(4), 101797. https://doi.org/10.1016/j.pubrev.2019.101797

Reber, B. H., Yarbrough, C. R., Nowak, G. J., & Jin, Y. (2021). Complex and challenging crises: A call for solutions. In Y. Jin, B. H. Reber, & G. J. Nowak (Eds.), *Advancing crisis communication effectiveness: Integration of public relations scholarship and practice* (pp. 3–16). Routledge.

Overview of Social Media Research in Crisis Communication

1
SOCIAL MEDIA AND CRISIS COMMUNICATION (SMCC) RESEARCH IN A GLOBAL CONTEXT

An Updated Review and Critique

Yang Cheng, Tomeeka Spruill, and Cheyenne Dalton

Introduction

At the beginning of 2021, according to the global digital overview, 4.66 billion people have access to the Internet (Chaffey, 2021). Most significantly, more than half of the world's total population (4.2 billion), which includes 90% Internet users, is actively adopting social media tools and the annual growth in the number of users is 13% (Kemp, 2021). Regionally, data demonstrates that the social media penetration rate varies in Eastern Asia (66%), North America (74%), South America (72%), North Europe (79%), Western Europe (79%), Western Africa (16%), and Middle Africa (8%) (Chaffey, 2021).

With the steadily increasing use of social media worldwide, organizations are adopting these media tools to communicate with their stakeholders such as consumers, employees, and investors for marketing and public relations activities (Godey et al., 2016). For instance, a recent study of social media use among practitioners found that professionals viewed Facebook as one of the most essential platforms for delivering information to stakeholders, especially in global health crises (Avery, 2017). Meanwhile, in regards to stakeholders or the general public, social media have played a significant role in influencing how stakeholders respond to crisis situations. In times of crises, stakeholders rely on social media to seek information and express their views in reaction to these situations (Liu et al., 2016). Social media have proven themselves as significant communication tools, creating dialogues for both organizations and their stakeholders in recent crises such as the Boston terror bombing in 2013 (Liu et al., 2016), Ebola virus outbreak in 2014–2016 (Tully et al., 2019), Hurricane Harvey in 2017 (Chen et al., 2019), and child abuse scandal in 2017 (Cheng et al., 2020).

DOI: 10.4324/9781003043409-3

As the use of social media between organizations and stakeholders in crises has significantly increased, there has been a growth in literature to uncover how and why social-mediated communication is applied during crisis situations (Cheng & Cameron, 2016). When analyzing social media use in crises on a global scale, scholars noticed that it is significant to consider not only the messages being exchanged but also the contexts within which information is transmitted online (Huang et al., 2015; Zhu et al., 2017). A variety of contextual factors (e.g., political, social, cultural, and economic) have been found to play a crucial role in influencing how organizations, governments, corporations, and stakeholders respond to crisis situations (Cheng, 2020). In addition to the regional differences in crisis communication practice, there are also variations in the adoption of social media platforms such as Facebook and Twitter (Eriksson & Olsson, 2016).

As the field of social media and crisis communication (SMCC) expands and evolves in the recent four years, it is important to understand the state of current SMCC research and the potential for differences in social media usage and practices depending on the context of the crisis at hand and the region. Using a global lens to uncover and explore the implications of SMCC research during worldwide crisis situations, this chapter conducts a content analysis of 135 articles published in 15 journals, indexed by Social Science Index Citation from 2016 to 2020. The following three questions are proposed to serve research purposes:

- What is the general picture of SMCC research in a global context in terms of author affiliations, theoretical, and methodological approaches?
- What are the crises and types of social media studied by SMCC research?
- What kind of contextual factors were mentioned and how did these factors influence SMCC research?

Data Collection and Content Analysis

A quantitative content analysis was conducted by searching the *Web of Science Core Collection* electronic database using the search terms "social media," "communication," and "crises or crisis." This dataset was selected because it records over 20,000 high-standard journals published worldwide in multi-disciplines and contains the social science citation index as well (Clarivate, 2020). In addition, the search was limited to articles written in English and published in the field of public relations and crisis communication (i.e., the *Journal of Public Relations Research, Public Relations Review, Journal of Contingencies and Crisis Management,* and *Disasters*), international communication (i.e., *International Communication Gazette, International Journal of Communication, Asian Journal of Communication, Chinese Journal of Communication, International Journal of Business Communication,* and *European Journal of Communication*), new media technologies (i.e., *New Media & Society, Computers in Human Behaviors, Social Media + Society,*

TABLE 1.1 Percentage of Articles in Each Journal

Journal title	Number of articles	Percentage (%)
Asian Journal of Communication	3	2
Chinese Journal of Communication	3	2
Computers in Human Behaviors	27	20
Communication Research	2	1.5
Disasters	5	4
European Journal of Communication	2	1.5
International Communication Gazette	2	1.5
International Journal of Communication	9	7
International Journal of Business Communication	2	1.5
Journal of Public Relations Research	1	1
Journal of Contingencies and Crisis Management	27	20
New Media & Society	3	2
Public Relations Review	39	29
Social Media + Society	4	3
Telematics and Informatics	6	4
Total	**135**	**100**

and *Telematics and Informatics*), and general communication (i.e., *Communication Research and Communication Theory*). The initial search provided us with 157 articles available from 2016 to June 2020. Two coders then checked all the collected articles to see whether they had addressed the research field of SMCC or not. This final refining process resulted in a total sample of 135 articles from 15 journals. We then selected 15 articles for a reliability check of the content analysis and resulted in a composite inter-coder reliability score of 0.85 Krippendorff's alpha.

Table 1.1 presents the collected number of articles from each journal. Results indicated that a majority of analyzed articles came from *Public Relations Review* ($n = 39$, 29%), *Computers in Human Behavior* ($n = 27$, 20%), and *Journal of Contingencies and Crisis Management* ($n = 27$, 20%). The vast majority of SMCC research in the recent four years (2016–2020) was published in 2019 ($n = 41$, 30.3%), which made up nearly a third of all the articles analyzed, trailed closely by 2016 ($n = 36$, 26.7%), 2018 ($n = 32$, 23.7%), 2017 ($n = 18$, 13.3%), and 2020 ($n = 8$, 6%).

The State of SMCC Research

First Authorship and Affiliation

To explore the representation among global institutions, this study analyzed the country and the affiliated institution with the most publications. It is revealed that among the 135 articles, authors' institutions within the U.S. had the most publications ($n = 65$, 48%), followed by Greater China ($n = 21$, 15%), the Netherlands ($n = 9$, 7%), Germany ($n = 6$, 4%), Belgium ($n = 5$, 4%), South Korea ($n = 5$, 4%), and Sweden ($n = 5$, 4%) (see Table 1.2 for more details).

TABLE 1.2 Country Affiliation and Continental Region of First Authorship

Location of continental region	Country affiliation	Number of articles
North America	**Total**	**65**
	U.S.	63
	Canada	2
Europe	**Total**	**32**
	U.K.	2
	The Netherlands	9
	Germany	6
	Belgium	5
	Sweden	5
	Portugal	1
	Spain	1
	Greece	1
	Ireland	1
	Norway	1
Asia	**Total**	**36**
	Hong Kong	9
	Mainland China	8
	South Korea	5
	Singapore	4
	Taiwan	4
	Malaysia	1
	Kuwait	1
	Thailand	1
	Cyprus	1
	Israel	1
	Jordan	1
Africa	**Total**	**1**
	South Africa	1
Oceania	**Total**	**3**
	Australia	3

Note: Two articles in the SMCC Research had an author with two institution affiliations.

Using the first author for each publication, it is revealed that the institution affiliation with the most publications is Hong Kong Baptist University ($n = 6$, 4.4%), followed by University of Kentucky ($n = 5$, 3.7%), University of Maryland ($n = 5$, 3.7%), University of Amsterdam ($n = 5$, 3.7%), North Carolina State University ($n = 5$, 3.7%), and Ghent University ($n = 4$, 3.0%) (see Table 1.3).

Theoretical Application and Frameworks

In terms of the trends of theoretical approaches, we first examined hypotheses or research questions applied in the current SMCC research. Data indicate that 70 out of 135 articles (52%) applied research questions only, followed by 22 articles (16%) with hypotheses only, 19 articles (14%) with both hypotheses

TABLE 1.3 Most Represented Institutions in the SMCC Research

Author affiliations	No. of articles	Location/country
Hong Kong Baptist University	6	Hong Kong
University of Maryland	5	Maryland, U.S.
University of Amsterdam	5	The Netherlands
North Carolina State University	5	North Carolina, U.S.
University of Kentucky	5	Kentucky, U.S.
Ghent University	4	Belgium
University of Connecticut	3	Connecticut, U.S.
University of Georgia	3	Georgia, U.S.
Syracuse University	3	New York, U.S.
Nanyang Technological University	3	Singapore
National Chiao Tung University	3	Taiwan

and research questions, and 24 of 135 articles (18%) provided neither research questions nor hypotheses. The results also demonstrate that a significant portion of the SMCC research applied a specific theory ($n = 97$, 72%) in comparison to articles that did not specify one ($n = 38$, 28%). Among the collected articles with a theoretical framework, the most frequently used theory was the Situational Crisis Communication Theory (SCCT) (Coombs, 2007) ($n = 29$, 30%). Scholars also adopted blog/social-mediated crisis communication (SMCC) model (Austin et al., 2012) ($n = 12$, 12%), framing theory (Johnson-Cartee, 2005) ($n = 11$, 11%), uses and gratification theory (Katz et al., 1973) ($n = 7$, 7%), dialogue theory ($n = 7$, 7%), image repair strategies (Benoit, 1997) ($n = 6$, 6%), and attribution theory (Weiner, 1985) ($n = 5$, 5%). Other theoretical frameworks, such as grounded theory and the crisis and emergency risk communication (CERC) model, were also mentioned in the SMCC research.

Research Methods and Sampling

Regarding the methodological approach, we analyzed the research method, sampling technique, and type of sample in each article. Results showed that 109 out of 135 articles applied single-method in their research, among which content analysis was the most frequently used method ($n = 40$, 36.7%), followed by experiment ($n = 20$, 18%), survey ($n = 18$, 16.5%), interviews ($n = 10$, 9%), computational method ($n = 10$, 9%), case study ($n = 4$, 4%), literature review ($n = 3$, 2.8%), sentiment analysis ($n = 2$, 2%), and rhetorical/textual analysis ($n = 2$, 2%). It is also noted that global scholarship that adopted mixed-research methods accounted for 20% of the total number. For example, in the U.S., scholars such as Liu et al. (2020) adopted both quantitative content analysis and interviews to study governmental crisis communication responses to a wildfire on social media and websites. In the Netherlands, van der Meer (2018) relied on both advanced automated content analyses and the quasi-experimental design to investigate how public frame built crisis-related tweets.

Among the 135 coded articles, data indicate that the non-probability sampling method appeared in over half of the articles ($n = 75$, 55.5%), followed by probability ($n = 40$, 30%), and mixed-sampling methods ($n = 3$, 2%). Seventeen articles (12.5%) did not use a sampling method.

Among all the collected samples (e.g., people, traditional media or social media contents, or both), we found that the most frequently used sample type was social media content ($n = 54$, 40%).

Crises and Social Media in the SMCC Research

In the SMCC research, the majority of scholars ($n = 114$, 84%) mentioned a specific crisis in their studies and the others referred to a general crisis without specifying a country or continent in their research. The time of these crises ranged from 2008 to 2017 (e.g., financial crisis in 2008, BP oil spill crisis in 2011, Boston Marathon bombing in 2013, Ebola outbreak in 2014, and Manchester Arena bombing in 2017) and natural crises (e.g., Hurricane Sandy in 2012 or Hurricane Harvey in 2017) were mostly studied.

There were 31 locations of crises mentioned in the SMCC research. In specific, four articles discussed crises and collected relevant data in more than one continent (e.g., U.S. and China, see Lin et al., 2016). Research on a single continent represented crises in the U.S. ($n = 45$, 33%), Asia ($n = 32$, 24%), Europe ($n = 28$, 21%), Africa ($n = 2$, 1%), and Oceania ($n = 3$, 2%, see Figure 1.1).

Within each continent, we also analyzed the type of social media. In North America including the U.S., Gulf coast, and Canada, Twitter, Facebook, blog, 360° video, and Instagram were mainly investigated. Spence and colleagues (2016) argued that social media provided opportunities for researchers to collect randomized sampling on their research subjects in crises. Twitter, in particular, can be used to track affected public responses via unobtrusive observations. Wukich (2016), for instance, collected tweets on government online messages across disaster stages. Their findings supported that all agencies on Twitter most frequently posted messages for situational awareness and protective actions in crises. Fraustino et al. (2018) demonstrated the effects of artificial reality (i.e., 360° omnidirectional video) in enhancing the publics' positive attitudes toward content featuring consequences of a natural disaster.

In Asia, scholars such as Pang and Ng (2016) analyzed audiences' responses to a little India riot. Jin et al. (2018) focused on emotions on Twitter during the MH370 airplane crash incident. Within the Chinese context, Weibo was mostly examined in the SMCC research; scholars such as Zheng et al. (2018) explored how corporate reputation might influence public crisis responses on Weibo and

FIGURE 1.1   Crises Discussed in the SMCC Research Globally

Note: The Background image of this figure was adopted from *Free world map stock photo*. Retrieved from: https://www.freeimages.com/photo/world-map-1577937

their findings supported the positive impact of firm reputation on preventing secondary crisis communication.

In Europe, studies focused on Twitter or Facebook mediated crisis communication. Hänska and Bauchowitz (2019) mapped the geospatial structure of publics' tweets on the internet of Greece and found that these social media activities facilitated a European public sphere as Twitter users across countries tweeted about the bailout negotiations. Gaspar et al. (2016) conducted a sentiment analysis of social media users' affective responses to crises in Germany. Their research indicated that social media data not only provided results of sentiments but also enhanced our understanding of adaptive functions of affective expressions of coping. In Africa (i.e., Kenya and Côte d'Ivoire) and Oceania (i.e., Australia and Samoa), Facebook or Twitter was utilized for data collection in crises. Schreiner (2018) focused on the African continent and demonstrated that Twitter served for multi-purposes such as verifying false information, spreading rumors, facilitating political debate, and crowdsourcing information in a post-electoral crisis.

In summary, the most frequently studied social media platform in the SMCC research is Twitter ($n = 32$, 24%), followed by Facebook ($n = 16$, 12%), and Weibo ($n = 4$, 3%). These results refer to articles that focused on only one type of social media platform. Of the articles that included two or more media platforms, the most frequent combination of social media is Facebook and Twitter ($n = 18$, 13%).

Contextual Impact on SMCC Research

It is noted that 102 articles (76%) in recent SMCC research (2016–2020) addressed the contextual impact on crisis communication. Cultural elements and political environments are mostly perceived as significant factors that influence organizational crisis communication strategies, stakeholder responses, and applications of social media in diversified context(s). Following Hofstede's (2001) model of national culture, power distance, collectivism-individualism, masculinity–femininity, and uncertainty avoidance were frequently discussed by the global scholarship of SMCC. Cheng and Lee (2019), for instance, suggested that power distance and relationships (i.e., *Guanxi*) determined the dialogue between organizations and their publics in China's crises. Chinese crisis communication practitioners preferred indirect and abstract communication strategies such as diversion and avoidance for face-saving (Wu et al., 2016). Triantafillidou and Yannas (2020) pointed out that high levels of uncertainty avoidance and collectivism that featured Greece's culture make stakeholders on social media prefer corrective crisis communication responses rather than punishment for wrongdoings in racially charged crises. In addition, Kim and colleagues (2016) suggested that social media culture, such as a sense of humor, was useful for managing a paracrisis on social media in China.

Political context also has a profound influence on the SMCC research. Scholars found that political parties, on the one hand, utilized social media to share information and interact with the publics in countries such as Africa (Schreiner, 2018), Malaysia (Valaei & Baroto, 2017), Spain (Gálvez-Rodríguez et al., 2019), Thailand (Kaewkitipong et al., 2016), China (Cheng, 2020), and so on. On the other hand, propaganda and censorship occurred on the social media landscape for political control online (Cheng, 2020; Schreiner, 2018).

Social media in global crisis communication thus served as a double-edged sword. It enabled dialogic communication between organizations and publics and allowed citizens to develop online communities to seek and share crisis information online (Kaewkitipong et al., 2016) while also reinforcing political control, facilitating a widespread of misinformation, disinformation, or violent and hostile speech online (Chen & Cheng, 2019; Lev-On, 2018), and exposing viral gang activities among the youth (Patton et al., 2016).

Discussion and Future Directions

Through content analyzing 135 articles from 15 journals in the recent 4 years, this study focuses on an updated review of global SMCC scholarship. We find that compared to results on the review of SMCC research from 2002 to 2014 (Cheng & Cameron, 2016), the number of publications in recent four years has significantly increased. Furthermore, the recent SMCC research frequently adopted hypotheses or research questions in their theoretical framework and often utilized mixed research methods. Quantitative methods, such as content analysis and experiment, dominated this field and new approaches, such as computational methods, began to emerge. A significant majority of authors were affiliated with U.S. institutions and scholars frequently adopted Twitter or Facebook as main platforms of study. Results also conclude that despite increased technological advancement and globalization, many scholars in the field of SMCC mainly collected research data from North America. The Western-originated communication theories, such as the SCCT theory or framing theory, are the predominant tools used to measure social-mediated crisis communication process. This study argues that this field is in much need of diversification among the region of focus, social media platforms, and theoretical development. Viable suggestions for future research directions of the global SMCC research are presented below.

To Enhance Global Representation of the SMCC Research

Data demonstrate that a significant majority of first authors' institutions were located in the U.S. Most of the SMCC research focused on this single country. Of the 135 articles, a large portion of them examined a crisis or phenomenon located in the U.S. as a whole or in a specific state or region. Based on this study, we discover that there is a notable lack of representation among the SMCC research from countries outside of the U.S. Furthermore, there is a lack of focus and representation when it comes to crisis communication research in Africa, the Middle East, and South America. Although a majority of these articles provide implications, their results and suggested practices might not fully be adopted globally. Additionally, methods and theories that were used by U.S. scholars might not be applied to non-U.S. or non-Western societies (Cheng, 2018). Consequently, this global SMCC research reveals that the field is in great need of diversification. By expanding research to less represented areas, scholars and academics could develop a more holistic view of social media and its use during crisis communication situations on a global scale.

To Conduct Comparative Studies in Global Crises

When the world is exacerbated by globalization and becoming more and more mediated by social networking sites, public relations and crisis communication practitioners have had to quickly evolve alongside the normalization of everyday social media use, especially during crisis situations. The recent global crises, such as the climate crisis and the coronavirus pandemic, were tougher with a flood of misinformation spread online, making SMCC research invaluable. Future studies might utilize the advantages of social media platforms to track and compare global communicative responses to this coronavirus pandemic via machine learning techniques and big data analysis. Twitter, for instance, could be utilized for such comparative studies. Due to the platform's open nature and the ability for users to communicate with each other in real time, Twitter has played a major role in the communication and construction of online public discourse (López-Rabadán & Mellado, 2019). Additionally, Twitter is often used by government officials, organizations, and media professionals to mitigate and communicate with the public throughout various stages of a crisis (Liu et al., 2018). Consequently, Twitter use in comparative SMCC research should be given more attention by both professionals and scholars to better determine its usefulness and application.

To Further Develop Theories and Models

Through this study, we demonstrate that theoretical frameworks and models were applied in more than half of the coded articles. Out of all of the theories used in these articles, SCCT was applied the most frequently. Developed by Coombs (2007), SCCT tries to predict how stakeholders react to different crisis management strategies based on levels of attributed responsibilities. Image repair theories proposed by Benoit (1997) provided five general approaches of crisis communication strategies for organizations. However, these traditional crisis communication theories and strategies have originated from Western societies (Huang et al., 2015), which has resulted in a lack of focus on non-Western and non-democratic societies. This study shows that in the current SMCC research, there is a lack of theoretical development and model explorations originated from non-Western contexts. To gain a more comprehensive understanding of theoretical frameworks and applications on a global scale, crisis communication scholars should expand their reach to include theories that are used in non-U.S. studies. This will help to diversify crisis communication scholarship and encourage the need for theoretical development (Jain et al., 2014).

References

Austin, L., Liu, B. F., & Jin, Y. (2012). How audiences seek out crisis information: Exploring the social-mediated crisis communication model. *Journal of Applied Communication Research*, 40(2), 188–207. https://doi.org/10.1080/00909882.2012.654498

Avery, E. J. (2017). Public information officers' social media monitoring during the Zika virus crisis, a global health threat surrounded by public uncertainty. *Public Relations Review*, 43(3), 468–476. https://doi.org/10.1016/j.pubrev.2017.02.018

Benoit, W. (1997). Image repair discourse and crisis communication. *Public Relations Review*, 23(2), 177–186. doi: 10.1016/S0363-8111(97)90023-0

Chaffey, D. (2021, March 11). *Global social media summary 2021*. Retrieved from: https://www.smartinsights.com/social-media-marketing/social-media-strategy/new-global-social-media-research/

Chen, Z. F., & Cheng, Y. (2019). Consumer response to fake news about brands on social media: The effects of self-efficacy, media trust, and persuasion knowledge on company trust. *Journal of Product & Brand Management, 29*(2), 188–198. https://doi.org/10.1108/JPBM-12-2018-2145

Chen, Y.-R., Cheng, Y., Hung-Baesecke, R., & Jin, Y. (2019). Engaging international publics via mobile-enhanced CSR (mCSR): A cross-national study on stakeholder reactions to corporate disaster relief efforts. *American Behavioral Scientist, 63*(12), 1603–1623. https://doi.org/10.1177/0002764219835258

Cheng, Y. (2018). How social media is changing crisis communication strategies: Evidence from the updated literature. *Journal of Contingencies and Crisis Management, 26*, 58–68. https://doi.org/10.1111/1468-5973.12130

Cheng, Y. (2020). The social-mediated crisis communication research: Revisiting dialogue between organizations and publics in crises of China. *Public Relations Review, 46*(1), 1–9. https://doi.org/10.1016/j.pubrev.2019.04.003

Cheng, Y., & Cameron, G. (2016). The status of social mediated crisis communication (SMCC) research: An analysis of published articles in 2002–2014. In L. Austin and Y. Jin (Eds.), *Social media and crisis communication*. Routledge.

Cheng, Y., & Lee, C. J. (2019). Online crisis communication in a post-truth Chinese society: Evidence from interdisciplinary literature. *Public Relations Review, 45*(4), 1–10. https://doi.org/10.1016/j.pubrev.2019.101826

Cheng, Y., Shen, H. M., & Jiang, Q. L. (2020). Corporate dialogue in crises of China: Examining dialogic strategies and communicative outcomes in a child abuse scandal. *Public Relations Review, 46*(1), 1–9. https://doi.org/10.1016/j.pubrev.2019.101816

Clarivate. (2020). *Web of science core collection*. Retrieved from: https://clarivate.com/webofsciencegroup/solutions/web-of-science-core-collection/

Coombs, W. T. (2007). Protecting organization reputations during a crisis: The development and application of situational crisis communication theory. *Corporate Reputation Review, 10*, 163–177. https://doi.org/10.1057/palgrave.crr.1550049

Eriksson, M., & Olsson, E. K. (2016), Facebook and Twitter in crisis communication: A comparative study of crisis communication professionals and citizens. *Journal of Contingencies and Crisis Management, 24*, 198–208. https://doi.org/10.1111/1468-5973.12116

Fraustino, J. D., Lee, J. Y., Lee, S. Y., & Ahn, H.-M. (2018). Effects of 360° video on attitudes toward disaster communication: Mediating and moderating roles of spatial presence and prior disaster media involvement. *Public Relations Review, 44*(3), 331–341. https://doi.org/10.1016/j.pubrev.2018.02.003

Gálvez-Rodríguez, M., Haro-de-Rosario, A., & Caba-Pérez, M. (2019). The Syrian refugee crisis: How local governments and NGOs manage their image via social media. *Disasters, 43*, 509–533. https://doi.org/10.1111/disa.12351

Gaspar, R., Pedro, C., Panagiotopoulos, P., & Seibt, B. (2016). Beyond positive or negative: Qualitative sentiment analysis of social media reactions to unexpected stressful events. *Computer in Human Behavior, 54*, 179–191. https://doi.org/10.1016/j.chb.2015.11.040

Godey, B., Manthiou, A., Pederzoli, D., Rokka, J., Aiello, G., Donvito, R., & Singh, R. (2016). Social media marketing efforts of luxury brands: Influence on brand equity and consumer behavior. *Journal of Business Research, 69*(12), 5833–5841. https://doi.org/10.1016/j.jbusres.2016.04.181

Hänska, M., & Bauchowitz, S. (2019). Can social media facilitate a European public sphere? Transnational communication and the Europeanization of Twitter during the Eurozone crisis. *Social Media + Society, 5*(3), 1–14. https://doi.org/10.1177/2056305119854686

Hofstede, G. (2001). *Culture's consequences: Comparing values, behaviors, institutions, and organizations across nations* (2nd ed.). SAGE Publications.

Huang, Y. H., Wu, F., & Cheng, Y. (2015). Crisis communication in context: Some aspects of cultural influence underpinning Chinese PR practice. *Public Relations Review, 42*(1), 201–213. https://doi.org/10.1016/j.pubrev.2015.11.015

Jain, R., De Moya, M., & Molleda, J. (2014). State of international public relations research: Narrowing the knowledge gap about the practice across borders. *Public Relations Review, 40*(3), 595–597. https://doi.org/10.1016/j.pubrev.2014.02.009

Jin, B., Chung, S., & Byeon, S. (2018). Media influence on intention for risk-aversive behaviors: The direct and indirect influence of blogs through presumed influence on others. *International Journal of Communication, 12*, 2443–2460. https://ijoc.org/index.php/ijoc/article/view/7763

Johnson-Cartee, K. (2005). *News narrative and news framing: Constructing political reality.* Rowman & Littlefield.

Kaewkitipong, L., Chen, C. C., & Ractham, P. (2016). A community-based approach to sharing knowledge before, during, and after crisis events: A case study from Thailand. *Computer in Human Behavior, 54*, 653–666. https://doi.org/10.1016/j.chb.2015.07.063

Katz, E., Blumler, J. G., & Gurevitch, M. (1973). Uses and gratifications research. *The Public Opinion Quarterly, 37*(4), 509–523. https://doi.org/10.1086/268109

Kemp, S. (2021). *Digital 2021: Global digital overview.* Retrieved from: https://wearesocial.com/blog/2021/01/digital-2021-the-latest-insights-into-the-state-of-digital

Kim, S., Zhang, X. A., & Zhang, B. W. (2016). Self-mocking crisis strategy on social media: Focusing on Alibaba chairman Jack Ma in China. *Public Relations Review, 42*, 903–912. https://doi.org/10.1016/j.pubrev.2016.10.004

Lev-On, A. (2018). The anti-social network? Portraying social media in wartime. *Social Media and Society, 4*(3), 1–12, https://doi.org/10.1177/2056305118800311

Lin, X., Lachlan, K. A., & Spence, P. R. (2016). Exploring extreme events on social media: A comparison of user reposting/retweeting behaviors on Twitter and Weibo. *Computers in Human Behavior, 65*, 576–581. https://doi.org/10.1016/j.chb.2016.04.032

Liu, B. F., Fraustino, J. D., & Jin, Y. (2016). Social media use during disasters: How information form and source influence intended behavioral responses. *Communication Research, 43*(5), 626–646. https://doi.org/10.1177/0093650214565917

Liu, B. F., Iles, I. A., & Herovic, E. (2020). Leadership under fire: How governments manage crisis communication. *Communication Studies, 71*(1), 128–147. https://doi.org/10.1080/10510974.2019.1683593

Liu, W., Lai, C., & Xu, W. (2018). Tweeting about emergency: A semantic network analysis of government organizations' social media messaging during hurricane Harvey. *Public Relations Review, 44*(5), 807–819. https://doi.org/10.1016/j.pubrev.2018.10.009

López-Rabadán, P., & Mellado, C. (2019). Twitter as a space for interaction in political journalism. Dynamics, consequences and proposal of interactivity scale for social media. *Communication & Society, 32*, 1–18. https://doi.org/10.15581/003.32.1.1-18

Pang, N., & Ng, J. (2016). Twittering the Little India Riot: Audience responses, information behavior and the use of emotive cues. *Computer in Human Behavior, 54*, 607–619. https://doi.org/10.1016/j.chb.2015.08.047

Patton, D. U., Eschmann, R. D., Elsaesser, C., & ve Bocanegra, E. (2016). Sticks, stones and Facebook accounts: What violence outreach workers know about social media and urban-based gang violence in Chicago. *Computers in Human Behavior, 65*, 591–600. https://doi.org/10.1016/j.chb.2016.05.052

Schreiner, T. (2018). Information, opinion, or rumor? The role of Twitter during the post-electoral crisis in Côte d'Ivoire. *Social Media + Society, 4*(1), 1–16. https://doi.org/10.1177/2056305118765736

Spence, P. R., Lachlan, K. A., & Rainear, A. M. (2016). Social media and crisis research: Data collection and directions. *Computer in Human Behavior, 54,* 667–672. https://doi.org/10.1016/j.chb.2015.08.045

Triantafillidou, A., & Yannas, P. (2020). Social media crisis communication in racially charged crises: Exploring the effects of social media and image restoration strategies. *Computers in Human Behavior, 106,* 1–10. https://doi.org/10.1016/j.chb.2020.106269

Tully, M., Dalrymple, E. K., & Young, R. (2019). Contextualizing nonprofits' use of links on Twitter during the West African Ebola virus epidemic. *Communication Studies, 70*(3), 313–331. https://doi.org/10.1080/10510974.2018.1539021

Valaei, N., & Baroto, M. B. (2017). Modelling continuance intention of citizens in government Facebook page: A complementary PLS approach. *Computer in Human Behavior, 73,* 224–237. https://doi.org/10.1016/j.chb.2017.03.047

van der Meer, T. G. L. A. (2018). Public frame building: The role of source usage in times of crisis. *Communication Research, 45*(6), 956–981. https://doi.org/10.1177/0093650216644027

Weiner, B. (1985). An attributional theory of achievement motivation and emotion. *Psychological Review, 92*(4), 548–573. https://doi.org/10.1037/0033-295x.92.4.548

Wu, F., Huang, Y.-H., & Kao, L. (2016). East meets West: A new contextual perspective for crisis communication theory. *Asian Journal of Communication, 26*(4), 350–370. https://doi.org/10.1080/01292986.2016.1148186

Wukich, C. (2016), Government social media messages across disaster phases. *Journal of Contingencies and Crisis Management, 24,* 230–243. https://doi.org/10.1111/1468-5973.12119

Zheng, B., Liu, H., & Davison, R. M. (2018). Exploring the relationship between corporate reputation and the public's crisis communication on social media. *Public Relations Review, 44*(1), 56–64. https://doi.org/10.1016/j.pubrev.2017.12.006

Zhu, L., Anagondahalli, D., & Zhang, A. (2017). Social media and culture in crisis communication: McDonald's and KFC crisis management in China. *Public Relations Review, 43,* 487–492. https://doi.org/10.1016/j.pubrev.2017.03.006

2

CURRENT ISSUES OF SOCIAL MEDIA AND CRISIS COMMUNICATION

Itsaso Manias-Muñoz and Bryan H. Reber

Why Study Social Media and Crisis Communication?

In a 2021 global crisis study, PwC found that 95% of 2,800+ corporate respondents said their crisis communication capabilities need improvement (PwC, 2021). The traditional crisis communication toolkit includes strategies primarily employing media relations, internal communication, and consumer relations, depending on the nature of the crisis. Press releases, press conferences, FAQs, and spokespersons have always been among the common tactics employed by crisis communicators. The traditional strategies and tactics remain, but they have been joined by others.

In an October 2020 Global Digital Report, the total number of social media users worldwide was cited as 4.14 billion. That is more than half (53%) of the world's population. That growth rate is accelerating. Between October 2019 and 2020 Global Digital Reports, "more than 14 people started using social media *every second*" (Kemp, October 2020, para. 16). Active social media users increased by more than 12% during that year (ibid).

In PwC's 2019 Global Digital Report, 69% of respondents reported experiencing a crisis within the past five years (PwC, 2019). Combine the fact that more than two-thirds of corporate executives said they had faced at least one crisis in the preceding half a decade and the phenomenal growth in the number of social media users and the opening question answers itself. "Why study social media and crisis communication?" Because there is a synergy between the medium and the issue that can be harnessed to improve crisis communication or ignored, potentially accelerating the crisis spread.

DOI: 10.4324/9781003043409-4

The pandemic of 2020–2021 contributed to growth and use of social media. A global study co-sponsored by Hootsuite and We Are Social found that social media use increased at double the rate "and represents the largest quarter-on-quarter increase that we've seen since we started producing these reports back in 2011" (Kemp, October 2020, para. 19). Changes like these, brought on at least in part by the need to socially distance during the pandemic, makes the employment of social media in crisis communication all the more relevant and urgent.

The Intersection of Theory and Practice

As noted above, there are many important reasons to study social media and crisis communication. Likewise, there are important reasons to look at these media and situations from the perspective of both academics and crisis communicators. In the remainder of this chapter, we will summarize some crisis communication theories, apply them to specific cases, and finally hear from crisis experts via depth interviews.

Theories

Image Repair Theory

Image Repair Theory was introduced by William L. Benoit in his book, *Accounts, excuses, apologies: A theory of image restoration discourse* (1995). The theory assumes that (1) communication is goal-directed and that (2) positive reputation maintenance is a central goal of communication (Benoit, 2015). The theory is based on the scholarship of rhetorical discourse and persuasion. Rhetorical strategies to repair damaged corporate images fall into three categories, according to Benoit: (1) denial, (2) evasion of responsibility, and (3) reducing offensiveness of event (ibid, p. 308).

Contingency Theory of Strategic Conflict Management

The Contingency Theory of Strategic Conflict Management grew from the Contingency Theory of Accommodation (Cancel et al., 1997) and describes the dynamic nature of crisis communication. The theory describes a continuum with endpoints of pure accommodation and pure advocacy. The communication stance of an organization runs up and down the continuum, as the situation merits. The Contingency Theory is a positive descriptive theory rather than a normative one. "Contingency theory reasons that the first strategic choice might not be the best, but that it will be tested in operation. If it is found to be inadequate, or unhelpful to conflict management, other hybrid options are available" (Shin & Health, 2021, p. 90). Pang et al. (2012) claimed that the theory's relevance to crisis communication included its strategic flexibility "through the adoption of stances along a continuum instead of adhering to a set model of communication" (p. 542).

Theory of Crisis Response Narratives

The Theory of Crisis Response Narratives was introduced by Robert L. Heath in the book *Responding to Crisis: A Rhetorical Approach to Crisis Communication* (2004). Heath wrote: "Narratives are the basis for how organizations are enacted, interpreted, and responded to (Heath, 1994). A crisis shifts the narrative being enacted by an organization from one of routine events to one that is not routine... For this reason, crisis is a narrative event that demands unique and strategically appropriate rhetorical enactments" (Heath, 2004, p. 175).

With the Theory of Crisis Response Narratives, Heath extended the way narrative theory had been applied. Narratives, or stories, may be told by an organization or some set or subset of its stakeholders. Based on a narrative of stakeholders, an organization may not – at least initially – believe it is in crisis. The preferred narrative flow for the organization would be from routine narrative to crisis narrative and back to routine narrative (ibid, p. 168). As Heath further noted, "Narrative – as enacted by a crisis response and communication team – gives us a means for understanding, interpreting, and critiquing the response in a manner that is coherent and systematic" (ibid, p. 187).

Situational Crisis Communication Theory

W. Timothy Coombs first proposed the Situational Crisis Communication Theory (SCCT) in 2007. Coombs and his colleagues suggest that crisis communication managers should evaluate crisis type, crisis history, and prior relational reputation between stakeholders and the entity in crisis. By doing this, Coombs says, crisis communicators and managers can predict the threat of a crisis to the reputation of the entity involved and how publics will perceive the crisis.

Coombs identified three clusters of crisis types – victim cluster, accident cluster, and intentional cluster. Similarly, prescribed crisis responses are classified by Coombs as deny, diminish, and rebuild.

Social-Mediated Crisis Communication Model

The Social-Mediated Crisis Communication (SMCC) model grew out of an earlier Blog-Mediated Crisis Communication Model (Jin & Liu, 2010). The broader SMCC framework identifies communication flow between and among a variety of online and offline media as well as influential publics (Liu et al., 2021).

Three types of people are identified in SMCC: Influential Social Media Creators, Social Media Followers, and Social Media Inactives. The model also describes how messages flow both directly and indirectly among concerned publics and between the organization and its publics (Reber et al., 2021).

Behavioral Crisis Communication Theory

Claeys and Coombs (2020) proposed a descriptive theory of Behavioral Crisis Communication with roots in behavioral economics theory. Claeys and Coombs asked why "crisis managers utilize suboptimal rather than the theoretically prescribed optimal crisis response strategies" (ibid, p. 291). Because people are generally loss averse, they are not always looking to maximize gains but rather to minimize losses. Claeys and Coombs suggested that this human nature is especially relevant during the highly ambiguous conditions surrounding most crises. As they further articulated, "Research confirms that organizational public relations professionals experience more uncertainty in times of crisis compared to under routine circumstances (van der Meer et al., 2017)" (ibid, p. 301).

Theory-Informed Practice

Crisis case studies provide insight into situational decision-making and instances in which theory did or could have informed crisis communication response. Three distinctly different cases provide some opportunity for analysis of current issues of social media and crisis communication.

European Super League

On Sunday, April 18, 2021, a press release was distributed that announced the formation of a European Super League (ESL) consisting of 12 European football clubs. The League would be governed by its Founding Clubs – AC Milan, Arsenal FC, Atletico de Madrid, Chelsea FC, FC Barcelona, FC Internazionale Milano, Juventus FC, Liverpool FC, Manchester City, Manchester United, Real Madrid CF, and Tottenham Hotspur. Joel Glazer, co-chairman of Manchester United and vice chairman of the Super League, said, "By bringing together the world's greatest clubs and players to play each other throughout the season, the Super League will open a new chapter for European football, incurring world-class competition and facilities, and increased financial support for the wider football pyramid" (The "Super League" Announcement, *New York Times*, April 19, 2021).

There was a minor problem, stakeholders. The Union of European Football Associations (UEFA) and Federation Nationale de Football Association (FIFA), the governing bodies for these 12 clubs, were surprised. Team players and managers were surprised. Fans were outraged. Thousands of Manchester United supporters protested the club owners, the Glazer family. Likewise Chelsea fans protested owner Roman Abromovich and Arsenal fans protested owner Stan Kroenke (BBC.com, European Super League…, April 25, 2021).

By late afternoon Sunday, UEFA announced it would use "all measures" to stop the "cynical project." By midnight Sunday, FIFA condemned the ESL, too. Midday Monday, William the Duke of Cambridge tweeted, "Now, more than ever, we must protect the entire football community – from the top level to the grassroots – and the values of competition and fairness at its core. I share the concerns of fans about the proposed Super League and the damage it risks causing to the game we love. W." Players expressed their displeasure on Twitter and Instagram and to the traditional media. Former U.K. player and current U.S. franchise owner David Beckham posted on his Instagram account that football was "nothing without the fans" (BBC.com, European Super League timeline…, April 21, 2021).

Tuesday, April 20, Manchester City and Chelsea announced they were pulling out of the new League. Manchester City defender Benjamin Mendy tweeted, "what a beautiful day for football let's keep playing, let's keep fighting, let's keep dreaming. That's the very first reason why we do this!! #supergone." By the end of Tuesday, all six UK teams had withdrawn (ibid).

By 10 a.m. Wednesday, April 21, Andrea Agnelli, chairman of Juventus and ESL founder, told Reuters, "I remain convinced of the beauty of that project, of the value that it would have developed to the pyramid, of the creation of the best competition in the world, but evidently no. I don't think that project is now still up and running" (ibid). Joel Glazer distributed a letter of apology, saying it was a mistake for Manchester United to join the ESL. Former co-owner of Arsenal FC, David Dein, told the BBC, "The Super League project is a lesson on how not to launch a campaign. …All the way through there was no-one ever speaking up for them to defend them. In all my years in football I've never seen something so major start and finish so quickly" (European Super League…, April 25, 2021). A lack of understanding of the power of stakeholders and of protest and social media brought the Super League to a close in three days.

The ESL crisis was like most organizational crises – self-inflicted. The crisis falls into the SCCT's intentional cluster. The response was not uniform, which Dein noted was part of the problem. Little to no coordination was apparent. At best, the owners attempted to diminish the crisis. Behaviorally, the club owners quickly exhibited their aversion to loss. While the ESL was created to make the most profitable clubs more so, the owners followed a suboptimal tactic of quickly folding rather than engaging in dialogue as they should have before the announcement. The crisis response narrative was owned by external publics. Narratives created highlighted the fact that the clubs were created and maintained by the fans, not the owners. The owners were simply exhibiting greed.

The ESL could not seem to turn this narrative around and therefore was forced to shift from pure advocacy for the new league to pure accommodation of fan demands – within 72 hours.

This case demonstrates the importance of influential social media creators, as noted in the SMCC model. Social media posts by Prince William, David Beckham, and current player Benjamin Mendy all served to reinforce the fans' positions. To maintain the support of those whose concerns they had not addressed, the club owners had little option but to employ Benoit's Image Restoration tactic to attempt to reduce the offensiveness of the plan.

WhatsApp Update

On January 4, 2021, the messaging application WhatsApp was the most popular in its category, with 2 billion users. That same day, it announced a new privacy policy. The app, owned by Facebook, was popular because of its end-to-end encryption. Conversations using the app were unable to be collected and monetized for their data value. But the new privacy policy required WhatsApp users to share data with Facebook, which would then use the data to assist advertisers in targeting their audience. WhatsApp users weren't happy.

A global boycott movement emerged. In the ten days following the January 4 announcement, WhatsApp installs dropped by 16%. "Privacy-conscious consumers demand companies and brands to provide more transparency and granular consent," Forrester senior analyst Xiaofeng Weng told *PRWeek*. The PR trade publication reported, "Confusion over WhatsApp's data collection practices and how long it has been sharing data with Facebook points to the need for 'better transparency and communication,'" according to Weng (Goodfellow, January 20, 2021).

In the days following WhatsApp's announcement, Tesla CEO Elon Musk and Twitter CEO Jack Dorsey each promoted the use of WhatsApp competitors. Musk simply tweeted, "Use Signal," a competing encrypted messaging app. Dorsey posted a screenshot of the App Store charts showing Signal at the top. He added a heart emoji (Nguyen, January 15, 2021). Following such high-profile endorsements, The Signal app reached 1.3 million downloads in one day. Its previous daily download average was 50,000. A second WhatsApp rival, Telegram, also saw remarkable growth as WhatsApp users migrated away (Hodge, January 15, 2021).

Over those ten days following the announcement, Signal installs grew by 19.3 million. The company had only 317,000 installs during the entire preceding month of December 2020. Likewise, Telegram installs grew by 17.4 million over the same time (Goodfellow, January 20, 2021). In April 2021, Indian tech publication *Trak.in* ran this headline: "It's Official: Signal Beats WhatsApp to Become World's Fastest Growing Messenger App" (Kulkarni, April 4, 2021). India was WhatsApp's biggest market, with 340 million users in January 2021 (Goodfellow, January 20, 2021).

On January 15, 2021, WhatsApp published its response to the furor in a blog post. "We've heard from so many people how much confusion there is around our recent update. There's been a lot of misinformation causing concern and we want to help everyone understand our principles and the facts… We're also going to do a lot more to clear up the misinformation around how privacy and security works on WhatsApp. We'll then go to people gradually to review the policy at their own pace before new business options are available on May 15," the company reported (Statt, January 15, 2021).

PRWeek predicted that WhatsApp's user base would take no "meaningful hit" from the crisis because shifting messaging applications is challenging due to the need to shift contacts, too. Jason Davey, head of experience technology at Ogilvy Australia, told *PRWeek*, "Messaging platform adoption depends on your complete circle of friends and family following in your footsteps. With over 2 billion users globally, it will take more than this policy update issue for non-savvy WhatsApp users to bother switching, learning a new app, setting up new contacts, etc." (Goodfellow, January 20, 2021).

The negative response to WhatsApp's change in privacy policy was likely linked to the poor pre-existing relational reputation of Facebook. The SCCT links the depth of a crisis to the preexisting reputation of an organization. The response from WhatsApp users suggests feeling betrayed by a company that purports to be about privacy and security of messaging. WhatsApp employed a rebuilding strategy. The behavioral crisis communication linked to the WhatsApp policy change was shifted from a February start to a May start. The policy remained in place, so the suboptimal response was simply putting off what would become inevitable for WhatsApp users.

The narrative of the crisis response attempted to meet the ideal of routine communication, crisis communication, and return to routine communication. By shifting the implementation date, WhatsApp employed a modest shift from pure advocacy to very partial accommodation of WhatsApp users. As Contingency Theory predicts, the disparity of power between WhatsApp/Facebook and boycotting consumers allowed the social media titans to be somewhat dismissive of user concerns.

The role of influential social media creators, as outlined in the SMCC model, is once again illustrated in this case. When Musk and Dorsey promoted WhatsApp competitor Signal, consumers listened. Nevertheless, WhatsApp did little to address image repair beyond working to reduce the offensiveness of the policy by delaying it.

Fagor Electrical Appliances

The bankruptcy of Fagor Electrical Appliances (FEA) cooperative company in 2013 put Mondragon Corporation (MC), the world's largest conglomerate of cooperatives, in jeopardy. The Basque MC is a megastructure employing about 80,000 workers around the world and comprising over 260 companies.

It is often said that the Mondragon Corporation has a very complex organizational structure, whereas actually it is just an inverted pyramid structure, which is a system of democracy based on representation: at the top are cooperatives with their own sovereignty, sectoral divisions are in the middle, and the corporate center is at the bottom.

The failed cooperative Fagor Electrical Appliances was the key cooperative in the corporation. It was the first cooperative project, created in 1956; it was also the catalyst for the creation of all the other cooperatives, due to its rapid expansion and financial success, among other reasons. In its factories, spanning the length and breadth of the Basque Country there were 2,000 workers. Solidarity and participatory democracy were at the heart of this cooperative company; worker-members were actively involved in the management and development of the company and the group.

Although the crisis situation was evident, it needed to be made public, reported on and clearly explained. It was unclear whether the Fagor cooperative would completely collapse. There was disbelief among citizens, the media, and cooperative stakeholders because the Mondragon Group cooperatives had always been financially solvent and had always coped well with economic crises. During the crisis, their main task was to protect FEA's most important asset: the Fagor brand. This was done by transmitting positive values of its corporate image.

Prior to filing for bankruptcy, the FEA crisis managers did not gather to analyze data and user feedback from social media. They received monthly data reports on the impact of social media activity. After filing for bankruptcy, the volume of social media traffic became impossible to manage. Twitter comments were collected and analyzed. Simultaneously, the cooperative had to communicate legal decisions, manage the brand and minimize any negative effects, and remain optimistic about Fagor's legacy.

During the crisis, the strategy followed by the Fagor and the Mondragon Corporation concurred with two defensive tactics found in Benoit's (1995) Image Repair Theory: (1) avoiding responsibility and (2) corrective action. FEA and the MC dodged any semblance of responsibility for the crisis and eluded the media in an aim to deflect any responsibility. They used social media as a listening device and attempted some accommodation of stakeholders.

According to the SCCT, there are several ways in which companies can apologize. Although FEA and MC did not clearly request any forgiveness or engage in self-criticism, they did express grief. The purpose of this strategy is to express grief or sorrow at what has happened, which would demonstrate the aim to minimize the damage done.

A meta-organization such as the MC has shown that putting crisis communication and crisis management principles into practice can be a complex task, especially when the structure of the organization itself regulates and limits the relationship with other organizations. In this case, the dependence on worker-members and the horizontal organization of the corporate governing bodies also had a great impact on decision-making. In fact, the rapid response times required by a crisis situation clashed with the procedures of cooperative decision-making. However, the cooperative did recognize the need to minimize clashes with the media and to maximize social media outreach, employing a more proactive communication policy.

Listening to Experts

The expansion of crisis communication research over the last decade shows its growing influence within public relations (Coombs, 2010; Heath, 2010; Pasadeos et al., 2010). Today, crisis communication, which is recognized as both an organizational practice and as an academic discipline at universities (Frandsen & Johansen, 2017), continues to engender interest among professionals, researchers, and students. However, there is a lack of qualitative studies examining the discipline.

Attempting to address that void, an international Delphi study (Manias-Muñoz et al., 2019) was conducted among 23 seasoned crisis scholars to explore the state of crisis communication research in Africa, Australia, Europe, and North America. The study aimed to get a better understanding of the quality and methodological application of the contributions; how the body of knowledge is built; what are gaps in current research; and what undermines or facilitates crisis communication scholarship and practice.

In 2018 a qualitative questionnaire with 10 open-ended questions accompanied by a Likert Scale was put into circulation to stimulate, broaden and collect insights linked to the advancement of crisis communication research and education.

A Call for More and Better Dialogue between Scholars and Practitioners

The research showed a gap between theory (academia) and practice (industry) continues to be pronounced in crisis communication research. Knowledge transfer between scholars and practitioners appears to be insufficient and unsuccessful. Crisis researchers' opinions show two crisis communication bodies of knowledge, one that emerges from scholarship and one that arises from practice. These two approaches, however, are often walled off from one another in academic journals or trade publications. Additionally, some participants mentioned that the body of knowledge of crisis communication is focused mostly on academic theories or over-generalized case studies, and thus crisis communication scholarship seems to be out of touch with what occurs in practice.

According to experts in the U.S., the body of knowledge there is built largely through individual research agendas, and theories tend to be idiosyncratic of the prominent researchers, whose directions vary. Experts noted that professional research is more influential because it reaches more practitioners. European experts described a similar relationship between academics and professionals.

Additionally, experts said crisis communication has abandoned its self-centric approach and has begun to discuss how to profit from other academic fields and interdisciplinary research. Crisis scholars in nearly all countries cite and use, in similar ways, ideas and theories from different disciplines, like management, psychology, public relations, and communication theory. In the U.S., the interplay between disciplines tends to be less flexible and some experts in the U.S. claimed they often fail to cite each other's work.

Some Future Perspectives

Crisis experts believe crisis communication research is too dominated by case studies, and as a result, the research is difficult to be generalized in building a strong, global, crisis communication theoretical framework. It does not mean, however, that case studies are not valid, but future research should be focused more on fundamental research and theory development and less on narrow case studies. According to experts one methodological approach applied too often in crisis communication research is the experimental approach using a student sample. Respondents claimed these studies are not addressing nor testing what crisis communication research requests, that is, meta-theoretical issues.

A future challenge is developing more sophisticated methods of data collection and data analysis; getting access to the field before, during, and after crises or disasters; and considering international and cultural diversity. The challenge is to effectively respond with accurate information and define what fact and speculation are, to know what news suggests real threats and how to avoid noise. This also means paying attention to organizational learning, to community practices and making them valuable at a global scale, and listening to crisis communication management teams. In the same way, some experts find that crisis researchers need to be more active in industry discussions, identifying pressing crisis research topics and even collaborating with practitioners to design research projects.

In the future, crisis experts would like to see new theory and strategy development; new research designs; more triangulation approaches using multiple research methods; more inward insights in studies concerning organizational crises; more expansion of crisis communication directions, more interdisciplinary studies, and eventually more societal contribution.

Speed and Control: The Blessing and Curse of Social-Mediated Crisis Communication

As illustrated in this chapter, theory and practice do go hand in glove whether scholars or practitioners know it or not. Current issues of social media and crisis communication are challenging but hopeful. Social-mediated crisis communication can be nearly instantaneous and highly targeted by stakeholder groups. But this near-instant distribution of information cuts two ways. Whether it is Jack Dorsey celebrating the rise of a social media app, to the detriment of the app's challenger, or the Duke of Cambridge cheering on football fans in their challenge of club owners, social media posts are often disruptors and sources of crisis. Understanding the intersection of crisis communication scholarship and practice will benefit both.

References

BBC.com (April 21, 2021). European Super League timeline: Game changer – football's volatile 72 hours. Last accessed: May 2, 2021. https://www.bbc.com/sport/football/56825570

BBC.com (April 25, 2021). European Super League: Manchester United fans protest against Glazer family. Last accessed: May 2, 2021. https://www.bbc.com/sport/football/56870465

Benoit, W. L. (1995). *Accounts, excuses, apologies: A theory of image restoration discourse*. State University of New York Press. https://doi.org/10.5860/choice.33-1337

Benoit, W. L. (2015). Image repair theory in the context of strategic communication. Handbook of strategic communication, In D. Holtzhausen & A. Zerfass (Eds.), *The Routledge handbook of strategic communication* (pp. 303–311). Routledge. https://doi.org/10.4324/9780203094440-28

Cancel, A. E., Cameron, G. T., Sallot, L. M., & Mitrook, M. A. (1997). It depends: A contingency theory of accommodation in public relations. *Journal of Public Relations Research*, 9(1), 31–63. doi: https://doi.org/10.1207/s1532754xjprr0901_02

Claeys, A.-S., & Coombs, W. T. (2020). Organizational crisis communication: Suboptimal crisis response selection decisions and behavioral economics. *Communication Theory*, 30(3), 290–309. doi: https://doi.org/10.1093/ct/qtz002

Coombs, W. T. (2007). Protecting organization reputations during a crisis: The development and application of situational crisis communication theory. *Corporate Reputation Review*, 10(3), 163–176. doi: https://doi.org/10.1057/palgrave.crr.1550049

Coombs, W. T. (2010). Parameters for crisis communication. In W. T. Coombs, & S. J. Holladay (Eds.), *The handbook of crisis communication* (pp. 17–53). Wiley-Blackwell.

Frandsen, F., & Johansen, W. (2017). *Organizational crisis communication: A multivocal approach*. Sage.

Goodfellow, J. (January 20, 2021). WhatsApp privacy crisis could erode Facebook's dominance over user time, PRWeek. Last accessed: May 2, 2021. https://www.prweek.com/article/1704991/whatsapp-privacy-crisis-erode-facebooks-dominance-user-time

Heath, R. L. (1994). *Management of corporate communication: From internal contacts to external affairs*. Erlbaum Associates.

Heath, R. L. (2004). Telling a story: A narrative approach to communication during crisis. In D. P. Millar D. P. & R. L. Heath (Eds.), *Responding to crisis: A rhetorical approach to crisis communication* (pp. 167–187). https://doi.org/10.4324/9781410609496-17

Heath, R. L. (2010). Crisis communication: Defining the beast and de-marginalizing key publics. In W. T. Coombs, & S. J. Holladay (Eds.), *The handbook of crisis communication* (pp. 1–13). Wiley-Blackwell.

Hodge, R. (January 15, 2021). After Musk tweet, Signal and Telegram see millions of new downloads, CNET. Last accessed: May 3, 2021. https://www.cnet.com/news/after-musk-tweet-signal-and-telegram-see-millions-of-new-downloads/

Jin, Y., & Liu, B. F. (2010). The blog-mediated crisis communication model: Recommendations for responding to influential external blogs. *Journal of Public Relations Research, 22,* 429–455. https://doi.org/10.1080/10627261003801420

Kemp, S. (October 2020). Digital 2020: Global Digital Statshot Report. Last accessed: May 1, 2021 https://thenextweb.com/news/more-than-50-of-humans-in-the-world-use-social-media-heres-what-you-need-to-know

Kulkarni, R. (April 4, 2021). It's Official: Signal Beats WhatsApp To Become World's Fastest Growing Messenger App. Trak.in. Last accessed: May 3, 2021. https://trak.in/tags/business/2021/04/04/its-official-signal-beats-whatsapp-to-become-worlds-fastest-growing-messenger-app/

Liu, B. F., Jin, Y., Austin, L., Kuligowski, E., & Young, C. E. (2021). The social-mediated crisis communication (SMCC) model: Identifying the next frontier. In Y. Jin, B. H. Reber, & G. J. Nowak (Eds.), *Advancing crisis communication effectiveness: Integrating public relations scholarship with practice* (pp. 214–230). Routledge.

Manias-Muñoz, I., Jin, Y., & Reber, B. H. (2019). The state of crisis communication research and education through the lens of crisis scholars: An international Delphi study. *Public Relations Review, 45*(4), 101797. doi: https://doi.org/10.1016/j.pubrev.2019.101797

Nguyen, N. (January 15, 2021). WhatsApp, Signal, Telegram and iMessage: Choosing a Private Encrypted Chat App, Wall Street Journal. Last accessed: May 3, 2021. https://www.wsj.com/articles/signal-telegram-whatsapp-and-imessage-choosing-a-private-encrypted-chat-app-11610550076

Nytimes.com (April 19, 2021). The "Super League" Announcement. Last accessed: May 2, 2021. https://www.nytimes.com/interactive/2021/04/19/sports/soccer/super-league-announcement.html

Pang, A., Jin, Y., & Cameron, G. T. (2012). Contingency theory of strategic conflict management: Directions for the practice of crisis communication from a decade of theory development, discovery, and dialogue. In W. T. Coombs, & S. J. Holladay (Eds.), *The handbook of crisis communication* (pp. 527–549). John Wiley & Sons, Ltd.

Pasadeos, Y., Berger, B., & Renfro, R. B. (2010). Public relations as a maturing discipline: An update on research networks. *Journal of Public Relations Research, 22*(2), 136–158. doi: https://doi.org/10.1080/10627261003601390

PwC (2019). Global Crisis Survey 2019. Last accessed: May 1, 2021. https://www.pwc.com/gx/en/news-room/press-releases/2019/global-crisis-survey.html

PwC (2021). Global Crisis Survey 2021: Building Resilience for the Future. Last accessed: May 1, 2021. https://www.pwc.com/gx/en/issues/crisis-solutions/global-crisis-survey.html

Reber, B. H., Yarbrough, C. R., Nowak, G., & Jin, Y. (2021). Complex and challenging crises: A call for solutions. In Y. Jin, B. H. Reber, & G. J. Nowak (Eds.), *Advancing crisis communication effectiveness: Integrating public relations scholarship with practice* (pp. 3–16). Routledge.

Shin, J.-H., & Health, R. L. (2021). *Public relations theory: Capabilities and competencies.* John Wiley & Sons.

Statt, N. (January 15, 2021). WhatsApp to delay new privacy policy amid mass confusion about Facebook data sharing. *The Verge.* Last accessed: May 2, 2021. https://www.theverge.com/2021/1/15/22233257/whatsapp-privacy-policy-update-delayed-three-months

van der Meer, T. G. L. A., Verhoeven, P., Beentjes, H. W. J., & Vliegenthart, R. (2017). Communication in times of crisis: The stakeholder relationship under pressure. *Public Relations Review, 43*(2), 426–440. doi: https://doi.org/10.1016/j.pubrev.2017.02.005

SECTION II

Current Issues of Social Media

3

ETHICAL AND LEGAL PRINCIPLES FOR THE PRACTITIONER

Consumers, Organizations, and Platforms

Taylor S. Voges and Jonathan Peters

Social media saw stratospheric growth in the first 20 years of the twenty-first century. The early 2000s marked the beginning of the social media age. Platforms quickly became dominant, and by 2010 Facebook had amassed 500 million users, YouTube had 400 million, and Twitter had 40 million. Not even ten years later, in 2019, Facebook had amassed 2.38 *billion* users, YouTube had 2 *billion*, and Twitter had 330 million (Ortiz-Ospina, 2019). Further, these social media platforms have become increasingly important to organizations and their communication practitioners (Coombs & Holladay, 2012).

Social media can be used in a variety of ways, but the type of interaction of interest here is among consumers, organizations, and platforms. Practitioners can use social media to scan for potential crises (Coombs & Holladay, 2012). These scans are important for the organization as they can help practitioners identify consumer concerns that may read as a crisis but ultimately do not warrant the same response (Coombs & Holladay, 2012). This is known as a *paracrisis*: a situation similar to a crisis that is not an actual one. These distinctions are important because of the difference in responses. Consider, for example, that truthful comments posted on social media can have appreciably different implications than untruthful comments. Truthful but negative comments have produced litigation, while extreme untruthful comments have resulted in weaponization and unethical uses of social media, with serious impacts on an organization's reputation.

This chapter explores how user comments made on social media have differing legal and ethical implications for both the organization and the practitioner. Those of focus include: how consumers use platforms to communicate with

DOI: 10.4324/9781003043409-6

organizations; how platforms moderate consumer communications; how organizations respond through litigation; and the practical and legal effectiveness of that litigation in view of the corresponding First Amendment and procedural challenges.

Consumer Use of Platforms to Review Products and Services

A unique feature of consumer-organization interactions on social media is the inclusion of a third party, the social media platform. The organization's communication practitioners are engaging with consumers in a mediated space. The organization is responsible for its page or account, but the platform sets the rules of engagement for the organization and its consumers (or users). It is important for practitioners to be aware of the differences between these platforms in order to engage appropriately and effectively.

Yelp

Yelp, founded in 2004 by Jeremy Stoppelman and Russel Simmons, is a platform that crowdsources reviews of businesses (About Yelp, n.d.). Yelp reported an average of 28 million monthly users and $169 million in revenue for the first two quarters of 2020 (Yelp, n.d.). Yelp allows consumers to interact with organizations by posting information, pictures, and reviews ("Yelp Metrics," n.d.).

Organizations can use Yelp to support their missions by posting content, interacting with consumers, and buying advertisements. Consumers can use Yelp in the marketplace by finding and scrutinizing businesses based on user reviews and by posting about their own experiences with businesses.

TripAdvisor

TripAdvisor, founded in 2000 by Stephen Kaufer and Langley Steinert, offers a variety of services that include travel information, travel forums, and reviews and opinions (TripAdvisor Media Center, n.d.). The platform is home to over 860 million reviews and 463 million monthly users ("Media Center," n.d.), and in 2019 it reported $1.56 billion in revenue (Lock, 2020).

There are two ways for a business to be listed: one is for the business to request a listing, and the other is for a user to create a listing by reviewing the business (TripAdvisor Help Center, n.d.). Users post about their experiences with hotels, airlines, restaurants, tour guides, and more. TripAdvisor moderates the reviews to ensure that they are unbiased and are based on actual experiences (TripAdvisor, n.d.).

Facebook

Mark Zuckerberg, along with Andrew McCollum, Eduardo Saverin, Dustin Moskovitz, and Chris Hughes, founded Facebook in 2004. The platform has changed significantly, starting as a site exclusively for Harvard students and evolving to include all manner of users worldwide (Barr, 2018). Zuckerberg has said that Facebook's mission is to give people a voice and to build community (About Facebook, n.d.).

Facebook users can be individuals or businesses, in the latter case through brand pages and the opportunity to advertise on the platform and to allow consumers to shop the brand while still on Facebook (Help Center n.d.). Users, in turn, can also review businesses on the platform.

Ethics and Consumer Communication on Social Media Platforms

Social media has been a locus of organizational issues (Burns, 2008). Organizations have posted on social media sites falsely claiming to be consumers (Burns, 2008). Consumers have weaponized social media platforms to attack organizations (Aarts, 2015). Consumers have paid to post about organizations without disclosure (Toledano & Avidar, 2016), and much more.

Consumers post reviews for various reasons, but there are two motivations especially worth exploring: good and bad faith. When posting in good faith, consumers can offer businesses feedback and offer information to other consumers that help them make informed decisions. Good-faith comments, however, may be negative. The practitioner must choose how to engage with negative good-faith comments about their experiences with the organization.

When posting in bad faith, consumers can weaponize reviews to attack an organization for reasons not related directly to its products and services, with the possible effect of harming the business (Aarts, 2015). In one case, political activists posted thousands of false reviews of the restaurant Red Hen, after its co-owner asked Sarah Huckabee Sanders, then the White House press secretary under President Donald Trump, to leave (Matsakis, 2020). Supporters of Sanders posted one-star reviews, while supporters of the co-owner posted five-star reviews. The Red Hen case is not isolated but demonstrates how the manipulation of reviews presents ethical concerns.

Indeed, unethical decision-making can result in organizational reputation concerns, as happened with Red Hen (Aarts, 2015). Ethics on social media (or a lack thereof) can come from within the organization or from outside the organization. Practitioners need to be prepared to make decisions that are founded on ethical principles.

Ethics is a determination of right and wrong (Bowen, 2004; Duncan & Voges, 2020; Josephson, 2002). It is a question of rightness in deciding which choice is best. There are many different approaches and theories of ethics, and all provide insight into right and wrong and the decision-making process. Two discussed here are deontology and utilitarianism, both of which are widely used approaches in the field of communication (Bowen, 2004; Christians, 2007).

Deontology

Through Immanuel Kant's work, ethics can be seen as a responsibility of the actor's, a duty, to uphold moral principles like truth-telling (Bowen, 2004). The concern, for deontology, is evaluating decisions by thinking through how they reflect agreed-upon moral principles. If there is a question regarding *to tell the truth or to lie*, the deontologist would consider how the choices reflect and affect the overall moral principle. If truth is a moral principle, deontology suggests that it is humanity's duty to uphold it and to avoid lying. Should a lie be chosen, then the moral principle of truth would degrade and ultimately hurt society.

For a communication practitioner, the moral principles typically of interest are advocacy, transparency, and honesty – which can be found in various codes of ethics (e.g., the PRSA Code of Ethics). Each principle, or value, can be threatened in times of crisis, so it is up to practitioners to discern how to uphold the principles.

Utilitarianism

Utilitarianism is popularly traced back to philosopher John Stuart Mill. This perspective of ethics evaluates decision-making from the potential consequences of an action (Mill, 1863/2002). Based in part around the Greatest Happiness Principle, decisions are made by determining how much goodness (or happiness) the action will bring to others. And others, in this context, are evaluated by like desires that typically result in majority and minority groups.

For the communication practitioner, these groups might manifest as an organization's employees, consumers, and shareholders. The goodness, or rightness, of an action is then thought of in conjunction with how the consequences affect the identified groups.

Ethics Applications

These two approaches to ethics offer insights into how decisions can be made. However, the Potter Box (see Table 3.1) offers a more hands-on approach to decision-making in times of crisis (Franquet-Santos-Silva & Ventura-Morujao, 2017). It is a model of moral reasoning and can help practitioners develop better analysis and deeper understandings of questionable scenarios (Franquet-Santos-Silva & Ventura-Morujao, 2017).

TABLE 3.1 The Potter Box (Franquet-Santos-Silva & Ventura-Morujao, 2017)

Definitions	Values
What is important to know?	*What core ideas do you need to think about when making this decision?*
Principles	Loyalties
What framework will guide the practitioner to the best decision?	*Who matters in this decision? Who does this situation affect?*

The Potter Box presents decision-making in four separate but related quadrants: (1) definition, (2) values, (3) principles, and (4) loyalties. The first quadrant requires a practitioner to describe the situation at hand: *What is important to know?* The second quadrant requires insight into what is being affected: *What core ideas do you need to think about when making this decision?* There is the possibility that the values conflict, which could be indicative of an ethical dilemma and a harder decision (Franquet-Santos-Silva & Ventura-Morujao, 2017). The third quadrant requires an application of principles, i.e., theories like deontology and utilitarianism. Here, the practitioner uses the theories for guidance: *What framework will guide the practitioner to the best decision?* Decisions without guiding principles lack moral grounding and cannot be sufficiently justified (Christians et al., 2005). The fourth quadrant requires the practitioner to reflect on the parties involved in or affected by the decision: *Who matters in this decision? Who does this situation affect?* Examples of such parties include the organization, segmented consumer groups, the communications team, and the practitioner.

The Potter Box can be used to evaluate decisions normatively or to examine current choices prescriptively (Franquet-Santos-Silva & Ventura-Morujao, 2017). When a practitioner conducts scans of social media, as recommended by Coombs and Holladay (2012), the practitioner can use the Potter Box to guide his or her choices. In situations like the Red Hen example, practitioners are expected to respond. How to respond to social media uncertainties, issues, and crises needs to be explicitly guided by moral principles or the resulting decisions cannot be easily justified.

After orienting oneself to ethical principles that will improve decision-making and the rightness of the corresponding choices, the practitioner and the organization have a variety of principles, actions, and responses to consider. But in the context of consumer comments posted to a social media platform like Facebook, it is necessary first to understand how those platforms engage with consumer content.

Content Moderation and Consumer Reviews

Content moderation is the "practice of screening user generated content (UGC) posted to Internet sites, social media and other online outlets, in order to determine the appropriateness of the content for a given site, locality, or jurisdiction"

(Roberts, 2017). When a user signs up for an account on a platform, she must agree to its terms of service, and they almost always include content-related rules and speak to how the platform may address violations of those rules.

Content moderation is commonly carried out in two ways: by people and artificial intelligence (Gerrard & Thornham, 2020). Human content moderators review potentially objectionable content and apply relevant rules to it, moving at a fast pace and in difficult working conditions (Newton, 2019). They consider context and nuance better than artificial intelligence, though artificial intelligence reduces the amount of disturbing content that humans view (York & McSherry, 2019). But artificial intelligence also makes more errors due to machine learning limits (Gerrard & Thornham, 2020).

Platforms engage in content moderation for assorted reasons, among them to manifest their community values, to offer users and businesses better experiences, to comply with the law, and to manage the volume of user posts (Cobbe, 2020). On Facebook alone, there are roughly 2.85 billion active monthly users, and they create a lot of content. Brands publish around 52 posts per week, media organizations around 53 posts per week, and sports teams around 18 posts per week (Omnicore Agency, 2021). The content runs the gamut from photos and videos to narrative status updates and comments.

Unfortunately, mistakes are too often made: Zuckerberg once estimated that one in ten of Facebook's content-moderation decisions turns out to be a mistake (Koetsier, 2020). In addition, some users are wary and suspicious of how content moderation works (Koetsier, 2020). In the context of user reviews, platforms tend to focus on moderating content that is abusive, content that is uncivil or vulgar or coarse, and content that is a threat to safety, authenticity, information integrity, or trustworthiness. The standard language attempts to nip bad-faith reviews by forbidding untruthful or unauthentic reviews and/or by requiring that a poster have personal experience with a business or its products and services. Depending on the platform, flagged or offending posts may be moderated by human beings, artificial intelligence, or a combination.

Responding Through Litigation

Platforms conduct private speech regulation through the enforcement of their content rules and community guidelines (Benesch & MacKinnon, 2012). They are able to decide what may be posted, when to honor requests to remove content, and how to display and prioritize information using algorithms (Peters, 2014) and are unconstrained by constitutional limits, including those imposed by the First Amendment (Sengupta, 2012). Users cannot call on the First Amendment to constrain content policies and practices of platforms like Yelp, TripAdvisor, and Facebook. Platforms have the right to set and enforce their content rules.

They also enjoy a broad legal immunity under Section 230 of the Communications Decency Act, passed in 1996, which says "[n]o provider or user of an interactive computer service shall be treated as the publisher or speaker of any information provided by another information content provider" (47 U.S.C. § 230; Harmon, 2018). Platforms are not liable for most of the user-generated content that they host. The law also states that platforms will not lose these protections even if they moderate their user content (Harmon, 2018). If a business wanted to file a defamation action over a review, the business would not prevail against the platform hosting the review.

Businesses occasionally initiate legal actions related to offending reviews (when in a crisis or when a review is causing one), and usually the actions are defamation claims. This kind of litigation can be effective regardless of its outcome. It invokes the judicial system's formality to legitimize – to some extent – the claims made by the business. It can also have the effect of chilling criticism of the business by sending the message that consumers may review it at their peril. This is often true where a plaintiff is not likely to win on the merits and instead is wanting to retaliate against critics or to intimidate critics from speaking out.

But that is unprincipled as a communications practice and unwise as a legal strategy because these suits frequently fail under Section 230; under procedures allowing for the swift dismissal of claims lacking merit and designed to chill protected speech (Vining & Matthews, n.d.); under laws that block compelled disclosure of anonymous users (Vining & Matthews, n.d.); and under First Amendment doctrines both hostile to prior restraints and protective of opinions expressed in exaggerated, figurative, and hyperbolic language.

Defamation

Defamation is the umbrella term for a legal claim involving injury to a person's or entity's reputation caused by a false statement of fact. It includes libel (traditionally written) and slander (traditionally spoken). In any event, defamation is a state law claim limited by federal constitutional principles. States define their defamation laws as long as they do not run afoul of the First Amendment (Peters, 2015).

Courts have established doctrines and elements that attempt to balance a plaintiff's interest in protecting her reputation with a defendant's interest in her own speech (Schauer, 1978). What has emerged is a highly complex area of law in which it is difficult for plaintiffs to win as well as expensive and time-consuming simply to bring or defend a claim. To prevail in most states, a plaintiff must prove that the statement at issue is defamatory, false, presented as a matter of fact, and published; that it is of and concerning the plaintiff; and that the defendant is at fault and caused the plaintiff to suffer harm (Lee et al., 2020).

It is notable that falsely accusing a person or organization of a serious moral failing or job-related incompetence is seen by courts as highly likely to harm reputation (Peters, 2015). In some states, the plaintiff would not have to prove actual harm and the court would simply presume harm because of the inherently injurious nature of the claims (Peters, 2015). But a key element, always, is falsity. A statement must be factually false for there to be defamation.

Case Studies

Consider the following cases (see Table 3.2), generally representative of the significant challenges of prevailing in defamation claims related to online reviews.

These cases show that organizations have the right to defend their reputations in the courts, but it is difficult for plaintiffs to find success in defamation claims related to online reviews. Courts are not friendly to injunctions that restrict or remove reviews. They use Section 230 to dismiss claims against platforms acting as intermediaries and content moderators, and courts recognize broad First Amendment protections for reviews using exaggerated, figurative, and hyperbolic language. Courts recast reviewers as sources, too, to invoke a reporter's shield law to prevent compelled disclosure of anonymous users, and still other courts dismiss claims lacking merit and designed to chill constitutionally protected speech.

TABLE 3.2 Reputation Crisis Litigation Case Studies

Case	Facts	Outcome	Implications
Perez v. Dietz Development LLC (Supreme Court of Virginia, 2012)	Dietz is a construction contractor that provided Perez with services. Perez posted criticism of the services on Yelp, among other platforms, and said Dietz's company "is not legitimate in lacking BBB Accreditation" and that Dietz had once been sanctioned by a state regulator. Dietz felt this presented a crisis to both his business and name, so he sued for defamation and sought an injunction against Perez – to remove the posts and to prevent any further posts while the lawsuit was pending.	The trial court granted the injunction in part, but the state supreme court reversed and vacated it, finding that the injunction was "not justified" and that it apparently constituted a prior restraint in violation of the First Amendment.	Businesses should proceed carefully when considering legal actions against former customers who post unfavorable reviews because rushing to court can result in a high-profile defeat. This is true where the desired remedy is a prior restraint, which is presumptively unconstitutional.

(Continued)

TABLE 3.2 Reputation Crisis Litigation Case Studies *(Continued)*

Case	Facts	Outcome	Implications
Reit v. Yelp!, Inc. (New York Supreme Court, 2010)	Reit is a dentist with reviews on Yelp, one of which is negative and calls his office "small," "old," and "smelly," with "old and dirty" equipment. Reit alleged that the negative reviews were causing him to lose 5 to 11 calls per day, so, to try to address such a crisis, he sued Yelp and a John Doe user for defamation. Reit said he complained to Yelp about the negative review and that the platform eventually removed all of the reviews, even the positive ones. In addition to money damages, Reit sought an order requiring Yelp to delete all references to him and his office.	The court dismissed the defamation claims against Yelp based on Section 230 of the Communications Decency Act.	These claims were clearly barred by Section 230, so Reit appears thin-skinned for bringing them. This is true where the desired remedy is an order to remove speech, requiring the plaintiff to clear a prohibitively high bar.
Seaton v. TripAdvisor LLC (U.S. Court of Appeals for the Sixth Circuit, 2013)	TripAdvisor published a list titled "Dirtiest Hotels, as reported by travelers on TripAdvisor." Grand Resort Hotel in Pigeon Forge, Tennessee, topped the list. It included a user photo of a bedspread and a quote from a review: "There was dirt … in the bathtub which was filled with lots of dark hair." In an accompanying press release, TripAdvisor stated, "If you are looking for a hotel with chewing tobacco spit oozing down the halls and corridors … carpeting so greasy and dirty you wouldn't want to sit your luggage down - let alone walk around barefoot … by all means stay at the Grand Resort." The hotel's proprietor, Seaton, in a crisis caused by the bad publicity, sued the platform for defamation.	TripAdvisor filed a motion to dismiss, asserting that Grand Resort Hotel's placement on the list was protected under the First Amendment. The trial court granted the motion, and the appeals court affirmed, focusing only on TripAdvisor's own statements, not those of its users. The appeals court held that a reasonable person would not understand the language in question as assertions of fact but as hyperbole or rhetorical exaggeration that is constitutionally protected.	The court acknowledged the problems in attacking a platform's efforts to provide illuminating metadata, observing that "top ten lists and the like appear with growing frequency on the web. It seems to us that a reasonable observer understands that placement on and ranking within the bulk of such lists constitutes opinion, not a provable fact."

(Continued)

TABLE 3.2 Reputation Crisis Litigation Case Studies *(Continued)*

Case	Facts	Outcome	Implications
Lincoln City Lodging Ltd. P'ship I v. Doe (Multnomah County Circuit Court, Oregon, 2014)	The Ashley Inn in Lincoln City, Oregon, sued for defamation a John Doe user who posted under a pseudonym several negative and crisis-inducing TripAdvisor reviews about the Inn. They said that the "laundry and housekeeping are either high or drunk," that "the owner smokes weed," and that the front-desk associate "had phone sex with someone." TripAdvisor refused to reveal the poster's identity, so the Inn sought in court to compel disclosure of the identity to proceed with its defamation action.	The trial court declined to compel disclosure, and in doing so, the court applied the state reporter's shield law. It protects a reporter from compelled disclosure of sources. The court found that the shield law applied to TripAdvisor on the theory that it is a form of media and that the pseudonymous poster was its source.	This is among the first and most notable rulings to apply a state reporter's shield law to block the compelled disclosure of the identity of an anonymous online reviewer. It prevented the Inn from proceeding with its defamation action because the Inn could not identify the party responsible for the alleged defamation in the review.

Conclusion

User reviews can make or break a business, and they can help consumers make informed choices about the products they buy and the services for which they contract. In order to respond appropriately, communication practitioners need to first understand the legal and ethical repercussions of crisis situations. As online communication evolves, and as platforms continue for many people to be their principal means of public communication (Electronic Frontier Foundation, n.d.), businesses increasingly will have to navigate crises and paracrises related to consumer comments and reviews. Platforms will have to refine continuously their content moderation policies and practices to safeguard the authenticity and informational integrity of the reviews.

This chapter shows how consumers use platforms to post reviews, in good and bad faith; how practitioners can navigate these consumer comments using ethical principles and theories; how platforms moderate the reviews; how businesses respond through litigation; and why that litigation so often is unsuccessful, all against the background of First Amendment doctrines highly protective of individual speech interests.

References

Aarts, D. (2015, Feb. 19). Online review sites allow bad customers to become blackmailers. *Canadian Business.* https://www.canadianbusiness.com/blogs-and-comment/yelp-tripadvisor-review-blackmail/

About Facebook (n.d.). Our Mission. *Facebook.* Retrieved on September 26, 2020, from http://about.fb.com/company-info/

About Yelp (n.d.). Content Guidelines. Yelp. Retrieved on September 26, 2020, from https://www.yelp.com/guidelines

Barr, S. (2018, Aug. 23). When Did Facebook Start? The Story Behind a Company That Took Over the World. *Independent.* https://www.independent.co.uk/life-style/gadgets-and-tech/facebook-when-started-how-mark-zuckerberg-history-harvard-eduardo-saverin-a8505151.html

Benesch, S., & MacKinnon, R. (2012, Oct. 5). The Innocence of YouTube. *Foreign Policy.* http://foreignpolicy.com/2012/10/05/the-innocence-of-youtube/

Bowen, S. A. (2004). Organizational factors encouraging ethical decision making: An exploration into the case of an exemplar. *Journal of Business Ethics, 52*(4), 311–324.

Burns, K. S. (2008). The misuse of social media: Reactions to and important lessons from a blog fiasco. *Journal of New Communications Research, 3*(1), 41–54.

Christians, C. (2007). Utilitarianism in media ethics and its discontents. *Journal of Mass Media Ethics, 22*(2/3), 113–131. https://doi-org.proxy-remote.galib.uga.edu/10.1080/08900520701315640

Christians, C., Rotzoll, K., Fackler, M., McKee, K. B., & Woods, R. H. (2005). *Media ethics: Cases and moral reasoning.* Longman.

Cobbe, J. (2020). Algorithmic censorship by social platforms: Power and resistance. *Philosophy & Technology.* https://doi.org/10.1007/s13347-020-00429-0

Coombs, T. W., & Holladay, S. J. (2012). The paracrisis: The challenges created by publically managing crisis prevention. *Public Relations Review, 38*(3), 408–415. doi: https://doi.org/10.1016/j.pubrev.2012.04.004.

Duncan, J., & Voges, T. S. (2020). EULAs as Unbalanced Contractual Power Between an Organization and Its (Unannounced and Underage) Users: A Mobile Game Textual Analysis. Paper presented to the Critical and Cultural Studies Division of the Association for Education in Journalism and Mass Communication.

Electronic Frontier Foundation (n.d.). Third-Party Platforms. *Electronic Frontier Foundation.* Retrieved on September 29, 2020, from https://www.eff.org/freespeech-weak-link#platforms

Franquet-Santos-Silva, M., & Ventura-Morujao, C. (2017). The Potter Box model of moral reasoning. *El Profesional de La Información, 26*(2), 328–335. doi: https://doi.org/10.3145/epi.2017.mar.2.

Gerrard, Y., & Thornham, H. (2020). Content moderation: Social media's sexist assemblages. *New Media & Society, 22*(7), 1266–1286. doi: http://doi.org:10.1177/1461444820912540.

Harmon, E. (2018, Apr. 12). No, Section 230 Does Not Require Platforms to be Neutral. *EFF.* https://www.eff.org/deeplinks/2018/04/no-section-230-does-not-require-platforms-be-neutral

Help Center. (n.d.). Run an Existing Shoppable Post as an Ad with Product Tags. Retrieved October 21, 2021, from https://www.facebook.com/help/instagram/3847932154942 12?helpref=search&sr=317&query=How+do+I+acctivate+temporarily+disable+my+acc ount%3F&search_session_id=bf869d4e3369f654ac0b899663de38e8.

Josephson, M. (2002). *Making ethical decisions.* Josephson Institute of Ethics.

Koetsier, J. (2020, Jun. 9). Report: Facebook Makes 300,000 Content Moderation Mistakes Every Day. *Forbes.* https://www.forbes.com/sites/johnkoetsier/2020/06/09/300000-facebook-content-moderation-mistakes-daily-report-says/#3b42ea3a54d0

Lee, W., Stewart, D., & Peters, J. (2020). *The law of public communication* (11th ed.). Routledge.

Lincoln City Lodging Ltd. P'ship I v. Doe, No. 14CV4902 (Or. Cir. Ct. Oct. 1, 2014)

Lock, S. (2020, Feb. 24). TripAdvisor's Global Revenue 2008–2019. *Statista.* Retrieved on September 22, 2020, from https://www.statista.com/statistics/225435/tripadvisor-total-revenue/

Matsakis, L. (2020, Jun. 26). The Red Hen and the Weaponization of Yelp. *Wired.* https://www.wired.com/story/red-hen-trump-and-weaponization-of-yelp/

Mill, J. S. (2002 [Originally published 1863]). Utilitarianism. In *The basic writings of John Stuart Mill: On liberty, the subjection of women, and utilitarianism*, introduction by J. B. Schneewind, notes and commentary by D. E. Miller. Modern Library.

Newton, C. (2019, Feb. 25). The Trauma Floor. *The Verge.* https://www.theverge.com/2019/2/25/18229714/cognizant-facebook-content-moderator-interviews-trauma-working-conditions-arizona

Omnicore Agency. (2021, Jan. 4). 63 Facebook Statistics you Need to Know in 2021. Retrieved on October 22nd, 2021 from https://www.omnicoreagency.com/facebook-statistics/

Ortiz-Ospina, E. (2019, Sept. 18). The Rise of Social Media. *Our World in Data.* Retrieved on September 20, 2020, from https://ourworldindata.org/rise-of-social-media#:~:text=Social%20media%20started%20in%20the,%2C%20by%20platform%2C%20since%202004

Perez v. Dietz Development LLC, 2012 WL 6761997 (Va. 2012).

Peters, J. (2014). All the news that's fit to leak. In C. N. Davis, & D. Cuillier (Eds.), *Transparency 2.0: Digital data and privacy in a wired world* (pp. 117–129). Peter Lang Inc.

Peters, J. (2015, Nov. 9). Can I Say That? A Legal Primer for Journalists. *Columbia Journalism Review.* https://www.cjr.org/united_states_project/can_i_say_that_a_legal_primer_for_journalists.php

Reit v. Yelp!, Inc., 2010 WL 3490167 (N.Y. Sup. Ct. Sept. 2, 2010).

Roberts, S. T. (2017). Content moderation. In L. A. Schintler, & C. L. McNeely (Eds.), *Encyclopedia of big data* (pp. 44–49). Springer.

Seaton v. TripAdvisor LLC, 728 F.3d 592 (6th Cir. 2013).

Sengupta, S. (2012, Sept. 16). On Web, a Fine Line on Free Speech Across the Globe. *The New York Times.* http://www.nytimes.com/2012/09/17/technology/on-theweb-a-fine-line-on-free-speech-across-globe.html

Schauer, F. (1978). Fear, risk and the first amendment: Unraveling the chilling effect. *Boston University Law Review 58*(685–732).

Toledano, M., & Avidar, R. (2016). Public relations, ethics, and social media: A cross-national study of PR practitioners. *Public Relations Review, 42*(1), 161–169. doi: https://doi.org/10.1016/j.pubrev.2015.11.012.

TripAdvisor (n.d.). Journey of a Review. *TripAdvisor.* Retrieved on September 22, 2020, from https://www.tripadvisor.com/TripAdvisorInsights/w795

TripAdvisor Help Center. (n.d.). Listing a Business/Place on TripAdvisor. Retrieved on October 21, 2021, from https://www.tripadvisorsupport.com/en-US/hc/owner/articles/403.

TripAdvisor Media Center (n.d.) About TripAdvisor. Retrieved on September 22, 2020, from https://tripadvisor.mediaroom.com/us-about-us

Vining, A., & Matthews, S. (n.d.). Introduction to Anti-SLAPP Laws. *Reporters Committee for Freedom of the Press.* Retrieved on September 26, 2020, from https://www.rcfp.org/introduction-anti-slapp-guide/

Yelp. (n.d.). *Yelp connects people with great local businesses.* Retrieved September 23, 2020, from https://www.yelp.com/about.

York, J. C., & McSherry, C. (2019). Content Moderation is Broken. Let Us Count the Ways. *EFF.* https://www.eff.org/deeplinks/2019/04/content-moderation-broken-let-us-count-ways

4

CORPORATE SOCIAL RESPONSIBILITY AND CRISIS

Seoyeon Kim and Lucinda Austin

CSR as Crisis Risk

Corporate social responsibility (CSR) refers to the discretionary acts and business practices for corporations to address social and environmental causes cherished by their stakeholders (e.g., Commission of the European Communities, 2001; Coombs & Holladay, 2012b). Although economic (providing quality products/ services to be profitable) and legal responsibilities (abiding by laws and regulations) are certainly corporate responsibilities in a broad sense (Carroll, 1991), the modern concept of CSR concerns corporate activities performed on a voluntary basis and beyond legal obligations (Carroll & Shabana, 2010).

The idea that CSR can serve as crisis risk has recently received scholarly attention (e.g., Coombs & Holladay, 2015; Sohn & Lariscy, 2014), as it has been increasingly reported that consumers are willing to reward or punish a company based on its CSR performance (Edelman, 2018); failures in fulfilling stakeholder expectations for CSR may result in reputational threats and even crises. Coombs and Holladay (2015) classified CSR-involved crises as paracrises and distinguished them from operational crises. A paracrisis is "a publicly visible crisis threat that charges an organization with irresponsible or unethical behavior" (Coombs & Holladay, 2012a, p. 409). What is unique about a paracrisis is that, unlike most operational crises accompanying immediate concerns in health, safety, security, or personnel change, it rarely brings immediate impact to business operation; that is, a paracrisis may or may not escalate into an actual crisis depending on how visible the paracrisis is and how well the paracrisis is managed. For example, the environmental activist group Greenpeace's claim against Nestlé's palm oil sourcing and deforestation in 2010 did not affect the corporate

DOI: 10.4324/9781003043409-7

routines until the claim received attention from a larger number of consumers/ social media users and finally got the company alerted.

Sometimes, CSR challenges emerge from an operational crisis, as the company's pre-existing irresponsibilities are newly reported during investigation of the operational crisis or the company's responses to the operational crisis lack ethical/philanthropic responsibilities. In fact, many high-profile operational crisis cases have been labeled as "CSR crises" or "ethical crises." Particularly, the following crisis examples suggest that there are various ways CSR-involved crises may begin and develop and that ethical and responsible everyday business routine and decision making plays a critical role for stakeholders in judging ethical culpability of a company.

The automaker Volkswagen's cheat on emissions test in 2015 was, technically, a crisis caused by legal transgressions (using an illegal software and organizational conniving of it). However, many stakeholders blamed the company not only for its unlawful acts (violation of legal responsibilities) but also for its lack of ethical/environmental responsibilities, which are not codified but socially cherished (violation of CSR).

Another example that shows complex aspects of a CSR-involved crisis is the case of Oxy Reckitt Benckiser (Oxy in short), a South Korean subsidiary of the British consumer goods company Reckitt Benckiser. Oxy's toxic humidifier disinfectants have been accused of scores of deaths and lung impairments in South Korea. The crisis was initially stemmed from product harms and legal/ procedural issues on safety testing. But, it has ignited moral outrage among consumers and severely damaged the corporate reputation, as the company took two years to announce funds for the affected consumers and more than four years to make an official apology after the recall order made by the governmental health authority in 2011 (Chaudhuri, 2016); the crisis response strategy the company chose was to deny responsibility and minimize its legal liability. Based on the crisis typology of Coombs (2019), the beginning of the Oxy crisis was an operational crisis, with ethical culpabilities unknown; but more significant loss of reputational assets occurred by the company's irresponsible crisis response.

Crisis Perceptions: CSR-Involved Versus Operational Crises

Research has suggested that CSR-involved crises are likely to result in higher blame than operational crises, as individuals differently weigh positive and negative information about ability/competence versus integrity (e.g., Folkes & Kamins, 1999; Sohn & Lariscy, 2014). The hierarchically restrictive schematic model of dispositional attribution posits that individuals tend to weigh positive attributes more heavily in ability-related judgment, whereas negative attributes tend to be more pronounced in integrity judgment (Folkes & Kamins, 1999; Reeder & Brewer, 1979). According to the hierarchically restrictive schemas approach, a single success in ability (e.g., a company's positive market competence) is likely to be appreciated more than a failure in ability (e.g., a company's poor market competence), in the belief that the high level of ability/competence is not something that anyone can achieve. A failure in ability is more likely to be discounted because even a competent one can sometimes poorly perform due to certain hindering circumstances. On the other hand, when it comes to the integrity domain, the amount of negative information a single violation of integrity communicates is likely to be larger than the amount of positive information a single observation of integrity communicates; it is assumed that even one with low integrity can act morally from time to time in different situations (e.g., for image promotion or incentives), while one with high integrity is believed to act morally in any situation. In the context of a corporate crisis, a company's violation of integrity is likely to be viewed as a reflection of its stable, and not situational, nature of low integrity, leading to more negative perceptions of the company. The cue–diagnosticity approach provides a similar explanation about the way ability-related versus integrity-related behaviors are interpreted (see Skowronski & Carlston, 1987, 1989).

The Role of Prior CSR: Pre-Crisis CSR Communication

Many studies have reported buffering effects of prior CSR, suggesting that CSR history serves as a reputational asset and thus reduces reputational damages during corporate crises (e.g., Kim, 2014; Klein & Dawar, 2004; Vanhamme & Grobben, 2009). And, more recently researchers have begun to investigate the boundary/contingent conditions where prior CSR may backfire.

A factor that has been found to moderate the effects of prior CSR on crisis outcomes is the type of crisis. Specifically, researchers have suggested that prior CSR may differently affect stakeholder perceptions about the crisis and the company in the context of a corporate ability (CA) crisis versus CSR crisis, where a CA crisis is concerned with a failure in providing quality products/services (e.g., product harm, technical error) while a CSR crisis is violating CSR expectations of stakeholders (e.g., transgressions; Sohn & Lariscy, 2014, 2015; Tao & Song, 2020). For example, Sohn and Lariscy (2015) found the buffering effect of prior CSR in the CA crisis condition, while the backfiring effect was found in the CSR crisis condition. The researchers explained the result on the buffering effect, using the cognitive dissonance theory (Festinger, 1957); consumers may have discounted negative information about the CA crisis in order to maintain their favorable company perceptions previously formed based on the company's positive CSR records.

On the other hand, the expectancy violations (EV) theory (Burgoon, 1993; Burgoon & LePoire, 1993) is often employed to explain the backfiring effect of prior CSR during a crisis. In the context of CSR-involved crisis, the EV theory suggests that stakeholder expectations about a company are violated to a greater extent during a CSR-involved crisis, resulting in greater loss of stakeholder support; consumer expectation once raised based on the company's prior CSR creates a larger discrepancy between expected (consistent commitment to CSR) and observed conduct (inconsistent and violated CSR) of the company after a CSR-involved crisis. For a company with little or negative CSR records, the level of perceived discrepancy would be lower during a similar (CSR-involved) crisis. (Sohn & Lariscy, 2015; Tao & Song, 2020).

Another possible factor bringing the backfiring effect of prior CSR during a crisis is the congruence between pre-crisis CSR and crisis (Kim & Choi, 2018; Kim & Lee, 2015). Kim and Lee (2015) found that consumers were led to more negative CSR perceptions and higher CSR skepticism when the crisis and the company's pre-crisis CSR shared the same attributes (i.e., prior CSR on obesity prevention and a crisis with cardiovascular risk of the product). The EV theory explains such a condition where a crisis is associated with the company's pre-crisis CSR; the perceived discrepancy between advocacy for a value and a violation of the same versus different values would be greater. The Volkswagen emissions scandal adds an anecdotal support for more negative crisis outcomes generated from the high congruence between pre-crisis CSR and crisis; the company communicated its environmental awareness through its years of Clean Diesel marketing campaign prior to the emissions scandal, possibly increasing consumers' perceived corporate hypocrisy and feelings of being deceived (Biesecker, 2016).

The Role of CSR as Crisis Response: Post-Crisis CSR Communication

CSR is "reactively" communicated when it is part of a response to a CSR-involved reputational threat (e.g., a new CSR campaign launched in response to a CSR-involved crisis), while CSR is considered as "proactive" when communicated in the absence of visibly negative CSR issues. In general, reactive CSR is known to be viewed more unfavorably and skeptically than proactive CSR; CSR communicated *after* a known CSR concern negatively paints the voluntary and altruistic nature of CSR (Becker-Olsen et al., 2006; Groza et al., 2011; Ricks, 2005; Wagner et al., 2009).

More recent studies have extended prior research on reactive CSR by investigating boundary conditions in which the effects of reactive CSR may diverge (e.g., Kim & Choi, 2018; Oh et al., 2017; Rim & Ferguson, 2017). For example, it has been found that the way stakeholders perceive reactive/post-crisis CSR may depend on whether the post-crisis CSR is congruent with the crisis issue. Oh and colleagues (2017) conducted in-depth interviews with millennial consumers in regards to a hypothetical drink company's crisis over food safety. The qualitative study reported that the interviewees were most likely to forgive the company when its post-crisis CSR initiatives were relevant to the crisis (e.g., employee training to improve knowledge and skills for producing safer and higher quality food products); post-crisis CSR irrelevant to the crisis would seem like a hypocritical act to cover up the crisis. Similarly, Kim and Choi (2018), through their experimental research, showed that high congruence between crisis and post-crisis CSR led to more altruistic perceptions about the CSR activity and higher consumer support for the company (e.g., company attitudes, purchase intentions).

In addition, reactive CSR may be differently perceived, depending on what types of CSR initiative are used, as certain CSR initiative types may communicate organizational commitment more than others and may be perceived to be a more sincere response to the crisis (Kim & Austin, 2019; Lin-Hi & Blumberg, 2018). Kim and Austin (2019) examined consumer responses to the socially responsible business practices type of CSR initiative (CSR fulfilled within business operation; e.g., making less waste in production processes) and philanthropic type of initiative (cause-supporting activities occurring outside business operation; e.g., charitable giving) in the context of proactive versus reactive CSR. The researchers found the generally known negative outcomes of reactive CSR, such as more negative attitudes toward the company and lower levels of supportive intentions, but *only* in the philanthropic initiatives condition. The CSR initiative type socially responsible business practices were perceived as favorably as in the proactive CSR setting; for the particular CSR initiative type, the levels of perceived public-serving motives and consumer support were similar in the proactive as well as in the reactive setting, suggesting the potential effectiveness of the socially responsible business practices type of CSR initiatives for reactive CSR communication.

Responding to CSR-Involved Crises

There have been research attempts to help companies more appropriately respond to CSR-involved crises. Though different in terms and concepts used, studies often emphasize acknowledgment of moral responsibility for negative impact the company has brought to the stakeholders.

Coombs and Tachkova (2019) argued that, during a situation where the corporate reputation is greatly threatened for the company's morally offensive conduct, acknowledging the moral violation and taking corrective actions to prevent future violations have the potential to reduce negativity and facilitate forgiveness. Also, Kim et al. (2004) examined the relative effects of apology versus denial on trust repair, given the availability of guilt and innocence information. Overall, Kim et al.'s (2004) findings suggest that inconsistency between initial response and subsequent evidence can further hinder trust repair, even if the subsequent evidence indicates innocence. The study found that trust repair was more successful when subsequent evidence of guilt was present and the trust violator had apologized for the violation (initial response consistent with the subsequent evidence). Also, trust repair was successful when subsequent evidence revealed innocence and the trust violator had denied culpability, rather than apologized, for the violation (initial response consistent with the subsequent evidence).

A lesson these aforementioned research findings suggest is that the company needs to acknowledge their moral responsibility as a crisis breaks out unless they are completely sure that they are free of moral guilt. This lesson also hints at why operational crisis cases ended up in scathing criticism and CSR stigma for some companies. For example, the two crashes of Boeing 737 Max jets, which occurred in the years 2018 and 2019 within five months of each other, stripped the aerospace conglomerate Boeing of its core values. After the first accident, the 737 Max airliners continued to fly, as Boeing deflected blame and no promise for a thorough safety investigation was ensured (Gates, 2019). Even after the second accident and groundings of the Max in many countries, Boeing still delayed efforts to show sympathy for the victims and ground the airliner. Social media provided the company with a convenient way to monitor what stakeholders are saying to and expecting from the company: more than 870,000 tweets – mostly negative – were made about 737 MAX within a week after the second crash (Stoll, 2019). However, it took eight days for the company to issue an open letter to address its awareness of victims and safety concerns (*Chicago Tribune*, 2019). As in the Oxy case mentioned earlier in this chapter, Boeing has brought the moral outrage upon itself not only by missing an opportunity to appropriately respond to the raised safety concerns before another accident but also by overlooking the moral imperative to recognize hundreds of lives lost by its aircrafts.

Apology or acknowledgment of moral responsibility made during an early phase of crisis does not necessarily indicate that the company admits its full responsibility for everything that happened. Corporate apology communicates the company's regret for any negative impact brought to stakeholders by an event in which the company is involved. Furthermore, making an apology can help the company reassure stakeholders by signaling the company's willingness to prevent future trust violations (Kim et al., 2004). For example, Swaminathan and Mah (2016) reported that Tweeter users' sentiment toward the company during the Volkswagen's emissions scandal shifted from the extremely negative immediately after the outbreak of the scandal to the more neutral, following the company's recovery efforts including issuing apologies and initiating recalls.

Research calls for more active adoption of moral recognition and engagement with stakeholders during ethics-related crises (Snyder et al., 2006; Tao & Kim, 2017). Tao and Kim (2017) found that, during ethical crises, crisis responses based on the ethics of care, an approach focusing on organizational engagement with the affected stakeholders' feelings and situational needs, were sparsely used, compared to crisis responses based on the ethic of justice emphasizing objective evaluations of the situation to ensure impartiality and fairness between different parties.

Social Media and CSR-Involved Crisis Management

What we often observe during corporate crises – especially when the crisis involves CSR – are companies being extremely vigilant and hesitant about publicly communicating their thought process to minimize any potential liabilities. However, today's stakeholders, particularly consumers, increasingly expect companies to initiate external crisis communication as quickly as possible and to continue the conversation via media throughout the crisis (Crisp, 2019; Freshfields Bruckhaus Deringer, 2013). The international law firm Freshfields Bruckhaus Deringer (2013), based on its survey of crisis communications professionals, emphasizes that assessment of legal implications should keep pace with prompt crisis responses via news and social media. The survey results reported that 69% of crises are thought to go round the world within 24 hours, and 28% within an hour. Active crisis communication through social media helps the company connect with stakeholders in real time and prevent spread of false information during a crisis. Furthermore, crisis management through active two-way communication is likely to generate more positive reactions among stakeholders (Ki & Nekmat, 2014).

Many recent cases of paracrisis and CSR-involved crisis were sparked or amplified on social media. United Airlines' forcible removal of a passenger in 2017 went viral on YouTube, generating outrage among airline consumers. When the clothing company H&M used a black child model for a sweatshirt with the printed phrase "coolest monkey in the jungle" in 2018 on its website, many social media users circulated the image and spread the company's racial insensitivity.

As social media allows two-way interaction between a company and its stakeholders, companies can use social media as a tool to scan emerging CSR concerns and monitor current and potential claims regarding the company's CSR activities (Coombs & Holladay, 2012b). Some issues spotted on social media may turn out to be paracrises and raise the alarm, directing the company to plan appropriate responses. Other issues might not be directly related to the company but offer an opportunity to assess the company's current CSR in relations to stakeholder concerns and sentiments, which may evolve or constantly change over time. To help with effective prioritization of CSR concerns found on social media, companies can evaluate: the likelihood of the CSR concern to be the interests of the company's stakeholders; and the anticipated impact of the CSR concern on society and the company (Coombs & Holladay, 2012b).

It needs to be noted though, even well-intended CSR activities or attempts to integrate widely cherished values into the company's CSR do not always guarantee positive stakeholder outcomes. Stakeholder reactions to a CSR activity may vary depending on different factors, such as pre-existing perceptions of the company and contexts where the CSR issue is talked about. For example, the razor maker Gillette uploaded a #MeToo-inspired commercial film on YouTube in 2019 in a reflection of the public empathy for the social movement against sexual harassment and sexual assault committed by men. The film presented examples of undercutting toxic masculinity. Despite the widespread consensus on the significance of the #MeToo movement at that time, many consumers uncomfortably viewed the company's shift from how it had previously positioned itself in promoting masculinity and the brand (Smith, 2019). Similarly, not all consumers were happy when Nike began an advertising campaign and voiced its stance against racial discrimination in 2018, with the football player Colin Kaepernick being the campaign model. Kaepernick had history of kneeling during the national anthem in NFL games in protest of racial discrimination and police brutality. Some consumers with more conservative viewpoints claimed that the company was advocating someone who disrespected the country; and the company began to be tagged on social media posts featuring Nike products burned or destroyed (Abad-Santos, 2018).

These examples suggest that some causes a company envisions to contribute to are not universally cherished and may require principles and guidelines different than those for general CSR communication. Making a corporate statement or action to take a public stance on a potentially controversial social/political issue is called "corporate social advocacy" (Dodd & Supa, 2014), and scholarly examination of this topic has recently begun, furthering the understanding of multiple facets inherent in CSR communication (e.g., Dodd & Supa, 2015; Gaither et al., 2018).

In Summary

CSR is now a commonly expected realm of corporate activity, and how the company performs CSR, rather than whether the company addresses CSR or not, has become a more important determinant of corporate reputation. Poorly performed CSR or inadequate management of CSR issues can result in threats to the corporate reputation; research has supported greater and more negative crisis outcomes involved in crises with more versus less ethical culpability. Hence, good CSR communication includes managing current and potential CSR concerns as well as appropriately responding to CSR-involved crises. In relation to social media, CSR challenges and CSR-involved crisis information can be quickly disseminated through social media, increasing the visibility and impact of certain CSR concerns or a crisis. Therefore, corporate communication professionals should be aware of CSR as a crisis risk and closely examine social/environmental concerns and CSR issues discussed on social media. CSR in relation to crisis is still an emerging area of research, and thus more extensive investigation is called into the roles of different aspects of CSR communication before, during, and after a crisis.

References

Abad-Santos, A. (2018, September 4). Why the social media boycott over Colin Kaepernick is a win for Nike. *Vox*. https://www.vox.com/2018/9/4/17818148/nike-boycott-kaepernick

Becker-Olsen, K. L., Cudmore, B. A., & Hill, R. P. (2006). The impact of perceived corporate social responsibility on consumer behavior. *Journal of Business Research, 59*(1), 46–53. https://doi.org/10.1016/j.jbusres.2005.01.001

Biesecker, M. (2016, March 29). FTC sues VW over false "Clean Diesel" advertising claims. *Associated Press*. https://apnews.com/article/215c28386408435292334cfef7850b72

Burgoon, J. K. (1993). Interpersonal expectations, expectancy violations, and emotional communication. *Journal of Language and Social Psychology, 12*(1–2), 30–48. https://doi.org/10.1177%2F0261927X93121003

Burgoon, J. K., & LePoire, B. A. (1993). Effects of communication expectancies, actual communication, and expectancy disconfirmation on evaluations of communicators and their communication behavior. *Human Communication Research, 20*(1), 67–96. https://doi.org/10.1111/j.1468-2958.1993.tb00316.x

Carroll, A. B. (1991). The pyramid of corporate social responsibility: Toward the moral management of organizational stakeholders. *Business Horizons, 34*(4), 39–48. https://doi.org/10.1016/0007-6813(91)90005-G

Carroll, A. B., & Shabana, K. M. (2010). The business case for corporate social responsibility: A review of concepts, research and practice. *International Journal of Management Reviews, 12*(1), 85–105. https://doi.org/10.1111/j.1468-2370.2009.00275.x

Chaudhuri, S. (2016, September 21). Reckitt Benckiser apologizes for disinfectant deaths: More than 100 people have been killed in South Korea by Reckitt's humidifier disinfectant. *The Wall Street Journal*. https://www.wsj.com/articles/reckitt-benckiser-struggles-to-move-past-disinfectant-deaths-1474480171

Chicago Tribune. (2019, October 14). Timeline: Boeing 737 Max jetliner crashes and aftermath. https://www.chicagotribune.com/business/ct-biz-viz-boeing-737-max-crash-timeline-04022019-story.html

Commission of the European Communities. (2001). *Green paper: Promoting a European framework for corporate social responsibility*. europa.eu/rapid/press-release_DOC-01-9_en.pdf

Coombs, W. T. (2019). *Ongoing crisis communication: Planning, managing, and responding* (5th ed.). Sage.

Coombs, W. T., & Holladay, J. S. (2012a). The paracrisis: The challenges created by publicly managing crisis prevention. *Public Relations Review, 38*(3), 408–415. https://doi.org/10.1016/j.pubrev.2012.04.004

Coombs, W. T., & Holladay, S. J. (2012b). *Managing corporate social responsibility: A communication approach*. John Wiley & Sons.

Coombs, W. T., & Holladay, S. (2015). CSR as crisis risk: Expanding how we conceptualize the relationship. *Corporate Communications: An International Journal, 20*(2), 144–162. https://doi.org/10.1108/CCIJ-10-2013-0078

Coombs, W. T., & Tachkova, E. R. (2019). Scansis as a unique crisis type: Theoretical and practical implications. *Journal of Communication Management, 23*(1), 72–88. https://doi.org/10.1108/JCOM-08-2018-0078

Crisp. (2019). The 2019 crisis impact report: How customers react to a brand crisis. https://info.crispthinking.com/crisis-impact-report-2019

Dodd, M. D., & Supa, D. (2015). Testing the viability of corporate social advocacy as a predictor of purchase intention. *Communication Research Reports, 32*(4), 287–293. https://doi.org/10.1080/08824096.2015.1089853

Dodd, M. D., & Supa, D. W. (2014). Conceptualizing and measuring "corporate social advocacy" communication: Examining the impact on corporate financial performance. *Public Relations Journal, 8*(3), 2–23. https://doaj.org/article/3996d156ea764f7f9ae5dfdc94299e2a

Edelman. (2018, October). 2018 Edelman Earned Brand: Brands take a stand. https://www.edelman.com/sites/g/files/aatuss191/files/2018-10/2018_Edelman_Earned_Brand_Global_Report.pdf

Festinger, L. (1957). *A theory of cognitive dissonance.* Stanford University Press.

Folkes, V. S., & Kamins, M. A. (1999). Effects of information about firms' ethical and unethical actions on consumers' attitudes. *Journal of Consumer Psychology, 8*(3), 243–259. https://doi.org/10.1207/s15327663jcp0803_03

Freshfields Bruckhaus Deringer. (2013). Containing a crisis: Dealing with corporate disasters in the digital age. https://www.freshfields.com/globalassets/campaign-landing/cyber-security/containing-a-crisis.pdf

Gaither, B. M., Austin, L., & Collins, M. (2018). Examining the case of Dick's sporting goods: Realignment of stakeholders through corporate social advocacy. *The Journal of Public Interest Communications, 2*(2), 176–201. https://doi.org/10.32473/jpic.v2.i2.p176

Gates, D. (2019, November 8). After Lion Air crash, Boeing doubled down on faulty 737 MAX assumptions. *Seattle Times.* https://www.seattletimes.com/business/boeing-aerospace/after-lion-air-crash-boeing-doubled-down-on-faulty-737-max-assumptions/

Groza, M. D., Pronschinske, M. R., & Walker, M. (2011). Perceived organizational motives and consumer responses to proactive and reactive CSR. *Journal of Business Ethics, 102*(4), 639–652. https://doi.org/10.1007/s10551-011-0834-9

Ki, E. J., & Nekmat, E. (2014). Situational crisis communication and interactivity: Usage and effectiveness of Facebook for crisis management by Fortune 500 companies. *Computers in Human Behavior, 35*, 140–147.

Kim, S. (2014). What's worse in times of product-harm crisis? Negative corporate ability or negative CSR reputation? *Journal of Business Ethics, 123*(1), 157–170. https://doi.org/10.1007/s10551-013-1808-x

Kim, S., & Austin, L. (2019). Effects of CSR initiatives on company perceptions among millennial and Gen Z consumers. *Corporate Communications: An International Journal, 25*(2), 299–317. https://doi.org/10.1108/CCIJ-07-2018-0077

Kim, S., & Choi, S. M. (2018). Congruence effects in post-crisis CSR communication: The mediating role of attribution of corporate motives. *Journal of Business Ethics, 153*(2), 447–463. https://doi.org/10.1007/s10551-016-3425-y

Kim, P. H., Ferrin, D. L., Cooper, C. D., & Dirks, K. T. (2004). Removing the shadow of suspicion: The effects of apology versus denial for repairing competence-versus integrity-based trust violations. *Journal of Applied Psychology, 89*(1), 104–118. https://doi.org/10.1037/0021-9010.89.1.104

Kim, H. S., & Lee, S.Y. (2015). Testing the buffering and boomerang effects of CSR practices on consumers' perception of a corporation during a crisis. *Corporate Reputation Review, 18*(4), 277–293. https://doi.org/10.1057/crr.2015.18

Klein, J., & Dawar, N. (2004). Corporate social responsibility and consumers' attributions and brand evaluations in a product–harm crisis. *International Journal of Research in Marketing, 21*(3), 203–217. https://doi.org/10.1016/j.ijresmar.2003.12.003

Lin-Hi, N., & Blumberg, I. (2018). The link between (not) practicing CSR and corporate reputation: Psychological foundations and managerial implications. *Journal of Business Ethics, 150*(1), 185–198. https://doi.org/10.1007/s10551-016-3164-0

Oh, H. J., Chen, R., & Hung-Baesecke, C. J. F. (2017). Exploring effects of CSR initiatives in strategic postcrisis communication among millennials in China and South Korea. *International Journal of Strategic Communication, 11*(5), 379–394. https://doi.org/10.1080/1553118X.2017.1360892

Reeder, G. D., & Brewer, M. B. (1979). A schematic model of dispositional attribution in interpersonal perception. *Psychological Review, 86*(1), 61–79. https://doi.org/10.1037/0033-295X.86.1.61

Ricks, J. M. (2005). An assessment of strategic corporate philanthropy on perceptions of brand equity variables. *Journal of Consumer Marketing, 22*(3), 121–134. https://doi.org/10.1108/07363760510595940

Rim, H., & Ferguson, M. A. T. (2017). Proactive versus reactive CSR in a crisis: An impression management perspective. *International Journal of Business Communication, 57*(4), 545–568. https://doi.org/10.1177/2329488417719835

Skowronski, J. J., & Carlston, D. E. (1987). Social judgment and social memory: The role of cue diagnosticity in negativity, positivity, and extremity biases. *Journal of Personality and Social Psychology, 52*(4), 689–699. https://doi.org/10.1037/0022-3514.52.4.689

Skowronski, J. J., & Carlston, D. E. (1989). Negativity and extremity biases in impression formation: A review of explanations. *Psychological Bulletin, 105*(1), 131–142. https://doi.org/10.1037/0033-2909.105.1.131

Smith, T. (2019, January 17). Backlash erupts after Gillette launches a new #MeToo-inspired ad campaign. *NPR.* https://www.npr.org/2019/01/17/685976624/backlash-erupts-after-gillette-launches-a-new-metoo-inspired-ad-campaign

Snyder, P., Hall, M., Robertson, J., Jasinski, T., & Miller, J. S. (2006). Ethical rationality: A strategic approach to organizational crisis. *Journal of Business Ethics, 63*(4), 371–383. https://doi.org/10.1007/s10551-005-3328-9

Sohn, Y. J., & Lariscy, R. W. (2014). Understanding reputational crisis: Definition, properties, and consequences. *Journal of Public Relations Research, 26*(1), 23–43. https://doi.org/10.1080/1062726X.2013.795865

Sohn, Y. J., & Lariscy, R. W. (2015). A buffer or boomerang?: The role of corporate reputation in bad times. *Communication Research, 42*(2), 237–259. https://doi.org/10.1177/0093650212466891

Stoll, J. D. (2019, March 15). Did Twitter Help Ground the Boeing 737 MAX?: Corporate executives must respond in real time or risk being overrun by criticism. *The Wall Street Journal.* https://www.wsj.com/articles/ill-tweet-to-that-social-media-gives-consumers-newfound-reach-11552667731

Swaminathan, V., & Mah, S. (2016, September 2). What 100,000 tweets about the Volkswagen scandal tell us about angry customers. *Harvard Business Review*. https://hbr.org/2016/09/what-100000-tweets-about-the-volkswagen-scandal-tell-us-about-angry-customers

Tao, W., & Kim, S. (2017). Application of two under-researched typologies in crisis communication: Ethics of justice vs. care and public relations vs. legal strategies. *Public Relations Review*, *43*(4), 690–699. https://doi.org/10.1016/j.pubrev.2017.06.003

Tao, W., & Song, B. (2020). The interplay between post-crisis response strategy and pre-crisis corporate associations in the context of CSR crises. *Public Relations Review*, *46*(2), 101883. https://doi.org/10.1016/j.pubrev.2020.101883

Vanhamme, J., & Grobben, B. (2009). Too good to be true!: The effectiveness of CSR history in countering negative publicity. *Journal of Business Ethics*, *85*(2), 273–283. https://doi.org/10.1007/s10551-008-9731-2

Wagner, T., Lutz, R. J., & Weitz, B. A. (2009). Corporate hypocrisy: Overcoming the threat of inconsistent corporate social responsibility perceptions. *Journal of Marketing*, *73*(6), 77–91. https://doi.org/10.1509/jmkg.73.6.77

5

ONLINE ACTIVISM AND A CONCEPTUAL TYPOLOGY OF PUBLIC RELATIONS ACTIVIST ROLES

Melissa D. Dodd, Dean Mundy, and Eve R. Heffron

Introduction

An activist is someone who campaigns to bring about political or social change. Social media has revolutionized the modern communication and activist landscape, yet academics and professionals alike remain divided on whether social media augments traditional activism or represents a revolutionary paradigm shift for sociopolitical issues engagement (Allsop, 2016; Kent & Li, 2020). More so, public and academic debate as to the societal impacts of social media abound (McCabe & Harris, 2021), alongside public relations scholarship that debates the generally positive value of social media to the field (Valentini, 2015), its effective use during organizational crises (Crijns et al., 2017; Jin et al., 2011) or for the emergent concept of corporate social advocacy (CSA) and the politicized corporation (Dodd, 2018; Scherer & Palazzo, 2011).

To the extent that it is clear that there is much research to still be done, it is also clear that activism and social media are inextricably linked. According to a Pew Research report, more than 50% of Americans engage in sociopolitical issues on social media (Anderson et al., 2018). Thus, public relations professionals may serve in increasingly distinctive activist-oriented roles of which each has a growing body of literature: (1) the Social Movement Activist Role, the professional employs traditional and modern public relations strategies and techniques on behalf of social movement organizations (SMOs) and as related to the maturation of those organizations and issues lifecycles; (2) the Activist Corporate Boundary Spanner Role, the (re)definition of traditional roles where professionals serve as the internal-external boundary spanner on behalf of the organization and its stakeholders addressing business-related issues in the added context of

DOI: 10.4324/9781003043409-8

online activism; and (3) the CSA role, the evolution of the professional as activist on behalf of the corporate organization engaging in controversial social-political issues otherwise divorced from traditional, non-controversial corporate social responsibility initiatives.

An evaluation of the relationship between traditional public relations roles and emergent public relations roles in the context of today's online activist climate provides an initial classification schema based on the existing academic literature applied to the roles of public relations professionals as part of it. These roles are clearly not one size fits all and may often overlap in meaningful ways that should be addressed by future research alongside the evolution of emerging and social media – as well as the potential theoretical and practical changes in issues lifecycles and identification of stakeholder groups for which it gives rise to. This research categorizes the evolution of public relations roles and online activism in order to raise further questions about the emergent role of public relations professionals as related to online activism and crisis communication.

The Social Movement Activist Role

Arguably until the late 20th century, advocacy/activist organizations and corporations operated largely in separate realms. Given power differentials and a lack of government interference in many instances, corporations had much greater flexibility of when and how to engage in issue discourse, if they engaged at all. Their mission remained focused predominantly on profit and growth. However, one particularly noteworthy timeframe in the development of public relations was the 1960s when anti-corporate sentiment was at an all-time high, and companies were compelled to acknowledge public attitudes and claims toward the organization (Heath & Palenchar, 2009; Park & Dodd, 2017). Clark (2000) explained, "The much-publicized era of activism began to change the way in which corporations interacted with society, and thus how they communicated with society. [...] Nuclear power, civil rights abuses, regulation of business' activities, the consumer rights movement, and the women's movement were just a few key developments that contributed to the tension between business and society" (p. 365).

In response SMOs arose with issues life cycles (cf. the evolution of issues and SMOs in Hallahan, 2001, and oligarchization of SMOs in early research, Zald & Ash, 1966) and with time, often became more formalized, powerful entities (e.g., non-governmental activist/advocacy organizations) that adopted their own public relations functions and tactics in the pursual of corporate acknowledgment of issues that is beyond the scope of this chapter.

With a more level playing field and the advent of social media, activist organizations and corporations have become inevitably intertwined, where public relations roles, strategies, and tactics are more readily employed by activist organizations to apply public pressure to businesses surrounding a host of issues, a leveling of the public power dynamic where public relations professionals served as the key communicators, utilizing similar strategies and tactics on both sides. Thus, corporations evolved to become more receptive to engagement with activist organizations that were traditionally viewed as "the enemy." Using public relations best practices of issues management, corporate social responsibility, and crisis communication, companies today often seek to proactively engage with activist organizations, generating dialogue and forging partnerships around issues before they become crises.

For instance, The Human Rights Campaign (HRC), a national organization advocating for LGBTQ+ protections, provides a good example and reflects in three ways today's new context for advocacy organizations. First, beginning in 2006, they developed an annual "Corporate Equality Index," which scores corporations based on a set of criteria regarding LGBTQ-inclusive policies and protections (i.e., HRC, 2021). Similar to many other advocacy organizations, they understood the powerful shift toward the public voice, and the public wanting to support those corporations that shared their values. Accordingly, the index has become a reliable source and guide for consumers who value LGBTQ+ inclusion. It also helps serve as a watchdog and call to action when corporations are perceived to express anti-LGBTQ+. In 2019, for example, when the Hallmark corporation bowed to pressure by the conservative group One Million Moms and pulled an ad featuring a same-sex couple (Voss, 2019), the HRC announced that they were suspending Hallmark's rating. At the same time, they announced that more than 60,000 HRC supporters had joined the organization's letter-writing campaign to have Hallmark put the ad back into their line-up. Other high-profile influencers and companies joined the call, and Hallmark quickly re-routed its course.

The second way the HRC reflects today's advocacy context is how they are able to leverage corporations to advance their agenda and seek new LGBTQ+ protections. As mentioned, social media has given the public an immense amount of power, particularly the role they play in influencing corporate advocacy/activism initiatives. Consequently, the HRC periodically updates the criteria for its Equality Index – raising the stakes, per se, regarding what workplace policies and protections afford a company a high score. Moreover, to be included in the index, companies must apply for certification, which expires every three years at which time companies must apply for recertification. This strategy, in turn, allows the HRC to advance its social agenda incrementally, addressing new issues while holding corporations accountable.

Finally, the HRC reflects today's advocacy context through the partnership coalition they have built with Fortune 500 companies. For example, they have 57 corporate sponsors, including Apple, Coca-Cola, and Nike. While seeking corporate sponsors is not new necessarily, the visibility provided with social media allows the HRC to leverage these partnerships, and these corporations' vast followings, to spread their message to bigger audiences. In turn, by helping spread advocacy messages, corporations demonstrate to their followers that they are in tune with and support their followers' social values. The power of this coalition also is reflected by the composition of activist organizations' boards of directors. Having influential corporate leaders on an advocacy organization's board can lend legitimacy to an organization's cause. Here, the HRC again reflects this relationship. In July 2020, for example, they announced 13 new board members, including executives from high profile companies such as Deloitte, Invesco, Twitter, and Diageo (Bibi, 2020).[1]

Ultimately, the activist role of public relations within the issues lifecycle and formalization of SMOs is central to the achievement of advocacy organization goals outside the corporate context. Social media has elevated public relations into the Social Movement Role where online activists are able to decrease power differentials, expedite issues lifecycles, and more quickly formalize the organization. Social media provides three key opportunities for the activist organization and corporate relationships. First, as the HRC example demonstrated, social media helps activist organizations forge partnerships with corporations that raise visibility for their issues, lend legitimacy for their issues, and help advance their broader issue agenda. Second, social media helps activist organizations large and small create strategic, polished calls to action that can reach vast audiences quickly. Finally, social media can quickly help activists and activist organizations put pressure on organizations to action. These activists may be voices trying to bridge the external call for attention on an issue with the internal operation and decision-making of an organization, a more traditional corporate boundary spanning role as follows.

Activist Corporate Boundary Spanner Role

A traditional function public relations practitioners perform is that of boundary spanner, linking organizational structure and operation with external environmental issues and pressures in a way that can either mitigate effect on an organization or help an organization change course altogether. "Public relations professionals are the primary internal and external communicators in organizations, which allows them to represent the publics' opinions, interests, and values to the organization (and vice versa). Public relations professionals may therefore act as the corporate conscience for an organization" (Park & Dodd, 2017); otherwise differentiated from other traditional public relations roles and termed "boundary spanner" (Broom & Dozier, 1986). The traditional boundary spanner often addressed issues under the purview of corporate social responsibility (e.g., environmental sustainability, fair labor, supply chain management). However, early research and guiding models were less proactive and too often approached activism and advocacy as aggressive, violent, and threatening to the organization (Ganesh & Zoller, 2012; Grunig, 1992). The corporate-activist power differential was not adequately acknowledged, nor was the practicality of two-way symmetrical communication strategies to create "win–win" solutions.

That said, perspectives regarding this boundary-spanning role have evolved in recent years, and there is considerably more room for practitioners to act as an internal force for social change. In fact, Coombs and Holladay (2012) argued that activism provides an opportunity to advance public relations theory and practice itself, focusing on increased stakeholder expectations for corporate social responsibility. As some scholars argue (e.g., Holtzhausen & Voto, 2002; Toledano, 2016) the practitioner can (and should) act as an internal activist. Giving voice to activist groups internally can help organizational reputation while advancing needed change.

With the rise of online activism, the traditional corporate boundary spanner role is increasingly important. Environmental scanning in online spaces, where activist attention has the potential to generate corporate crises, may occur entirely online or transfer to offline activist engagement (Dookhoo & Dodd, 2019). Negotiating if, how, and the extent to which external online activism influences organizational operations (and communication priorities) – has become particularly crucial to an organization's public relations function. Online activism perhaps necessitates a redefinition of the traditional corporate boundary spanner role. As internal/external boundary spanner that not only increasingly monitors issues in an online activist context, the activist boundary spanner may also represent public interests and negotiate in a fully online context, embedded in the dynamics of power balance.

Whereas the rise of online activism has allowed for more expedited issues lifecycles and formalization of the public relations role within SMOs, as well as has potentially necessitated a redefinition of the traditional corporate boundary spanner role, online activism may also be attributed to the rise of an emergent activist role for public relations: the CSA Role.

CSA Role

The traditional role of business in society has predominantly included avoiding participation in highly divisive and politicized social issues (Palazzo & Scherer, 2006), which may isolate some stakeholders and attract new stakeholder activist group attention. Where a lack of government action existed (e.g., gun policy reform) and mistrust in traditional institutions alongside corporate multinational power were on the rise, public expectations of business in society evolved to include corporate engagement in controversial sociopolitical issues, termed CSA.

An emergent public relations role, CSA, is when companies and/or their CEOs intentionally or unintentionally (Dodd, 2018) "align themselves with a controversial social-political issue outside their normal sphere of CSR interest" (Dodd & Supa, 2015, p. 288). Industry research indicates that the majority of the American public believes companies should step up and effect social change by taking stances on sociopolitical issues and should do so regardless of controversy (Global Strategy Group, 2020). Likewise, a nationally representative survey of U.S. adults found that people do want corporations to address the important social issues facing society today (Austin et al., 2019). Social media and online activists, more than ever before, may now publicly target corporations for societal-level changes to include issues such as climate change, health care reform, gun violence prevention, race relations, LGBTQ+ issues, gender and marriage equality, and reproductive rights, among others. Research supports the power of companies to impact societal issues by way of influencing the public's issues awareness, attitudes, and behaviors (Heffron & Dodd, 2021; Overton et al., 2020; Parcha & Kingsley Westerman, 2020).

For instance, on May 25, 2020, Minneapolis police officers arrested George Floyd, a 46-year-old Black man, after a convenience store clerk called 911 and told the police that Floyd had used a counterfeit $20 bill to make a purchase. Floyd died in police custody after officer Derek Chauvin knelt on his neck for 8 minutes and 46 seconds – a length of time that became a rallying cry for protestors – as Floyd pleaded: "I can't breathe." A bystander recorded the police brutality against Floyd and shared it online, where the video went viral on social media, attached to the #BlackLivesMatter hashtag (founded by the SMO Black Lives Matter Global Network, Inc.) that had formerly garnered widespread attention following the death of Trayvon Martin in 2012. On May 28, 2020, just three days after the murder of George Floyd, the hashtag reached its highest number of uses ever recorded – 8.8 million tweets containing the #BlackLivesMatter hashtag (Anderson et al., 2020). The online, viral spread of the video of George Floyd's murder powerfully re-ignited the Black Lives Matter civil rights movement and made policing and racial injustice a focal point of modern discourse.

Provided both the online tools for organization and voice by social media platforms, tens of thousands of activist protestors of all ages, races, ethnicities, and backgrounds took to the streets to protest the injustice of Floyd's killing and the controversial histories, policies, and systems of racism that exist globally.

Entering the fray, corporate organizations issued statements of support in online spaces and on social media; pledged donations to the Black Lives Matter movement and relevant organizations such as the National Association for the Advancement of Colored People (NAACP); reviewed internal policies and structures; and some companies went as far as to advise consumers (e.g., Ben & Jerry's) not to buy their products if they do not agree with the major tenets of the BLM movement, The forced transparency of social media (DiStaso & Messner, 2010) further allowed for the questioning of the authenticity of corporate issues engagement (Vasquez & Dodd, 2019), and companies perceived as hypocritical or inauthentic are often publicly confronted on social media (Elston & Dodd, 2021). For instance, SpaghettiOs posted an image of their mascot holding a BLM flag to Twitter. In a response that garnered widespread negative online attention, a user stated: "Thank you for your Black Lives Matter graphic. May I please see a picture of your executive leadership team and company board?"

Other recent instances of public relations professionals working as the activist on behalf of a company's CSA efforts are demonstrated in the public relations research in the cases of the Starbucks Race Together Initiative (Logan, 2016), DICK's Sporting Goods and gun control (Gaither et al., 2018), Nike's campaign featuring Colin Kaepernick (Kim et al., 2020; Overton et al., 2020), the Dove Real Beauty Campaign (Taylor et al., 2016), Ben & Jerry's support of the Black Lives Matter movement on social media (Ciszek & Logan, 2018), and Starbucks and Budweiser's responses to President Donald Trump's immigration ban executive order (Rim et al., 2020), to list a few.

Each of these studies signifies the critical activist role public relations professionals must maintain to legitimize the company and effect positive social change, communicated widely using hashtags to connect to the conversation in an online activist era. Public relations professionals engaging in the CSA role must identify and understand underlying corporate values systems in order to engage meaningfully with controversial issues. Professionals must consider numerous complex factors when communicating on behalf of the company in public online spaces. Social media gives voice and spaces for organization to a public frustrated by government inaction and social injustices. It allows online activists to publicly apply pressure to powerful companies with boycott/buycott hashtags aplenty. Companies and public relations professionals today seek to be more proactive in addressing sociopolitical issues in order to avoid these hashtags and associated crisis communication. As online activism and public expectations of corporate engagement in CSA continue to grow, the activist role of the public relations professional communicating issues on behalf of the organization offers much room for further research.

Discussion

This chapter conceptualizes three distinctive public relations roles related to online activism: (1) Social movement activist role, the employment of traditional and modern online public relations strategies and techniques on behalf of activist organizations; (2) corporate boundary spanner activist, the professional as traditional internal-external activist on behalf of the organization and its stakeholders in an online activist context; and (3) the CSA role, the professional as issues manager and values enforcer on behalf of businesses engaging in controversial social-political issues. Additional research is needed to further explore and explicate these roles as related to modern online activism, paving the way for a better understanding of the evolution of public relations roles and online activism in order to raise more questions about the emergent role of public relations professionals as related to online activism and crisis communication.

Given this typology and evaluation of the relationship between traditional public relations roles and emergent public relations roles in the context of today's online activist climate, the researchers also identify areas for future research as related to the activist roles identified in this chapter. For instance, beyond formal, long-term partnerships, corporate engagement with activist publics can be tricky. As part of their environmental scanning role, corporations must maintain a pulse of public discourse regarding social issues, and of course, social media is a key tool in the process. The challenge becomes when and how to engage with activist publics on social media; there is a fine line between being perceived to truly care and exploiting a community. This risk is particularly heightened when engaging with "social media subcultures," where individuals representing the same group or groups discuss social issues relevant to their social group(s). These subcultures are considered, for example, gay Twitter, black Twitter, feminist Twitter, etc. One study (Rogers, 2016) found that when corporations try to engage with these subcultures – through the use of a hashtag, trying to engage in a certain conversation, or even promoting an initiative they feel is relevant to that group – they need to have a well-established reputation of prior engagement with that population over the long term. Moreover, they must deliver a truly sincere message devoid of commercial intent. Otherwise, they risk immediate and widespread backlash from the broader subgroup. And because of these tight-knit groups, reputational damage could be swift.

Theoretically and practically, the application and implications of this as related to the roles outlined in this chapter may draw on research related to proactivity in the more traditional boundary spanner role as activist (e.g., relationship and community building). However, given the controversiality of issues surrounding an online social group (or that a corporation would need to authentically engage with issues important to that group) might better draw on research related to corporate issues engagement as activist roles. Meanwhile, on the "other side" is the social movement activist role, employing traditional public relations strategies and tactics in an environment more fertile for engagement and perhaps, employing more modern online activist engagement strategies than other activist roles identified here by way of the nature and goals of their organizations.

Note

1 Of course, today's social media age does not just benefit large, national, advocacy organizations such as the Human Rights Campaign. Social media have allowed small advocacy organizations paths for growth as well. In particular, arguably, social media have

heightened the importance of coalitions have become even more of a strategic priority for smaller organizations. A small or new advocacy, organization must foster relationships with like-minded organizations of all sizes. Doing so gives them much-needed visibility in the advocacy community. Along the way, it provides an opportunity via social channels to reach new supporters who would not see their message otherwise. For example, a small, new organization focused on racial justice can follow/friend the national ACLU account and develop a relationship by liking, commenting, reposting their content. Once the relationship is established, the ACLU might do the same, and a repost by an organization with as large a following as the ACLU is invaluable to a small organization trying to get its footing and spread its message.

References

Allsop, B. (2016). Social media and activism: A literature review. *Social Psychology Review, 18*(2), 35–40. https://cpb-us-e1.wpmucdn.com/cobblearning.net/dist/0/696/files/2017/09/social-media-2-1ig7dxn.pdf

Anderson, M., Barthel, M., Perrin, A., & Vogels, E. A. (June 10, 2020,). #BlackLivesMatter surges on Twitter after George Floyd's death. Pew Research Center. Retrieved from https://www.pewresearch.org/fact-tank/2020/06/10/blacklivesmatter-surges-on-twitter-after-george-floyds-death/

Anderson, M., Toor, S., Rainie, L., & Smith, A. (July 11, 2018). Activism in the social media age. Pew Research Center. Retrieved from: https://www.pewresearch.org/internet/2018/07/11/public-attitudes-toward-political-engagement-on-social-media/

Austin, L. J., Miller Gaither, B., & Gaither, K. (2019). Corporate social advocacy as public interest communications: Exploring perceptions of corporate involvement in controversial social-political issues. *Journal of Public Interest Communications, 3*(2). https://doi.org/10.32473/jpic.v3.i2.p3

Bibi, E. (July 15, 2020). Human Rights Campaign Announces 13 New Members of Board of Directors. Human Rights Campaign. Retrieved April 7, 2021 from: https://www.hrc.org/news/human-rights-campaign-announces-13-new-members-of-board-of-directors

Broom, G. M., & Dozier, D. M. (1986). Advancement for public relations role models. *Public Relations Review, 12*(1), 37–56. https://doi.org/10.1016/S0363-8111(86)80039-X

Ciszek, E., & Logan, N. (2018). Challenging the dialogic promise: How Ben & Jerry's support for Black Lives Matter fosters dissensus on social media. *Journal of Public Relations Research, 30*(3), 115–127. https://doi.org/10.1080/1062726X.2018.1498342

Clark, C. E. (2000). Differences between public relations and corporate social responsibility: An analysis. *Public Relations Review, 26*(3), 363–380. https://doi.org/10.1016/S0363-8111(00)00053-9

Coombs, W. T., & Holladay, S. J. (2012). Fringe public relations: How activism moves critical pr toward the mainstream. *Public Relations Review, 38*, 880–887. https://doi.org/10.1016/j.pubrev.2012.02.008

Crijns, H., Cauberghe, V., Hudders, L., & Claeys, A.-S. (2017). How to deal with online consumer comments during a crisis? The impact of personalized organizational response on organizational reputation. *Computers in Human Behavior, 75*, 619–631. https://doi.org/10.1016/j.chb.2017.05.046

DiStaso, M., & Messner, M. (2010). Forced transparency: Corporate image on Wikipedia and what it means for public relations. *Public Relations Journal, 4*(2). https://apps.prsa.org/Intelligence/PRJournal/past-editions/Vol4/No2/

Dodd, M. D. (2018). Globalization, pluralization, and erosion: The impact of shifting societal expectations for advocacy and public good. *Journal of Public Interest Communications, 2*(2), 221–238. https://doi.org/10.32473/jpic.v2.i2.p221

Dodd, M. D., & Supa, D. (2015). Testing the viability of corporate social advocacy as a predictor of purchase intention. *Communication Research Reports, 32*(4), 287–293. https://doi.org/10.1080/08824096.2015.1089853

Dookhoo, S. R., & Dodd, M. D. (2019). Slacktivists or activists? Millennial motivations and behaviors for engagement in activism. *Public Relations Journal, 13*(1). https://prjournal.instituteforpr.org/wp-content/uploads/Slacktivists-or-Activist.pdf

Elston, A., & Dodd, M. D. (March 2021). Corporate social advocacy: Analyzing corporate responses to the Black Lives Matter civil rights movement. International Public Relations Research Conference. Virtual.

Gaither, B. M., Austin, L., & Collins, M. (2018). Examining the case of DICK's sporting goods: Realignment of stakeholders through corporate social advocacy. *The Journal of Public Interest Communications, 2*(2), 176–201. https://doi.org/10.32473/jpic.v2.i2.p176

Ganesh, S., & Zoller, H. M. (2012). Dialogue, activism, and democratic social change. *Communication Theory, 22*(1), 66–91. https://doi.org/10.1111/j.1468-2885.2011.01396.x

Global Strategy Group. (2020). Call out culture: Brands and politics collide in 2020. 7th Annual Business & Politics Study. https://www.globalstrategygroup.com/wpcontent/uploads/2020/01/2020-GSG-Business-and-Politics-Study.pdf

Grunig, L. A. (1992). Activism: How it limits the effectiveness of organizations and how excellent public relations departments respond. In J. E. Grunig (Ed.), *Excellence in public relations and communication management* (pp. 503–530). Lawrence Erlbaum Associates.

Hallahan, K. (2001). The dynamics of issues activation and response: An issues processes model. *Journal of Public Relations Research, 13*(1), 27–59. https://doi.org/10.1207/S1532754XJPRR1301_3

Heath, R. L., & Palenchar, M. J. (2009). *Strategic issues management: Organizations and public policy change* (2nd ed.). Sage.

Heffron, E. R., & Dodd, M. D. (2021). The impact of corporate social advocacy on stakeholders' issue awareness, attitudes, and voting behaviors. *Public Relations Journal, 12*(4). https://prjournal.instituteforpr.org/wp-content/uploads/Heffron_PRJ14.2.pdf

Kent, M. L., & Li, C. (2020). Toward a normative social media theory for public relations. *Public Relations Review, 46*(1). https://doi.org/10.1016/j.pubrev.2019.101857

Kim, J. K., Overton, H., Bhalla, N., & Li, J. Y. (2020). Nike, Colin Kaepernick, and the politicization of sports: Examining perceived organizational motives and public responses. *Public Relations Review, 46*(2), 1–10. https://doi.org/10.1016/j.pubrev.2019.101856

Holtzhausen, D. R., & Voto, R. (2002). Resistance from the margins: The postmodern public relations practitioner as organizational activist. *Journal of Public Relations Research, 14*(1), 57–84. https://doi.org/10.1207/S1532754XJPRR1401_3

HRC. (2021). Corporate Equality Index. Human Rights Campaign. Retrieved April 7, 2021 from: https://www.hrc.org/resources/corporate-equality-index

Jin, Y., Liu, B. F., & Austin, L. L. (2011). Examining the role of social media in effective crisis management: The effects of crisis origin, information form, and source on publics' crisis responses. *Communication Research, 41*(1), 74–94. https://doi.org/10.1177/0093650211423918

Logan, N. (2016). The Starbucks race together initiative: Analyzing a public relations campaign with critical race theory. *Public Relations Inquiry, 5*(1), 93–113. https://doi.org/10.1177/2046147X15626969

McCabe, A., & Harris, K. (2021). Theorizing social media and activism: where is community development? *Community Development Journal, 56*(2), 318–337. https://doi.org/10.1093/cdj/bsz024

Overton, H., Choi, M., Weatherred, J. L., & Zhang, N. (2020). Testing the viability of emotions and issue involvement as predictors of CSA response behaviors. *Journal of Applied Communication Research, 48*(6), 695–713. https://doi.org/10.1080/00909882.2020.1824074

Palazzo, G., & Scherer, A. (2006). Corporate legitimacy as deliberation: A communicative framework. *Journal of Business Ethics, 66*(1), 71–88. https://doi.org/10.1007/s10551-006-9044-2

Parcha, J. M., & Kingsley Westerman, C. Y. (2020). How corporate social advocacy affects attitude change toward controversial social issues. *Management Communication Quarterly, 34*(3), 350–383. https://doi.org/10.1177/0893318920912196

Park, Y. E., & Dodd, M. D. (2017). The historical development of corporate social responsibility as a strategic function of public relations. In B. Brunner (Ed.), *The moral compass of public relations* (pp. 15–27). Routledge Research in Public Relations Series.

Rim, H., Lee, Y., & Yoo, S. (2020). Polarized public opinion responding to corporate social advocacy: Social network analysis of boycotters and advocators. *Public Relations Review, 46*(2), 1–10. https://doi.org/10.1016/j.pubrev.2019.101869

Rogers, A. (2016). *Understanding the Intersection of Twitter Advocacy Subcultures and Corporate Social Responsibility* (Senior Honors Thesis). University of Oregon.

Scherer, A. G., & Palazzo, G. (2011). The new political role of business in a globalized world: A review of a new perspective on CSR and its implications for the firm, governance, and democracy. *Journal of Management Studies, 48*(4), 899–931. https://doi.org/10.1111/j.1467-6486.2010.00950.x

Taylor, J., Johnston, J., & Whitehead, K. (2016). A corporation in feminist clothing? Young women discuss the dove "real beauty" campaign. *Critical Sociology, 42*(1), 123–144. https://doi.org/10.1177/0896920513501355

Toledano, M. (2016). Advocating for reconciliation: Public relations, activism, advocacy and dialogue. *PR Inquiry, 5*(3), 277–294. https://doi.org/10.1177/2046147X16666595

Valentini, C. (2015). Is using social media "good" for the public relations profession? A critical reflection. *Public Relations Review, 41*(2), 170–177. https://doi.org/10.1016/j.pubrev.2014.11.009

Vasquez, R. A., & Dodd, M. D. (2019). *Communicating corporate social advocacy: Perceptions of authenticity and corporate outcomes.* Orlando, FL: International Public Relations Research Conference.

Voss, B. (December 15, 2019). Hallmark pulls gay wedding ads under pressure from Christian moms. *NewNowNext.* Retrieved April 7, 2021 from: http://www.newnownext.com/hallmark-gay-lesbian-wedding-one-million-moms-zola/12/2019/.

Zald, M. N., & Ash, R. (1966). Social movement organizations: Growth, decay, and change. *Social Forces, 44*, 327–341. https://doi.org/10.2307/2575833

SECTION III

Foundations and Frameworks

SECTION III-A

Foundations and Frameworks: Organizational Approaches and Considerations

6

ORGANIZATIONAL PURPOSE, CULTURE, CRISIS LEADERSHIP, AND SOCIAL MEDIA

LaShonda L. Eaddy, Karla K. Gower, and Bryan H. Reber

Communicate Organization Values Through Using Social Media

Organizations have long noted their mission in statements, routinely noting why they exist, goals and services, and maybe even something about their primary customers. Vision statements or statements of organizational purpose are a more recent phenomenon and seem to be more and more an essential part of any successful organization's raison d'etre. Forbes contributor Afdhel Aziz wrote that purpose should, at its best, be an organization's North Star. "Having a clear and compelling purpose is now becoming increasingly essential for any company or brand which seeks to attract talent, inspire its community and out-innovate its competition," Aziz wrote (The Power of Purpose …, 2020, para. 1).

Organizational Purpose

Consumers today reward organizations that demonstrate and communicate their purpose. There are classic examples such as the TOMS one-for-one shoe program. Since the company's inception in 2006, it pledged that when consumers buy a pair of TOMS, the company donates shoes, water, or eye care to those in need. In its 2019–2020 Impact Report, TOMS announced a new model. One-third of the company's profits would be used "in support of grassroots good, creating change from the ground up," providing local leaders the financial resources for positive change in a variety of purpose areas. The company's new purpose statement is "1/3 of profits for grassroots good" (TOMS Impact Report, 2019–2020, p. 4).

DOI: 10.4324/9781003043409-10

Organizations are using social purpose to guide marketing communication, product innovation, and cause investment (Rodriguez-Vila & Bharadwaj, 2017). They identify "social purpose natives" and "social-purpose immigrants." Social purpose immigrants are "established brands [that] have grown without a well-defined social-purpose strategy and are now seeking to develop one" (ibid., para. 6). Whether a social purpose native or immigrant, businesses know they must deliver not only quality products or services but also quality purpose.

Organizational Culture

According to Gallup, fewer than half of U.S. employees "strongly agree that the mission or purpose of their company makes them feel their job is important" (Gallup's approach ..., 2018, p. 6). The value of strong, positive organizational culture can be measured in decreased absenteeism among employees, better employee retention, and loyal consumers. Cultural alignment means that everyone "thinks and talks about the company in the same way," meaning employees, customers, industry leaders, and journalists all share a common opinion of the organization's culture (ibid., p. 8).

Culture is driven by leadership and communication, values and rituals, human capital, work teams and structures, and performance (ibid., p. 13). External forces also affect organizational culture. Seventy percent of surveyed PR professionals predict employees' expectations of companies taking a role in societal issues to increase, according to the USC Annenberg Center for Public Relations' 2021 survey. They also expect an increase in CEOs taking a public stand on societal issues (Politics ..., April 2021). Organizational culture is important, perhaps more so than ever. For example, George Floyd's May 2020 murder in Minneapolis invigorated the Black Lives Matter movement and corporate sensitivity to diversity, equity, and inclusion issues. The USC survey revealed that 60% of PR professionals expect an increase in hiring a more diverse staff.

Crisis Leadership in Organizations

Organizational crisis leadership is sometimes dispersed: messaging decisions made by the communication function, efforts to limit legal exposure by internal counsel, business continuity overseen by line management, and everything orchestrated and approved by a chief executive. At all levels, some common leadership behaviors are useful (Nichols et al., 2020).

During the COVID-19 pandemic, crisis leadership came to the forefront. Traditional crisis communication leadership advises that spokespersons focus only on what they know are facts. That doesn't change, but Nichols et al. urge leaders to "decide with speed over precision;" arguing that if COVID-19 has shown us anything it's that a crisis situation may change daily or hourly. "The best leaders quickly process available information, rapidly determine what matters most, and make decisions with conviction," according to Nichols et al. (2020, para. 4).

The best crisis leaders are able to "adapt boldly." With the aforementioned rapidly changing circumstances, equally rapid adaptation is needed. As businesses changed strategies during COVID-19, the phrase "pandemic pivot" joined the business lexicon. Suddenly curbside pickup, home delivery, video meetings, and working from home were the norm. "The actions that previously drove results may no longer be relevant. The best leaders adjust quickly and develop new plans of attack" (Nichols et al., 2020, para. 11). They adapt boldly. Crisis leaders also "reliably deliver"; they expect a culture of accountability.

COVID-19 highlighted the need for emotional intelligence in crisis leadership. Leaders take care of their teams and, usually, their teams return the favor. Crisis leaders "engage for impact." "Effective leaders are understanding of their team's circumstances and distractions, but they find ways to engage and motivate, clearly and thoroughly communicating important new goals and information" (ibid.). Crisis often strikes on multiple fronts. COVID-19 is a health crisis that could impact team members in various ways. The best crisis leaders connect with individual team members to support them personally and reinforce their roles in the tasks at hand.

Changing Workplace and Marketplace Expectations

Organizations are experiencing changing expectations in the workplace and in the marketplace. The changes are being fueled by millennials (a cohort born roughly between 1983 and 1995) and Generation Z (those born approximately between 1996 and 2003). Failing to acknowledge and address these expectations is impacting corporate reputations worldwide. According to the 2020 Deloitte Global Millennial Study, barely half of the millennials said that business is a force for good, a striking decline from 2017 when three-quarters of millennials believed businesses could positively impact society.

Millennials and Gen Z now make up nearly half of the full-time workforce in the U.S. (O'Boyle, 2021). These groups expect open, transparent, and ethical leadership, but millennials and Gen Z conceptualize ethics differently from the earlier generations. Ethics, for the younger generations, is broader, and it's about treating individuals and the planet with respect. They believe businesses owe a duty of care to their stakeholders, including employees, not just to avoid harm but to actively work to promote care (Deloitte, 2020).

Gen Z and millennials want employers who care about them as individuals. Well-being in their eyes includes all aspects of their lives and is tied to the idea of "individualized respect" (O'Boyle, 2021, para. 4). Thus, a diverse, equitable, and inclusive workplace is expected and demanded because it affects how employees accomplish their daily work. As O'Boyle (2021) noted, for millennials and Gen Z, "disrespect breeds distrust, which destroys collaboration and honest communication. Respect and recognition matter from every direction—peers, managers, policies, systems, and leaders" (para. 4).

Ultimately, these young employees are concerned about environmental, social, and governance (ESG) issues. Their recruitment and ultimately retention is directly related to how employers plan to address such issues. A 2018 study of millennial communication professionals found that job decisions were driven by the reputation of the employer, its culture, and the job's location (Meng & Berger, 2018). This finding was reinforced in the 2020 Deloitte study, which found that job loyalty rose as businesses addressed employee needs, including diversity and inclusion, sustainability, and reskilling. Together, these new employee expectations are driving a shift in corporate purpose toward serving all stakeholders (Sims, 2020).

At the same time, millennial and Gen Z consumers are increasingly well-informed about company policy (Gold Standard, 2019). A company that appears to share their values will be supported, while a business that does not will be penalized (Deloitte, 2020). For example, millennials say they patronize businesses whose products and services have a positive impact on the environment and who achieve a balance between doing good and making a profit. But a third have stopped or lessened business relationships when they perceive a company as doing harm to the environment, and a quarter have done the same with companies who fail to safeguard consumers' personal information or reward senior executives with exorbitant bonuses or salaries while underpaying employees (Deloitte, 2020).

Although increasingly companies are taking political and social stands on issues, almost a quarter of millennials surveyed indicated they have reacted negatively to a CEO's public position on a political issue and stopped or lessened their relationship with the business. Only 12% said they were attracted to a business because of its CEO's political standpoint (Deloitte, 2020).

As indicated, publics increasingly expect businesses to make a positive impact on society via action. Checking a compliance box on a legal form is no longer sufficient. Compliance from a legal perspective is usually a minimum ethical standard. Stakeholder theory, which emphasizes the needs of stakeholders in relation to businesses, is often used in public relations to justify corporate ethical behavior. But millennials' and Gen Z's emphasis on respect suggests a turn toward human rights theory, which shifts the focus to stakeholder "rights" from "needs." The idea underlying human rights theory is that individuals are autonomous beings and therefore worthy of respect from others, including organizations (Arnold, 2010). Leaders should keep respect at the forefront when messaging during any crisis.

Leadership During Crises

The COVID-19 pandemic has presented a unique crisis situation that is different than the typical crisis as it has had significant impacts but also spawned off many other crises. Reber and colleagues (2021) suggest that the pandemic is a "sticky" crisis. "Sticky" crises are characterized by their severity, recurrence, and complexity, simultaneously resulting in a ripple effect of ancillary crises that impact both organizations and industries. "Sticky" crises require a near-immediate response and also might compel crisis managers to explore and understand the possible breadth and scope of emerging crises. These additional complexities and communication demands impact the way leaders prepare for potential crises. In early 2021, PRNEWS and the University of Georgia's Crisis Communication Coalition partnered to survey more than 400 public relations professionals regarding timely issues such as crisis leadership; diversity, equity, and inclusion (DEI); organizational preparedness, and ethics in the "sticky" crisis context (Eaddy et al., 2021).

Resourceful and Sensemaking Leadership

PR professionals were asked about sensemaking and resourceful leadership qualities that are pertinent in conflict and crisis management. Sensemaking refers to leaders' ability to examine and evaluate circumstances and situations so that organizations can spring into action if necessary. Resourcefulness involves leaders' ability to make quick decisions, adapt to changing circumstances, and use resources effectively. The survey results showed that 75.4% strongly agreed or agreed that sensemaking leaders see how events link together even when others do not and are able to identify something that does not fit with normal routines. Also, more than 80% strongly agreed or agreed that resourceful leaders adapt very quickly to pending crisis developments and deploy resources easily to respond to opportunities and threats encountered. Although many of these attributes have been traditionally associated with good leaders, "sticky" crises like the COVID-19 pandemic require leaders to have more foresight regarding the potential crisis threats' scopes, ancillary crisis developments, and seemingly unrelated crisis impacts. As leaders continue to strategize and navigate "sticky" crises' unprecedented impacts, they also face the additional challenge of publics' dwindling trust in CEOs and organizations.

Mistrust in Leaders

According to Edelman's 2021 Trust Barometer, there continue to be global trust gaps and declines, and people are more concerned with quality leadership and effective solutions rather than hearing from the typical "talking heads" that often lack authenticity and credibility (2021 Edelman Trust Barometer, n.d.). The study also shows that societal leaders such as CEOs are not trusted to do what's right. Despite the concerning perceptions of CEOs and mistrust, there's a silver lining; businesses are the most trusted institutions and are the only institution viewed as competent and ethical. Herein lies an opportunity for leaders to continue sharing organizational mission, vision, and values while also infusing them with notions of ethics and competence.

Enhancing Communication, Avoiding Crises

Research is clear; existing reputation affects how well an organization avoids or weathers a crisis (e.g., Claeys & Cauberghe, 2015). According to Claeys and Cauberghe (2015), a favorable pre-existing reputation serves to inoculate an organization during a crisis. If an organization has a favorable pre-existing reputation, it will suffer less reputational loss during a crisis than will an organization with an unfavorable pre-existing reputation (p. 64). Enhancing communication to build a stockpile of goodwill or favorable pre-existing reputation would be helped by transparent communication, holistic impact management, governance, and redressing stakeholders' grievances.

Transparency

The Annenberg Center for Public Relations surveyed PR professionals and found 39% of respondents expected an increase in demand for transparent communication. "Transparency is most often associated with three tenets: Being open and honest; reporting the bad with the good; and providing information in a timely manner," according to McCorkindale and DiStaso (2014, p. 2). Men and colleagues (2020) examined transparency between an organization and its employees and found that higher use of internal social media led employees to perceive their employer to be more transparent. They also noted employees are more likely to identify with employers when there is a perceived willingness to disclose truthful, complete, and useful information, be open, accountable, and demonstrate care for employees' voice and information needs (2020, p. 46).

Impact Relations

Benjamin Franklin is credited with first counseling to "do well by doing good." As implied elsewhere in this chapter, that sentiment is no longer just an aphorism; it's a dictum. It is a demand by both consumers and employees, especially among the youngest within the workforce. Into this arena has arrived a practice called "Impact Relations." Impact relations is more than corporate social responsibility (CSR). The Global Impact Relations Network (GIRN) is "a nonprofit organization created to legitimize, govern, educate, and scale the practice of Impact Relations" (https://impactrelations.org/about-us/). Companies are understanding that taking a stand is expected, as demonstrated by The New Plastics Economy Global Commitment is comprised of 118 business signatories that "produce, use, and recycle large volumes of plastic packaging".

In 2019, the group published its first Global Commitment Progress Report. Campaigns such as "The Trash Isles" developed by The Plastic Oceans Foundation in partnership with the LADBible Group and creative agency AMV BBDO have been successful in raising awareness of the breadth of the plastics problem in the oceans. This program proposed The Trash Isles as the 196th country and petitioned to join the United Nations. The campaign blasted onto the internet. The Trash Isles reached more than half a billion people worldwide and garnered over 50 million online views. The impact was amplified by social media and search engines. Plastic producers such as soft drink companies decided to join the effort to tackle plastic pollution.

Organization Governance

Leadership during times of crisis doesn't always stop in the CEO's office. Governance boards are also charged with helping manage crises. PwC found that corporate executives were unsettled about the crisis management oversight provided by their boards. Only 37% of PwC survey respondents said their board of directors' crisis management expertise was good or excellent, and only 57% believed their board understood the company's crisis plan very or somewhat well (DeNicola, 2021, para. 2).

The COVID-19 pandemic exposed organizations' crisis management vulnerabilities. PwC asked executives about pandemic-specific vulnerabilities, and respondents "cited crisis management more often than anything else" (ibid.). While governing boards may make missteps during the opening days or hours of a crisis, over time they often recalibrate to right the organization. PwC's Paul DeNicola wrote that focus on communication and paying attention to the entire organization are central to board success as they manage crises.

An example of successful organizational governance during a crisis is illustrated by Papa John's Pizza. Papa John's Pizza's governing board faced a series of controversies surrounding the brand's namesake, CEO, chairman, and company spokesman John Schnatter. Schnatter was accused of making two racist public statements. The board of directors first asked Schnatter to step down as CEO and eventually to relinquish his chairmanship as well. He was removed from all marketing efforts. Schnatter countered by turning to digital media. He created a website SavePapaJohns.com where he countered moves, legal and communication, made by the Papa John's board (Mowery, 2018, para. 3). The board of directors approved a poison pill strategy to thwart any effort at a hostile takeover by Schnatter, who owned 29% of shares (Mowery, 2018, para. 7). Basketball legend Shaquille O'Neal was added as the first African American board member; he began to make marketing appearances for the brand. The board's intervention kept the brand in good stead; Papa John's held its same spot – fourth-largest pizza company – at the end of 2019 with $3.70 billion gross revenue.

Leadership, Social Media, and Crises: Seizing Opportunities, Avoiding Pitfalls, and Mitigating Threats

Many tried-and-true standards of leadership in crisis apply in the social media context too. Social media presents opportunities for leaders to share important information about what distinguishes their organization from others, as discussed in this chapter's previous sections. However, serious consideration must be given to the potential opportunities and threats that social media poses. Although social media isn't a new phenomenon, it continues to evolve, nearly constantly, so organizations' social media strategies must be revisited often. Moreover, it's important to consider what constitutes a social media crisis and what type of problems present threats that could result in social media crises. Challenge crises occur when stakeholders believe organizations have acted unethically or irresponsibly and have become more visible with social media. Oftentimes, if stakeholders perceive organizations' responses to challenges as inadequate or inappropriate, they bring more awareness to the issue. Social media provides the perfect opportunity for this to occur quickly and with no costs incurred. Despite the prevalence of issues "going viral" on social media, it's crucial for leaders to consider several factors to identify and mitigate potential social media crises and respond appropriately. Coombs and Holladay (2012) suggest that many "so-called" social media crises are, in fact, paracrises:

> A paracrisis is like a crisis. It can "look like" a crisis and does require action from the organization. However, a paracrisis does not warrant convening the crisis team and operating in a crisis mode.
>
> (Coombs & Holladay, 2012, p. 408)

Paracrises mimic crises primarily due to high visibility, which is usually present with social media and must be managed publicly, often resulting from challenges, customer service complaints, and dissatisfied customers (Coombs, 2014). Leaders must recognize such threats and respond accordingly to be good stewards of organizational resources like time, money, and personnel. If handled well, threats posed by paracrises can be mitigated without becoming social media crises.

Social Media Crisis Prevention and Mitigation Perspectives

Leaders must distinguish between paracrises and social media crises and incorporate considerations into pre-crisis planning. Most organizations have some form of social media presence or are aware of online stakeholder sentiment. Social media monitoring runs the gambit between informal scanning to sophisticated monitoring and data analytics. Regardless of the monitoring complexity, leaders must develop criteria to gauge whether a problem is a crisis or a paracrisis. Furthermore, leaders must identify the respective operational units that are essential to mitigating paracrises; to ensure those leaders know their role in mitigation and understand the dire consequences of not handling paracrises in a timely and appropriate manner. Augmenting existing monitoring and mitigation strategies with these considerations can further protect organizations' financial and reputational assets. CEOs and other c-suite members also warrant discussion when examining crisis communication, proactive crisis management, and crisis strategy development in the social media context.

Chief Executive Officers Considerations

Although this chapter hasn't detailed CEOs' role in determining organizations' purpose, fostering a positive culture, and communicating organizational values, it goes without saying that CEOs are integral to these. Therefore, not only must CEOs (and c-suite) be prepared to communicate well regarding these aspects, they must also be keenly aware of the potential resulting impacts, both positive and negative, when relaying them via social media. Prior to the social media era, most organizations and CEOs were reluctant to offer support or advocate for polarizing topics. However, the social media landscape along with stakeholders' evolving preferences, have ushered in new expectations for corporate social advocacy and CEO activism. Larcker and colleagues (2018) define CEO activism as:

> the practice of CEOs taking public positions on environmental, social, and political issues not directly related to their business.
>
> *(Larcker et al., 2018, p. 1)*

CEO activism can be a double-edged sword, potentially accentuating organizations' positive attributes or detracting from them. CEO activism becomes a reputational threat when it doesn't align with organizational values or isolates stakeholders. While authenticity is paramount to CEO activism, crisis leaders must ensure that CEOs are aware of the potential costs (Branicki et al., 2021; Chatterji & Toffel, 2019). However, organizational and executive social media presence has become expected, if not demanded; therefore, it is critical for leaders to recognize that the ease of posting or sharing on social media still requires intentionality and sound strategy. Not only does social media present reputational threats, but it also can jeopardize regulatory standing or cause litigation.

Legal Perspectives

From a legal standpoint, leaders must be aware of potential lawsuits arising from crises or organizations' responses to them. Social media posts can be discoverable in the event of a trial, which means social media managers must be careful about what is posted and retweeted. Although an employee's statements on social media are usually seen as personal, they may be considered as emanating from the company if the account makes it appear as though the person is speaking in their official capacity (Windon, 2018). Netflix CEO Reed Hastings found that out the hard way when he used his personal Facebook account to celebrate a record month of streaming. The U.S. Securities and Exchange Commission (SEC) started an investigation into the post because it appeared that Hastings' "friends" were getting access to inside information. The SEC ultimately closed the investigation, but not before reminding companies that their social media posts must comply with the rules (Robertson, 2013).

Leaders must also consider issues such as timing, accuracy, and geographic reach. There is no set timeline for disclosing information to the public, but delays can result in greater legal jeopardy. Equifax, for example, discovered its massive data breach in July 2017 but didn't disclose it publicly for two months. Numerous lawsuits resulted because the delay prevented the public from taking steps to mitigate personal damages (O'Brien, 2017; Windon, 2018). The speed of disclosure, however, must be balanced with accuracy. Being fast but wrong can lead to unnecessary legal action as well. In 2015, Kanye West announced his new album would be available exclusively on the paid music-streaming service Tidal. But when the album was released, it appeared on several services at once. West was sued by people who joined Tidal solely to gain access to his music (Sanchez, 2019; Windon, 2018).

Strategic Social Media Perspectives

It's also critical for organizations to communicate organizational vision, mission, and values via online platforms. These important components of organizations' purpose and culture must be interwoven into key messaging, advertising, and all other communication channels. Social media provides opportunities to reach the masses quickly and also relay targeted messaging to niche audiences. However, social media responsibilities are oft given to PR technicians who are viewed as social media "experts" based upon their age and technological savvy. When leaders delegate social media entirely to entry-level or junior employees, organizations run the risk of relegating social media to a tactical vehicle void of strategic direction. Not only is this a missed opportunity, but it could also result in crises if there's misalignment with stakeholders' expectations. Prior to the social media age, this risk might not be viewed seriously, especially if the stakeholder group involved was considered insignificant or "on the fringes." However, social media is a proven ally, helping organizations gain legitimacy and visibility that formerly was elusive. Even a cursory glance of an organization's social media crisis such as Cinnamon Toast Crunch's (CTC) sugary shrimp tails fiasco demonstrates the continued importance of sound social media strategy and the repercussions of not following said strategy. Therefore, it's critical for leaders to be intimately involved in social media strategy development, ensuring that organizational vision, mission, and values are not only being communicated but also to decrease the likelihood of stakeholder expectation gaps leading to crises.

Social Media Crisis Snapshot: *Cinnamon Toast Crunch's Sugary Shrimp Tails*

In March 2021, Jensen Karp tweeted that his family's CTC cereal appeared to have shrimp tails inside it. The following day, a social media specialist followed up with Karp regarding his concern. Two days later, CTC's parent company, General Mills (GM), CEO Jeff Harmening responded to the claim:

> It is amazing the amount of news coverage that this story has generated. I must admit that some of it is kind of humorous, but what I want you to know … is that we take food safety very seriously … it is highly unlikely this occurred at a General Mills facility … We're in the process of working with that consumer to try to figure out what happened between when it left our docks and when he opened it.

Although Harmening responded fairly quickly, GM missed several opportunities to potentially keep the story from going viral. Primarily, the prominence of the tweeter; the potential and perceived risk to consumers; and the organizational response helped this story gain traction and be seen by thousands (if not millions) of consumers.

Key Considerations:

- Jensen Karp is a TV Writer and podcast host with over 203,000 engaged Twitter followers. His wife, actress Danielle Fishel, played Topanga on *Boy Meets World*. The combination of the couple's celebrity and creativity also made the story interesting to follow for consumers and news organizations alike. It's also likely that Gen Z and Millennial consumers would see the claim and be concerned about the potential impact and whether GM met its duty of care to not just avoid harm but to actively work to promote care.

- GM failed to acknowledge the true risk posed to consumers (i.e., those with seafood allergies, etc.) if the claim was true. GM espouses a "Consumer First" strategy, but it didn't seem to have been executed (General Mills, n.d.). Additionally, GM missed opportunities to reiterate its mission, vision, goals, and quality standards.
- GM's initial response was timely but lacked strategy and forethought. It appears that GM handled the consumer complaint just like all others. Although Harmening references food safety in his response, it could be perceived as disingenuous based on the rest of his statement.

Conclusion

Organizational purpose and culture inform crisis leadership and vice versa. Employees, consumers, shareholders, and other stakeholders now demand organizational purpose. Gen Z and millennials have used their numbers and values to shift organizational culture. These values set the standard for rapid but transparent communication at all times, but particularly during crises. Organization leaders can use social media to reassure or enflame emotions when faced with crises. The value-driven changes and attendant social media platforms offer a solid foundation for successful crisis communication leadership.

References

Arnold, D. G. (2010). Transnational corporations and the duty to respect basic human rights. *Business Ethics Quarterly, 20*(3), 371–399. https://doi.org/10.5840/beq201020327

Aziz, A. (February 18, 2020). *The power of purpose: The 7 elements of a great purpose statement (Part 1)*. Last accessed: 5/5/2021. Retrieved from: https://www.forbes.com/sites/afdhelaziz/2020/02/18/the-power-of-purpose-the-7-elements-of-a-great-purpose-statement/?sh=107e27693fad

Branicki, L., Brammer, S., Pullen, A., & Rhodes, C. (2021). The morality of "new" CEO activism. *Journal of Business Ethics, 170*(2), 269–285. https://doi.org/10.1007/s10551-020-04656-5

Chatterji, A. K., & Toffel, M. W. (2019). Assessing the impact of CEO activism. *Organization & Environment, 32*(2), 159–185. https://doi.org/10.1177/1086026619848144

Claeys, A.-S., & Cauberghe, V. (2015). The role of a favorable pre-crisis reputation in protecting organizations during crisis. *Public Relations Review, 41*, 64–71. http://dxdoi.org/10.1016/j.pubrev.2014.10.013

Coombs, W. T., & Holladay, J. S. (2012). The paracrisis: The challenges created by publicly managing crisis prevention. *Public Relations Review, 38*(3), 408–415. https://doi.org/10.1016/j.pubrev.2012.04.004

Coombs, W. T. (2014). *Ongoing crisis communication: Planning, managing, and responding.* Sage Publications.

Deloitte. (2020). *Deloitte global millennial study 2020.* Retrieved from: https://www2.deloitte.com/global/en/pages/about-deloitte/articles/millennialsurvey.html

DeNicola, P. (April 21, 2021). *The crisis management crisis – and how boards can overcome it. PwC.* Last accessed: 5/7/2021. Retrieved from: https://www.pwc,com/us/en/services/governance-insights-center/blog/crisis-management-boards.html

Eaddy, L. L., Ervin, S., Lee, J., & Kim, S. (April, 2021). *Survey notes diversity issues, importance of leaders in "Sticky" crises.* Crisis Insider.

2021 Edelman Trust Barometer. (n.d.). https://www.edelman.com/trust/2021-trust-barometer.

Gallup's approach to culture: Building a culture that drives performance (2018). Last accessed: 5/7/2021. Retrieved from: https://thepowerscompany.com/wp-content/uploads/2019/12/Culture_POV_External-Digital_MK_POV_032918.pdf

General Mills. (n.d.). *General Mills: A U.S.-based food company.* Retrieved from: https://www.generalmills.com/en/Company/Overview

Gold Standard. (2019). Transform 2019. In *Ethical corporation.* Amsterdam, Netherlands.

Larcker, D. F., Miles, S. A., Tayan, B., & Wright-Violich, K. (November 1, 2018). *The double-edged sword of CEO activism.* Stanford Graduate School of Business. https://www.gsb.stanford.edu/faculty-research/publications/double-edged-sword-ceo-activism

McCorkindale, T., & DiStaso, M. W. (2014). The state of social media research: Where are we now, where we were and what it means for public relations. *Research Journal of the Institute for Public Relations, 1*(1), 1–17.

Men, R. L., O'Neil, J., & Ewing, M. (2020). Examining the effects of internal social media usage on employee engagement. *Public Relations Review, 46*(2), 101880. https://doi.org/10.1016/j.pubrev.2020.101880

Meng, J., & Berger, B. K. (2018). Maximizing the potential of millennial communication professionals in the workplace: A talent management approach in the field of strategic communication. *International Journal of Strategic Communication, 12*(5), 507–525. https://doi.org/10.1080/1553118X.2018.1508467

Mowery, M. (August 22, 2018). *Our timeline of the Papa John's controversy now includes a head-scratching website.* Retrieved July 26, 2020, from https://adage.com/article/digital/a-history-papa-john-s-controversy/314260

Nichols, C., Hayden, S. C., & Trendler, C. (April 2, 2020). 4 Behaviors that help leaders manage a crisis. *Harvard Business Review.* Last accessed: 5/5/2021. Retrieved from: https://hbr.org/2020/04/4-behaviors-that-help-leaders-manage-a-crisis

O'Boyle, E. (March 30, 2021). *4 things Gen Z and Millennials expect from their workplace.* Gallup.com https://www.gallup.com/workplace/336275/things-gen-millennials-expect-workplace.aspx

O'Brien, S. A. (September 8, 2017). *Giant Equifax breach: 143 million people could be affected.* https://money.cnn.com/2017/09/07/technology/business/equifax-data-breach/index.html

Politics, polarization & purpose: 2021 Global communication report (April 2021). USC Annenberg Center for Public Relations.

Reber, B. H., Yarbrough, C. R., Nowak, G. J., & Jin, Y. (2021). Complex and challenging crises: A call for solutions. In Y. Jin, B. H. Reber, & G. J. Nowak (Eds.), *Advancing crisis communication effectiveness: Integration of public relations scholarship and practice* (pp. 3–16). Routledge.

Robertson, A. (2013, April 2). SEC clears Reed Hastings and Netflix to share investor information on Facebook. *Wall Street Journal.* https://www.theverge.com/2013/4/2/4175630/sec-clears-reed-hastings-netflix-to-share-investor-information-on-facebook

Rodriguez-Vila, O., & Bharadwaj, S. (September–October. 2017). Competing on social purpose. *Harvard Business Review.* Last accessed: 5/4/2021. https://hbr.org/2017/09/copeting-on-social-purpose

Sanchez, D. (January 31, 2019). Kanye West and Tidal quietly settle the Life of Pablo lawsuit. *Digital Music News.* https://www.digitalmusicnews.com/2019/01/31/kanye-west-tidal-lawsuit-settlement/

Sims, M. P. (January 21, 2020). Davos: Sustainability momentum will drive "conscious capitalism." *PRovoke Media.* https://www.provokemedia.com/latest/article/davos-sustainability-momentum-will-drive-%27conscious-capitalism%27

TOMS Impact Report 2019–2020. Last accessed: 5/7/2021. Retrieved from: https://www.toms.com/on/demandware.static/-/Library-Sites-toms-content-global/default/pdfs/TOMS_Impact_Report.pdf

Windon, R. (2018). Legal considerations for crisis communicators in the digital age. In R. Culp (Ed.), *New rules of crisis management: Issues & crisis planning and response in the digital age* (pp. 32–37). RockDove Solutions.

7

SOCIAL MEDIA INFLUENCERS IN CRISIS

Providing Counsel on Instagram

Augustine Pang, Debbie Lee, Gindelin Low, and Valerie Hum

Introduction

Increasingly, organizations are harnessing social media influencers (SMIs) as third-party advocates or key opinion leaders (KOLs). Consumers view them as knowledgeable sources of information (Tuten & Solomon, 2017). In the United States, the Kardashians are used by a number of organizations to promote their products. Yang (2019) noted that while Western influencers are mostly video bloggers on Instagram or YouTube, Chinese KOLs have multiple channels, including social media platforms WeChat and Weibo, social networking sites Douban or TikTok. Figures from 2016 point to it as a US$8.6 billion industry in China (Yang, 2019). The incomes of SMIs have soared too, as organizations pay top dollars to sponsor posts, videos, stories, and blogs (Wakefield, 2019):

- The average cost from 2018 to 2019 for a sponsored Instagram photo rose by 44%
- A sponsored blog post increased from $7.39 in 2006 to $1,442 in 2019
- YouTube videos commanded the highest fees – four times that of the next highest-priced form of sponsored content – up from $420 in 2014 to $6,700 in 2019
- A Facebook status update rose from $8 in 2014 to $395 in 2019
- A Twitter post went up from $29 in 2014 to $422 in 2019
- Blog posts increased from $407 to $1,442

Sng et al. (2019) argued that besides speaking on behalf of organizations, SMIs had been used extensively in influencer marketing. The pervasive use of

DOI: 10.4324/9781003043409-11

social media has enabled KOLs to amplify an organization's marketing messages through paid word-of-mouth (WOM) (Scott, 2015).

However, SMIs carry certain risks to the organizations. Some of them have found themselves in crises through personal indiscretions (Ang, 2019). Sng et al. (2019) described SMIs as leveling potential paracrisis threats, undermining the organizations' strategic communication efforts. "Engagement of SMIs can be a boon or bane in the organizations' strategic communication efforts. A well-conceived SMI-based communication initiative can benefit organizations because SMIs have the connections to reach and influence their specific community and followers" (Uzunoğlu & Kip, 2014, p. 316). Their study found that SMIs become organizational risks when their indiscretions spillover on social media, triggering a paracrisis that developed into a crisis.

The question remains: When SMIs face crises, where can they seek help? This study examines micro-influencers who bring in the greatest value for organizations with their high engagement rate and low endorsement costs (Pierucci, 2018). A preliminary study was conducted to better understand their mindset – their motivations, awareness of crisis threats, information consumption habits, and preferred medium of engagement. Instagram is the most used influencer channel (Mediakix, 2019). Since micro-influencers are active on Instagram, we propose using this platform to house crisis counsel information relevant to them.

The crisis manual is constructed by leveraging various Instagram functions like Instagram Highlights. Bite-sized crisis advice is conceived across the crisis cycle (Coombs, 2019; Wilcox et al., 2015). Counsel is anchored on key crisis theories like image repair theory (Benoit & Pang, 2008), delivered in the language SMIs understand.

Literature Review

Defining Social Media Influencers

An SMI is a KOL who amasses influence and has a strong following on their content (Engle, 2019). According to "The Pyramid of Influence" (StarNgage, n.d.), *mega-influencers*, *macro-influencers*, *micro-influencers*, and *brand advocates* constitute the social media landscape.

At the top of the pyramid are *mega-influencers*, celebrities who possess half a million or more followers, like Ellen DeGeneres and PewDiePie. *Macro-influencers* are those who have amassed a 50,000 to 500,000 strong following, such as Ava Louise. *Micro-influencers* are everyday influencers with 1,000 to 100,000 followers, such as Carrine Low, a Singaporean lifestyle influencer who has brand affiliations with McDonald's, PepsiCo, and Lazada. Finally, *brand advocates* are individuals who do not have a dedicated following but are passionate about sharing about their favorite brands (StarNgage, n.d.).

Why Focus on Micro-influencers Rather Than Macro-influencers?

Although micro-influencers do not have as many followers, this has not stopped brands from endorsing them. Pierucci (2018, para. 12) suggested: "…the Game isn't just getting eyeballs; but getting eyeballs that care." Simply put, engagement matters more than reach.

Micro-influencers are viewed as knowledgeable sources of information (Tuten & Solomon, 2017). Being "a group of passionate people dedicated to writing topics and issues relevant to the community" (Loh, 2019), they drive more conversations and higher brand engagement. It is less costly to engage them as they are not celebrities or macro-influencers. With the value they bring, investing in micro-influencers may be considered a sound investment. Pierucci perfectly summarized micro-influencers' influence (Pierucci, 2018, para. 9):

> 60 per cent higher campaign engagement rates are driven by micro-influencers; those campaigns are 6.7 times more efficient per engagement than influencers with larger followings, which makes them more cost effective; and micro-influencers drive 22.2 times more weekly conversations than the average consumer.

Micro-influencers are the subject of this project since they drive more engagement, stimulate online conversations, and are worth the value for brands (Pierucci, 2018).

SMIs as Brands

Micro-influencers engage in a technique known as *self-branding* (Khamis et al., 2017). By crafting themselves as an authentic "personal" brand (Hearn & Schoenhoff, 2016), they amass a loyal following on their social media platforms.

Self-branding by SMIs, micro or macro, leverages the crucial aspect of "authenticity" (Khamis et al., 2017). SMIs are perceived as "real" as they provide followers with an insight into their private lives and constantly engage with them (Marwick, 2015). However, reputational implications are involved when they carry themselves as a brand. Hence, micro-influencers are expected to "always be on work mode" to vigilantly monitor their "authentic" self, which is "paradoxically both edited (since it is outward looking) and real" (Khamis et al., 2017, p. 203).

Followers have a strong belief that whatever the SMIs are advocating is authentic and a reflection of their real lives, such that when they diverge from their established online image, it results in an explosion of outrage. An example would be 29-year-old Yovana Mendoza Ayres (Pseudonym: *Yovana*, previously known as *Rawvana*), a mega-influencer. She built an empire of over a million followers from advocating her plant-based diet, which she claimed transformed her health for the better (Rosenberg, 2019). When she was caught eating fish on video, outrage ensued. The misalignment between Ayres' online persona and real identity resulted in a backlash, thrusting her into a crisis (Chen, 2019). Given that micro-influencers leverage authenticity more heavily than macro-influencers, parallels can be drawn from Ayres' crisis that an online persona who strays from reality serves as a threat to their reputation.

SMIs as a Crisis Risk

Organizations are constantly identifying new ways to engage their audiences (Stacks & Bowen, 2013), and SMIs are increasingly employed as organizational advocates to shape stakeholder attitudes and persuade audiences to support organizational initiatives (Booth & Matic, 2011; Freberg et al., 2011). Nielsen (2012) showed that WOM and personal recommendations trumped traditional advertising. In a similar light, Millner and colleagues (2011) described SMIs as "proxy communicators" who speak on behalf of organizations and are seen as independent third-party endorsers. Considering the above factors, Sng et al. (2019) posited that an SMI's extensive network of followers is perceived as an asset. However, it is important to be aware of the pitfalls when engaging SMIs who, like celebrities, can face reputational crises that may affect the affiliated brand (Jiang et al., 2015; Sato et al., 2015).

Paracrisis is defined as a "publicly visible crisis threat that charges an organization with irresponsible or unethical behavior" (Coombs & Holladay, 2012, p. 414). Social media has five characteristics: Participation, conversation, openness, communication, and connectedness (Coombs, 2019). These characteristics, coupled with the fact that SMIs are perceived as representatives of the organization, make any reputational crises they face a paracrisis threat to the organization. Although SMI-triggered organizational crises may be uncommon, there still lies a risk that paracrises caused by SMIs could escalate into a crisis for the organization (Sng et al., 2019).

Sng et al. (2019) posited that the key factor in differentiating a paracrisis from a crisis is when the SMI's crisis threatens the business continuity of the affiliated organization. Although arguable that the personal indiscretion of the SMI is beyond the organization's control, stakeholders still hold the organization responsible (Sng et al., 2019) – see the case of PewDiePie. After publishing anti-Semitic YouTube videos, YouTube faced a crisis, which resulted in revenue loss as advertisers pulled out. The British government also held Google, YouTube's parent company, responsible (Grierson, 2017).

While SMIs can pose crisis risk to organizations, brands can also damage SMIs' reputations. In 2015, SingTel, a telecommunications company in

Singapore, engaged Gushcloud, a digital talent agency, then-micro-influencers Saffron Sharpe and Eunice Lim, to promote its latest Youth Plan. Gushcloud instructed them to "lament about competitors' (M1/StarHub) services" (Tan, 2015, para.6). When the instructions were leaked by blogger Wendy Cheng, many netizens labeled Gushcloud as unethical and Sharpe and Lim deceitful.

Another example, in 2017, Kendall Jenner, who was featured in Pepsi's "Live for Now" advertisement, was excoriated by netizens for trivializing the Black Lives Matter movement – where she handed a can of Pepsi to a policeman in a scene that appeared to replicate protest frontlines. Jenner apologized.

The Evolution of a Paracrisis into a Crisis

To explain micro-influencers' relevance to crises, we referenced three concepts – "the strength of weak ties" by Granovetter (1973), "social media hype" by Pang (2013a), and the concept of information vacuum by Pang (2013b).

First, "the strength of weak ties" theory by Granovetter (1973) argued that acquaintances are more influential than close friends in spreading information through social networks. "Strong ties" are trusted individuals with similar social circles, likes, and interests (p. 1368). Conversely, "weak ties" are defined as "mere acquaintances" that provide "novel information not circulating in the closely-knit network of strong ties" (p. 1368). Weak ties are crucial in bringing networks of strong ties into contact with one another. More importantly, these ties encourage sharing of information across different groups (Gilbert & Karahalios, 2009). In the context of social media, Levin and Cross (2004) argued that weak ties expedite the transfer of "novel and potentially useful knowledge" across groups (p. 1480), spreading the news of a paracrisis in the quickest way possible since social networks thrive on weak ties. If an SMI is involved in a paracrisis, such newsworthy information tends to circulate faster since negative emotions have a stronger ability to connect users together (Fan et al., 2014).

Second, Pang (2013a) posited that a social media hype is generated by netizens that grabbed attention; it is "triggered by a key event and sustained by a self-reinforcing quality in its ability for users to engage in conversation" (p. 333). It has three defining characteristics – a trigger event that resonates with netizens' emotions; spaces for discussion; and diverse opinions (Pang, 2013a, p. 332). SMIs may trigger social media hype, as exemplified in Daryl Yow's photoshop scandal. The Singaporean influencer was caught passing off stock images as his own on Instagram (Teo, 2018). This incident satisfied the three characteristics (How, 2018). Within 24 hours of the discovery, Sony, a major sponsor, was pressured for an explanation. This threw Yow and his sponsors into a paracrisis. Thus, it is crucial to educate SMIs on crisis preparation and reputational risks.

Lastly, a lack of response to a paracrisis results in an information vacuum. An information vacuum exists when organizations fail to respond to a crisis promptly, allowing others to control their narrative and cause reputational risk (Pang, 2013b). Yow's scandal was promptly reported by *Mothership*, an online Singapore news site. This led to an information vacuum – Yow only responded five days later through an interview with *MustShareNews*, another local online news site. He should have controlled the narrative, i.e., stealing the thunder, which is described as "making rapid, full disclosure first" (Arpan & Pompper, 2003, p. 294).

The Application

Seeking SMIs Thoughts

Conversations were conducted with nine SMIs to better understand micro-influencers' thoughts from February 28, 2020, to March 5, 2020. Of the nine influencers, six were female and three were male, aged between 21 and 26 years old.

Preliminary Thoughts

Five key insights inform our application:

1. *SMIs lacked knowledge in image cultivation.* The SMIs stated that they do not actively cultivate a relationship with stakeholders or consider how they were viewed by the public. Instead, they trust that being true to who they are is sufficient. Having a positive relationship with stakeholders is important, which helps ameliorate the negative effects during a crisis (Coombs, 2013). Already poor reputation can exacerbate during a crisis, i.e., the *"Velcro effect"* (Coombs, 2013). Similar to "credits" in a bank account, reputational currency accumulated by SMIs before a crisis acts as a ready stock they can tap on in the event of a crisis (Coombs, 2013, p. 269; Coombs & Holladay, 2006).

2. *SMIs do not understand that a crisis is perceptual.* During interviews, Yow was presented as a case study. Insights gathered showed that SMIs viewed this as a trivial matter. Although SMIs agreed that it was a transgression, they believe that photo-editing and the use of stock images are common occurrences in the industry. This shows that SMIs failed to take into account the audience's perception of Yow's scandal. SMIs need to understand that crisis is perceptual, and stakeholders are the ones constructing the events as crises (Coombs, 2019).

3. *SMIs tend to adopt a reactive stance.* From the interviews, it was deduced that none of the SMIs knew how to manage a crisis should it occur. When asked where they would look for information on managing their crisis, some cited the internet or fellow influencers as trusted channels. They believed that sourcing for help *during* the crisis would suffice.

4. *SMIs view crisis response as an either-or approach: To apologize or not to apologize.* To understand the response that SMIs would employ during a crisis, the respondents were shown two case studies – Yow's photoshop debacle and the Singtel-Gushcloud saga. While most SMIs recognized the importance of apologizing, one of the respondents insisted that he would not apologize since his clients were aware that he was using stock images. From these responses, it could be deduced that SMIs are "locked into thinking that there is only a set way(s) of communicating during crises," which is similar to how organizations and practitioners often approach crisis communication (Pang et al., 2021). However, Cancel et al. (1997) posited that public relations is more accurately represented along a continuum due to the fluidity of each crisis situation. Therefore, this similar approach could be extrapolated for an SMI's crisis to better craft their response.

5. *SMIs do not realize the potential repercussions of a mismanaged crisis.* The respondents did not see the severity of a mismanaged crisis, citing reasons that "they do not plan to make social media influencing into a full-time career" or that they could "easily drop out of the social media scene to pursue other career paths." However, during a crisis, the accused is under constant public scrutiny, and on a platform like social media, speculations can be exaggerated within a short time (Siah et al., 2010). Through every crisis, an enduring image – a picture that is forever etched in the minds of the public – is formed "at first mention" and defines the accused even after the crisis is over. (Ho et al., 2014; Pang, 2012).

Project SMIs: Providing Counsel

How Can Instagram Provide Counsel?

To ensure the content housed on @howtocrisis resonated with our target audience, we chose an appropriate tone of voice, as academic jargon could render the tone of our content dull or uninteresting.

To sustain the interest of SMIs in our posts, we emulated the casual tone of the influencers' Instagram profiles when crafting the text. Witty hashtags, emojis, and attractive visuals and graphics to make information absorption easier were included.

Why Instagram?

In 2019, Instagram topped the list for the most used influencer marketing channel, ahead of YouTube and Facebook (Mediakix, 2019). This is supported by the spike in global Instagram influencer market value, estimated at US$1.07 billion in 2017 and a predicted value of US$2.38 billion by 2019 (Statista, 2017).

TABLE 7.1 Insights and Corresponding Crisis Concepts

Key insight	Crisis concept
SMIs lacked knowledge in image cultivation	Velcro effect analogy (Coombs, 2013) Bank account analogy (Coombs, 2013; Coombs & Holladay, 2006)
SMIs do not understand that a crisis is perceptual	Crisis (Coombs, 2019) Situational Crisis Communication Theory (Coombs, 2013)
SMIs tend to adopt a reactive stance	Pre-crisis scanning (Coombs, 2019)
SMIs view crisis response as an either-or approach: To apologize or not to apologize	Crisis response strategies (Pang et al., 2012) Contingency theory (Pang et al., 2021)
SMIs do not realize the potential repercussions of a mismanaged crisis	Integrated crisis mapping model (Jin et al., 2012) Enduring image (Ho et al., 2014) Building dialogic relationships (Kent & Taylor, 1998) Post-crisis communication (Coombs, 2019) Mediating the media model (Pang, 2010)

Instagram, with its varying media forms and sizable word count, is an effective and convenient medium for influencers to deliver content in a relatable tone to the target audience.

Functions of Instagram

Instagram has several functions that we could use – *Instagram posts, Instagram Highlights,* and *Instagram TV (IGTV).*

Crisis Concepts

From insights garnered from the conversations, the following concepts were chosen to provide SMIs with the necessary crisis knowledge (see Table 7.1).

How Crisis Counsel Is Provided

Crisis counsel is provided through *Instagram posts, Instagram Highlights,* and *Instagram TV (IGTV).* Constant across our visuals is the customized copy for captions, casual tone, and interesting images that parallel concepts shared. Academic jargon and complex concepts were presented in layman speak to avoid coming across as instructive. Case studies were distilled into a step-by-step explanation. We also leveraged the interactivity of the platform to engage with SMIs (Figure 7.1).

FIGURE 7.1 Screenshot of the Platform

Instagram Posts

The *Instagram posts* on @howtocrisis made use of striking images with short headers to capture the attention of SMIs. Each post included emojis and was written in a casual tone. Analogies such as a vacuum cleaner to explain the information vacuum concept and other fictional situations to get SMIs thinking were used. A call-to-action was included at the end of each caption to direct SMIs to the Instagram Highlights to learn more about the crisis concepts (Figures 7.2 and 7.3).

FIGURE 7.2 Screenshot of Instagram Posts

If the media frames their story with you as the victim, it stirs the emotion of sadness within your followers who will tend to process information more carefully, leading to a fairer evaluation of you.

If you are interested in learning more about emotions and the media, refer to Integrated Crisis Mapping (ICM) model by Jin, Pang, and Cameron (2007) and Appraisal-Tendency Framework by Lerner and Kelter.

Now that you are aware of how the media influence your followers, are you able to influence the media to frame your crisis more favourably?

There must be something you can do... right? Or do you just have to suck it up and deal?

Stay tuned for our next highlight to find out!

FIGURE 7.3 Screenshot of Instagram Highlights – Fictional Scenario and Polls
(Continued)

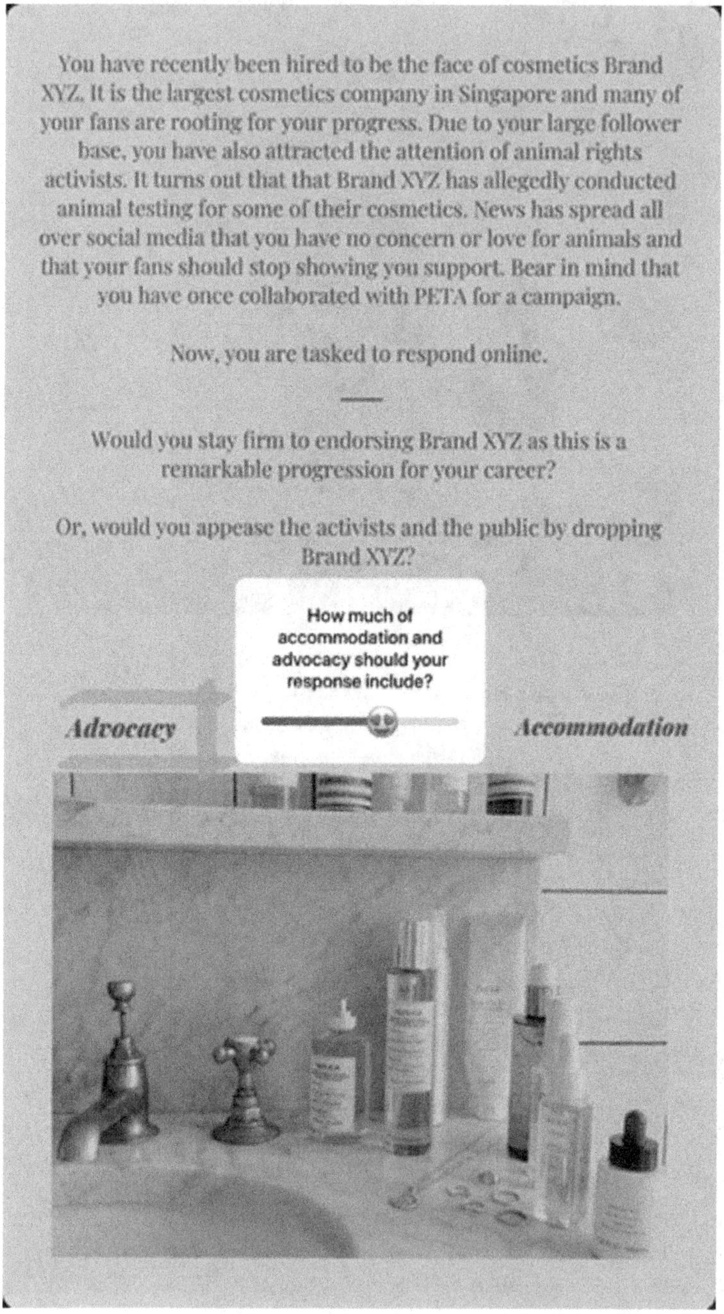

You have recently been hired to be the face of cosmetics Brand XYZ. It is the largest cosmetics company in Singapore and many of your fans are rooting for your progress. Due to your large follower base, you have also attracted the attention of animal rights activists. It turns out that that Brand XYZ has allegedly conducted animal testing for some of their cosmetics. News has spread all over social media that you have no concern or love for animals and that your fans should stop showing you support. Bear in mind that you have once collaborated with PETA for a campaign.

Now, you are tasked to respond online.

Would you stay firm to endorsing Brand XYZ as this is a remarkable progression for your career?

Or, would you appease the activists and the public by dropping Brand XYZ?

How much of accommodation and advocacy should your response include?

Advocacy   *Accommodation*

FIGURE 7.3   *(Continued)*

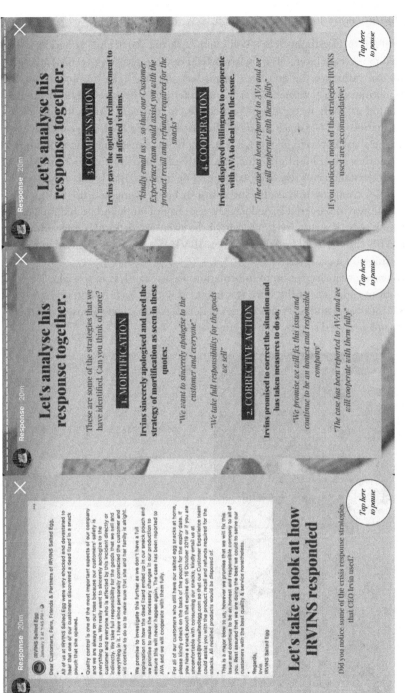

FIGURE 7.4 Screenshot of Instagram Highlights – IRVINS Case Study

Instagram Highlights

For Instagram Highlights, the "Poll" and "Ask me Anything" functions were utilized to increase interactivity with SMIs. For example, to show SMIs that the media can influence the emotions of readers and that crisis responses can fall on a continuum, a fictional scenario and slider poll were used. This facilitated interaction as SMIs were able to participate anonymously and without fear of recrimination. The *"Ask me Anything"* function allowed SMIs a personal avenue to deepen their knowledge of crisis concepts while remaining unidentified.

In another set of highlights, the case study of a crisis was shared for SMIs to better understand crisis response strategies. For context, IRVINS is a Singapore-based food company that is also successful in Hong Kong and the Philippines. Jane Holloway discovered a fried lizard in her bag of chips and posted images on Facebook, which went viral. This caught the attention of South China Morning Post, ABS-CBN, and The Straits Times. IRVINS's apology was used as a real-life example of a crisis response.

To ensure that absorption of information was as seamless as possible, a spot at the bottom right side of the story was included within each Instagram highlight for SMIs to pause and read the content in detail. Again, the response was broken down and analyzed step by step (Figure 7.4).

FIGURE 7.5 Screenshot of IGTV

Instagram TV (IGTV)

Finally, through IGTV, case studies adopted a storytelling approach for SMIs easy comprehension – with the use of eye-catching video clips and voiceover to break the monotony of Instagram posts and highlights. IGTVs showcased selected case studies on how influencers previously embroiled in crises managed the scenarios, with bite-sized learnings, tips, and relevant concepts at the end of each segment (Figure 7.5).

Conclusion

It is important to provide counsel on Instagram for SMIs as they are likely to handle crises on their own without the help of external consultants or agencies. By presenting crisis concepts in a digestible manner on a platform SMIs are already active on, they will be able to equip themselves with how to respond and establish their position in the case of a crisis. Case studies and concepts are provided to show them that crisis responses fall on a continuum and not an either-or approach. Recommendations are:

- Be proactive when it comes to managing reputations,
- Being mindful they are public figures and of their image prior to the crisis as it is critical in shaping stakeholders' perceptions of them,
- They should fill the information vacuum (Pang, 2013b) as soon as they can,
- Like any public figure, seek counsel when in trouble (Pang et al., 2017),
- While professional counsel can be helpful (Pang & Yeo, 2012), this platform can be their first point of help.

For future research, cultural impacts on the perception of apologies could be explored to further shape the responses SMIs could employ. Scholarly articles have shown that the "function and meaning" of apologies differ in individualistic and collectivistic cultures, posing implications for effective trust repair (Maddux et al., 2011). Therefore, apologies made during a crisis should be relevant to the cultural context of the SMI to ensure effectiveness.

Another unexplored area for future research could be examining the social and emotional impacts of crises on SMIs. SMIs are public figures subject to strong emotions, and research can uncover where they are most likely to be vulnerable before they face crises.

References

Ang, B. (2019, August 25). Influencers behaving badly. Retrieved September 30, 2020, from https://www.straitstimes.com/lifestyle/influencers-behaving-badly

Arpan, L. M., & Pompper, D. (2003). Stormy weather: Testing "stealing thunder" as a crisis communication strategy to improve communication flow between organizations and journalists. *Public Relations Review*, *29*, 291–308. https://doi.org/10.1016/S0363-8111(03)00043-2

Benoit, W. L., & Pang, A. (2008). Crisis communication and image repair discourse. In T. Hansen-Horn, & B. Neff (Eds.), *Public relations: From theory to practice* (pp. 244–261). Pearson Allyn & Bacon.

Booth, N., & Matic, J. A. (2011). Mapping and leveraging influencers in social media to shape corporate brand perceptions. *Corporate Communications: An International Journal, 16*(3), 184–191. https://doi.org/10.1108/13563281111156853

Cancel, A. E., Cameron, G. T., Sallot, L. M., & Mitrook, M. A. (1997). It depends: A contingency theory of accommodation in public relations. *Journal of Public Relations Research, 9*(1), 31–63

Chen, T. (2019, April 10). A famous vegan YouTuber was forced to explain herself after angry fans caught her allegedly eating meat on camera. Retrieved March 8, 2020, from https://www.buzzfeednews.com/article/tanyachen/famous-vegan-youtuber-rawvana-allegedly-caught-eating-fish

Coombs, W. T. (2013). Situational theory of crisis: Situational crisis communication theory and corporate reputation. In C. E. Carroll (Ed.), *Handbook of communication and corporate reputation* (pp. 262–278). Malden, MA: Wiley-Blackwell.

Coombs, W. T. (2019). *Ongoing crisis communication* (5th ed). Thousand Oaks, CA: Sage.

Coombs, W. T., & Holladay, S. (2006). Unpacking the halo effect: Reputation and crisis management. *Journal of Communication Management, 10*(2), 123–137. https://doi.org/10.1108/13632540610664698

Coombs, W. T., & Holladay, J. S. (2012). The paracrisis: The challenges created by publicly managing crisis prevention. *Public Relations Review, 38*(3), 408–415. https://doi.org/10.1016/j.pubrev.2012.04.004

Engle, J. (2019). Should kids be social media influencers? Retrieved March 8, 2020, from https://www.nytimes.com/2019/03/08/learning/should-kids-be-social-media-influencers.html

Fan, R., Zhao, J., Chen, Y., & Xu, K. (2014). Anger is more influential than joy: Sentiment correlation in Weibo. *PLoS One, 9*(10), E110184. https://doi.org/10.1371/journal.pone.0110184

Freberg, K., Graham, K., McGaughey, K., & Freberg, L. A. (2011). Who are the social media influencers? A study of public perceptions of personality. *Public Relations Review, 37*(1), 90–92. https://doi.org/10.1016/j.pubrev.2010.11.001

Gilbert, E., & Karahalios, K. (2009, April). Predicting tie strength with social media. In *Proceedings of the SIGCHI conference on human factors in computing systems*, ACM, 211–220.

Granovetter, M. S. (1973). "The strength of weak ties," *Social networks*, Academic Press, 347–367. https://doi.org/10.1086/225469

Grierson, J. (2017, March 17). Google summoned by ministers as government pulls ads over extremist content. *The Guardian*, Retrieved March 8, 2020, from https://www.theguardian.com/technology/2017/mar/17/google-ministers-quiz-placement

Hearn, A., & Schoenhoff, S. (2016). From celebrity to influencer. In P. D. Marshall, & S. Redmond (Eds.), *A companion to celebrity* (pp. 194–212). Malden, MA: Wiley-Blackwell.

Ho, B., Pang, A., Auyong, G., & Lau, L. T. (2014). Enduring image: Capturing defining moments in crises. *Public Relations Review, 40*, 519–525. https://doi.org/10.1016/j.pubrev.2014.03.008

How, M. (2018, June 21). Sony "surprised & disappointed" by Daryl Aiden Yow saga, says it's looking into the matter. Retrieved April 14, 2019 from https://mothership.sg/2018/06/daryl-aiden-yow-sony-creative-ally/

Jiang, J., Huang, Y. H., Wu, F., Choy, H. Y., & Lin, D. (2015). At the crossroads of inclusion and distance: Organizational crisis communication during celebrity-endorsement crises in China. *Public Relations Review, 41*(1), 50–63. https://doi.org/10.1016/j. pubrev.2014.11.003

Jin, Y., Pang, A., & Cameron, G. T. (2012). Toward a publics-driven, emotion-based conceptualization in crisis communication: Unearthing dominant emotions in multi-staged testing of the Integrated Crisis Mapping (ICM) model. *Journal of Public Relations Research, 24*(3), 266–298. https://doi.org/10.1080/1062726x.2012.676747

Kent, M. L., & Taylor, M. (1998). Building dialogic relationships through the World Wide Web. *Public Relations Review, 24*(3), 321–334. https://doi.org/10.1016/ s0363-8111(99)80143-x

Khamis, S., Ang, L., & Welling, R. (2017). Self-branding, "micro-celebrity" and the rise of social media influencers. *Celebrity Studies, 8*(2), 191–208. https://doi.org/10.1080/1939 2397.2016.1218292

Levin, D. Z., & Cross, R. (2004). The strength of weak ties you can trust: The mediating role of trust in effective knowledge transfer. *Management Science, 50*(11), 477–1490. https:// doi.org/10.1287/mnsc.1030.0136

Loh, T. (2019). Seminars 7–9: management & strategies II – Content management. *Presentation*, Singapore.

Maddux, W. W., Kim, P. H., Okumura, T., & Brett, J. M. (2011). Cultural differences in the function and meaning of apologies. *International Negotiation, 16*(3), 405–425. https://doi. org/10.1163/157180611X592932

Marwick, A. E. (2015). You may know me from YouTube: (Micro-)celebrity in social media, *A Companion to Celebrity*, 333–350. https://doi.org/10.1002/9781118475089.ch18

Mediakix. (2019, August 7). How to choose the right social media channels for influencer marketing. Retrieved March 8, 2020, from https://mediakix.com/blog/ how-to-choose-social-media-channels-influencer-marketing/

Millner, A. G., Veil, S. R., & Sellnow, T. L. (2011). Proxy communication in crisis response. *Public Relations Review, 37*(1), 74–76. https://doi.org/10.1016/j.pubrev.2010.10.005

Nielsen. (2012, October 4). Reports and insights: Global trust in advertising and brand messages. Retrieved March 8, 2020, from https://www.nielsen.com/us/en/insights/ report/2012/global-trust-in-advertising-and-brand-messages-2/

Pang, A. (2010). Mediating the media: A journalist-centric model in managing the media by corporate communication practitioners. *Corporate Communications: An International Journal, 15*(2), 192–204. https://doi.org/10.1108/13563281011037955

Pang, A. (2012). Towards a crisis pre-emptive image management model. *Corporate Communications: An International Journal, 17*(3), 358–378. https://doi.org/10.1108/ 13563281211253584

Pang, A. (2013a). Social media hype in times of crises: Nature, characteristics and impact on organizations. *Asia Pacific Media Educator, 23*(2), 309–336. https://doi.org/10.1177/ 1326365X13517189

Pang, A. (2013b). Dealing with external stakeholders during the crisis: Managing the information vacuum. In A. J. DuBrin (Ed.), *Handbook of research on crisis leadership in organizations* (pp. 209–229). Northampton, MA: Edward Elgar Publishing.

Pang, A., Damayanti, R., & Woon, E. (2017). When a nation's leader is under siege: Managing personal reputation and engaging in public diplomacy. In B.V. Ruler, I. Smit, S. Romenti, & O. Ihlen (Eds.), *How strategic communication shapes value and innovation in society* (pp. 37–67). Advances in Public Relations and Communication Management book series. Bingley, UK: Emerald.

Pang, A., Ho, B., & Malik, N. (2012). *Repairing an organization's image in times of crises: What strategies to use when? Proceedings of the 11th Conference on Corporate Communication*, 485–507.

Pang, A., Jin, Y., & Cameron, G. T. (2021). Contingency theory of strategic conflict management: Explicating a "grand" theory of public relations. In C. Valentini (Ed.), *Public relations* (pp. 381–398). Berlin, Germany: De Gruyter Mouton.

Pang, A., & Yeo, S. L. (2012). Examining the expertise, experience and expedience of crisis consultants in Singapore. *Public Relations Review, 38*, 853–864. https://doi.org/10.1016/j.pubrev.2012.06.009

Pierucci, S. (2018, January 17). Why micro-influencer marketing is still the game? in 2019. Retrieved March 8, 2020, from https://medium.com/swlh/why-micro-influencer-marketing-is-the-game-in-2018-fdeda0993c36

Rosenberg, E. (2019, March 22). A vegan YouTube star went to Bali. A video of her there brought her platform crashing down. Retrieved March 8, 2020, from https://www.washingtonpost.com/technology/2019/03/22/vegan-youtube-star-rawvana-gets-caught-eating-meat-camera/?utm_term=.88eb9e8729a3

Sato, S., Ko, Y. J., Park, C., & Tao, W. (2015). Athlete reputational crisis and consumer evaluation. *European Sport Management Quarterly, 15*(4), 434–453. https://doi.org/10.1080/16184742.2015.1065895

Scott, D. M. (2015). *The new rules of marketing and PR*. New York: Wiley.

Siah, J., Bansal, N., & Pang, A. (2010). New media: A new medium in escalating crises? *Corporate Communications: An International Journal, 15*(2), 143–155. https://doi.org/10.1108/13563281011037919

Sng, K., Au, T. Y., & Pang, A. (2019). Social media influencers as a crisis risk in strategic communication: Impact of indiscretions on professional endorsements. *International Journal of Strategic Communication, 13*(4), 301–320. https://doi.org/10.1080/1553118X.2019.1618305

Stacks, D. W., & Bowen, S. A. (2013). Dictionary of public relations measurement and research. Institute for PR. Retrieved from http://www.instituteforpr.org/wpcontent/uploads/Dictionary-of-Public-Relations-Measurement-and-Research-3rdEdition.pdf

Statista. (2017, May). Global Instagram influencer market size from 2017 to 2019 (in billion U.S. dollars). Retrieved March 8, 2020, from https://www.statista.com/statistics/748630/global-instagram-influencer-market-value/

StarNgage. (n.d.). Influencer marketing in Singapore. Retrieved March 8, 2020, from https://starngage.com/influencer-marketing-singapore/

Tan, M. (2015, March 15). Xiaxue's exposé Part 2: Singtel clarifies that it didn't issue the brief to smear its competitors. Retrieved April 13, 2019, from https://mothership.sg/2015/03/xiaxues-expose-part-2-singtel-clarifies-that-it-didnt-issue-the-brief-to-smear-its-competitors/

Teo, J. (2018, December 14). Daryl Aiden Yow spills all in his first interview after Photoshop saga – of his scandal, hiatus and first photo exhibition since the comeback. Retrieved April 14, 2019, from https://www.todayonline.com/8days/seeanddo/thingstodo/daryl-aiden-yow-spills-all-his-first-interview-after-photoshop-saga-his

Tuten, T., & Solomon, M. (2017). *Social media marketing*. Sage.

Uzunoğlu, E., & Kip, S. M. (2014). Brand communication through digital influencers: Leveraging blogger engagement. *International Journal of Information Management, 34*(5), 592–602. https://doi.org/10.1016/j.ijinfomgt.2014.04.007

Wakefield, J. (2019, November 14). Social media influencers: Incomes soar amid growing popularity. *BBC News*. Retrieved February 12, 2020, from https://www.bbc.com/news/technology-50418807.

Wilcox, D., Cameron, G. T., & Reber, B. H. (2015). Conflict management: Dealing with issues, risks, crises. *Public relations: Strategies and tactics* (11th ed., pp. 248–276). Pearson Allyn & Bacon.

Yang, Y. (2019, March 13). How China's opinion leaders convert fans to sales. Retrieved September 30, 2020 from https://sg.style.yahoo.com/china-online-opinion-leaders-kols-205742411.html

8

THE IMPORTANCE OF AUTHENTICITY IN ORGANIZATIONAL CRISIS COMMUNICATION VIA SOCIAL MEDIA

An-Sofie Claeys and Aurélie De Waele

When organizations want to build or restore relationships, they must communicate and behave in an authentic manner (Kent & Taylor, 2002). Perceived authenticity can be defined as, "the extent to which one acts in accord with the true self" (Shen & Kim, 2012, p. 375). Because organizations are increasingly being pressured by stakeholders in terms of transparency, openness, and responsibility, authenticity should receive more attention in public relations (PR) research (Molleda, 2010), and in the context of social media and crisis communication especially.

Authenticity has been widely discussed in domains such as art, discourse studies, tourism, and branding (Peterson, 2005; Shen & Kim, 2012). Definitions of the term often reflect the multidimensional nature of the construct. Brand authenticity is defined as, "the extent to which consumers perceive a brand to be faithful toward itself (continuity), true to its consumers (credibility), motivated by caring and responsibility (integrity), and able to support consumers in being true to themselves (symbolism)" (Morhart et al., 2015, p. 203). Definitions of authentic talk are characterized by three dimensions (Montgomery, 2001). First, talk is considered to be authentic when it sounds natural and spontaneous as opposed to contrived and performed. Second, authentic talk truly captures the speaker's experience. Finally, authentic talk appears to project the true self of the speaker in an existential manner.

PR researchers acknowledge the importance of authenticity. The authenticity of supervisors in organizations is determined by their consistency in terms of matching words with actions and matching core values and beliefs with their behavior (Thelen, 2019). Authenticity is also considered a key concept in understanding the process of organizational relationship building (Shen & Kim, 2012).

DOI: 10.4324/9781003043409-12

The omnipresence of social media has further increased the need to take authenticity into account in PR (Gilpin et al., 2010). On the whole, social media has revolutionized PR "through the manner in which authentic organizations can act as authentic people to instill spirit and emotions in the communication messages to generate public resonance, understanding, and identification" (Men & Tsai, 2014, p. 430). The role of authenticity becomes especially relevant in the practice of crisis communication. Public figures, CEOs, and spokespersons often turn to social media platforms to apologize for crises and to express emotions regarding those events (Sandlin & Gracyalny, 2018, 2020). We argue that authenticity is a key feature by which the public evaluates such socially mediated crisis communication efforts.

Based on the definitions of authenticity, we propose that a social media audience will evaluate the authenticity of an organizational crisis response on three distinct levels: the source, the message, and the nonverbal cues of message delivery. First, the public will assess who is behind an official social media profile and then they will evaluate the authenticity of the source. Is the CEO actually writing the messages on her or his official Twitter account, or has the crisis response been written or edited by PR practitioners (Sebastião et al., 2017)? Second, members of the public will evaluate the actual response in terms of authenticity. Authentic communication should correspond to organizational values and beliefs and it should be consistent (Thelen, 2019). Over the years, scholars have prescribed a number of optimal crisis communication strategies (Claeys & Coombs, 2020). In reality, however, tension can arise between those strategies and organizational values and beliefs. What happens when the public demands that an organization takes responsibility, but evaluates corporate apologies as fake because they don't match with what is known or expected of the organization?

Finally, the public will evaluate how the message is delivered nonverbally, in order to determine whether the spokesperson or CEO meant what they said (Schoofs et al., 2020). Nonverbal behaviors expressed during a crisis response will be evaluated in terms of how real a potential expression of emotions is on the one hand and in terms of spontaneity (e.g., is the CEO reading from an autocue?) on the other. In order for the message to be effective, both the actual message and the way it is communicated to the public should be considered as authentic.

With this chapter, we discuss these distinct characteristics of crisis communication, each of which can cause a social media audience to question the authenticity of an organization in trouble. This discussion does not only bring forth suggestions for research on authenticity in crisis communication, but also raises an interesting paradox for PR practitioners: While the conclusions are interesting for consideration when drafting an authentic crisis response, they also serve as a warning that organizations should avoid creating the impression that crisis response messages are merely the result of a full-blown PR machine.

Authenticity of the Source

Organizations can cultivate strong relationships with their publics through social media because these platforms allow them to increase perceived transparency and authenticity (Men & Tsai, 2014). Research on the impact of CEOs' personal social media messages shows that authenticity is indeed crucial to their success (Men & Tsai, 2016). Specifically, CEOs who manage to engage the public with their social media messages can foster stronger relationships with them through the perceived increase in authenticity. Hence, the key to success for CEOs on social media is to not come across as virtual figures but rather as real people, each with a genuine personality.

In the original conceptualizations of the term, written texts were considered as authentic when they could be traced back to a trustworthy and accredited source (Montgomery, 2001). These questions might be even more important for social media, because research findings suggest that social media messages trigger more source-related thoughts than those from traditional media (Lee & Shin, 2014). The identity behind a post on social media is often a source of distrust (Gilpin et al., 2010). Even when a profile on social media clearly belongs to an organization or CEO, questions can be raised as to who wrote the messages on that profile. Organizations and their CEOs often employ professional assistance to deliver social media messages (Sebastião et al., 2017). Even though many users are aware that such assistance is needed to provide continual updates, they may reduce the authenticity of the messages and the messenger.

Results from a study in the field of political communication, for example, illustrate that social media blunders made by politicians using Twitter (i.e., inappropriate tweets) lead to better evaluations of those politicians compared to typical, carefully designed tweets (Lee et al., 2020). This effect was explained by the higher perceived authenticity of the politician. This finding can be related to the success of Donald Trump (Theye & Melling, 2018). Analyses of the 2016 U.S. presidential election suggest that while the political incorrectness and bumptious language of Trump's discourse did not concur with most PR guidelines, his amateurish style increased his authenticity. Trump's tweets were his own and had not been written or adapted by PR professionals. In fact, his authenticity during that campaign was placed opposite Hillary Clinton's inauthentic PR machine.

Even though the assistance of PR professionals may be required to guarantee the continuity of social media profiles from a CEO or a public figure (Sebastião et al., 2017), the actual content and message must align with how that person is perceived by the public and her or his style of communicating. When people do not believe that a social media post containing an important response to a crisis is authentic, the outcome may be problematic. Even though authenticity has not specifically been the focus of crisis communication research, related perceptions such as sincerity have been deemed important for the acceptance of CEO communication (e.g., Claeys et al., 2013; Sandlin & Gracyalny, 2018, 2020). We therefore argue that ideally, the CEO holds the pen when writing important social media responses to a crisis, based on the advice of communication specialists.

Consistency of the Response

A social media audience will not only look for authenticity in the source behind a message, but also in the actual message itself. Authenticity can be derived from the degree to which the words of a spokesperson or CEO align with the organizational values and beliefs (Thelen, 2019) and the level of consistency of the organizational reaction (Jones, 2016; Shen & Kim, 2012). When spokespersons or CEOs apologize on YouTube, for example, the public will estimate the degree to which the apology accords with the organization's values, the organization's words and actions before the crisis, and other comments made throughout the crisis life cycle.

An authentic crisis response should first correspond with the organizational values and beliefs (Thelen, 2019). Crisis communication researchers have put great emphasis on determining which crisis communication strategies are appropriate, and under what conditions (Avery et al., 2010; Claeys & Coombs, 2020). One consistent recommendation is that organizations should apologize and accept full responsibility when they are to blame for a crisis. While findings from several studies offer support for this advice, others indicate that apologies may not be as effective under all circumstances and that sincerity of the response is vital (cf. Sandlin & Gracyalny, 2018, 2020). This shows that while indeed some crisis communication strategies are better than others, there is not one that can serve as a cure-all. When the public assesses the appropriateness of crisis communication, they will not only evaluate whether the response is suitable for the situation but also whether it is authentic. The question then becomes, if there is a mismatch between what the public finds suitable to say (e.g., apologies) and what an organization actually believes (e.g., not feeling responsible), which will be more decisive for the reputational outcome: the appropriateness of the response or its authenticity?

Second, an authentic organizational crisis response is one that does not only correspond with the organization's core values and beliefs but is consistent as well. As a matter of fact, we infer authenticity of a response in terms of its alignment with organizational values and beliefs through consistency (Jones, 2016). The public's perception of organizational values develops over time through consistent communicative behavior from organizations (Ulmer, 2001). When an organization has always communicated a certain perspective or consistently followed a certain course of action, a crisis response that deviates from that pattern may be considered as inauthentic. As such, an authentic crisis response should be consistent with an organization's past messages and behaviors.

Finally, people may also assess the consistency of the organizational crisis response throughout the crisis life cycle. Some organizations tend to take different stances or send different messages as a crisis develops (Ihlen, 2002). A fair share of organizations in crisis initially denies that a crisis exists or that they bear any responsibility for it, only to end up with an apology when pressured by the press or through social media. Best practices already reflect the importance of coordinating messages during a crisis, because inconsistency creates confusion among members of the public (Seeger, 2006). With regard to crisis response strategies, organizations have been urged to maintain consistency in order to ensure effectiveness (Coombs, 2007). We want to add that inconsistency in terms of the crisis response strategy could negatively affect the authenticity of the response. Organizations that apologize only after they have initially denied or diminished their responsibility can be considered as less authentic.

Real Emotions

A social media audience will estimate the authenticity of crisis communication not only through an assessment of the source and the message, but also by assessing how those messages are delivered. We distinguish between the role of emotions in crisis communication and the spontaneity of the message.

Written expressions of emotion can help reduce crisis damage (e.g., Claeys et al., 2013; Van der Meer & Verhoeven, 2014). Social media allows organizations to express emotions both verbally and nonverbally. Corporate crisis responses on YouTube, for example, are often accompanied by nonverbal emotional displays (Sandlin & Gracyalny, 2018). Researchers have examined the impact of such nonverbal cues of emotion as well. Exercising restraint in the expression of sadness in audiovisual crisis responses can enhance credibility (Stephens et al., 2019), and when a CEO communicates with a sad voice, the public experiences more empathy (De Waele et al., 2020).

While emotional crisis communication can thus reduce reputational damage, we should consider the importance of authenticity in this regard. Psychological research reveals that not all emotional expressions are considered to be authentic (e.g., Anakin & Lima, 2018; Bryant et al., 2018). Research in this field indicates that there are perceptual and acoustic differences between emotions that are real and those that are acted (Anikin & Lima, 2018). Depending on the emotion (e.g., laughing, anger, fear, sadness), there are acoustic differences with regard to several parameters, such as pitch, harmonicity, spectral slope, and amplitude. There are also perceptual differences, meaning that listeners can distinguish between real and staged emotions, with accuracy levels beyond those attributable to chance. Several researchers have concluded that these perceptual differences affect authenticity, in the sense that real emotions are indeed perceived as more authentic than acted emotions (e.g., Anikin & Lima, 2018; Bryant et al., 2018).

The perception of the authenticity of emotions in turn affects the evaluation of the person expressing the emotions. According to psychological research, for example, people evaluate a crying person more negatively when they perceive the tears as fake and inauthentic (Van Roeyen et al., 2020). Research in the context of service encounters also shows that the authenticity of emotional displays is important because people feel less positive about others who offer insincere smiles (Grandey et al., 2005). Social media followers may similarly assess whether emotions expressed by organizational spokespersons in times of crisis are real or fake, which could determine the overall organizational evaluation. For example, when YouTuber Faze Jarvis apologized in a social media video for cheating in the game Fortnite, his apparent "crocodile tears" cost him a lot of sympathy among the social media audience (Worrall, 2019). It thus seems important to add to findings from prior research on emotional crisis communication, according to which expressions of sadness especially can increase reputation repair, that these emotions should be real and authentic.

Spontaneous Reactions

A social media audience in pursuit of authenticity will not only differentiate between real and staged emotions, but also between an overall response that is spontaneous and one that is overly rehearsed. Many organizational spokespersons and CEOs, as well as public figures, prepare to face the media through professional training (De Waele et al., 2020). These training sessions contain recommendations regarding verbal aspects of delivery (e.g., the use of key messages), visual cues (e.g., adopting an open and relaxed posture), and sometimes even vocal cues (e.g., the use of a lowered voice pitch). Such standardized recommendations can help increase the effectiveness of a crisis response. Messages that are well-rehearsed and messengers that are well-trained may, for example, better succeed at minimizing harmful nonverbal displays of deception (De Waele & Claeys, 2017). Spokespersons may thus be able to prevent PR disasters through media training, the use of an audio cue, or by developing the perfect corporate video in several takes. While preparation may reduce the likelihood of failure, however, we argue that the lack of authenticity may hinder true success.

This apparent opposition between spontaneous and rehearsed communication can be connected to discussions regarding authentic talk in the area of discourse studies. Although authenticity cannot be considered an objective feature of talk, spontaneity and the lack of premeditation are often considered key conditions for authenticity (Van Leeuwen, 2001). In the context of media, a distinction has been made between authentic speech on the one hand and media language or broadcast talk on the other. Conversations in a mediated context are frequently staged and characterized by a perceived sense of scriptedness (Montgomery, 2001). Such broadcast talk is often considered to be inauthentic, whereas authentic talk does not sound simulated or performed but rather natural and spontaneous.

We argue that organizations' audiovisual crisis responses should be professional, but they should also avoid coming across as overly rehearsed and prepared. An authentic crisis response thus leaves room for spontaneity and stays close to the personality, style, and values of the spokesperson or CEO. For that reason exactly, professional media trainers are hesitant to train nonverbal behaviors all too vigorously (De Waele et al., 2020). While certain vocal or visual behaviors may be more effective than others, they might be inauthentic and hence ineffective when they conflict with the natural style of the speaker.

Implications for Theory and Practice

The results from crisis communication research have been used to produce specific guidelines for what to say, when to say it, under what conditions, through which medium, and in what way (Avery et al., 2010; Claeys & Coombs, 2020). An overview of the extant literature may create the impression that there is a one-size-fits-all solution for each crisis. Within the context of the analyses presented in this chapter, we argue that offering a crisis response that "ticks all the boxes" may, however, not be enough and could sometimes even backfire. Publics will evaluate a crisis response based not only on its appropriateness but also on its authenticity. As a consequence, a textbook apology might fail once people get the impression that a spokesperson or CEO did not "mean it."

In this chapter we discussed elements of a crisis response that may trigger a social media audience to question organizational authenticity. One element of doubt may be the identity behind a social media profile or the author of a social media message. While it is no exception that messages on the social media profiles of CEOs are written or edited by PR professionals (Sebastião et al., 2017), during crises it might be advisable for corporate executives to hold the pen when the most important reactions are written. PR professionals must think carefully about when their input regarding social media messages is more or less warranted. Communications advisors could recommend that CEOs express empathy with victims and their families, for example, and then encourage them to actually place themselves in the shoes of victims and formulate a genuinely empathic response in their own words.

The level of consistency can be a second important gauge by which the public assesses the authenticity of a crisis response. A crisis response should align not only with the expectations and demands of the public, but also with the values and beliefs of the organization. PR counselors should therefore survey what values and beliefs the public associates with an organization and then suggest a crisis response strategy that is both adapted to stakeholder attributions of organizational responsibility (cf. Coombs, 2007) and consistent with how the organization is perceived. Inauthentic apologies might backfire because they could come across as a trick. That does not imply that an organization whose apologies can come across as inauthentic should just issue a denial. Rather, it means that such organizations will probably have to explain what caused their change of heart, accept actual responsibility, and add actions to their words. A simple sorry may not be enough for them.

Finally, when the organizational spokesperson or CEO brings the message across through social media, emotions must be real and spokespersons should avoid coming across as all too rehearsed. Expressions of sadness in response to corporate crises can minimize reputational harms, irrespective of whether sadness is expressed verbally (e.g., Claeys et al., 2013), vocally (e.g., De Waele et al., 2020), or visually (e.g., Schoofs & Claeys, 2021). While authenticity will be important when expressing sadness in either of those manners, a social media audience may especially assess the authenticity of emotions expressed through audiovisual messages (e.g., YouTube). An all-too-expressive visual display of emotion, for example, may backfire (Stephens et al., 2019). And acoustic differences between real and staged emotions can affect their perceived authenticity (cf., Anikin & Lima, 2018; Bryant et al., 2018). PR practitioners can therefore recommend that CEOs express sadness in a corporate video, but only when it is, in fact, how they feel. When a CEO or spokesperson is not really touched by the events or when they are not naturally inclined to show those emotions, it might be better to bring the message across in a rational manner.

Crisis responses that are communicated via social media through videos (e.g., YouTube), should also consider the importance of the overall message delivery. The speaker should find the right balance between being professional and prepared as well as being spontaneous and authentic. In practice, media trainers seem to be aware of this important balance. With regard to the appearance of a spokesperson, for example, they argue that this should align with the personality of that person in order to come across as authentic (De Waele et al., 2020). Vocal cues also appear to be too closely linked to the personality of a spokesperson to vigorously train them. At the same time, however, the findings from content analyses indicate that preparation may minimize the occurrence of nonverbal cues that indicate deception (De Waele & Claeys, 2017). PR professionals should therefore make sure that CEOs and spokespersons are well-prepared to offer an effective and professional response in a corporate video, but leave enough room for spontaneity and the personality of the speaker.

To conclude, we propose that the importance of authenticity should be examined by crisis communication researchers. First, we suggest that scholars examine what makes an organizational crisis response more or less authentic. Second, researchers should not only examine how the public evaluates the authenticity of crisis communication but also how crucial that might be for reputational outcomes. We propose that a crisis response should be suitable in terms of the harm that was caused and the responsibility taken, and it should be authentic. The question then remains as to how important each of the elements are in stakeholders' evaluations of an organization in crisis.

References

Anakin, A., & Lima, C. F. (2018). Perceptual and acoustic differences between authentic and acted nonverbal emotional vocalizations. *Quarterly Journal of Experimental Psychology, 71*(3), 622–641. https://doi.org/10.1080/17470218.2016.1270976

Avery, E. J., Lariscy, R. W., Kim, S., & Hocke, T. (2010). A quantitative review of crisis communication research in public relations from 1991 to 2009. *Public Relations Review, 36*(2), 190–192. https://doi.org/10.1016/j.pubrev.2010.01.001

Bryant, G. A., Fessler, D. M. T., Fusaroli, R., Clint, E., Amir, D., Chavez, B., Denton, K. K., Díaz, C., Duran, L. T., Fančovićová, J., Fux, M., Ginting, E. F., Hasan, Y., Hu, A., Kamble, S. V., Kameda, T., Kuroda, K., Li, N. P., Luberti, F. R., …Zhou, Y. (2018). The perception of spontaneous and volitional laughter across 21 societies. *Psychological Science, 29*(9), 1515–1525. https://doi.org/10.1177/0956797618778235

Claeys, A.-S., Cauberghe, V., & Leysen, J. (2013). Implications of stealing thunder for the impact of expressing emotions in organizational crisis communication. *Journal of Applied Communication Research, 41*(3), 293–308. https://doi.org/10.1080/00909882.2013.806991

Claeys, A.-S., & Coombs, W. T. (2020). Organizational crisis communication: Suboptimal crisis response selection decisions and behavioral economics. *Communication Theory, 30*(3), 290–309. https://doi.org/10.1093/ct/qtz002

Coombs, W. T. (2007). Protecting organization reputations during a crisis: The development and application of situational crisis communication theory. *Corporate Reputation Review, 10*(3), 163–176. https://doi.org/10.1057/palgrave.crr.1550049

De Waele, A., & Claeys, A.-S. (2017). Nonverbal cues of deception in audiovisual crisis communication. *Public Relations Review, 43*(4), 680–689. https://doi.org/10.1016/j.pubrev.2017.06.004

De Waele, A., Claeys, A.-S., & Opgenhaffen, M. (2020). Preparing to face the media in times of crisis: Training spokespersons' verbal and nonverbal cues. *Public Relations Review, 46*(2), 101871. https://doi.org/10.1016/j.pubrev.2019.101871

De Waele, A., Schoofs, L., & Claeys, A.-S. (2020). The power of empathy: The dual impacts of an emotional voice in organizational crisis communication. *Journal of Applied Communication Research, 48*(3), 350–371. https://doi.org/10.1080/00909882.2020.1750669

Gilpin, D. R., Palazzolo, E., & Brody, N. (2010). Socially mediated authenticity. *Journal of Communication Management, 14*(3), 258–278. https://doi.org/10.1108/13632541011064526

Grandey, A. A., Fisk, G. M., Mattila, A. S., Jansen, K. J., & Sideman, L. A. (2005). Is "service with a smile" enough? Authenticity of positive displays during service encounters. *Organizational Behavior and Human Decision Processes, 96*, 38–55. https://doi.org/10.1016/j.obhdp.2004.08.002

Ihlen, O. (2002). Defending the Mercedes a-class: Combining and changing crisis-response strategies. *Journal of Public Relations Research, 14*(3), 185–206. https://doi.org/10.1207/S1532754XJPRR1403_2

Jones, B. (2016). Authenticity in political discourse. *Ethical Theory and Moral Practice, 19*(2), 489–504. https://doi.org/10.1007/s10677-015-9649-6

Kent, M. L., & Taylor, M. (2002). Toward a dialogic theory of public relations. *Public Relations Review, 28*(1), 21–37. https://doi.org/10.1016/s0363-8111(02)00108-x

Lee, E.-J., Lee, H.-Y., & Choi, S. (2020). Is the message the medium? How politicians' Twitter blunders affect perceived authenticity of Twitter communication. *Computers in Human Behavior, 104*, 106188. https://doi.org/10.1016/j.chb.2019.106188

Lee, E.-J., & Shin, S.Y. (2014). When the medium is the message: How transportability moderates the effects of politicians' Twitter communication. *Communication Research, 41*(8), 1088–1110. https://doi.org/10.1177/0093650212466407

Men, L. R., & Tsai, W.-H. S. (2014). Perceptual, attitudinal, and behavioral outcomes of organization-public engagement on corporate social networking sites. *Journal of Public Relations Research, 26*(5), 417–435. https://doi.org/10.1080/1062726X.2014.951047

Men, L. R., & Tsai, W.-H. S. (2016). Public engagement with CEOs on social media: Motivations and relational outcomes. *Public Relations Review, 42*, 932–942. https://doi.org/10.1016/j.pubrev.2016.08.001

Molleda, J.-C. (2010). Authenticity and the construct's dimensions in public relations and communication research. *Journal of Communication Management, 14*(3), 223–236. https://doi.org/10.1108/13632541011064508

Montgomery, M. (2001). Defining "authentic talk." *Discourse Studies, 3*(4), 392–397. https://doi.org/10.1177/1461445601003004004

Morhart, F., Malär, L., Guèvremont, A., Girardin, F., & Grohmann, B. (2015). Brand authenticity: An integrative framework and measurement scale. *Journal of Consumer Psychology, 25*(2), 200–218. https://doi.org/10.1016/j.jcps.2014.11.006

Peterson, R. A. (2005). In search of authenticity. *Journal of Management Studies, 42*(5), 1083–1098. https://doi.org/10.1111/j.1467-6486.2005.00533.x

Sandlin, J. K., & Gracyalny, M. L. (2018). Seeking sincerity, finding forgiveness: YouTube apologies as image repair. *Public Relations Review, 44*(3), 393–406. https://doi.org/10.1016/j.pubrev.2018.04.007

Sandlin, J. K., & Gracyalny, M. L. (2020). Fandom, forgiveness and future support: YouTube apologies as crisis communication. *Journal of Communication Management, 24*(1), 1–18. https://doi.org/10.1108/JCOM-06-2019-0096

Schoofs, L., & Claeys, A.-S. (2021). Communicating sadness: The impact of emotional crisis communication on the organizational post-crisis reputation. *Journal of Business Research, 130*, 271–282. https://doi.org/10.1016/j.jbusres.2021.03.020

Schoofs, L., Claeys, A.-S., & Koppen, E. (2020). How does the public perceive audio-visual crisis responses? An exploration through focus group research. International Communication Association, converted from Australia to virtual due to COVID-19, May 21–25, 2020.

Sebastião, S. P., Zulato, G., & Santos, T. B. (2017). Public relations practitioners' attitudes towards the ethical use of social media in Portuguese speaking countries. *Public Relations Review, 43*, 537–546. https://doi.org/10.1016/j.pubrev.2017.03.012

Seeger, M. W. (2006). Best practices in crisis communication: An expert panel process. *Journal of Applied Communication Research, 34*(3), 232–244. https://doi.org/10.1080/00909880600769944

Shen, H., & Kim, J.-N. (2012). The authentic enterprise: Another buzz word, or a true driver of quality relationships? *Journal of Public Relations Research*, *24*, 371–389. https://doi.org/10.1080/1062726X.2012.690255

Stephens, K. K., Waller, M. J., & Sohrab, S. G. (2019). Over-emoting and perceptions of sincerity: Effects of nuanced displays of emotions and chosen words on credibility perceptions during a crisis. *Public Relations Review*, *45*(5), 101841. https://doi.org/10.1016/j.pubrev.2019.101841

Thelen, P. D. (2019). Supervisor humor styles and employee advocacy: A serial mediation model. *Public Relations Review*, *45*, 307–318. https://doi.org/10.1016/j.pubrev.2019.02.007

Theye, K., & Melling, S. (2018). Total losers and bad hombres: The political incorrectness and perceived authenticity of Donald J. Trump. *Southern Communication Journal*, *83*(5), 322–337. https://doi.org/10.1080/1041794x.2018.1511747

Ulmer, R. R. (2001). Effective crisis management through established stakeholder relationships. *Management Communication Quarterly*, *14*(4), 590–615. https://doi.org/10.1177/0893318901144003.

Van der Meer, T. G. L. A., & Verhoeven, J. W. M. (2014). Emotional crisis communication. *Public Relations Review*, *40*(3), 526–536. https://doi.org/10.1016/j.pubrev.2014.03.004

Van Leeuwen, T. (2001). What is authenticity? *Discourse Studies*, *3*(4), 392–397. https://doi.org/10.1177/1461445601003004003

Van Roeyen, I., Riem, M. M. E., Toncic, M., & Vingerhoets, A. J. J. M. (2020). The damaging effects of perceived crocodile tears for a crier's image. *Frontiers in Psychology*, *11*(172). https://doi.org/10.3389/fpsyg.2020.00172

Worrall, W. (November 10, 2019). Banned Fortnite YouTuber Faze Jarvis made good money with crocodile tears. CCN. https://www.ccn.com/fortnite-youtuber-faze-jarvis-makes-20000-crocodile-tears-apology-video/

Foundations and Frameworks: Audience-Oriented Approaches and Considerations

9

PARACRISIS AND CRISIS

Guidance from Situational Crisis Communication Theory

Feifei Chen, W. Timothy Coombs, and Sherry J. Holladay

Theories, particularly social scientific theories, are not meant to be static. As research and practice expose new aspects of a phenomenon, theories must seek to accommodate this new knowledge. The second edition of this book is testament to the way online communication platforms (social media) have demanded the attention of crisis communication theorists. Social media must be integrated into crisis communication theories for those theories to fully capture the phenomenon we call crisis communication. The focus of this chapter is the way situational crisis communication theory (SCCT) has adapted to the influences of social media/online communication platforms. Central to integration of social media into SCCT is the concept of paracrisis.

There is a long discussion thread in crisis and crisis communication about what constitutes a crisis. Part of that discussion includes crisis managers arguing that people, including academics, are far too willing to label a situation as a "crisis" when really it is an incident or a bad day. It is important to reserve the term crisis for those events worthy of the time and resources the label evokes (Coombs, 2019). Early discussions of social media and crises tended to reflect the overuse of the crisis label. Not every negative event transpiring on a social media platform was or is a crisis (Coombs & Holladay, 2012). This blurring of the term crisis hampered efforts to integrate social media into crisis communication theories because it included situations that were not actual crises. Theorizing demands clarity in conceptualization, hence mixing crises and non-crises was problematic. We explore the integration of SCCT and social media through the concept of paracrisis. Paracrisis captures situations that are not actual crises but demand the attention and even action

DOI: 10.4324/9781003043409-14

of managers – they are like crises. The lens of paracrises helps to create the conceptual clarity necessary to merge social media with SCCT. The first part of the chapter articulates paracrises followed by an explication of SCCT and how it accommodates paracrises.

Conceptualizing Paracrises: Definition, Types, and Response Strategies

Popular use of the term "social media crisis" has hindered attempts to distinguish channels and platforms from organizational crises, including types of crises. This differentiation is crucial because first, social media platforms themselves are not a crisis and second, the messages communicated via social media rarely lead to an actual crisis. The tendency for extremely negative information to generate attention and spread rapidly via social media means that an organization's tweet gaffes, angry customer complaints, and unsolicited support from controversial politicians and interest groups to be labeled "social media crises" is evident in popular, trade, and even academic publications. Despite intense public attention, often these "crises" are actually risks or incidents that can be properly managed to preclude possible escalation into crises that potentially could generate severe ramifications for the organization and/or its important stakeholders. There are similar problems with the term "reputational crisis" (Sohn & Lariscy, 2014). Reputation damage is a common crisis outcome and any crisis can negatively affect a reputation. Hence, the term reputational crisis creates more confusion than clarity.

As social media continue to reduce the opacity of the pre-crisis stage, the overly generic use of the terms "social media crisis" and "reputational crisis" inappropriately catastrophizes publicly visible risks that might be easily managed and thus blurs significant differences between both the nature of and appropriate responses to risks and crises. To describe more accurately the risks socially constructed on and off social media, Coombs and Holladay (2012) advanced the concept of "paracrisis." Initially, paracrisis was conceptualized as a challenge, "a publicly visible crisis threat that charges an organization with irresponsible or unethical behavior" (Coombs & Holladay, 2012, p. 409).

Because paracrises are *risks* that might evolve into crises if not managed properly, paracrises response strategies should be variations of crisis response strategies that focus on risk mitigation (Coombs, 2017). Coombs and Holladay (2015) proposed six response strategies for addressing challenge paracrises: refusal, refutation, repression, recognition, reform, and revision. *Refusal* is used when an organization deliberately makes no response and remains silent. *Refutation* argues the challenge against an existing organizational practice is invalid via two sub-strategies: Denial with evidence and dispute.

Denial with evidence presents evidence to demonstrate the challenged practice is not irresponsible or unethical, whereas *dispute* questions the validity of challengers' expectations. *Repression* summarizes the efforts to halt the dissemination of a challenge, such as a lawsuit threat or deleting negative social media comments. This strategy is generally not recommended because it is against the ethos of social media and can be seen as a move against free speech. *Recognition* is applied when an organization acknowledges a problem exists but cannot change its practice. *Revision* is used when an organization cannot fully meet the challenger's expectation but is willing to make minor modification. Finally, *reform* is delivered when an organization acknowledges the legitimacy of a challenge and promises to overhaul its practice. To make appropriate responses, managers should consider various contextual factors, such as a challenger's salience, cost of and feasibility for making possible changes, and the organizations' prior CSR efforts (Coombs, 2019; Coombs & Holladay, 2012).

When a challenge emerges, an organization should first assess the challenger's salience affected by three attributes: legitimacy, power, and urgency (Coombs & Holladay, 2012; Mitchell et al., 1997). A public response is warranted when the challenge is deemed *legitimate* by other stakeholders and the challenger has the *power* and the willingness or *urgency* to harm the organization. Additionally, managers should also reassess their internal environment to decide if the organization can afford the proposed change financially and logistically. Recognition or revision is recommended if the change is not feasible yet. When a challenge is relevant to an organization's values and corporate social responsibility (CSR) commitments, managers must strive for message consistency so that the paracrisis response would not render perception of CSR-washing and risk further reputation erosion.

Later, the paracrisis concept was expanded beyond the challenge paracrises (Coombs & Holladay, 2012, 2015) to include additional risk types such as customer service, misuse of social media, venting (Coombs, 2015), organizational faux pas, rumor, and collateral damage (Coombs, 2019). Unlike crises posing *survival* reputational and/or financial threats, these paracrisis clusters only engender different levels of *thrive* threats (Coombs, 2002). This premise was confirmed though subsequent research demonstrating that for publicly listed companies, paracrises were found to pose only insignificant and negligible impacts on stock price values (Selaković et al., 2019).

While some paracrises may be managed relatively easily with a sincere apology, others could require more sophisticated consideration of various contextual factors. Given the volume and variety of paracrises, using empirical methods to categorize paracrises into identifiable clusters is an important step toward systematic development of appropriate response strategies.

This effort would parallel the initial processes used by Coombs and Holladay (1996, 2002) to develop SCCT where they first identified crisis clusters and then examined response strategies.

Refining Typologies of Paracrisis Clusters and Response Strategies

To refine, reformulate, and more precisely describe existing typologies of paracrisis clusters and response strategies with strong external validity, Chen (2019) conducted a systematic examination of 143 paracrisis cases reported by traditional media, digital-born media, and trade publications over a four-year time span. Chen's rigorous case series method produced six paracrisis clusters: faux pas (two types), challenge, guilt by association, misinformation, social media misuse, and social media account hacking. Chen (2019) also used the cases to identify response strategies used to address the paracrises. Previously identified response strategies were re-evaluated and reformulated, and two additional strategies were added in light of the findings from the case series. Tables 9.1 and 9.2

TABLE 9.1 Typology on Paracrisis Clusters

Paracrisis cluster	Description
Faux pas	An organization takes an action with a good or no bad intention but is perceived by at least some publics as embarrassing, offensive, or insensitive (Type I); an organization unintentionally allows someone to generate embarrassing, offensive, or insensitive content that can be attributed to the organization (Type II)
Challenge	An organization's existing practice is charged by discontented stakeholders as unethical or irresponsible
Guilt by association	A negatively viewed actor is publicly associated with an organization
Misinformation	A crisis risk triggered by the circulation of messages about the organization that lack veracity
Social media misuse	A situation where an organization incurs crisis risk because it violates social media ethos or rule(s)
Social media account hacking	A situation where an organization's social media account is hacked and generates crisis risk

TABLE 9.2 Typology on Paracrisis Response Strategies

Response strategy	Description
Refusal	An organization deliberately ignores a paracrisis by not making any direct response
Refutation	An organization denies a challenge accusation, an accused bad intention, or attacks the accuser
Repression	An organization attempts to silence discontented stakeholders through actions such as deleting negative social media posts
Recognition	An organization acknowledges the validity of a challenge accusation or an accused negative intention
Revision	An organization takes action to make change(s) regarding a faux pas or a challenged existing organizational practice
Reference to organizational values[a]	An organization refers to its organization values and/or its long-termed commitment to pursue the values to address an accused negative intention or a challenge
Disassociation[a]	An organization denies its connection with a negatively perceived actor or action that generates crisis risk

a Two new strategies identified through the case series.

respectively report the definitions for the six paracrisis clusters and the descriptions for the seven paracrisis response strategies.

The faux pas cluster (Coombs, 2019) was further refined into two types (Table 9.1) that differ in locus of control and thus might be addressed differently. A Type I faux pas features full organizational responsibility for its inappropriate action and can be addressed by using *refutation* to deny a deliberate intention, *recognition* to acknowledge the validity of publics' accusations, and *revision* to retract the action and/or promise to avert similar mistakes. Yet because the responsibility for a Type II faux pas is less on the organization and more on those who abuse the organization's action, refutation in the form of attacking the abusers might be adopted to reduce the organization's perceived responsibility for spreading inappropriate social media content.

The collateral damage cluster (Coombs, 2019) was renamed as *guilt by association* to emphasize *risks* arising from an organization's connection with a negatively viewed actor. This cluster may be addressed with *disassociation,* a newly identified strategy that denies the organization's connection to the actor. But this strategy cannot be used without sufficient consideration over the possible costs of severing ties and the effectiveness of doing so.

The *misinformation* cluster expands the rumor cluster (Coombs, 2019) to include risk situations caused by the purposefully spread of all types of unverified messages, such as rumor, gossip, disinformation, propaganda, and factitious information blend generated by elites and "opinion entrepreneurs" who seek to discredit political rivals (Rojecki & Meraz, 2016). We recommend this cluster can be addressed by refutation that denies a false accusation and corrects the misinformation.

Social media account hacking is a newly emergent cluster that occurs when a hacked social media account provokes short-term attention for posting insensitive, controversial, or even egregious content. This cluster can be managed by using *recognition* to acknowledge the inappropriateness of the social media content, *disassociation* to state the content is not created by the organization, and *revision* to remove the content and promise caution to preclude another incident.

The revised typologies of paracrisis clusters and response strategies contribute to developing more sophisticated understanding on "social media crises" and help to reduce practitioners' uncertainty when faced with a sudden, unexpected online threat. Moving further, more empirical research is needed to explore the connections between the two typologies and articulate more nuanced response strategy recommendations. Furthermore, different contextual modifiers should be explored, because paracrises, as reputational threats, are also constructed through different publics' sensemaking processes.

Development of SCCT

SCCT was driven by Benson's (1988) observation that we did not have a serious and systematic means of connecting crisis response strategies (what crisis communicators say and do during a crisis) and crisis situations. By the late 1990s, researchers had created inventories of both crisis response strategies and crisis types. However, what had yet to emerge was a theoretical framework to link crisis response strategies and crisis types in a systematic manner. SCCT draws upon Attribution Theory to make the connection between crisis types and crisis response strategies. Attribution Theory is a socio-cognitive approach that describes people's general tendencies – their sense-making process – when ascribing causality for events. Attribution Theory holds that people seek reasons for events, especially negative events. People attribute events to either external factors (situational concerns) or internal factors (something about the people involved in the event) (Weiner, 1986). For instance, a favorite sports team is defeated. Was the loss a result of poor play and coaching (internal) or weather conditions and improper officiating (external)? The attributions are important because they shape people's cognitions, emotions, and reactions to the event (Weiner, 1995). SCCT argues that crises are negative events for which people seek causes and this leads them to make attributions about the crisis responsibility of the organization involved in the crisis. SCCT's initial development and testing pre-dates the explosion of social media platforms, hence, social media were not included in its original conceptualization.

Crisis responsibility, the degree to which stakeholders attribute responsibility for the crisis to the organization in crisis, is *the* pivotal variable in SCCT. SCCT posits that the amount of crisis responsibility generated by the crisis situation determines the nature of the crisis response that will be optimal for the crisis. An *optimal crisis response* serves to maximize protection for stakeholders and the organization from the harm the crisis can inflict (Claeys & Coombs, 2020).

SCCT recommends that crisis communicators examine the crisis type and the contextual modifiers relevant to the organization and the situation to assess the level of crisis responsibility stakeholders are likely to attribute to the organization in crisis. Though crisis responsibility attributions may not be uniform across all stakeholders, a general assessment of crisis responsibility can be established, thus paralleling Attribution Theory's identification of patterns of causal explanations for events. The crisis type is the *frame* being used by stakeholders to interpret the crisis situation. Crisis *types* can be divided into three categories: minimal crisis responsibility (disasters, workplace violence, and malevolence), low crisis responsibility (technical-error accidents and technical-error product harm), and high crisis responsibility (human-error accidents, human-error product harm, management misconduct, and scansis). See Coombs (2019) for a more detailed discussion of the SCCT crisis types. SCCT has undergone revisions since it first appeared in 1995. SCCT crisis types have been refined to include only *operational crises*. Though misinformation (rumor) was originally proposed as a crisis type, it has shifted to paracrises. Additionally, *contextual modifiers* that cause people to increase their attributions of crisis responsibility have been identified. Crisis history (whether or not an organization has had similar crises previously) and prior reputation (was the organization perceived unfavorably before the crisis) are proven intensifying factors (Coombs, 2007; Eaddy & Jin, 2018). A history of crises or an unfavorable pre-crisis reputation will intensify stakeholder attributions of crisis responsibility. Contextual modifiers matter most with crises that involve low levels of crisis responsibility. Contextual modifiers would move a crisis with a low level of crisis responsibility to a crisis with a high level of crisis responsibility, thereby precipitating a significant shift in what would be the optimal crisis response strategy. Because crises with both minimal and low levels of crisis responsibility should utilize similar response strategies, little shift of crisis response strategies is required when one moves from minimal to low levels of crisis responsibility.

The crisis response strategies can be divided into (1) instructing information, (2) adjusting information, and (3) reputation repair (Holladay, 2009; Sturges, 1994). Instructing information helps stakeholders to cope physically with a crisis. Product recall statements and evacuation signals are examples of instructing information. Adjusting information helps people to cope psychologically with a crisis. Expressions of sympathy, corrective action, information about the crisis event, counseling services, and to some degree compensation are examples of adjusting information (Holladay, 2009; Holladay & Coombs, 2013). It should be noted that instructing and adjusting information seem to overlap, hence, it is best to consider them together. SCCT refers to the combined use of adjusting and instructing information as the *ethical base response*. It is an ethical base response because it reflects the ethic of care. The ethic of care focuses on protecting those with less power. In a crisis, the stakeholders are typically the party with less power relative to the organization in crisis. The ethical base response should be used any time a crisis creates victims, those who suffer from the crisis in some way, and should be the first response offered by crisis managers (Coombs, 2017). For crises with minimal to low crisis responsibility, the ethical base response alone serves as the optimal crisis response for protecting stakeholders and the organization (Coombs, 2019).

There are now two primary reputation repair strategies in SCCT: Diminish and rebuild. Diminish strategies attempt to reinforce the view that the organization has low responsibility for the crisis and include excuses and justification. Rebuild strategies seek to create positive information about the organization and include apologies and compensation. Bolstering is considered a secondary strategy, one that can be combined with other strategies but should not be used alone. Bolstering attempts to flatter those who have helped with the crisis or to remind stakeholders of past good works by the organization (Benoit, 1995). As with rebuild strategies, the bolstering strategies attempt to create positive perceptions of the organization (Kim & Woo, 2019). (See Coombs (2019) for more a more detailed discussion of the SCCT crisis response strategies.)

SCCT recommends that crisis managers match the crisis response(s) to the attributions of crisis responsibility. As noted earlier, when attributions of crisis responsibility are minimal to low, the ethical base response is an effective crisis response. Diminish strategies can be added to crises with low crisis responsibility. However, there is little evidence that diminish strategies add much to the effects of a crisis response. Diminish strategies have limited utility as they work best in technical-error accidents or product harm crises. There are very few accidents or product harm crises that are predominantly caused by technical-errors. Rebuild strategies should be reserved for crises that generate strong attributions of crisis responsibility due to the high cost of those response strategies for the organization (Coombs, 2007; Tyler, 1997). Bolstering, as a secondary strategy, can be combined with any of the two primary crisis response strategies.

Recent Developments: Moral Outrage as a Boundary

Recently, *moral outrage* has been added to the cognitive appraisals associated with SCCT. SCCT is a socio-cognitive model because it draws upon attributions. However, recent research has demonstrated that crises that generate strong attributions of crisis responsibility can produce perceptions of strong moral outrage as well. Moral outrage is a specific emotion emerging from the cognitive appraisal research. Moral outrage is likely to emerge when people perceive cues that indicate the situation is both an injustice and motivated by greed (Antonetti & Maklan, 2016). Hence, moral outrage acts as a boundary condition for SCCT because it represents the limits of a theory. The communicative recommendations for SCCT do not hold when a crisis evokes moral outrage. The accommodative strategies have no effect on the common outcomes of post-crisis reputation, purchase intention, or negative word-of-mouth with moral outrage crises (Coombs & Tachkova, 2019).

The recognition of the impact of moral outrage has led to reformulating SCCT through the lens of triadic appraisal. The first appraisal is when people assess the situation as *negative*. A negative situation triggers an appraisal of *responsibility*, the second appraisal. The third appraisal occurs if people perceive the cues of *injustice and greed* that feed the feeling of moral outrage. The consideration of moral outrage has resulted in two significant changes to SCCT. First, the preventable crisis cluster is divided between technical-error crises (low moral outage) and management misconduct and scansis (high moral outrage). Second, for crises generating high moral outrage, the recommended response becomes the *ethical base response* coupled with *acknowledging the moral violation* the organization committed. Managers must publicly confess to what they have done wrong. There also is a need to shift outcome variables. Because moral outrage causes stakeholders to question their *value congruence* with the organization, the result is decreased identification with the organization. Thus, perceived value congruence becomes an important new crisis outcome for moral outrage crises (Coombs & Tachkova, 2019).

Summary

This section provided a very brief review of the development and conceptualization of SCCT. Note how channel selection and social media platforms were not included in the original conceptualization and presentation of SCCT. However, paracrises demand a reconsideration of SCCT to integrate social media platforms into the theory along with revising the crisis types and crisis response strategies.

Conclusion

The revision of SCCT to incorporate paracrises necessitates a reconceptualization of crisis types. Historically, crisis management was designed to address operational concerns – the organization's ability to produce goods or deliver services.

Paracrises tend to be more reputational in nature than operational. SCCT has reformulated crisis types using the macro-categories of operational crises and paracrises. The revisions mean that SCCT is reserved for operational crises and misinformation and challenges are moved from being classified as crises to paracrises. SCCT now needs to account for the *management of risks* as well as the *management of crises*. Thus, SCCT is extended to the pre-crisis phase as response strategies are selected to address specific risks that emerge from a paracrisis.

While paracrises mirror crises by creating an exigence to respond, paracrises are about mitigating a risk rather than addressing a crisis. Success in managing a paracrisis can prevent the emergence of a crisis. Though there are similarities between the response options for crises and paracrises, there are significant differences as well. For instance, ignoring or denying can be viable options for addressing paracrises but are very ineffective crisis responses. The end results are separate, but somewhat overlapping, inventories of responses for addressing paracrises and crises. Moreover, crisis managers use different criteria when assessing paracrises and crises. Crisis assessments include crisis responsibility and moral outrage. In contrast, paracrisis assessments include stakeholder salience, the costs of making changes, and strategy compatibility of any changes. Managers are more likely to address a paracrisis when the stakeholders involved are highly salient. Furthermore, managers are more likely to implement the changes embedded in the paracrisis when the changes are inexpensive and consistent with the organization's strategy (Coombs & Holladay, 2015).

Online communication platforms (social media) have pushed the evolution of crisis communication. Crisis communication theories must account for how social media shapes crisis communication. In this chapter, we explain how social media facilitates the emergence of paracrises, the significance of distinguishing between paracrises and crises, and how paracrises have created an opportunity to revise SCCT. The term paracrisis is neither a semantic game nor a new name for an existing phenomenon. Social media amplifies the need for organizations to publicly manage risks as part of the larger crisis communication efforts. Paracrises highlight the close connection between risk and crisis communication and the benefits of integrating risk communication into crisis communication theories. SCCT has moved from a theory of crisis response to become a theory of risk and crisis communication by utilizing paracrises to develop its risk communication potential.

References

Antonetti, P., & Maklan, S. (2016). An extended model of moral outrage at corporate social irresponsibility. *Journal of Business Ethics*, *135*(3), 429–444. https://doi.org/10.1007/s10551-014-2487-y

Benson, J. A. (1988). Crisis revisited: An analysis of strategies used by Tylenol in the second tampering episode. *Central States Speech Journal*, *39*, 49–66. https://doi.org/10.1080/10510978809363234

Benoit,W.L. (1995). *Accounts, excuses, and apologies:A theory of image restoration*. State University of New York Press.

Chen, F. (2019). *Understanding paracrisis communication:Towards developing a framework of paracrisis typology and organizational response strategies* (Doctoral dissertation,Texas A&M University). TAMU Campus Repository. https://oaktrust.library.tamu.edu/handle/1969.1/186574

Claeys, A. S., & Coombs, W. T. (2020). Organizational crisis communication: Suboptimal crisis response selection decisions and behavioral economics. *Communication Theory, 30*(3), 290–309. https://doi.org/10.1093/ct/qtz002

Coombs, W.T. (2002). Deep and surface threats: Conceptual and practical implications for "crisis" vs. "problem." *Public Relations Review, 28*(4), 339–345. https://doi.org/10.1016/S0363-8111(02)00167-4

Coombs, W.T. (2007). Attribution theory as a guide for post-crisis communication research. *Public Relations Review, 33*, 135–139. https://doi.org/10.1016/j.pubrev.2006.11.016

Coombs, W. T. (2015). *Ongoing crisis communication: Planning, managing, and responding*. Sage Publications.

Coombs, W. T. (2017). Digital naturals and the rise of paracrises: The shape of modern crisis communication. In S. C. Duhe (Ed.), *New media and public relations* (3rd ed., pp. 281–290). Peter Lang.

Coombs, W. T. (2019). *Ongoing crisis communication: Planning, managing, and responding*. Sage Publications.

Coombs, W. T., & Holladay, S. J. (1996). Communication and attributions in a crisis: An experimental study in crisis communication. *Journal of Public Relations Research*, 8(4), 279–295. https://doi.org/10.1207/s1532754xjprr0804_04

Coombs, W. T., & Holladay, S. J. (2002). Helping crisis managers protect reputational assets: Initial tests of the situational crisis communication theory. *Management Communication Quarterly, 16*, 165–186. https://doi.org/10.1177/089331802237233

Coombs, W.T., & Holladay, S. J. (2012). The paracrisis: The challenges created by publicly managing crisis prevention. *Public Relations Review, 38*(3), 408–415. http://doi:10.1016/j.pubrev.2012.04.004

Coombs, W.T., & Holladay, S. J. (2015). CSR as crisis risk: Expanding how we conceptualize the relationship. *Corporate Communications: An International Journal, 20*(2), 144–162. http://doi:10.1108/CCIJ-10-2013-0078

Coombs, W. T., & Tachkova, E. R. (2019). Scansis as a unique crisis type: Theoretical and practical implications. *Journal of Communication Management, 23*(1), 72–88. https://doi.org/10.1108/JCOM-08-2018-0078

Eaddy, L. L., & Jin, Y. (2018). Crisis history tellers matter: The effects of crisis history and crisis information source on publics' cognitive and affective responses to organizational crisis. *Corporate Communications: An International Journal, 23*(2), 226–241. https://doi.org/10.1108/CCIJ-04-2017-0039

Holladay, S. J. (2009). Crisis communication strategies in the media coverage of chemical accidents. *Journal of Public Relations Research, 21*, 208–215. https://doi.org/10.1080/10627260802557548

Holladay, S. J., & Coombs, W. T. (2013). Successful prevention may not be enough: A case study of how managing a threat triggers a threat. *Public Relations Review, 39*(5), 451–458. https://doi.org/10.1016/j.pubrev.2013.06.002

Kim,Y., & Woo, C. W. (2019). The buffering effects of CSR reputation in times of product-harm crisis. *Corporate Communications:An International Journal*. https://doi.org/10.1108/CCIJ-02-2018-0024

Mitchell, R. K., Agle, B. R., & Wood, D. J. (1997). Toward a theory of stakeholder identification and salience: Defining the principle of who and what really counts. *Academy of Management Review, 22*(4), 853–886. http://doi:10.5465/amr.1997.9711022105

Rojecki, A., & Meraz, S. (2016). Rumors and factitious informational blends: The role of the web in speculative politics. *New Media & Society, 18*(1), 25–43. http://doi:10.1177/1461444814535724

Selaković, M., Ljepava, N., & Mateev, M. (2019). Implications of the paracrises on the companies' stock prices. *Corporate Communications: An International Journal, 25*(1), 3–19. https://doi.org/10.1108/CCIJ-07-2019-0080

Sohn, Y. J., & Lariscy, R. W. (2014). Understanding reputational crisis: Definition, properties, and consequences. *Journal of Public Relations Research, 26*(1), 23–43. http://doi:10.1080/1062726X.2013.795865

Sturges, D. L. (1994). Communicating through crisis: A strategy for organizational survival. *Management Communication Quarterly, 7,* 297–316. https://doi.org/10.1177/0893318994007003004

Tyler, L. (1997). Liability means never being able to say you're sorry: Corporate guilt, legal constraints, and defensiveness in corporate communication. *Management Communication Quarterly, 11*(1), 51–73. https://doi.org/10.1177/0893318997111003

Weiner, B. (1986). *An attributional theory of motivation and emotion.* Springer Verlag.

Weiner, B. (1995). *Judgments of responsibility: A foundation for a theory of social conduct.* Guilford Press.

10

CRISIS MISINFORMATION AND CORRECTIVE STRATEGIES IN SOCIAL-MEDIATED CRISIS COMMUNICATION

Toni G.L.A. van der Meer and Yan Jin

Even before "fake news" (Ireton & Posetti, 2018) became a widely recognized global challenge to the press and networked information systems, crisis scholars have cautioned the threat of false information to public communication, especially in times of crises. Coombs (2014) argued that the understanding of misinformation is essential to the base knowledge for crisis communicators. Focusing on the nature of false information and the negative consequences of its spread, communication and public relations scholars have studied informational falsehood under the umbrella of either misinformation or disinformation (e.g., Southwell et al., 2018; van der Meer & Jin, 2020), depending on whether it is unintentionally created/shared or deliberately created to harm others. Regardless, organizations and crisis practitioners must fight misinformation timely and strategically (Coombs, 2014).

The social-mediated crisis communication domain is flooded with misinformation in various forms, causing misperception and trigger negative crisis outcomes due to publics' emotional and behavioral reactions based on information disorder and perception distortion (van der Meer & Jin,2020). For a crisis-stricken organization, whose reputation, operation, and/or stakeholders may be threatened by misinformation, it becomes more important yet tougher than ever to fight back. Against the backdrop of far-reaching consequences of misinformation during a crisis, studies have addressed, for example, how to dispute crisis misinformation messages effectively online (van der Meer & Jin, 2020) and what type of corrective strategy is most successful (Jin et al., 2020).

To provide an overview and synthesis of existing misinformation and corrective communication theories and empirical evidences that are directly relevant to social-mediated crisis communication, this chapter defines crisis

DOI: 10.4324/9781003043409-15

misinformation, illustrates a typology of misinformation characteristics, identifies key actors in crisis misinformation spread, and recommends corrective communication strategies for organizations to consider in fighting misinformation in social-mediated crisis communication.

Defining Crisis Misinformation

In crisis communication, the term "misinformation" has been predominantly used to describe false information about a crisis (e.g., Coombs, 2014; van der Meer & Jin, 2020). In the context of social-mediated crisis, misinformation can include not only false information about a crisis (e.g., crisis severity) but also false information about an organization that is affected by a crisis and/or held responsible for crisis resolution (van der Meer & Jin, 2020).

Jin et al. (2020) provided a working definition of *crisis misinformation*: "false information about any aspect of an ongoing crisis or any incorrect information that can lead to a crisis according to factual evidence from credible source(s) (e.g., the organization, news media, third-party experts, and government agencies, and internal/external witnesses)." The scholars further argued that crisis misinformation can lead to publics' *crisis misperception* about any aspect of a crisis and might cause intentional/unintentional damage to an organization's reputation and/or operation if the crisis misinformation is not intervened and corrected effectively (Jin et al., 2020). Depending on the degree of information incorrectness, we further posit that two types of misinformation can occur in a given social-mediated crisis:

- *Completely false* information, which reflects Tan et al.'s (2015) definition of misinformation as "explicitly false" information as falsified by expert consensus (p. 675).
- *Incomplete* information, which is one type of misinformation that leads to individuals' false belief (Southwell et al., 2018), which can be regarded as partially correct or half-truth. However, if the missing part of the information is not supplied or the partial truth is intentionally promoted, there can be damaging consequences. Using an example from public health literature, doing exercise is a correct complementary therapy for depression treatment; however, when it is being communicated as an alternative therapy to the standard medical treatment, such information becomes incomplete, thus misleading and potentially causing harm (Glazer, 2013) such as antidepressant rejection.

To better understand misinformation types and, in turn, how to fight misinformation crises, we further elaborate on the most prominent characteristics of crisis misinformation by integrating current studies in crisis communication and misinformation.

Characteristics of Crisis Misinformation: Different Shades of Facticity

The concepts of crisis communication and misinformation are interrelated in various ways. First, during crisis situations, both public and private organizations commonly are challenged with the (online) presence of inaccurate information. The situational complexity and uncertainty that come with crises give rise to an immense information need among stakeholders to understand the situation at hand that often requires (immediate) action (Thelwall & Stuart, 2007). Yet, especially in the initial phase of a crisis, little information or conclusive knowledge is readily available. In an effort to nevertheless make sense of the crisis, misinformation might prevail in the absence of fact-based information. Accordingly, previous crisis research has demonstrated the omnipresence of inaccurate information in crisis communication. For example, during the Ebola outbreak, most (re)tweets were found to contain misinformation (Oyeyemi et al., 2014). The spread of inaccurate information can further complicate the solving of a crisis or even result in further escalation of the situation.

Second, not only can a crisis situation give rise to a flow of inaccurate information, but misinformation can also be considered the origin of a crisis. In today's information environment, commonly defined as a post-truth era (Van Aelst et al., 2017), every situation or organization can fall victim to misinformation. Inaccurate interpretation of situations or the spread of false information can form fertile ground for a crisis to originate. If such situations, often characterized as occurring in public or media debates and being emotionally loaded rather than data-based, remain unmanaged it could threaten an organization. In the time that the stricken organization is trying to provide factual evidence to debunk inaccurate information, the damage might have already been done. For example, an organization's reputation might have already been negatively affected in light of false accusations, consumers have grown skeptical about whether they can trust certain products, or panic has already broken out about a potentially dangerous situation while in fact nothing is the matter. A crisis caused by misinformation can be categorized as a victim-cluster crisis as the organization has overall weak attributions of crisis responsibility (Coombs, 2007). Yet, denying the accuracy of such information can be a communicative challenge that takes considerable effort and time, especially since (factual) information or (organizational) sources nowadays can easily be dismissed as "fake news" (Bennett & Livingston, 2018; Jahng et al., 2020). Particularly when organizations are accused or undergoing a crisis, they suffer a credibility disadvantage which will complicate fighting false information. In sum, misinformation can either further escalate an existing crisis or spark a new crisis situation. In order to understand how organizations should respond to the spread of inaccurate information, it is essential to recognize where and why such information gets circulated.

Misinformation can reach audiences via numerous channels and platforms. Overall, scholars are mainly concerned with the role social and new media play in the dissemination of inaccurate information (Lewandowsky et al., 2012; Vraga & Bode, 2018). While the internet has made information and news easily accessible to a large pool of audiences, it also brought forward an information environment that is flooded with, for example, biased narratives, false information, and conspiracy theories (Törnberg, 2018). The absence of gatekeeping functions and the option to self-select sources and content online give reason for concerns regarding the blurring of information and misinformation on online platforms (Vraga & Bode, 2018). The extent to which information is catchy, rather than its truthfulness, drives the spread of news on social media (Radzikowski et al., 2016). Accordingly, scholars agree that misinformation is generally fabricated and disseminated via social media (Tandoc et al., 2018) and research has observed how inaccurate information diffuses faster, farther, and deeper in digital news settings as compared to true news (Vosoughi et al., 2018). Hence, today's news environment is less organized through centralized processes of strict news verification; in the digital setting each news item, whether true or false, can spread like wildfire. In the context of issue management, it is essential that organizations monitor social media to see if any misinformation is fabricated or spread as correct that could potentially affect the organization's legitimacy (Jahng et al., 2020). Since anyone can circulate whatever untruthfulness they find online and easily reach a large audience, it is crucial for organizations to understand the intentions that underlie the design and spread of misinformation.

Key Actors in Crisis Misinformation Spread: Veracity Differed by Motivation

Misinformation can come from a wide array of actors (Ekström et al., 2020). Since receptivity of misinformation can vary strongly conditional upon the motivations of the sender of the message (Chou et al., 2018), it is important to differentiate actors based on their intention to spread misinformation. First, people may spread rumors to evaluate and interpret information in an effort to understand complex situations and, for example, solve crisis problems (Bordia & DiFonzo, 2004). During ambiguous and threatening situations, unverified information, which can end up being either accurate or false, is relied upon for processes of sense making (DiFonzo & Bordia, 2007). As rumors often claim facticity of unsubstantiated information, they can be considered a form of misinformation. Such claims gain their power through how wide the information is spread amongst a network of actors (Berinsky, 2017).

Second, inaccurate information can be created or spread unaware of its lack of veracity. Comparable to the conceptualization of rumors, information is being spread as accurate but, in this case, the information always turns out to be factually incorrect, which can happen outside of the creator's or sender's awareness. People might interpret certain information incorrectly or share statements they assume to be factual. Despite the accidental character of this form of misinformation, it can still cause substantial harm without the disseminators' knowledge. This accidental spread of untruthful information resonates with the definition of misinformation since it is defined as any type of inaccurate information that is spread without the intention to mislead (e.g., Freelon & Wells, 2020). Such "honest mistakes" in communication can be considered inevitable, especially during crises characterized by high levels of uncertainty and complexity (Hameleers et al., 2020; Hameleers, van der Meer, & Brosius, 2020).

Third, actors may also intentionally design or spread falsehoods. This form of misinformation resonates with what is defined as disinformation, where misleading information is intentionally created or spread to harm others (Freelon & Wells, 2020; Hameleers et al., 2020; Hameleers, van der Meer, & Brosius, 2020). Both financial and ideological reasons exist why actors knowingly spread inaccurate information (Vargo et al., 2018). Financial drivers of the rise of disinformation related to the combination of a higher need to generate traffic to news websites while the number of journalists decreases and ad revenues and readership of news media are sliding (Ihlen et al., 2019). Driven by economic incentives, like online advertising revenue based on page views, actors on (fake) news websites fabricate content that is sensational to attract more clicks and shares. The current state of clickbait-driven news incentivizes speedy publication of attention-grabbing news over fact-based news or processes of verification (Chen et al., 2015). Since large corporations and governmental actors have considerable news value, it can happen that false information about them is fabricated as traffic-generating news. Such falsehoods can have substantial negative effects; for example, when in 2008 it was falsely claimed that Apple CEO Steve Jobs had suffered a heart attack, this news resulted in a drop of 10% in Apple's stock price (Sandoval, 2008). Next to being financially motivated, actors disseminate false information to stir controversy (Vargo et al., 2018). Research in political communication has shown how disinformation can be spread aiming to attack outgroups or political opponents (Tandoc et al., 2018) or augment polarized divides among partisans (Bennett & Livingston, 2018). Accordingly, populist actors are found to intentionally spread false news to fuel dissent among citizens (Bennett & Livingston, 2018). Along the same line, falsehoods might be spread to harm an organization or escalate a public or organizational crisis. Those who hold populist or anti-establishment attitudes might consider corporations or governments as part of the corrupt and evil elites and evaluate them as basically self-interested, dishonest, and misleading publics. This might motivate certain actors or competitors to fabricate and spread disinformation about organizations that, in turn, can result in crises. As these forms of misinformation are intentionally manipulated, it is more likely that actors put considerable effort and resources into the design of disinformation to make it look authentic and real. For example, the reliance on manipulated visuals (Hameleers et al., 2020; Hameleers, van der Meer, & Brosius, 2020) or even deep fakes (Dobber, 2020) stand a high chance to stir a larger portion of their audience and therewith harm those who they intend to bring down.

As the intention related to the spread of false information can define the different types of misinformation actors or sources, some of them can be considered more harmful than others. The differences between intention to do harm (i.e., actors spreading disinformation) compared to being uninformed or less critical (i.e., actors spreading misinformation or rumors) might determine how difficult it is to persuade actors of what they should believe or understand as factual. Actors who spread honest mistakes or rumors might be easier informed about what is false and what is factual, which might prevent that the misinformation is maintained (online), compared to those sources who intentionally aim to harm certain organizations' reputations. When false information is professionally designed in such a way that it resembles real news, it might be challenging for corporations to persuade the general public about the veracity of this information. Therefore, it is essential for organizations that encounter potential harmful misinformation to monitor what type of actor they are up against when determining their correction strategy.

Corrective Communication and Misinformation Debunking Strategies

The prevalence and far-reaching consequences of misinformation are nothing new to academic research. Generally, literature acknowledges the complexity of debunking misinformation, especially since empirical results regarding the efficacy of corrective efforts are mixed. Beliefs in misinformation can prevail as corrections can be ineffective, even backfire, and strengthen falsehoods (Lewandowsky et al., 2012). Since questions concerning the effectiveness of debunking misinformation have been an integral aspect of misinformation literature from the start, we see several past meta-analyses that provide an overview of how effective corrective efforts are to fight misperceptions after exposure to misinformation. Taken together, correction attempts are found to help to reduce belief in misinformation when compared with experimental conditions where misinformation remains uncorrected (Blank & Launay, 2014; Walter & Murphy, 2018). The meta-analyses reveal how corrective attempts have a moderate-level effect reducing belief about misinformation (Walter & Murphy, 2018) and that such post corrections on average lessen the effect of misinformation to half of its size (Blank & Launay, 2014). However, in their meta-analysis on the continued influence of misinformation, Walter and Tukachinsky (2020) concluded that the misinformation remains to have a small effect after correction: "Overall, correction of misinformation does not entirely revert people's attitudes and beliefs to their baseline levels" (p.170).

Studying the aggregated results of multiple studies helped these meta-analyses to list several elements that determine the effectiveness of corrective attempts. First, misinformation is found to be more difficult to debunk for political and marketing topics compared to the context of health (Walter & Murphy, 2018). Second, with regard to the type of corrective strategy, corrective attempts combining retraction with an alternative explanation are most effective compared to fact-checking and appeals to credibility (Walter & Murphy, 2018). Comparably, corrections that rely on an enlightenment procedure, detailing not only that there was misinformation but also why, were more effective compared to warnings of the possible presence of misinformation and social discrediting of the misinformation source (Blank & Launay, 2014). Hence, a coherent description of what actually happened and why is crucial the correct misleading information. Next, it is recommended that a correction criticizes the misinformation source's credibility since source credibility plays a central role in how (mis)information is processed (Walter & Tukachinsky, 2020). Third, the perceived credibility of the source of misinformation is indeed important but the evaluation of the correcting source is found to be less essential in debunking incorrect information. Ideally, the correction comes from the same source as the misinformation (Walter & Tukachinsky, 2020).

Recent research has studied the phenomenon of correcting inaccurate information in the theoretical context of crisis situations and crisis communication. In line with the aggregated findings of the meta-analyses (Blank & Launay, 2014; Walter & Murphy, 2018; Walter & Tukachinsky, 2020), van der Meer and Jin (2020) showed the importance of providing a strong narrative as an alternative explanation for the misleading information. In their experimental design, van der Meer and Jin (2020) relied on two types of corrective information to see which one works best, not only for correcting beliefs but also to mobilize people in terms of engaging in protective actions. Inspired by previous misinformation literature (Lewandowsky et al., 2012), a distinction was made between simple rebuttal (i.e., brief corrective message where simplicity is valued over complexity in the context of information overload and clutter during crisis) and factual elaboration (i.e., a detailed correction reinforcing the correct facts that provide a new narrative that helps recipients abandon initial misinformation). Misinformation beliefs about the severity of a public-health outbreak were effectively countered with both types of corrective information. Yet, while the mere presence of a correction did counter misperception after misinformation, it did not result in behavioral effects. Only in the case of factual elaboration was it found to stimulate individuals' intention to take preventive actions. The new narrative provided in this form of correction was apparently crucial to mobilize respondents' behavioral intentions. Correspondingly, organizational-crisis research confirmed that factual elaboration outperformed simple rebuttal in correcting misinformation to avoid reputational damage and limit perceived crisis responsibility (Jin et al., 2020). Mediation analyses show that this more elaborated form of correction is more effective because it better sparks emotional responses among people (van der Meer & Jin, 2020) and such messages are perceived to be of higher quality (Jin et al., 2020).

Next, crisis research shows how the source of corrective information can play an important role. Contrary to Walter and Tukchinsky's (2020) conclusion based on previous misinformation research, crisis studies show that sources can make a difference in the context of correcting information during crises. As expertise is commonly related to levels of credibility, expert sources should enhance the efficacy of correction attempts (Vraga & Bode, 2018). Vraga and Bode (2018) showed how the inclusion of source information (Centers for Disease Control and Prevention [CDC] and Snopes.com) in the correction message is a necessity to ensure that beliefs based on misinformation about the Zika virus are corrected. Comparably, van der Meer and Jin (2020) demonstrated that both the news media and CDC are more effective in correcting misinformation beliefs about public-health crises compared to social peers. These findings suggest that expert and authority sources (e.g., national news media and government health organizations) are perceived as more reliable sources in times of crisis and are therewith more successful in debunking misinformation and correcting misperceptions. Next, not only is the correcting source found to play an important role, but also, supportive supplemental information from a third actor can boost the attempt to effectively debunk misinformation. In the context of an organizational crisis, the communicative backup of an employee in accompanying the organization in debunking misinformation can help to calibrate people's inaccurate response to a crisis in light of the spread of misinformation (Jin et al., 2020). Employees' authentic communication and first-hand experience can provide additional credibility to the correction attempt of the organization.

Another research avenue has explored the use of pre-warnings or news media literacy (NML) messages as a tool to fight misinformation. Most of the studies focusing on correcting misinformation looked at how post-warning can correct misinformation. Yet, since misinformation can still persist after correction (Walter & Tukachinsky, 2020), communicating the importance of media literacy and source criticism skills might also be a fruitful approach to ensure publics are less affected by misinformation. Although the meta-analysis showed how post-corrections often perform better than forewarnings do (Walter & Murphy, 2018), some studies did show the potential of such forewarning-based efforts. For example, short, scalable misinformation NML interventions can help to decrease the perceived accuracy of misinformation and distinguish it from factual information (Guess et al., 2020), general warnings about misleading information result in people perceiving false headlines as less accurate

(Clayton et al., 2019), and the combination between pre NML interventions and post-correction is the most effective way of fighting inaccurate beliefs based on misinformation (Hameleers, 2020). Such pre-warning messages could be considered by corporations when a crisis hits as strategic tools to beforehand fight the potential spread of false information in the clutter of (online) information during pressing times like crises.

Conclusion

We close this chapter by pointing out *corrective message credibility* and informational *competition/conflict* as two important future research directions for crisis scholars studying misinformation and social-mediated crisis. First, as van der Meer and Jin (2020) stressed, a crisis-stricken organization, by default, is in a disadvantageous position simply because publics are likely to expect them to fit back information against the organization. Therefore, organizational credibility, pre-crisis reputation, and existing organization-public relationships, among other organizational characteristics, matter to the success of an organization's debunking messages and overall corrective communication efforts. Second, the nature of public relations is centered on managing competition and conflict (Cameron et al., 2007). By fighting crisis misinformation, organizations often unavoidably add conflicting information to the crisis situation (Jin et al., 2020). Thus, organizations should be mindful about any side effect of debunking (or "over-correcting"), which might result in publics frustrated and confused, caught in between two contradictory pieces of information (misinformation [completely false or partially correct] vs. correct information), and feeling even more uncertain about whom to trust and which information should they use to cope with the crisis (Liu & Kim, 2011).

Rabindranath Tagore once said: "Facts are many, but the truth is one." In social-mediated crisis communication, misinformation, the opposite of facts and truth, takes many forms, but we believe the corrective communication approach we recommended – maneuvering debunking strategies according to misinformation characteristics and key players – provides a theory-driven, evidence-based system for crisis scholars and practitioners to further investigate crisis misinformation and devise more effective interventional strategies.

References

Bennett, W. L., & Livingston, S. (2018). The disinformation order: Disruptive communication and the decline of democratic institutions. *European Journal of Communication, 33*(2), 122–139. https://doi.org/10.1177/0267323118760317

Berinsky, A. J. (2017). Rumors and health care reform: Experiments in political misinformation. *British Journal of Political Science, 47*(2), 241–262. https://doi.org/10.1017/S0007123415000186

Blank, H., & Launay, C. (2014). How to protect eyewitness memory against the misinformation effect: A meta-analysis of post-warning studies. *Journal of Applied Research in Memory and Cognition, 3*(2), 77–88. https://doi.org/10.1016/j.jarmac.2014.03.005

Bordia, P., & DiFonzo, N. (2004). Problem solving in social interactions on the internet: Rumor as social cognition. *Social Psychology Quarterly, 67*(1), 33–49. https://doi.org/10.1177/019027250406700105

Cameron, G. T., Wilcox, D. L., Reber, B. H., & Shin, J.-H. (2007). *Public relations today: Managing competition and conflict.* London, UK: Pearson Publishing.

Chen, Y., Conroy, N. J., & Rubin, V. L. (2015). Misleading online content: Recognizing clickbait as "false news." *Proceedings of the 2015 ACM on Workshop on Multimodal Deception Detection*, 15–19.

Chou, W.-Y. S., Oh, A., & Klein, W. M. (2018). Addressing health-related misinformation on social media. *JAMA, 320*(23), 2417–2418. https://doi.org/10.1001/jama.2018.16865

Clayton, K., Blair, S., Busam, J. A., Forstner, S., Glance, J., Green, G., Kawata, A., Kovvuri, A., Martin, J., Morgan, E., Sandhu, M., Sang, R., Scholz-Bright, R., Welch, A. T., Wolff, A. G., Zhou, A., & Nyhan, B. (2019). Real solutions for fake news? Measuring the effectiveness of general warnings and fact-check tags in reducing belief in false stories on social media. *Political Behavior.* https://doi.org/10.1007/s11109-019-09533-0

Coombs, W. T. (2007). Protecting organization reputations during a crisis: The development and application of situational crisis communication theory. *Corporate Reputation Review, 10*(3), 163–176. https://doi.org/10.1057/palgrave.crr.1550049

Coombs, W. T. (2014). State of crisis communication: Evidence and the bleeding edge. *Research Journal of Institute of Public Relations, 1*(1), 1–12.

DiFonzo, N., & Bordia, P. (2007). Rumor, gossip and urban legends. *Diogenes, 54*(1), 19–35. https://doi.org/10.1177/0392192107073433

Dobber, T. (2020). *Data & democracy: Political microtargeting: A threat to electoral integrity?* Amsterdam School of Communication Research (ASCoR), University of Amsterdam. https://hdl.handle.net/11245.1/40d14da9-1fad-4b14-81bf-253b417f1708

Ekström, M., Lewis, S. C., & Westlund, O. (2020). Epistemologies of digital journalism and the study of misinformation. *New Media & Society, 22*(2), 205–212. https://doi.org/10.1177/1461444819856914

Freelon, D., & Wells, C. (2020). Disinformation as political communication. *Political Communication, 37*(2), 145–156. https://doi.org/10.1080/10584609.2020.1723755

Glazer, W. (2013). Scientific journalism: The dangers of misinformation: Journalists can mislead when They interpret medical data instead of just reporting it. *Current Psychiatry, 12*(6), 33–35.

Guess, A. M., Lerner, M., Lyons, B., Montgomery, J. M., Nyhan, B., Reifler, J., & Sircar, N. (2020). A digital media literacy intervention increases discernment between mainstream and false news in the United States and India. *Proceedings of the National Academy of Sciences, 117*(27), 15536–15545. https://doi.org/10.1073/pnas.1920498117

Hameleers, M. (2020). Separating truth from lies: Comparing the effects of news media literacy interventions and fact-checkers in response to political misinformation in the US and Netherlands. *Information, Communication & Society,* 1–17. https://doi.org/10.1080/1369118X.2020.1764603

Hameleers, M., Powell, T. E., van der Meer, T. G. L. A., & Bos, L. (2020). A picture paints a thousand lies? The effects and mechanisms of multimodal disinformation and rebuttals disseminated via social media. *Political Communication, 37*(2), 281–301. https://doi.org/10.1080/10584609.2019.1674979

Hameleers, M., van der Meer, T. G. L. A., & Brosius, A. (2020). Feeling "disinformed" lowers compliance with COVID-19 guidelines: Evidence from the US, UK, Netherlands and Germany. *Harvard Kennedy School Misinformation Review*. https://doi.org/10.37016/mr-2020-023

Ihlen, Ø, Gregory, A., Luoma-aho, V., & Buhmann, A. (2019). Post-truth and public relations: Special section introduction. *Public Relations Review*, *45*(4), 101844. https://doi.org/10.1016/j.pubrev.2019.101844

Ireton, C., & Posetti, J. (2018). *Journalism, fake news & disinformation: Handbook for journalism education and training*. UNESCO. https://unesdoc.unesco.org/ark:/48223/pf0000265552

Jahng, M. R., Lee, H., & Rochadiat, A. (2020). Public relations practitioners' management of fake news: Exploring key elements and acts of information authentication. *Public Relations Review*, *46*(2), 101907. https://doi.org/10.1016/j.pubrev.2020.101907

Jin, Y., van der Meer, T. G. L. A., Lee, Y.-I., & Lu, X. (2020). The effects of corrective communication and employee backup on the effectiveness of fighting crisis misinformation. *Public Relations Review*, *46*(3), 101910. https://doi.org/10.1016/j.pubrev.2020.101910

Lewandowsky, S., Ecker, U. K., Seifert, C. M., Schwarz, N., & Cook, J. (2012). Misinformation and its correction: Continued influence and successful debiasing. *Psychological Science in the Public Interest*, *13*(3), 106–131. https://doi.org/10.1177/1529100612451018

Liu, B. F., & Kim, S. (2011). How organizations framed the 2009 H1N1 pandemic via social and traditional media: Implications for US health communicators. *Public Relations Review*, *37*, 233–244.

Oyeyemi, S. O., Gabarron, E., & Wynn, R. (2014). Ebola, Twitter, and misinformation: A dangerous combination? *BMJ*, *349*, g6178. https://doi.org/10.1136/bmj.g6178

Radzikowski, J., Stefanidis, A., Jacobsen, K. H., Croitoru, A., Crooks, A., & Delamater, P. L. (2016). The measles vaccination narrative in Twitter: A quantitative analysis. *JMIR Public Health and Surveillance*, *2*(1), e1. https://doi.org/10.2196/publichealth.5059

Sandoval, G. (2008, Oct 7). Who's to blame for spreading phony Jobs story? CNET. http://www.cnet.com/news/whos-to-blame-for-spreading-phony-jobs-story.

Southwell, B. G., Thorson, E. A., & Sheble, L. (2018). *Misinformation and mass audiences*. University of Texas Press.

Tan, A. S., Lee, C. J., & Chae, J. (2015). Exposure to health (mis) information: Lagged effects on young adults' health behaviors and potential pathways. *Journal of Communication*, *65*(4), 674–698. https://doi.org/10.1111/jcom.12163

Tandoc, E. C., Ling, R., Westlund, O., Duffy, A., Goh, D., & Zheng Wei, L. (2018). Audiences' acts of authentication in the age of fake news: a conceptual framework. *New Media & Society*, *20*(8), 2745–2763. https://doi.org/10.1177/1461444817731756

Thelwall, M., & Stuart, D. (2007). RUOK? Blogging communication technologies during crises. *Journal of Computer-Mediated Communication*, *12*(2), 523–548. https://doi.org/10.1111/j.1083-6101.2007.00336.x

Törnberg, P. (2018). Echo chambers and viral misinformation: Modeling fake news as complex contagion. *PLOS ONE*, *13*(9), e0203958. https://doi.org/10.1371/journal.pone.0203958

Van Aelst, P., Strömbäck, J., Aalberg, T., Esser, F., de Vreese, C., Matthes, J., Hopmann, D., Salgado, S., Hubé, N., Stępińska, A., Papathanassopoulos, S., Berganza, R., Legnante, G., Reinemann, C., Sheafer, T., & Stanyer, J. (2017). Political communication in a high-choice media environment: A challenge for democracy? *Annals of the International Communication Association*, *41*(1), 3–27. https://doi.org/10.1080/23808985.2017.1288551

van der Meer, T. G. L. A., & Jin, Y. (2020). Seeking formula for misinformation treatment in public health crises: The effects of corrective information type and source. *Health Communication, 35*(5), 560–575. https://doi.org/10.1080/10410236.2019.1573295

Vargo, C. J., Guo, L., & Amazeen, M. A. (2018). The agenda-setting power of fake news: A big data analysis of the online media landscape from 2014 to 2016. *New Media & Society, 20*(5), 2028–2049. https://doi.org/10.1177/1461444817712086

Vosoughi, S., Roy, D., & Aral, S. (2018). The spread of true and false news online. *Science, 359*(6380), 1146–1151. https://doi.org/10.1126/science.aap9559

Vraga, E. K., & Bode, L. (2018). I do not believe you: How providing a source corrects health misperceptions across social media platforms. *Information, Communication & Society, 21*(10), 1337–1353. https://doi.org/10.1080/1369118X.2017.1313883

Walter, N., & Murphy, S. T. (2018). How to unring the bell: A meta-analytic approach to correction of misinformation. *Communication Monographs, 85*(3), 423–441. https://doi.org/10.1080/03637751.2018.1467564

Walter, N., & Tukachinsky, R. (2020). A meta-analytic examination of the continued influence of misinformation in the face of correction: How powerful is it, why does it happen, and how to stop it? *Communication Research, 47*(2), 155–177.

11

CRISIS INFORMATION VETTING

Extending the Social-Mediated Crisis Communication Model

Xuerong Lu, Yen-I Lee, Yan Jin, Lucinda Austin, and LaShonda L. Eaddy

The internet has become the main channel for people to get information, connect with others, seek entertainment, and purchase goods and services (BBVA, 2014). Information-wise, online channels, including online news platforms and social media, were reported as Americans' predominant and preferred sources for news and information (Pew Research Center, 2018). Around 43% of Americans identified online channels as their go-to channel for information, and 20% of them accessed news information on social media (Pew Research Center, 2018). During crises such as the 2011 Japanese tsunami, publics' activity on social media becomes more active because social media enables them to seek timely and unfiltered information, to check in with friends and family, and to cope with negative emotions through consuming and/or responding to information posted by others (Fraustino et al., 2012).

Due to social media's popularity, scholars believed that crises should be discussed as complex systems facilitated by social media's interactivity, where individuals and stakeholders co-create them through engaging and sharing information (Taylor, 2018). In order to understand the information role of social media in crisis, Liu et al. (2012) proposed the social-mediated crisis communication (SMCC) model to understand how crisis information is generated by influential content creators, and then influences both active and inactive publics through transmission among social media followers and media outlets. Extended studies have discussed how to tailor crisis message strategies when utilizing social media as the dissemination channel to repair organizational reputation, facilitate publics' coping with negative emotions, and shape publics' understanding of the crisis (Jin et al., 2020).

However, the lack of "gatekeepers" and explosive unfiltered information also facilitates the dark side of social media in crisis, such as crisis misinformation.

DOI: 10.4324/9781003043409-16

Misinformation here refers to false information "deliberately promoted and accidentally shared" (Southwell et al., 2018, p. 1), which might lead to false beliefs and misperceptions and could lead downstream to actions that may negatively affect public health, political functioning, and societal wellbeing (Southwell et al., 2018). Crisis misinformation, defined by Jin et al. (2020), is "false information about any aspect of an ongoing crisis or any incorrect information that can lead to a crisis according to factual evidence from credible source(s) (e.g., the organization, news media, third-party experts, and government agencies, and internal/external witnesses) (Defining Crisis Misinformation Section, para. 2)." During crises, misinformation might compete with factual information and interfere with publics' understanding of the crisis situation (van der Meer, 2018). When crisis misinformation becomes salient, it might lead to an unexpected communicative outcome (Liu & Kim, 2011), trigger negative emotions (van der Meer & Jin, 2020), and make publics overreact to the crisis emotionally, cognitively, and behaviorally (Merino, 2014). In the novel coronavirus (COVID-19) pandemic, misinformation regarding vaccines and related topics have been viewed 3.8 billion times on Facebook, which is four times more than authoritative content from institutions like World Health Organization (WHO) and Centers for Disease Control and Prevention (CDC) (Dwoskin, 2020). Meanwhile, the virality of coronavirus-related misinformation on social media led to hundreds dead around the world (Coleman, 2020). The way social media accelerated the global spread of misinformation, fueling panic and fear among publics amplify the infodemic during in the COVID-19 pandemic (e.g., Hao & Basu, 2020).

Although current SMCC literature has identified where and how publics seek and share crisis information when coping with crisis situations, little is known about how publics engage in the informational competition between factual information and misinformation before engaging in coping strategies. Given that informational engagement is a key component in the current media landscape, the general, unaffected public is more active in consuming information (Coombs, 2019). Publics' emotional, cognitive, and behavioral responses to initial crisis information should also be incorporated into the existing crisis information flow in the SMCC model. This chapter focuses on one specific process in such informational engagement – crisis information vetting.

Conceptualization: Information Vetting as a Key Component in SMCC

According to the Oxford dictionary (Hawkins & Le Roux, 1986), vetting is a careful and critical examination for errors. In computer science, data vetting is a step taken before using data purposefully, in which data is assessed for its quality and value, including accuracy and meaningfulness, under the guidance of established and acceptable principles (Di Zio et al., 2016). Analogically, vetting, as an information process, is posited as an evaluation procedure for information quality. In the context of SMCC, Lu and colleagues (2019) define *crisis information vetting* as an individual's two-stage psychological process of making judgment of (1) the accuracy of crisis information based on one's emotional and cognitive engagement with the information (i.e., primary); and (2) the validity of one's own judgment based on one's engagement with oneself (i.e., secondary) (see Figure 11.1). Lu and Jin (2020) further pointed out publics without the need

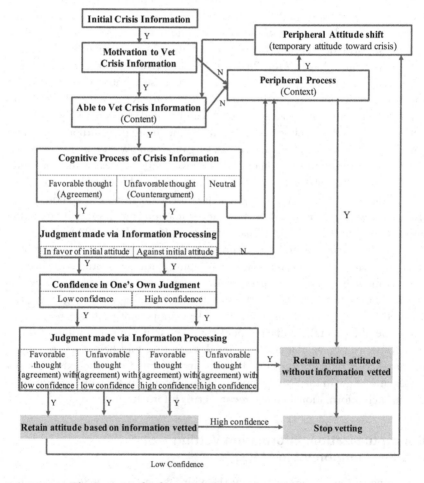

FIGURE 11.1 The Process of Information Vetting

Source: The figure was adapted from "Crisis Information Vetting in Social-Mediated Crisis and Risk Communication: A Conceptual Framework" by Lu et al. (2019), presented at The International Crisis and Risk Communication Conference. 9. https://stars.library.ucf.edu/icrcc/2019/posters/9

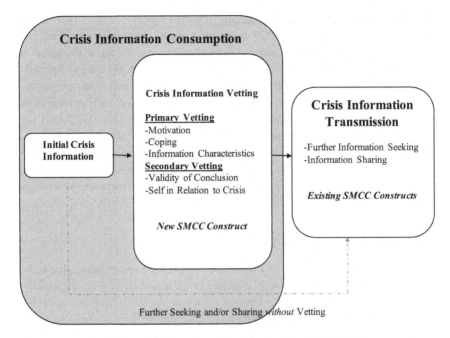

FIGURE 11.2 The Role of Crisis Information Vetting in the SMCC Context

Source: The figure was adapted from Lu and Jin (2020).[1]

for socialization or personal relevancy/importance may not undergo the vetting process (see Figure 11.2). However, publics motivated to vet crisis information are likely to assess the information in one or two stages (primary vetting and secondary vetting) in terms of (1) their perception of information features such as source, channel, and content [primary vetting], as well as (2) their perception of quality of their own judgment (e.g., objectivity) during the primary vetting stage [secondary vetting] (Lu & Jin, 2020).

Motivations for Crisis Information Vetting

Assuming that publics are actively involved in the battlefield of crisis information competition during crises, current SMCC model literature has revealed that publics' crisis information seeking and sharing through different media channels might be motivated by different psychological and social needs such as coping with crisis-triggered stress (Jin, 2010) and learning about the crisis magnitude as well as connecting with a community (Fraustino et al., 2012). Existing studies on social media communication suggest that gratifications provided by social media platforms might influence social media users' motivations and propensity to use a specific platform (Lin et al., 2017). For example, the gratification of information seeking and socialization provided might motivate individuals to use Facebook (Park et al., 2009), while the gratification of authenticity and enrichment provided might motivate individuals to use Pinterest (Sashittal & Jassawalla, 2015). SMCC model literature is consistent with the uses and gratification (U&G) theory's suggestion that individuals' choice and usage of specific media should vary with their different needs. In terms of crisis information vetting in social-mediated communication, Lu and Jin (2020) also found the same tendency in a qualitative study using in-depth interviews and focus groups. They found that predominant motivations mentioned by respondents included socialization needs (e.g., joining in discussion with other people), needs related to the acknowledgment of their personal relevancy and importance, and entertainment needs (Lu & Jin, 2020).

Primary Crisis Information Vetting

Consistent with the elaboration likelihood model (ELM)'s proposition that individuals' engagement, either low-elaborated (e.g., mood-driven) or high-elaborated (e.g., effortful thinking), is biased (Petty et al., 1998), individuals' crisis information vetting is also biased, which is dependent on the way they emotionally and cognitively engage with a situation and the information they received regarding the situation.

Lu and Jin (2020) found that publics might assess the accuracy of information exposed in terms of their perception of information source, channel, and message, consistent with existing findings in communication and information process literature that information features might influence the way individuals engage with the information. For example, studies found that individuals tended to engage with information delivered by a credible source (Petty & Cacioppo, 1996), a likable source (Roskos-Ewoldsen & Fazio, 1992), and a stakeholder group affiliated with a crisis-affected organization (e.g., employees) (Jin et al., 2020), and to perceive information from these sources as of high-quality. Current SMCC research has also pointed out that crisis information in varied forms, sources, and channels influences individuals' active communicative behavior, such as seeking and sharing (Austin et al., 2012). When it comes to crisis information vetting specifically, Lu and Jin (2020) found when vetting crisis information, publics might pay attention to (1) whether the information is from a good source (e.g., one they trust, are familiar with, or are members of a crisis-stricken organization; (2) whether the information looks objective by portraying news or lack of sensationalized content; (3) whether the information contains more than one side of an issue; (4) whether the information is consistent across different sources and channels; and (5) where information is delivered (e.g., via mass media or interpersonal channels).

Besides the crisis information content, individuals might also vet the crisis information based on the way they cope with the emotion in different crisis situations. Crisis scholars have pointed out that crisis information describing controllability and certainty (Smith & Ellsworth, 1985) in different crisis situations might evoke different emotions (Jin et al., 2012), which would consequently influence individuals' acceptance of information (Yeomans, 2007), and enactment of communicative behaviors (Smith & Ellsworth, 1985). For example, Guo (2017) suggested that exposure to positive information during a crisis could evoke individual positive emotions, which would make individuals further engage with other social media posts. Similarly, Jin et al. (2016) found that anger could motivate individuals to engage more with the information, while sadness could motivate individuals to seek more information. As Lu and Jin (2020) pointed out, in the stage of primary crisis information vetting by making the judgment on the truthfulness or falsity of the information, individuals actively cope with their perceived crisis uncertainty and uncontrollability, as well as with their expectations on the crisis event. Participants of their qualitative study mentioned that they would like to engage more with crisis information that was able to reduce their feelings of uncertainty or provide solutions for the crisis situation. Meanwhile, the discrepancy between individuals' expectations and the reality of a crisis situation described by crisis information might also lead to disbelief in crisis information truthfulness (Lu & Jin, 2020).

Secondary Crisis Information Vetting

While crisis information vetting in the primary stage is individuals' emotional and cognitive engagement with information content and information context, the one in the secondary stage is individuals' psychological engagement with themselves. Suggested by theories of meta-cognition, individuals might further give a second thought about the judgment they made earlier on whether the information they received is correct or not. The feelings related to certainty, confidence, or validity on the judgment made (Petty et al., 2007), can influence the consistency between one's attitudinal and behavioral outcomes (Doll & Ajzen, 1992). In other words, secondary "thoughts about thoughts" (Petty et al., 2007, p. 254) can also influence the degree of publics' sensemaking of social issues and their enactment of further information seeking and sharing activities. Petty et al. (2007) found that individuals' feelings of familiarity with information, whether it is consistent with their memory and knowledge, might also predict individuals' behaviors related to the initial information received. Existing studies have found the individuals' thoughts about their own judgments can be determined by information features. Borah (2011) found that by evoking feelings of uncertainty and ambivalence, a message with competitive information would facilitate individuals' information-seeking behaviors and interpersonal communication until they gained judgmental confidence.

Regarding crisis information vetting, empirical evidence has illustrated that individuals might vet crisis information in terms of (1) whether the information they have received is consistent with their memory and knowledge; (2) whether they feel certain after reading the information, and (3) whether the information could be associated with a positive self-identity when reading it (Lu & Jin, 2020). For example, individuals might compare the information they have received for emerging crises (e.g., Ebola outbreak) with familiar crises (e.g., seasonal flu) to see whether they are consistent with each other. The crisis message with inconsistent information could be regarded as misinformation by publics. In addition, individuals preferred crisis information that could make them feel more objective, satisfied, and confident when reading the information.

Operationalization: Scale Development for Measuring Individuals' Information Vetting

To refine the conceptualization and operationalization of crisis information vetting, Lu et al. (2020) developed a 26-item scale from 48 potential items generated by previous qualitative empirical evidence by gathering two survey data sets with U.S. adult samples ($N = 407$; $N = 410$, respectively). Following a systematic scale development and psychometric assessment procedure (i.e., item reduction, exploratory factor analysis [EFA] and confirmatory factor analysis [CFA]), four clusters for crisis information vetting behaviors were identified and confirmed with robust validity and reliability: (1) motivation, (2) primary vetting in terms of certainty, (3) primary vetting in terms of consistency, and (4) secondary vetting in terms of subjective feelings about one's self.

Item Reduction

To identify the final items for the crisis information vetting scale, Lu et al. (2020) applied a quantitative study, including item reduction, EFA, and CFA. Regarding an initial reduction method, first, the study used survey sample 1 ($N = 407$) to determine whether some items needed to be eliminated by following Clark and Watson's (1995) recommendations. The results showed normal distribution for all 48 items included in the scale in terms of the results of frequency tables and kurtosis (Lu et al., 2020).

Second, to ensure a theoretical solution uncontaminated by unique and error variability, the study's researchers conducted a principal component analysis (PCA) with Promax rotation to screen item by following Matsunaga's (2010) recommendation that factor correlation matrix values should be greater than 0.30 in a large dataset (Field, 2013; Meyers et al., 2013). In addition, to determine the appropriateness of factor analysis in terms of Kaiser and Rice's (1974) recommendation, the Kaiser-Meyer-Olkin (KMO) test of sampling adequacy and the Bartlett test of sphericity were used. The results showed that the factor analysis was appropriate for the data based on results of KMO level of 0.93 and the significance of the Bartlett test (0.00). In this initial step, the analysis determined 10 components with initial eigenvalues greater than 1 (explaining 63.78% of the variance) (Lu et al., 2020).

Exploratory Factor Analysis

After the item reduction, an EFA was then conducted using principal axis factoring with Promax rotation on the 48 items. Lu et al. (2020) deleted 22 items due to their comparatively lower factor loadings (<0.40) and communality (<0.50) or cross-loading with another component. Additionally, follow-up factor analyses on the remaining items suggested a 26-item scale with four underlying factors for information vetting behavior about the crisis situation, including the primary vetting process in terms of certainty by source perception and content (factor 1), the secondary vetting process (factor 2); the primary vetting process in terms of information consistency among channels (factor 3); and the motivation of information vetting (factor 4) (Lu et al., 2020).

Further analysis was conducted for internal consistency. The results showed the primary information vetting process consisted of 8 items ($\alpha = 0.92$, $M = 3.89$, $SD = 1.31$); the secondary information vetting process included 10 items ($\alpha = 0.91$, $M = 4.12$, $SD = 1.15$); the primary information vetting process was composed of 5 items ($\alpha = 0.84$, $M = 4.19$, $SD = 1.21$); and motivation of information vetting included 3 items ($\alpha = 0.85$, $M = 5.33$, $SD = 1.24$). The results indicated that the 26-item instrument measuring information vetting behavior satisfied internal consistency within each factor and that the subscales for each cluster of reasons causing information vetting behavior were reasonable and parsimonious (Lu et al., 2020).

Confirmatory Factor Analysis

To ensure the factor structure of the scale, the study used survey sample 2 ($N = 410$) to conduct a CFA (Lu et al., 2020). Using the software of AMOS 24, oblique models and maximum likelihood were adopted for these factors with a 26-item. Results indicated a good fit to the hypothesized four-factor oblique model with χ^2 (281, $N = 410$) = 516.84, p $\leq$ 0.001, with root mean square error of approximation (RMSEA) = 0.05, indicating an acceptable good fit using the cutoff of 0.06 (Hu & Bentler, 1999); comparative fit index (CFI) = 0.97; and goodness-of-fit index (GFI) = 0.91. Although according to Lu and Jin's (2020) qualitative findings, the scale for crisis information vetting was initially expected to have three clusters (i.e., motivation, primary vetting, and secondary vetting), items were loaded into four clusters with 26 items during EFA and reinforced by CFA (see the Appendix for the list of all items).

Results imply that the need for entertainment, acknowledgment, and socializing would motivate publics to engage in the judgment process on the accuracy of crisis information. When engaging in the vetting process, individuals tend to validate the information received when they perceive certainty induced through seemingly credible information and credible, familiar, and trustworthy sources, as well as when they perceive information consistency among different channels (e.g., interpersonal channels, mass media channels, and online news channels). Individuals may engage in additional information vetting steps, if triggered by their second thoughts about whether their initial judgments on the information are valid after all, factoring in whether they are satisfied and confident about themselves and whether they further confirm their initial judgments.

Conclusion

As noted in the chapter introduction, in order to better understand publics' informational and communicative behaviors in a highly competitive informational environment, the phase of information consumption was added to the existing SMCC model and transmission-based crisis information flow. In this chapter, we conceptualize and operationalize one key component in this new phase: crisis information vetting. Empirically, Eaddy et al. (2020) found that in the context of measles outbreak, individuals' crisis information vetting behavior, motivated by their relational history to infectious disease, and their involvement with a potentially infectious disease outbreak, might further facilitate their information seeking and sharing behaviors. However, more empirical studies are needed to provide support for this theoretical concept, as well as to generate insights for tailoring social-mediated corrective communication strategy for managing a misinformation crisis or crises threatened by misinformation spread on social media.

Note

1   This article was published in Lu, X. & Jin, Y. (2020). Information vetting as a key component in social-mediated crisis communication: An exploratory study to examine the initial conceptualization. *Public Relations Review*, *46*(2), 101910, Copyright Elsevier.

References

Austin, L., Liu, B. F., & Jin, Y. (2012). How audiences seek out crisis information: Exploring the social-mediated crisis communication model. *Journal of Applied Communication Research*, *40*(2), 188–207. http://doi.org/10.1080/00909882.2012.654498

BBVA. (2014). *Change: 19 Key Essays on How the Internet Is Changing Our Lives.* Retrieved from: https://www.bbvaopenmind.com/wp-content/uploads/2014/01/BBVA-OpenMind-book-Change-19-key-essays-on-how-internet-is-changing-our-lives-Technology-Internet-Innovation.pdf

Borah, P. (2011). Seeking more information and conversations: Influence of competitive frames and motivated processing. *Communication Research, 38*(3), 303–325. http://doi.org/10.1177/0093650210376190

Clark, L. A., & Watson, D. (1995). Constructing validity: Basic issues in objective scale development. *Psychological Assessment,* 7, 309–319. https://doi.org/10.1037/1040-3590.7.3.309

Coleman, A. (August 12, 2020). "Hundreds dead" because of Covid-19 misinformation. *BBC News.* https://www.bbc.com/news/world-53755067

Coombs, W. T. (2019). Ongoing crisis communication: Planning, managing, and responding (5th ed.). Sage.

Di Zio, M., Fursova, N., Gelsema, T., Gießing, S., Guarnera, U., Petrauskienė, J., et al. (2016). *Methodology for data validation 1.0.* Revised edition June 2016. Essnet Validat Foundation.

Doll, J., & Ajzen, I. (1992). Accessibility and stability of predictors in the theory of planned behavior. *Journal of Personality & Social Psychology, 63*(5), 754–765. https://doi.org/10.1037/0022-3514.63.5.754

Dwoskin, E (August 19, 2020). Misinformation about the coronavirus is thwarting Facebook's best efforts to catch it. The Washington Post. https://www.washingtonpost.com/technology/2020/08/19/facebook-misinformation-coronavirus-avaaz/

Eaddy, L. L., Austin, L., Jin, Y., & Lu, X. (March, 2020). True or false: How parents decide to seek, vet, or share infectious disease outbreak information. *International Crisis and Risk Conference 2020,* Orlando, FL.

Field, A. (2013). *Discovering statistics using IBM SPSS statistics* (4th ed.). Sage.

Fraustino, J. D., Liu, B. F., & Jin, Y. (2012). Social media use during disasters: A review of the knowledge base and gaps. Final report to Human Factors/Behavioral Sciences Division, Science and Technology Directorate, U.S. Department of Homeland Security. College Park, MD: START. http://www.start.umd.edu/start/publications/START_SocialMediaUseduringDisasters_LitReview.pdf

Guo, S. J. (2017). The 2013 Boston marathon bombing: Publics' emotions, coping, and organizational engagement. *Public Relations Review, 43*(4), 755–767. https://doi.org/10.1016/j.pubrev.2017.07.003

Hao, K., & Basu, T., (February 12, 2020). The coronavirus is the first true social-media "infodemic." *MIT Technology Review.* https://www.technologyreview.com/2020/02/12/844851/the-coronavirus-is-the-first-true-social-media-infodemic/

Hawkins, J., & Le Roux, S. (1986). Vetting. In J. Hawkins, & S. L. Roux (Eds.), *The Oxford reference dictionary* (p. 911). Clarendon Press.

Hu, L.-t., & Bentler, P. M. (1999). Cutoff criteria for fit indexes in covariance structure analysis: Conventional criteria versus new alternatives. *Structural Equation Modeling, 6*(1), 1–55. https://doi.org/10.1080/10705519909540118

Jin, Y. (2010). Making sense sensibly in crisis communication: How publics' crisis appraisals influence their negative emotions, coping strategy preferences, and crisis response acceptance. *Communication Research, 37*(4), 522–552. http://doi.org/10.1177/0093650210368256

Jin, Y., Austin, L., & Liu, B. F. (forthcoming). Social-mediated crisis communication research: How information generation, consumption, and transmission influence communication processes and outcomes. In W. T. Coombs, & S. J. Holladay. (Eds.). *The handbook of crisis communication* (2nd ed). Wiley-Blackwell.

Jin, Y., Fraustino, J. D., & Liu, B. F. (2016). The scared, the outraged, and the anxious: How crisis emotions, involvement, and demographics predict publics' conative coping. *International Journal of Strategic Communication, 10*(4), 289–308. https://doi.org/10.1080/1553118x.2016.1160401

Jin, Y., Pang, A., & Cameron, G. T. (2012). Toward a publics-driven, emotion-based conceptualization in crisis communication: Unearthing dominant emotions in multi-staged testing of the integrated crisis mapping (ICM) model. *Journal of Public Relations Research, 24*(3), 266–298. http://doi.org/10.1080/1062726X.2012.676747

Jin, Y., van der Meer, T. G. L. A., Lee, Y.-I., & Lu, X. (2020). The effects of corrective communication and employee backup on the effectiveness of fighting crisis misinformation. *Public Relations Review, 46*(3), 101910. http://doi.org/10.1016/j.pubrev.2020.101910

Kaiser, H. F., & Rice, J. (1974). Little jiffy, Mark IV. *Educational and Psychology Measurement, 34*, 111–117. https://doi.org/10.1177/001316447403400115

Lin, J.-S., Lee, Y.-I., Jin, Y., & Gilbreath, B. (2017). Personality traits, motivations, and emotional consequences of social media usage. *Cyberpsychology, Behavior and Social Networking, 20*(10), 615–623. https://doi.org/10.1089/cyber.2017.0043

Liu, B. F., Jin, Y., Austin, L. L., & Janoske, M. (2012). The social-mediated crisis communication model: Guidelines for effective crisis management in a changing media landscape. In Duhe, S. C. (Ed.), *New media and public relations* (2nd ed., pp. 257–266). Peter Lang.

Liu, B. F., & Kim, S. (2011). How organizations framed the 2009 H1N1 pandemic via social and traditional media: Implications for US health communicators. *Public Relations Review, 37*(3), 233–244. https://doi.org/10.1016/j.pubrev.2011.03.005

Lu, X., & Jin, Y. (2020). Information vetting as a key component in social-mediated crisis communication: An exploratory study to examine the initial conceptualization. *Public Relations Review, 46*(2), 101891. https://doi.org/10.1016/j.pubrev.2020.101891

Lu, X., Jin, Y., Eaddy, L., Austin, L., Liu, B. F., & van der Meer, T. G. L. A. (March, 2019). Crisis information vetting in social-mediated crisis and risk communication: A conceptual framework. *International Crisis and Risk Communication Conference*, Orlando, FL.

Lu, X., Lee, Y.-I., Jin, Y., van der, M., & T, G. L. A. (2020, May). To vet or not to vet: That is a process: Scale development for measuring individuals' information vetting. *70th Annual ICA Conference* (Virtual).

Matsunaga, M. (2010). How to factor-analyze your data right: Do's, don'ts, and how-to's. *International Journal of Psychological Research, 30*(1), 97–110. https://doi.org/10.21500/20112084.854

Merino, J. G. (2014). Response to Ebola in the US: Misinformation, fear, and new opportunities. *BMJ, 349*, g6712. https://doi.org/10.1136/bmj.g6712

Meyers, L. S., Gamst, G., & Guarino, A. J. (2013). *Applied multivariate research* (2nd ed.). Sage.

Park, N., Kee, K. F., & Valenzuela, S. (2009). Being immersed in social networking environment: Facebook groups, uses and gratifications, and social outcomes. *CyberPsychology & Behavior, 12*(6), 729–733. http://doi.org/10.1089/cpb.2009.0003

Petty, R. E., Briñol, P., Tormala, Z. L., & Wegener, D. T. (2007). The role of metacognition in social judgment. In A. W. Kruglanski & E. T. Higgins (Eds.), *Social psychology: Handbook of basic principles* (2nd ed., pp. 254–284). The Guilford Press.

Petty, R. E., & Cacioppo, J. T. (1996). *Attitudes and persuasion: Classic and contemporary approaches.* Routledge.

Petty, R. E., Wegener, D. T., & White, P. H. (1998). Flexible correction processes in social judgment. *Social Cognition, 16*(S1), 93–113. http://doi.org/10.1521/soco.1998.16.1.93

Pew Research Center. (December 10, 2018). Social media outpaces print newspapers in the U.S. as a news source. https://www.pewresearch.org/fact-tank/2018/12/10/social-media-outpaces-print-newspapers-in-the-u-s-as-a-news-source/

Roskos-Ewoldsen, D. R., & Fazio, R. H. (1992). The accessibility of source likability as a determinant of persuasion. *Personality and Social Psychology Bulletin, 18*(1), 19–25. https://doi.org/10.1177/0146167292181004

Sashittal, H. C., & Jassawalla, A. R. (2015). Why do college students use Pinterest? A model and implications for scholars and marketers. *Journal of Interactive Advertising, 15*(1), 54–66. http://doi.org/10.1080/15252019.2014.956196

Smith, C. A., & Ellsworth, P. C. (1985). Patterns of cognitive appraisal in emotion. *Journal of Personality and Social Psychology, 48*(4), 813–838. https://doi.org/10.1037/00223514.48.4.813

Southwell, B. G., Thorson, E. A., & Sheble, L. (2018). Misinformation among mass audiences as a focus for inquiry. In B. G. Southwell, E. A. Thorson, & L. Sheble (Eds.), *Misinformation and mass audiences* (pp. 1–14). University of Texas Press.

Taylor, M. (2018). Reconceptualizing public relations in an engaged society. In K. A. Johnston, & M. Taylor (Eds.), *The handbook of communication engagement* (pp. 103–114). Wiley Blackwell.

van der Meer, T. G. L. A. (2018). Public frame building: The role of source usage in times of crisis. *Communication Research, 45*(6), 956–981. http://doi.org/10.1177/0093650216644027

van der Meer, T. G. L. A., & Jin, Y. (2020). Seeking formula for misinformation treatment in public health crises: The effects of corrective information type and source. *Health Communication, 35*(5), 560–575. https://doi.org/10.1080/10410236.2019.1573295

Yeomans, L. (2007). Emotion in public relations: A neglected phenomenon. *Journal of Communication Management, 11*(3), 212–221. http://doi.org/10.1108/13632540710780201

Appendix: Information Vetting Scale

Please indicate how much you agree/disagree with each of the following actions when verifying the accuracy of the information (1 = Strongly disagree; 7 = Strongly agree).

Motivation: *"I would further vet the information if …"*

1. If the information is important to me personally.
2. If the information affects me.
3. If the information interests me.

Primary Information Vetting (Certainty and Source Perception): "I would check/verify how accurate the information is according to …"

1. Whether the information tells me exactly what happened.
2. Whether the information provides me a certain solution.

3. Whether the information is from a source I trust.
4. Whether the information is from a credible source.
5. Whether the information is from a source I am familiar with.
6. Whether the information is from an accountable/responsible source.
7. Whether the information is from a direct quote of stakeholder (people directly involved with the crisis-affected organization).
8. Whether the information is from an original/primary source (i.e., the one who create the information).

Primary Information Vetting (Channel Perception): "I would check/verify how accurate the information is according to ..."

1. Whether the same information is repeated by the same news channel multiple times.
2. Whether other people share the same argument and/or information.
3. Whether the same information is reported by traditional news media channels such as television and radio.
4. Whether the same information is delivered by online news sources such as e-news and google news.
5. Whether any of my family members tells me about the same information.

Secondary Information Vetting: "I would *further* check/verify how accurate the information is by ..."

1. Evaluating whether the information is consistent with my common sense.
2. Comparing the information with what I knew or experienced in a similar situation.
3. Checking on whether the information looks conclusive to me.
4. Seeking any conflicting information or argument against the information I received.
5. Detecting if the information was sent to deceive me.
6. Checking on whether the information makes me feel objective about the issue/situation at hand.
7. Checking on whether the information makes me feel satisfied with what I have learnt about the issue/situation at hand.
8. Checking on whether the information makes me feel confident in what I have learnt about the issue/situation at hand.
9. Checking on whether the information confirms my earlier thoughts about the issue/situation at hand.

Note: The scale was adapted from "To Vet or Not to Vet: That Is a Process: Scale Development for Measuring Individuals' Information Vetting" by Lu et al. (2020), presented at 70th Annual ICA Conference (Virtual).

Foundations and Frameworks: Characteristics and Types of Social Media

12

SOCIAL MEDIA PLATFORMS AND BROADER PARTICIPATION IN CRISIS COMMUNICATION

Keri K. Stephens and Brett W. Robertson

The field of crisis communication has undergone significant changes since 2000. As the internet became ubiquitous, and websites developed into communication platforms that were easy to create and access, it changed the level of control crisis communicators had over their messages (Stephens & Ford, 2014). Crisis communicators could still target audiences with messages, but there was no way of knowing what other information those audiences accessed. Social media added a new dimension to crisis communication as it further tipped the level of control toward the general public (Jin et al., 2014; Lachlan et al., 2018; Starbird & Palen, 2011; Stephens et al., 2020). By downloading an app, any member of the public can now broadly participate in crises when they seek, collect, create, and share online information during a crisis (Austin et al., 2012; Murthy, 2018; Neely & Collins, 2018).

This broad level of participation is particularly relevant when disasters strike. Disasters often involve multi-agency coordination, and they become crises for those governmental agencies, as well as communities and individuals, when they expand and continue over time (Coombs, 2010). This form of crisis communication can involve life and death, and since disasters often strike vast geographic areas, this means that multiple stakeholders will be involved in communicating during the crisis (Lachlan et al., 2018).

This chapter illustrates the breadth of social media platforms used in disasters that become crises. Our examples draw from data collected during a hurricane disaster that morphed into a flooding crisis for a large portion of the Texas Gulf Coast. Since our focus is on social media platforms, we begin by defining some of these platforms and explaining their capabilities using the perspective of affordances of technology (e.g., Gibson, 1986; Treem et al., 2020). We also provide

DOI: 10.4324/9781003043409-18

perspectives on different types of crisis communicators often present in disasters including public information officers (PIOs) and members of ad hoc volunteer responders. The case study serves to illustrate the role social media platforms have had in broadening participation in crisis communication.

Social Media Platforms Relevant for Disasters That Become Crises

During disasters and crises, the public increasingly uses social network sites (referred to as social media here), which are web-based platforms where individuals create public, semi-public, or shared-private profiles to connect with others (boyd & Ellison, 2007). One of the challenges with this trend is that the public believes that official emergency responders are monitoring social media, and if they post information, it will be seen ("New Study Shows," 2012). However, this is not often the case because emergency response organizations are uncomfortable saying they monitor social media because of potential liability, they lack the resources (both people and social listening technologies), and they lack training (Hiltz et al., 2014; Hughes & Tapia, 2015; Palen, 2012). To better understand these platforms, in general, we first discuss Twitter, a public social media platform, then we discuss more two-way communication platforms like Facebook, Instagram, WeChat, and WhatsApp. We also discuss the importance of shared documents where people who have the link can access and contribute to this shared platform. Our goal is to provide some context, but not go into detail about these platforms because they will likely change over time.

Understanding a Public Platform, Twitter

Twitter is still one of the only social media platforms where information shared is, by default, public; therefore, it offers a unique window into what the public thinks during crises and disasters (Murthy, 2018). Anyone with internet access and knowledge of the features of Twitter – e.g., hashtags, linking to URLs, retweeting, and @, mentions – can share information, but it is often considered more of a one-way or asymmetrical platform (White, 2012). Even though the public uses Twitter, and many volunteer groups use crowdsourcing to help during disasters, scholars suggest that Twitter, in particular, is underutilized by emergency managers and first responders (Lachlan et al., 2018).

Personal Social Media Use

In contrast to platforms like Twitter, many semi-private platforms are used heavily by the public during disasters, primarily because they support bi-directional information sharing, especially with friends and family (Eriksson & Olsson, 2016;

White, 2012). These include: Facebook, Instagram, WeChat, WhatsApp, and Snapchat. Past research has found that platforms like Facebook are perceived as useful during a crisis, especially because so many people use them. Twitter is better at providing timely alerts and warnings, but only for people who regularly use this platform (Eriksson & Olsson, 2016). Ephemeral platforms, like Snapchat, are often used to document a feeling or share an experience visually in real-time, which can be useful to capture the vantage point of users experiencing a crisis (Murthy et al., 2016; Villaespesa & Wowkowych, 2020).

Information Sharing Apps and Documents

The final platforms useful during disasters and crises are apps and documents that allow individuals to share data or see crowdsourced information. Past researchers have studied how crisis mappers, digital volunteers, and virtual operations support teams (VOSTs) interact with maps during disasters (Palen & Hughes, 2018). During Hurricane Harvey, apps were created (e.g., Crowdsource Rescue) that allowed members of the public to view updated information on shelter availability, people who needed to be rescued, and people who had boats (Smith et al., 2018). A walkie-talkie app, Zello, was used extensively by a volunteer rescue group, The Cajun Navy (Smith et al., 2018; Stone et al., 2019). Finally, shared spreadsheets and documents (e.g., Google Docs) created a common location for rescue and resource information to be cataloged and shared even as the volunteers changed over time (Stephens et al., 2020).

Affordances and Materiality

Each platform has different physical features – referred to as their materiality – that can influence how people use them (Leonardi, 2010). In social media, there are some shared material features, like hashtags, but their presence does not mean they will be used the same by different people. Individuals have choices in how they use these different platforms, thus, even though different technologies offer similar material features, the different uses are considered affordances (Gibson, 1986; Stephens et al., 2020; Treem et al., 2020). Affordances are often linked to perceptions people have about using these platforms, something that varies depending on context. For example, when people are trapped in their homes during a flood, they might evoke the affordance of locatability associated with a platform like Facebook because it could help others locate and rescue them. In other contexts, the same people might not want to be located because they value their privacy.

One study of people who needed to be rescued from floodwaters found that rescuees drew upon two amplification affordances: visibility and association. They used social media to post photos indicating their need for help, and those photos functioned to amplify their message and capture others' attention (Stephens et al., 2020). In addition, rescuees highlighted the groups where they belong – e.g., religious affiliation, running club – and this display of membership, called an association affordance, captured attention because others in that group felt a shared sense of belonging (Ellison & Vitak, 2015), and offered help.

In one of the first studies to develop a measure of communication affordances that extends across multiple types of communication channels, Fox and McEwan (2017) provide a comparison of how the affordances of Social Network Sites (SNS; specifically Facebook and Snapchat) compare to other communication channels. Facebook actually had the lowest mean (when compared to FtF, texting, email, phone, video conference, instant messaging, and Snapchat) for the affordance of privacy, but the highest mean for the affordance of network association.

Official Crisis Communicators

While communication platforms provide the tools for sharing information, in crises where public agencies are involved, the job role responsible for communicating information is the public information officer (PIO) – the public and community relations component of an agency like fire, police, or city offices. While it is reasonable to assume that a PIO has broad experience with social media, that is not always the case, since public agencies still lag private organizations (Hughes & Palen, 2012; Lachlan et al., 2018; Neely & Collins, 2018). Studies do show that more use of social media can help local city officials control a crisis and be evaluated more favorably in their response (Graham et al., 2015). In studies examining the specific platforms municipalities are using, Neely and Collins (2018) found that Facebook was the most popular platform (49.4% of the agencies using it), followed by Twitter (27.7% of the agencies reported using it).

However, growing evidence suggests that official crisis communicators constitute a small percentage of people participating in sharing, interpreting, and using crisis messages during disasters (Smith et al., 2018). Therefore, it is important to see the range of crisis communicators to better understand the trends and help project future actions. To accomplish this and see how affordances and materiality around social media function, we use a case study from a disaster, Hurricane Harvey, that became a serious crisis for Texas. Hurricane Harvey hit the Gulf of Texas in late August of 2017, and during the following two weeks, the rain resulting from it caused extensive flooding. An overwhelming number of people needed help and rescue, and since the official 911 emergency phone system was overloaded (Rhodan, 2017), many social media platforms emerged as crucial communication tools. The case study introduces people in diverse roles to bring affordances of social media to life.

Case Study[1]

PIOs' Roles as Official Crisis Communicators

Mandy, a 32-year-old "closet weather geek," lives an exciting entrepreneurial life in addition to managing the social media account and public relations efforts for one of the largest cities in the United States: Houston, Texas. As a PIO, and long-time Houstonian, her life moves fast, and she has multiple mobile devices with her always. "If I could have more arms, I could be faster and reach more people," she says. Every day in her job, she uses her iPhone, Android, and iPad, in addition to managing over 10 Facebook accounts, multiple Twitter and Instagram accounts, live streams from Periscope and Facebook, the neighborhood social media platform, Nextdoor, and when traveling internationally she uses platforms like WeChat.

While it makes sense that a city PIO would manage multiple social media accounts, her explanation for why she has different mobile devices is insightful. She explains that she must see what her posts look like on each social media platform, as well as on each device. "Emojis are really different on iPhones and Androids, and since our Mayor and Chief of Police are men of color, I want to respect them by representing them with an appropriate skin tone." She also explains that when they translate their messages into different languages, they need to be aware of character count differences, "Vietnamese takes many more characters than English or Spanish," so she is constantly reworking messages to reach her various constituents. The time spent being careful, conscientious, and respectful, while also working under deadlines makes her work both exciting and exhausting.

PIO Experiences Working a Major Crisis

Mandy had almost no emergency response training when she was called into the Joint Operations Center (JIC) for the Greater Houston Area. She was one of the few PIOs who could physically get to the JIC due to floodwaters, so she packed her overnight bag for five days anticipating that she would not be home while working the flooding crisis. "In the JIC," she described, "we have a system called WebEOC that allows us to see streams of social media coming in from multiple accounts and through different hashtags." There were also huge whiteboards on the walls of the JIC that kept running totals of the most important numbers like road closures, shelter availability, and death counts. "People were very fatigued, so they needed to be able to walk in and find answers visually without logging into a software system."

Triangulating Data from Multiple Platforms

Hurricane Harvey is considered an extreme disaster, and since there were so many people needing to be rescued, it illustrates the breadth and complexity involved in how social media is actually used for crisis communication. One of the biggest challenges she, along with her city and county PIO colleagues, faced during Hurricane Harvey was deciding when social media data was actionable, meaning when to notify emergency responders that their help was needed. She described a 10-hour timeframe where she and two colleagues divided tasks. She sought information from Twitter, her colleague looked through Facebook, and her third team member documented everything they found in a spreadsheet. Periodically, they stopped searching their designated social media platforms and tried to validate what they had found. They looked on other platforms, checked the 911 or 311 call logs, and when they found legitimate calls for rescue, they shared the information with the emergency responders. Actively looking for emergency situations was in addition to Mandy's primary job of handling calls from the media, providing updates on all social media platforms at least two times a day, and staying on top of the growing amount of misinformation and disinformation. Furthermore, she was also trying to communicate through two separate family and friend group chats because she had lots of family having to evacuate, and she tried to keep them updated with changing conditions.

Emergency Services District and Crisis Communication

While Mandy represents a PIO who is an official crisis communicator without any emergency response training, Harris, the PIO for an Emergency Services District (ESD), had extensive emergency response training, because he was a firefighter. Harris worked directly with his Fire Chief, and he was fortunate that in a time when, "PIOs tend to be a fifth or sixth tier job on one of the Chief's job descriptions," his Chief knew that he needed someone media trained, who could handle community relations along with crisis communication. Someone to "Tell their story," Harris explained.

Before Hurricane Harvey turned into an extended flooding crisis, Harris already had an established set of social media that were part of his repertoire as a PIO. When he joined the ESD, three years earlier, he created a news-based website so he could control his message. It was easy for him to share this site with the media, as well as port the information to platforms such as Facebook, Twitter, and Instagram. Working through his website provided him with key analytics that helped him better understand which social media platforms were read the most by residents in his district. He also relied heavily on a much more private, neighborhood-based platform, Nextdoor, but this functioned more like a one-way communication tool because Nextdoor restricts access to organizations like fire and police. He explained that "no one wants the police listening in on their conversations, and I get that, but in a disaster situation, it would be helpful for me know [who needs help]." The power of Nextdoor is that they have peoples' addresses, and no other platforms have addresses. Many older adults in his community are on Nextdoor because they do not like how public Facebook feels.

During Hurricane Harvey, he managed the crisis from his local ESD, in their District Emergency Operations Center. He was one of the few people in his office who could physically drive to their ESD, and he was both a part-time PIO, as well as a responder, jumping in to help rescue people. He used his ESD web page, and forwarded the information to Facebook, Twitter, and Instagram, to post updated road maps and inundation maps. Harris said that his ESD Facebook page ended up with 5000 likes by the end of this crisis, and for a fire department serving approximately 160,000 residents, that is huge. He explained that when he sat down to respond to comments made to his posts, one of them had over 800 comments. "As I would answer one and hit enter, there were five more that appeared." He heard from residents that his ESD was one of the only official response organizations answering questions posted on Facebook. Nicky, a community emergency response team (CERT) volunteer, also lived close to the ESD, and she was his 24/7 partner, trying to help as many residents as they could.

CERT Volunteers Running Social Media

Nicky was a CERT training coordinator who had worked with Harris since he became the PIO. She explained her role by saying, "I don't consider myself a first responder because I'm not. But I work with them." She was proficient with social media and she knew many members of the community. Concerned community members would post their addresses on the ESD's social media pages (or call into the station) and ask if they needed to evacuate. Nicky looked up their addresses, viewed the inundation maps, and helped them make informed decisions. She and Harris were in the DEOC together, so they could respond and collaborate during the rapidly changing flooding information. "I could have used 2–3 more Nicky's," Harris said. Trusted CERT volunteers were exactly the type of people needed; they want to help, are willing to train, and might not want to do the physical rescues.

In addition to running social media for the ESD, Nicky simultaneously played a dispatch role. Early in the crisis, her parents needed to be rescued, so she turned to a tool her CERT organization used during rescues, the Zello app, a walkie-talkie app that requires very low bandwidth. After her parents were rescued, she began monitoring all the social media channels, as well as Zello, wrote down addresses, and connected people who needed rescue with people who had boats.

Ad Hoc Emergency Response Groups and Shared Public Platforms

The extensive flooding meant that inland ESDs, police, and cities did not have the physical resources – like boats – to rescue victims. Therefore, the Mayor of Houston publicly asked for anyone to join the rescue effort (Rhodan, 2017).

As individuals and ad hoc groups rushed into the Greater Houston area to help, they also found themselves needing to be connected to other volunteers who could serve as their navigators. They had to figure out who needed to be rescued, and how they could best reach locations to launch their boats. Quite often, they teamed up with a family member, who was not in the field, and asked them to search social media to help make the most of rescue efforts.

There were also a host of groups that self-organized and allowed other volunteers to join their effort. One of the more formalized groups, the Cajun Navy, also used Zello. "I saw an article that people were using the Zello app to communicate with each other and request rescue because they couldn't get through 911," explained Harriett, a woman who joined the online rescue effort. She had no formal training in emergency response, but her work experience helped her serve as a form of dispatcher as she collected calls for help, documented them in a Google Doc, and shared them with the Cajun Navy.

Network Connections Matter

Having access to many social media platforms, including large numbers of followers, served to expand rescue opportunities during Hurricane Harvey. One individual used his followers on Facebook to orchestrate hundreds of rescues during a 48-hour time. "I place people on ships for a living," explained Mike, an entrepreneur who owned a maritime recruiting company. In his everyday work, he used social media to build his business, and then found the right employees for very specific maritime jobs. During Hurricane Harvey, Mike explained: "I have about 100,000 followers, so I put a blast out through my network, saying, if anyone's trapped, please contact me and give me your address...and almost immediately I had 70 responses." Then he worked the other side of his business and sourced boats, so he was "matchmaking boats to people."

Many other individuals and groups participated in these rescues. In previously published work, Smith and colleagues (2021) share examples of people who served in various rescue roles, and they called them disaster knowledge workers. Of particular note is how unofficial volunteers used a plethora of publicly available platforms – social media, shared Google Docs, locator apps, mapping apps, Zello, smartphones, and websites – to track rescue details, connect boats and people, and communicate those details to field-based volunteer responders. All these people became crisis communicators with a shared goal of rescuing others and saving lives.

Discussion

This chapter illustrates how the proliferation of social media and related platforms has allowed for much broader participation in disasters that turn into serious crises. There are people who are trained in emergency response or search and rescue who are using these platforms in either official or unofficial roles. Furthermore, there are PIOs and ad hoc dispatchers in official and unofficial roles who have no emergency response training, but they use their knowledge of social media to engage in rescue efforts in entirely new ways. Together, these stories demonstrate the considerable changes in crisis communication that have resulted from the affordances of public, semi-public, private, and shared social platforms. Anyone can now participate in crisis communication.

Public Accessibility of Platforms

These stories support prior findings that people use specific social media platforms for very different uses in crises (Eriksson & Olsson, 2016). Essentially, they draw upon different affordances to accomplish their goals. The fundamental reason that more people can participate as crisis communicators is that social media, apps, and shared documents either are, or can be made public, and thus people can rely on visibility affordances. Even information shared on more private platforms, like Nextdoor, can be screenshotted, and placed on more public distribution platforms. This is very different from the proprietary platforms that official emergency responders use such as radios and 911 dispatch systems; those platforms control access to information, and thus limit information sharing (Smith et al., 2018).

The accessibility of these communication platforms allows people to share information and engage in two-way information sharing and conversations. As this information is shared, people can then tap into their own networks and important crisis messages can be amplified and widely distributed. The finding that publicness both matters and varies within and across platforms raises concerns when scholars try to compare affordances between specific platforms. The way people draw upon affordances depends on context. During everyday life, individuals may value privacy and try to protect access to personal information, but when a crisis happens, they need those platforms to allow them to make the private information public or they risk not being reachable or rescuable.

As more official crisis communicators, e.g., PIOs, use social media and other public platforms, it also opens the possibility for more people to participate in these conversations. However, this still creates a dilemma for official crisis communicators because if they communicate publicly, the public will expect responses. When officials do not provide timely responses to the public, people can turn to social media to overcome the communication-vacuum deficit and thus, share their own stories with complex, incomplete, and often conflicting information of the crisis (Seeger & Sellnow, 2016).

Conclusion

Unfortunately, it is only a matter of time until the next disaster strikes. Given the rise of social media used in crises, affordances of these platforms allow broader participation in the crisis communication process. The public, semi-public, private, and shared nature of these platforms allow for an array of stakeholders to engage, create, and disseminate content about a crisis. Understanding how to leverage these platforms properly, regardless of formal media training, can ultimately provide people with the necessary information that may end up saving lives, as it did during Hurricane Harvey.

Note

1 This case study is written as accurately as possible from the interview and observational data collected by the authors. When text appears in quotes, it is exactly what the participants said in their interviews. All names in the case study are pseudonyms. This work was supported by a grant from the National Science Foundation [award # 1760453] RAPID/The Changing Nature of "Calls" for Help with Hurricane Harvey: 9-1-1 and Social Media. Any opinions, findings, and conclusions or recommendations expressed in this material are those of the authors and do not necessarily reflect the views of the National Science Foundation.

References

Austin, L., Fisher Liu, B., & Jin, Y. (2012). How audiences seek out crisis information: Exploring the social-mediated crisis communication model. *Journal of Applied Communication Research, 40*(2), 188–207. https://doi.org/10.1080/00909882.2012.654498

boyd, D. M., & Ellison, N. B. (2007). Social network sites: Definition, history, and scholarship. *Journal of Computer-Mediated Communication, 13*(1), 210–230. https://doi.org/10.1111/j.1083-6101.2007.00393.x

Coombs, W. T. (2010). Crisis communication and its allied fields. In W. T. Coombs, & S. J. Holladay (Eds.), *Handbook of crisis communication* (pp. 54–64). Blackwell Publishing.

Ellison, N. B., & Vitak, J. (2015). Social network site affordances and their relationship to social capital processes. In S. Sundar (Ed.), *The handbook of psychology of communication technology* (pp. 205–227). Wiley Blackwell.

Eriksson, M., & Olsson, E.-K. (2016). Facebook and Twitter in crisis communication: A comparative study of crisis communication professionals and citizens. *Journal of Contingencies and Crisis Management, 24*(4). https://doi.org/10.11111/1468-5973.12116

Fox, J., & McEwan, B. (2017). Distinguishing technologies for social interaction: The perceived social affordances of communication channels scale. *Communication Monographs, 84*(3), 298–318. https://doi.org/10.1080/03637751.2017.1332418

Gibson, J. J. (1986). *The ecological approach to visual perception.* Lawrence Erlbaum Associates.

Graham, M. W., Avery, E. J., & Park, S. (2015). The role of social media in local government crisis communications. *Public Relations Review, 41*(3), 386–394. https://doi.org/10.1016/j.pubrev.2015.02.001

Hiltz, R. S., Kushma, J. A., & Plotnick, L. (2014). Use of social media by US public sector emergency managers: Barriers and wish lists. In S. R. Hiltz, M. S. Pfaff, L. Plotnick, & P.C. Shih (Eds.), *Proceedings of the 11th International ISCRAM Conference.* http://idl.iscram.org/files/hiltz/2014/1171_Hiltz_etal2014.pdf

Hughes, A. L., & Tapia, A. H. (2015). Social media in crisis: When professional responders meet digital volunteers. *Journal of Homeland Security and Emergency Management, 12*(3), 679–706. https://doi.org/10.1515/jhsem-2014-0080

Lachlan, K. A., Spence, P., & Lin, X. (2018). Natural disasters, Twitter, and stakeholder communication: What we know and directions for future inquiry. In L. Austin, & Y. Jin (Eds.), *Social media and crisis communication* (pp. 296–305). Routledge.

Leonardi, P. M. (2010). Digital materiality? How artifacts without matter, matter. *First Monday, 15*(6). https://doi.org/10.5210/fm.v15i6.3036

Jin, Y., Liu, B. F., & Austin, L. L. (2014). Examining the role of social media in effective crisis management: The effects of crisis origin, information form, and source on publics' crisis response. *Communication Research, 41*(1), 74–94. https://doi.org/10.1177/0093650211423918

Murthy, D. (2018). *Twitter: Social communication in the Twitter age* (2nd ed.). Polity.

Murthy, D., Gross, A. J., & McGarry, M. (2016). Visual social media and big data: Interpreting Instagram images posted on Twitter. *Digital Culture & Society, 2*(2), 113–134. https://doi.org/10.14361/dcs-2016-0208

Neely, S. R., & Collins, M. (2018). Social media and crisis communications: A survey of local governments in Florida. *Journal of Homeland Security and Emergency Management, 15*(1), 1–13. https://doi.org/10.1515/jhsem-2016-0067

Palen, A. (2012). The evolving role of the public information officer: An examination of social media in emergency management. *Journal of Homeland Security and Emergency Management, 9*(1), 1547–7355. https://doi.org/10.1515/1547-7355.1976

Palen, L., & Hughes, A. (2018). Social media in disaster communication. In H. Rodriguez, D. William, & J. Trainor (Eds.), *Handbook of disaster research* (2nd ed., pp. 497–518). Springer.

Rhodan, M. (2017, August 30). Please send help: Hurricane Harvey victims turn to Twitter and Facebook. *Time.* http://time.com/4921961/hurricane-harvey-twitter-facebook-social-media/

Seeger, M., & Sellnow, T. L. (2016). *Narratives of crisis: Telling stories of ruin and renewal.* Stanford University Press.

Smith, W. R., Stephens, K. K., Robertson, B. W., Li, J., & Murthy, D. (2018). Social media in citizen-led disaster response: Rescuer roles, coordination challenges, and untapped potential. In K. Boersma & B. Tomaszewski (Eds.), *Proceedings of the 15th International ISCRAM Conference.* Rochester, NY. http://idl.iscram.org/files/williamrsmith/2018/2138_WilliamR.Smith_etal2018.pdf

Smith, W. R., Robertson, B. W., Stephens, K. K., & Murthy, D. (2021). A different type of disaster response digital volunteer: Looking behind the scenes to reveal coordinating actions of disaster knowledge workers. *Journal of Contingencies and Crisis Management, 29*(2). https://doi.org/10.1111/1468-5973.12352

Starbird, K., & Palen, L. (2011). Voluntweeters: Self-organizing by digital volunteers in times of crisis, *Proceedings of CHI 2011,* Vancouver, Canada.

Stephens, K. K., & Ford, J. L. (2014). Crisis communications and sharing message control. In M. Khosrow-Pour (Ed.), *Encyclopedia of information science and tech* (pp. 462–470). IGI Global.

Stephens, K. K., Robertson, B. W., & Murthy, D. (2020). Throw me a lifeline: Articulating mobile social network dispersion and the social construction of risk in rescue communication. *Mobile Media & Communication, 8*(2), 149–169. https://doi.org/10.1177/2050157919846522

Stone, J. T., Waldman, S., & Yumagulova, L. (2019). Filling the gaps: The potential and limitations of emergent, ICT-enabled organisation in disaster – A case study of The Cajun Army. *Environmental Hazards, 18*(5), 1–15. https://doi.org/10.1080/17477891.2019.1636758

Treem, J. W., Leonardi, P. M., & van den Hooff, B. (2020). Computer-mediated communication in the age of communication visibility. *Journal of Computer-Mediated Communication, 25*(1), 44–59. https://doi.org/10.1093/jcmc/zmz024

Villaespesa, E., & Wowkowych, S. (2020). Ephemeral storytelling with social media: Snapchat and Instagram stories at the Brooklyn Museum. *Social Media+Society, 6*(1), 1–13. https://doi.org/10.1177/2056305119898776

White, C. M. (2012). *Social media, crisis communications and emergency management: Leveraging Web 2.0 technology*. CRC Press.

13

VISUAL CRISIS COMMUNICATION

A Social Semiotic Approach to Visual Dialogues on Social Media

Silvia Ravazzani and Carmen Daniela Maier

Introduction

This chapter focuses on visual crisis communication and delves into its mani-festations in social media contexts. Platforms such as YouTube, Facebook, and Instagram have transformed the contemporary discursive landscape for news media, stakeholders, and organizations of all kinds. Social media increase the power of individual citizens and digital media actors (Castells, 2007), create augmented publics (Whelan et al., 2013) and rhetorical arenas (Frandsen & Johansen, 2010). More than that, social media are protagonists of the contem-porary visual culture as they incorporate, circulate, extend, and alter multiple forms of visuality (Hand, 2017) and thus offer new possibilities for communica-tion (Cassinger & Thelander, 2016).

In the realm of crisis communication, we are witnessing a fast-growing inter-est in social media due to their profound influence on this practice across organi-zations, industry areas, and countries (Austin & Jin, 2018). While social media enhance diverse aspects of crisis communication, such as expert information sharing and citizen engagement (White, 2012), its peculiarity lies in the visuals like photos and videos that can be shared and linked to text-based messages. By making communication more visual and interactive (Veil et al., 2011), social media deeply impacts crisis representation by news media and organizations on the one hand; and crisis perception and coping strategies by stakeholders on the other. Nonetheless, there is a lack of knowledge on visuals' role in social media (Cassinger & Thelander, 2016; Highfield & Leaver, 2016; Pearce et al., 2018) and in crisis communication in particular (Maier, 2020) coupled with an unbalanced methodological landscape favoring quantitative methodologies and

DOI: 10.4324/9781003043409-19

content analyses (Cheng & Cameron, 2018; Hand, 2017; Russmann & Svensson, 2017). We aim to revitalize both visual resources and qualitative approaches, in line with the general "visual turn" taking place in organization and management studies (Maier, 2020). We therefore suggest and apply a qualitative, social-semiotic approach to visual crisis communication that helps disentangle how the ongoing co-creation of meaning is subtly unfolded through visuals during crises. Our key contribution lies in enriching available methodological perspectives and analytical tools which are most needed today for better understanding visual crisis communication in social media contexts.

Social Media, Crisis, and Visual Communication

So much has been written about social media and how they have drastically changed people's online and offline relationships, conversations, peer influence, and socialization processes, not to mention the significant impact on organizations and the ways in which they act and communicate within and without their boundaries (Van Looy, 2016). As far as communication's modes are concerned, Russmann and Svensson (2017) highlight that "today social media platforms are becoming more multimodal as they now host pictures, videos, hashtags, emoticons as well as written text" (p. 2), also giving the possibility to edit and alter visuals.

Crisis communication researchers have studied social media's roles in organizations' crisis management and response (e.g., Cheng, 2018; George & Kwansah-Aidoo, 2017; Hess & Waller, 2015) as well as in stakeholders' reactions and behaviors (e.g., Austin et al., 2012; Coombs & Holladay, 2014). Following the "shift towards visual images" (Russmann & Svensson, 2017), crisis communication scholars have started to emphasize and research visuality as one of social media's defining features. Visuals enhance social media's "potential for encouraging preparedness, knowledge, and involvement in crisis response" (Veil et al., 2011, p. 112).

However, there has been little research so far on visual crisis communication, especially of qualitative nature and going beyond a textual focus (Cassinger & Thelander, 2016; Maier et al., 2019; Maier, 2020). Social media research in crisis communication too appears lacking, and generally dominated by quantitative approaches with an almost exclusive focus on verbal text through content analyses (Cheng & Cameron, 2018). As Frandsen and Johansen (2010) put it, "crisis communication is rarely subjected to more detailed textual or semiotic analysis, including not only verbal, but also visual aspects of crisis communication" (p. 428).

Jin et al. (2017) have clarified the role of strategic crisis visuals (CVs) and visual social media (VSM) in crisis by revisiting the social-mediated crisis communication model (Jin et al., 2014). The few other studies focusing on visual crisis communication have explored how visuals change the possibilities for crisis representation by news media and organizations on the one hand, and for crisis perception and coping strategies by stakeholders on the other. Researchers have variously studied CV reporting by traditional news media (e.g., Dahmen, 2016; Zeng & Akinro, 2013) and journalists in social media contexts too (e.g., Pantti, 2019), and CV representation by corporations (e.g., Lovegrove, 2018). Most recently, Maier et al. (2019) and Maier (2020) have employed a social semiotic approach to visual analysis on news media crisis reporting to shed light on visuals' usage to frame and symbolize crises. Visuals' effects on stakeholders' crisis perceptions have been explored through experimental crisis response research (Coombs & Holladay, 2009, 2011) and other studies testing the impact of visual imagery on stakeholders' crisis emotions and comprehension (e.g., Liu et al., 2017; Miller & LaPoe, 2016). Most recently, Janoske (2018) has explored visual crisis communication in a social media context to reveal individuals' coping strategies expressed through the crisis-related visuals' use and choice.

Acknowledging the need to enrich and advance the embryonic stream of research on visual crisis communication, and in social media contexts in particular, we introduce visual analysis and propose a qualitative social semiotic perspective to the study of visual crisis communication in social media.

Approaching Visual Crisis Communication

Visual analysis has attracted interest from several disciplines in social sciences and found application in multiple contexts, from ethnographic fieldwork to movies, advertising, and websites. Visuality has been gaining even more consideration with the modern rise and proliferation of social media, which amplify and change visuality "in ways that directly question existing methods of interpretation" (Hand, 2017, p. 2016). In social media contexts, social scientists are challenged because visuals assume many forms and specific qualities, are subject to circulation through different platforms and devices, and exist along with verbal semiotic resources (Hand, 2017; Ravazzani & Maier, 2017; Russmann & Svensson, 2017).

The study of visual communication so far has favored quantitative content analyses while also neglecting social media contexts (Cassinger & Thelander, 2016; Highfield & Leaver, 2016; Pearce et al., 2018; Russmann & Svensson, 2017) as similarly noted in relation to research in crisis communication. Taking our point of departure in this evident research gap, we propose a social semiotic perspective on visual crisis communication developed from Halliday's (1978) social semiotic view on language.

From this perspective, "language is a product of social processes" (Jewitt & Henriksen, 2016, p. 146) and has three specific metafunctions that fulfill the communicative requirements of social life: the *ideational* metafunction for representing the world; the *interpersonal* metafunction for representing interpersonal relations; the *textual* metafunction for organizing recognizable complexes of signs, namely "texts." Social semioticians have developed this approach investigating other semiotic resources than speech and writing in various contexts, from architectural design to mathematical symbolism and web communication. This perspective is very relevant for examining systematically social media communication because "humans can bend semiotic modes to do things that they originally do not seem to have been designed for" (Van Leeuwen, 2015, p. 107). In social media contexts, this happens on a regular basis: "a critical feature of social media is that publics dominate the creation and use of these channels" (Coombs & Holladay, 2014, p. 51).

Kress and Van Leeuwen (2006) have extended this perspective by focusing on visuals: the ideational metafunction can be visually fulfilled through narrative visual structures that present the unfolding of human or non-human participants' actions and events or conceptual visual structures that represent the world "in terms of more or less permanent states of affairs or general truths" (p. 109); the interpersonal metafunction can be visually fulfilled by designing viewers' desired position in their interactions with represented human or non-human participants; the textual metafunction can be visually fulfilled through integrating representational and interactive structures in a meaningful whole.

In our empirical application, we will focus only on visual manifestations of the ideational metafunction since the analytical work includes both visuals and their meaning-making connections with verbal or other visual resources that accompany them. Social semioticians have recurrently explored these connections acknowledging the complex functional interweaving between semiotic resources (Martinec & Salway, 2005; Royce, 2016; Van Leeuwen, 2005). In all communicative situations, "the value of information lies in its relation to its context" (Van Leeuwen, 2005, p. 219), no matter what semiotic resources are employed. The key conceptual labels meant to identify such connections are *elaboration* and *extension* (Van Leeuwen, 2005). Relations of elaboration appear when one semiotic resource makes the other one more specific by providing more details, or when one semiotic resource explains the other one by paraphrasing it. Relations of extension appear when the content of one semiotic resource is similar to, contrasts with, or complements that of the other semiotic resource.

The choices made at the level of the ideational metafunction in terms of intersemiotic relations are motivated in the context of the publics' responses to crises by different levels of emotions. Crisis communication researchers (e.g., Coombs & Holladay, 2005; Jin, 2009, 2010; Jin & Pang, 2010, 2012; Jin et al., 2007, 2010, 2014; Van der Meer & Verhoeven, 2014) have recognized affective states' impact on crisis communicative responses. Acknowledging that "emotions are one of the anchors in the publics' interpretation of what is unfolding, changing, and shaping" (Jin et al., 2010, p. 429), Jin, in collaboration with other researchers, has developed an integrated crisis mapping model identifying various emotions likely to be experienced by publics in crises. The negative emotions identified as those most likely to be experienced and communicated by the publics are *anger, fright, anxiety,* and *sadness.* Considering that emotions are "states varying along a set of continuous dimensions" (Frijda, 1986, p. 259), multiple variations of emotions (Shaver et al., 1987) can be manifested in different contexts. Emotions are also related to *cognitive* (interpretative) and *conative* (behavioral) coping strategies of the publics (Jin & Pang, 2010). Such a perspective can be fruitfully linked to the cognitive appraisal model of emotions (Bell & Song, 2005) that highlights the interdependence between specific emotions and people's *cognitive assessments* of situations (or of situations' representations) such as attribution of blame and concern over interests. Furthermore, "cognitions lead to emotions which in turn predispose or motivate the individual towards particular behaviors" (Bell & Song, 2005, p. 32). Due to the specificity of our visual data, the above categories of cognitive assessments have been complemented with a new category, namely *disengagement,* which indicates the publics' lack of involvement in cognitive assessments of visual crisis representations.

Data and Analysis

Based on the proposed methodological framework qualitative social semiotic approach to visual crisis communication, the following research question is posed: *How are visuals used to co-create meanings and express followers' cognitive assessments and emotions on Facebook during a crisis?*

To answer this, we apply the proposed perspective to the recent Australian bushfire crisis. Australia has been ravaged by massive wildfires sparked from September 2019 to the beginning of 2020. This crisis was described as the worst natural disaster in decades, leading nationwide to deaths, air pollution, destruction of homes, bushland, wooded areas (Yeung, 2020). For this study, 76 data items were collected from the Facebook page of *9news Australia,* the most trusted national source of news and current affairs (https://www.9news.com.au/about-us). Data included all still and moving images posted by followers as visual responses to two images posted by *9news Australia* in the two consecutive days of December 18 and 19, 2019, considered the hottest days registered during the bushfire crisis (BBC, 2019).

The two images posted by *9news Australia* are two different kinds of visual representations. The December 18 image displays Australia's temperature map, and is accompanied by the following text: *Australia has sweltered through its new hottest day on record, according to data from the Bureau of Meteorology. Yesterday's average maximum temperature across the country was 40.9°C, beating the previous record of 40.3°C from 2013.* **#9News** *Read more:* http://9Soci.al/f1MK30q2VfB. One thousand comments were added by followers out of which sixty embedding images too. The December 19 image depicts a firefighter in action with huge flames engulfing some trees in the background, and is accompanied by the following text: *COMING UP: An extra #NSWBushfire bulletin, to keep you across the bushfire crisis that's now on Sydney's doorstep. LIVE Stream from 8.35pm on 9now.com.au/live or tune into Channel 9*

TABLE 13.1 Sample of Analytical Table

No.	Visual responses and accompanying verbal comment(s)	Type of visual responses	Type of connection between main image and visual responses	Type of connection between visual responses and accompanying verbal comment(s)	Cognitive assessments and emotions
1.	Visual collage of two photos with superimposed labels: *Volunteer Fire Fighter* and *Australia's PM*	Conceptual representation with contrasting symbolic attributes (bushfire behind the volunteer and Hawaiian palm behind PM)	Extension through similarity at the level of first photo Extension through contrast at the level of second photo	Extension through similarity at the level of each photo	Blame Anger

on your *TV* set. *Latest RFS information and advice:* http://9Soci.al/cP8E30q3c6x *LIVE blog:* http://9Soci.al/th1M30q3c6j. Sixty-four comments were added by followers out of which fourteen embedding images too. The 76 images posted by followers as responses include a wide range of visual representations, from photos to cartoons, drawings, collages, gif images, and moving images.

Each of the 76 images was coded and examined along these parameters: type of visual response; main image-visual response relation; visual response-accompanying text relation; cognitive assessments and emotions. Table 13.1 displays an example of how the coding parameters were used to classify and annotate data in analytical tables.

The systematic data collection and analysis according to the above-mentioned criteria responds to the need for qualitative researchers to clearly identify, select, and organize visual materials in ways that effectively deal with the issues of sample, representation, authenticity, and "exhaustiveness" typical of image analysis in social media (Hand, 2017).

Findings

The manifestations of the ideational metafunction are different in the two main images posted by *9news Australia*: the first image visualizes the bushfires' cause, while the second visualizes its consequences. The first image (I1) is a *conceptual visual representation* displaying Australia's map characterized by a dimensional topographical accuracy with embedded numbers labeling extremely high-temperature degrees. The second image (I2) is *a narrative visual representation* displaying in the foreground a lone firefighter engaged in a seemingly futile action; the whole locative circumstance from the background, namely the trees engulfed by huge flames, has a symbolic value. In both cases, the visual responses posted by followers illustrate meaning co-creation as they indicate three cognitive assessments of the situations displayed in the two main images: *blame attribution, concern over interests,* and *disengagement*. Specific emotions are promoted by these particular "cognitive antecedents" (Bell & Song, 2005, p. 31): *anger* manifested through its subcategories of *scorn* and *contempt* in the case of blame attribution; *fear* through its subcategories of *anxiety* and *apprehension*; and *joy* through its subcategories of *contentment* and *amusement*.

The followers' visual responses to I1 are cognitively construing and appraising the alarming situation through *concern over interests, disengagement,* and *blame attribution*. Each of these cognitive appraisals is visualized through various types of images that reflect different emotions. Conceptual representations of the ideational metafunction are predominant and visualize various screens (from homes, cars, or mobile phones) displaying similar or contrasting temperatures to those displayed on I1. The followers' visualization of similar temperatures in their specific locations is implicit manifestation of their cognitive appraisal of *concern* toward the situation, appraisal that is associated with emotions of *anxiety* and *apprehension*. The accompanying texts labeling locations enhance their distressing meaning and their connection of extension through similarity with I1. For example, "Mildura Victoria. Not looking forward to Friday."

When cognitively assessing the alarming map through *disengagement*, the followers manifest their emotional states of *contentment* (when the displayed temperatures are lower) or *amusement* as they want to indicate their lighter mood. For example, a cartoon visualizing a melting car on the asphalt is accompanied by the words "It's summer."

Blame attribution as a cognitive assessment of I1 is also construed in the followers' visual responses that are angry manifestations of their *scorn* and *contempt* toward either the news channel or the Australian PM. These visual responses also include texts that enter in relations of elaboration through the specification with the images. When the news channel is the target of their *scorn* or *contempt*, the visualizations are displaying proofs of the fact that the situation displayed in I1 is not so unique or alarming. For example, the visualization of an old newspaper's page accompanied by the words: "You forgot 1939." In another angry visual response, a television set put on the ground with clear sky and a tree in the background has these words superimposed on it: "Tell Lies Vision." When the PM is the target of *scorn* or *contempt*, the visual responses shift the focus from the bushfire crisis to the political crisis. These responses include cartoons and collages of drawings and photos of the Australian PM that enter in relations of extension through contrast with I1 and in relations of elaboration through the specification with the accompanying texts. For example, the medium shot of the laughing PM with a Hawaiian flower crown on his head has the following superimposed text: "I'll be back for the ashes."

In most of their visual responses to I2, followers are cognitively construing the desperate situation of the lone firefighter through *blame attribution*, and thus also shifting the focus from the bushfire crisis to the political crisis. As in the case of I1, their main visualizing strategies of this cognitive appraisal are cartoons and collages of drawings and photos of the Australian PM manifesting their *scorn* and *contempt* toward the politician's lack of proper handling of bushfires. These narrative images extend through contrast the meaning of I2, as the embarrassing visualizations of the politician are incompatible with I2's content. This connective strategy of extension through contrast is enhanced by the connections between these visual responses and their accompanying texts. First, these responses have connections of elaboration through the specification with their accompanying texts. For example, the collage displaying the PM's closeup shot with the drawing of an opened door behind him has the following superimposed words: "I've been in Hawaii for six weeks. Did I miss anything?" Secondly, in other cases, the connection is one of contrast. For example, the collage displaying a medium shot of the smiling PM surrounded by big painted flames is accompanied by words coming out of the politician's mouth: "This is fine." The followers' anger is also manifested only visually as in the case of a cartoon which displays the head of the PM screaming while a koala bear with flames coming out of its back tries to hang on the politician's head.

Table 13.2 provides an overview of the main findings.

TABLE 13.2 Overview of the Study Results

Types of visual responses	Types of connections between main image and visual responses	Type of connections between visual responses and texts	Cognitive assessments	Emotions
Conceptual representations	Extension through similarity	Elaboration through specification	Concern	Anxiety and apprehension
	Extension through contrast	Elaboration through specification	Disengagement	Contentment and amusement
	Extension through contrast	Elaboration through specification Extension through contrast	Blame	Contempt and scorn
Narrative representations	Extension through contrast	Elaboration through specification Extension through contrast	Blame	Contempt and scorn

Conclusions

In this chapter, we have put forth a qualitative social semiotic perspective on visual crisis communication and showed how this could be effectively used for investigating how various semiotic resources, visuals above all, are used in specific crisis contexts as organized meaning systems (Höllerer et al., 2019) for encoding interpretations of experience and forms of social (inter)action. Clusters and/ or chains of information that are specific to social media cannot be approached without taking into consideration visuals and their meaning-making connections to other semiotic resources. Our proposed perspective responds to the call for methodological innovation in visual research and more specifically for qualitative approaches (Banks, 2014; Hand, 2017; Marotzki et al., 2014) among which social semiotics and multimodality stand out (Hand, 2017) because they allow researchers to carefully consider the aspects of intertextuality and broader contextualization of the visualized social practices.

While addressing this relevant research gap detected in both visual communication in general and crisis communication in particular, our social semiotic approach to visual crisis communication in social media offers researchers the possibility to perform fine-grained qualitative analyses; and news media and corporate practitioners new methodological tools to systematically monitor crisis reactions and manage communication strategies with enhanced awareness of the roles of visuals and emotions. Building on our perspective and empirical findings, we recommend future researchers to strengthen or revise the framework proposed by exploring additional cases and moving beyond single-platform visual analysis (Pearce et al., 2018) to eventually discern the special uses of visuals and visual crisis communication according to each platform's specificities, affordances, and constraints.

References

Austin, L., & Jin, Y. (2018). *Social media and crisis communication*. Routledge.

Austin, L., Liu, B. F., & Jin, Y. (2012). How audiences seek out crisis information: Exploring the social mediated crisis communication model. *Journal of Applied Communication Research, 40*(2), 188–207. https://doi.org/10.1080/00909882.2012.654498

Banks, M. (2014). Analysing images. In U. Flick (Ed.), *The SAGE handbook of qualitative data analysis* (pp. 394–408). SAGE.

BBC (2019, December 19). Australia heatwave: All-time temperature record broken again. Available at https://www.bbc.com/news/world-australia-50837025

Bell, C., & Song, F. (2005). Emotions in the conflict process: An application of the cognitive appraisal model of emotions to conflict management. *The International Journal of Conflict Management, 16*(1), 30–54. https://doi.org/10.1108/eb022922

Cassinger, C., & Thelander, Å (2016). Rotation curation on Instagram: A cultural practice perspective on participation. In W. T. Coombs, J. Falkheimer, M. Heide, & P. Young (Eds.), *Strategic communication, social media and democracy. The challenge of the digital naturals* (pp. 34–44). Routledge.

Castells, M. (2007). Communication, power and counter-power in the network society. *International Journal of Communication, 1*(1), 238–266.

Cheng, Y. (2018), How social media is changing crisis communication strategies: Evidence from the updated literature. *Journal of Contingencies and Crisis Management, 26*, 58–68. https://doi.org/10.1111/1468-5973.12130

Cheng, Y., & Cameron, G. (2018). The status of social-mediated crisis communication (SMCC) research: An analysis of published articles in 2002–2014. In L. Austin & Y. Jin (Eds.), *Social Media and Crisis Communication* (pp. 10–20). Routledge.

Coombs, W. T., & Holladay, S. J. (2005). An exploratory study of stakeholder emotions: Affect and crises. In N. M. Ashkanasy, W. J. Zerbe, & C. E. J. Härtel (Eds.), *Research on emotion in organizations*, Vol. 1 (pp. 263–280). Elsevier.

Coombs, W. T., & Holladay, S. J. (2009). Further explorations of post-crisis communication: Effects of media and response strategies on perceptions and intensions. *Public Relations Review, 35*(1), 1–6. https://doi.org/10.1016/j.pubrev.2008.09.011

Coombs, W. T., & Holladay, S. J. (2011). An exploration of the effects of victim visuals on perceptions and reactions to crisis events. *Public Relations Review, 37*(2), 115–120. https://doi.org/10.1016/j.pubrev.2011.01.006

Coombs, W. T., & Holladay, S. J. (2014). How publics react to crisis communication efforts. Comparing crisis response reactions across sub-arenas. *Journal of Communication Management, 18*(1), 40–57. https://doi.org/10.1108/JCOM-03-2013-0015

Dahmen, N. S. (2016). Images of resilience: The case for visual restorative narrative. *Visual Communication Quarterly, 23*(2), 93–107. https://doi.org/10.1080/15551393.2016.1190620

Frandsen, F., & Johansen, W. (2010). Crisis communication, complexity, and the cartoon affair: A case study. In W. T. Coombs, & S. J. Holladay (Eds.), *Handbook of crisis communication* (pp. 425–449). Wiley-Blackwell.

Frijda, N. H. (1986). *The emotions.* Cambridge University Press.

George, A. M., & Kwansah-Aidoo, K. (2017). "Almost without a trace": Missing flight MH370, culture and transboundary crisis communication in the era of social media. In A. M. George, & K. Kwansah-Aidoo (Eds.), *Culture and crisis communication: Transboundary cases from nonwestern perspectives* (pp. 184–208). Wiley.

Halliday, M. A. K. (1978). *Language as social semiotic.* Arnold.

Hand, M. (2017). Visuality in social media: Researching images, circulations and practices. In L. Sloan, & A. Quan-Haase (Eds.), *The SAGE handbook of social media research methods* (pp. 215–231). SAGE.

Hess, K., & Waller, L. (2015). Media targets: When a spark in social media develops into a mainstream media firestorm. In M. Sheehan, & D. Quinn-Allan (Eds.), *Crisis communication in a digital world* (pp. 94–106). Cambridge University Press.

Highfield, T., & Leaver, T. (2016). Instagrammatics and digital methods: Studying visual social media, from selfies and GIFs to memes and emoji. *Communication Research and Practices, 2*(1), 47–62. https://doi.org/10.1080/22041451.2016.1155332

Höllerer, M. A., Van Leeuwen, T., Jancsary, D., Meyer, R. E., Andersen, T. H., & Vaara, E. (2019). *Visual and multimodal research in organization and management studies.* Routledge.

Janoske, M. (2018). Visualizing response and recovery: The impact of social media–based images in a crisis. In L. Austin, & Y. Jin (Eds.), *Social media and crisis communication* (pp. 306–318). Routledge.

Jewitt, C., & Henriksen, B. (2016). Social semiotic multimodality. In N.-M. Klug, & H. Stöckl (Eds.), *Handbook of language in multimodal contexts* (pp. 145–164). DeGryter.

Jin, Y. (2009). The effects of public's cognitive appraisal of emotions in crises on crisis coping and strategy assessment. *Public Relations Review, 35*(3), 310–313. https://doi.org/10.1016/j.pubrev.2009.02.003

Jin, Y. (2010). Making sense sensibly in crisis communication: How publics' crisis appraisals influence their negative emotions, coping strategy preferences, and crisis response acceptance. *Communication Research, 37*(4), 522–552. https://doi.org/10.1177/00936502 10368256

Jin, Y., & Pang, A. (2012). Future directions of crisis communication research: Emotions in crisis – the next frontier. In W. T. Coombs, & S. J. Holladay (Eds.), *Handbook of crisis communication* (pp. 677–682). Wiley-Blackwell.

Jin, Y., Pang, A., & Cameron, G. T. (2007). Integrated crisis mapping: Towards a publics-based, emotion-driven conceptualization in crisis communication. *Sphera Publica, 7*, 81–95.

Jin, Y., & Pang, A. (2010). Future directions of crisis communication research: Emotions in crisis—The next frontier. In W. T. Coombs & S. J. Holladay (Eds.), *Handbook of crisis communication* (pp. 677–682). Wiley-Blackwell.

Jin, Y., Pang, A., & Cameron, G. T. (2010). The role of emotions in crisis responses. Inaugural test of the integrated crisis mapping (ICM) model. *Corporate Communications: An International Journal, 15*(4), 428–452. https://doi.org/10.1108/13563281011085529

Jin, Y., Liu, B. F., & Austin, L. L. (2014). Examining the role of social media in effective crisis management: The effects of crisis origin, information form, and source on publics' crisis responses. *Communication Research, 41*, 74–94. https://doi.org/10.1177 %2F0093650211423918

Jin, Y., Austin, L., Guidry, J., & Parrish, C. (2017). Picture this and take that: Strategic crisis visuals and visual social media (VSM). In S. Duhé (Ed.), *Crisis communication. New media and public relations* (3rd edition). Peter Lang Publishing Group.

Kress, G., & Van Leeuwen, T. (2006). *Reading images. The grammar of visual design.* Routledge.

Liu, B. F., Wood, M. M., Egnoto, M., Bean, H., Sutton, J., Mileti, D., & Madden, S. (2017). Is a picture worth a thousand words? The effects of maps and warning messages on how publics respond to disaster information. *Public Relations Review, 43*(3), 493–506. https://doi.org/10.1016/j.pubrev.2017.04.004

Lovegrove, N. (2018). A visual history of BP's use of public relations after deepwater horizon. In S. Collister & S. Roberts-Bowman (Eds.), *Visual public relations. Strategic communication beyond text* (chapter 8). Routledge.

Maier, C. D. (2020). Visual crisis communication. In F. Frandsen, & W. Johansen (Eds.), *Crisis communication* (pp. 213–237). De Gruyter.

Maier, C. D., Frandsen, F., & Johansen, W. (2019). Visual crisis communication in the Scandinavian press: Images of the MS disaster. *NordiCom Review, 40*(2), 91–109. https://doi.org/10.2478/nor-2019-0035

Marotzki, W., Holze, J., & Verständig, D. (2014). Analysing virtual data. In U. Flick (Ed.), *The SAGE handbook of qualitative data analysis* (pp. 450–463). SAGE.

Martinec, R., & Salway, A. (2005). A system for image-text relations in new (old) media. *Visual Communication, 4*, 337–371. https://doi.org/10.1177/1470357205055928

Miller, A., & LaPoe, V. (2016). Visual agenda-setting, emotion, and the BP oil disaster. *Visual Communication Quarterly, 23*(1), 53–63. https://doi.org/10.1080/15551393.2015.1128335

Pantti, M. (2019). The personalization of conflict reporting. Visual coverage of the Ukraine crisis on twitter. *Digital Journalism, 7*(1), 124–145. https://doi.org/10.1080/21670811.2017.1399807

Pearce, W., Özkula, S. M., Greene, A. K., Teeling, L., Bansard, J. S., Omena, J. J., & Rabello, E. T. (2018). Visual cross-platform analysis: Digital methods to research social media images. *Information, Communication & Society, 23*(2), 161–180. 10.1080/1369118X.2018.1486871

Ravazzani, S., & Maier, C. D. (2017). Strategic organizational discourse and framing in hypermodal spaces. *Corporate Communications, 22*(4), 507–522. http://dx.doi.org. ez.statsbiblioteket.dk:2048/10.1108/CCIJ-06-2017-0063

Royce, T. D. (2016). Intersemiotic complementarity in print advertisements. In N.-M. Klug, & H. Stöckl (Eds.), *Handbook of language in multimodal contexts* (pp. 348–371). DeGryter.

Russmann, U., & Svensson, J. (2017). Introduction to visual communication in the age of social media: Conceptual, theoretical and methodological challenges. *Media and Communication, 5*(4), 1–5. http://dx.doi.org/10.17645/mac.v5i4.1263

Shaver, P., Schwartz, J., Kirson, D., & O'Connor, C. (1987). Emotion knowledge: Further exploration of a prototype approach. *Journal of Personality and Social Psychology, 52*(6), 1061–1086. https://doi.org/10.1037//0022-3514.52.6.1061

Van der Meer, T., & Verhoeven, J. (2014). Emotional crisis communication. *Public Relations Review, 40*(3), 526–536. https://doi.org/10.1016/j.pubrev.2014.03.004

Van Leeuwen, T. (2005). *Introducing social semiotics.* Routledge.

Van Leeuwen, T. (2015). Theo van Leeuwen. In T. H. Andersen, M. Boeriis, E. Maagerø, & E. S. Tønnessen (Eds.), *Social semiotics. Key figures, new directions* (pp. 93–114). Routledge.

Van Looy, A. (2016). *Social media management. Technologies and strategies for creating business value.* Springer Texts in Business and Economics.

Veil, S. R., Buehner, T., & Palenchar, M. J. (2011). A work-in-process literature review: Incorporating social media in risk and crisis communication. *Journal of Contingencies & Crisis Management, 19*(2), 110–122. https://doi.org/10.1111/j.1468-5973.2011.00639.x

Whelan, G., Moon, J., & Grant, B. (2013). Corporations and citizenship arenas in the age of social media. *Journal of Business Ethics, 118*(4), 777–790. https://doi.org/10.1007/s10551-013-1960-3

White, C. M. (2012). *Social media, crisis communication, and emergency management. Leveraging Web 2.0 technologies.* Taylor & Francis.

Yeung, J. (2020, January 14). Australia's deadly wildfires are showing no signs of stopping. Here's what you need to know. CNN. https://edition.cnn.com/2020/01/01/australia/australia-fires-explainer-intl-hnk-scli/index.html

Zeng, L., & Akinro, N. A. (2013). Picturing the Jos crisis online in three leading newspapers in Nigeria: A visual framing perspective. *Visual Communication Quarterly, 20*, 196–204. https://doi.org/10.1080/15551393.2013.852444

14

NEW TECHNOLOGY, BIG DATA, AND ARTIFICIAL INTELLIGENCE

W. Scott Guthrie and John Rich

The industrial and information eras have begotten novel risks, a more informed public, new technologies, and novel strategies for dialogue, decision making, and risk assessment (Palenchar, 2009); forcing crisis communication theory and practice to evolve rapidly since the turn of the century (Coombs & Holladay, 2010). In this chapter, we explore three technologies – computational power, big data, and artificial intelligence (AI) – and their impact on how organizations conduct business, how humans interact, and how we define reality. Specifically, we investigate:

1. the explosion and analysis of "big data,"
2. the evolution of advanced AI, and
3. the emergence of extended reality (XR).

We begin with a brief review of the impetus driving these trends: computational power.

Computational Power

Moore's and Neven's Laws

Moore's law, named after Intel co-founder Gordon Moore, applies to traditional computing. It states that the number of transistors that can fit onto an integrated circuit doubles approximately every two years (Simonite, 2016). Integrated circuits are computer chips; transistors give computer chips power. The more transistors that fit onto a chip, the faster and more powerful the computer. Thus,

DOI: 10.4324/9781003043409-20

Moore's Law essentially posits that classical computers double in processing power every other year. For the past 50 years, Moore's law has served as a recurring progress marker for the computer industry. In 2016, however, Intel stated that computer chips could only continue to shrink for approximately another five years (Bourzac, 2016). Therefore, Moore's law is now outdated as more resources are being funneled toward the advancement of quantum computing.

Whereas traditional computers store data as bits in binary 0s and 1s, quantum computers store data as *qubits* (Ghose, 2019). A qubit can simultaneously be a 0, 1, and any number in between (Brassard et al., 1998). This allows quantum computers to deliver processing power that dwarfs that of even supercomputers. Hartmut Neven, director of Google's Quantum Artificial Intelligence Lab, declared in February 2019 that quantum computing is advancing at a doubly exponential rate (twice the speed of Moore's law), which is now known as *Neven's law* (Hartnett, 2019).

Data Growth with Big Data

Quantum computing is needed because traditional computers cannot process the exorbitant amount of data available today. More than 90% of the data in the world has been generated since 2016 and more than 2.5 *quintillion* bytes of data are created *every day* (Marr, 2018). *The Internet of Things* – the billions of devices interconnected through the internet – is largely driving the explosion of data, helping to create "big data."

Big data are extremely voluminous datasets containing highly varied information, analyzed at high velocity (Gartner, n.d.). Put simply, big data are large, complex datasets from new sources that traditional computers cannot process. *"Organic data,"* a type of big data, are often collected without the user's knowledge, a predetermined purpose, or a uniformed stimulus. For instance, *every minute of every day*:

- The Weather Channel receives more than 18 million forecast requests,
- Google conducts nearly 4 million searches, and
- YouTube plays approximately 4.4 million videos (DOMO, 2018).

This is organic big data. Quantum computers possess the processing power needed to extract value from big data, which experts predict will propel breakthroughs in fields such a science, medicine, and finance (IBM, n.d.). Google Flu and the MIT Billion Prices Index analyze big data to predict flu epidemics and to monitor inflation, respectively. Companies also can use big data to improve product development, customer experience, risk management, and operational efficiency.

Big Data Use Cases

Product Development and Customer Experience

Companies can analyze big data from social media, web traffic, and call logs to predict and prevent customer complaints, "improve the interaction experience, and maximize the value delivered" (Oracle, n.d.). Coca-Cola uses a digital loyalty program to collect data about consumer preferences. This helps the beverage company develop products, build customer loyalty, and provide a better customer experience. Furthermore, organizations can use big data to "build predictive models for new products and services by classifying key attributes of past and current products or services" (Oracle, n.d.). Netflix analyzes its subscribers' viewing data to steer its production decisions, and Volkswagen uses big data to produce more powerful batteries for electric cars.

Risk Management

Big data can improve risk management models, fortify areas of weakness, and identify potential risks (Kopanakis, 2018). With big data, UOB Bank in Singapore can conduct near real-time value at risk (VaR) analyses, a process that used to consume 18 hours (Huber et al., 2014). By consolidating big data across lines of business, a bank can better predict account holder behavior: a person who defaults on a credit card may be more likely to default on a mortgage (Latha & Lakshmi, 2016).

Operational Efficiency

Big data can increase operational efficiency by helping to make decisions that align with market demands. By analyzing big data, organizations can assess production, review customer feedback, prevent outages, and predict future demands (Oracle, n.d.). Additional insight into operational activities can lead to improved service levels, reduced processing times, streamlined supply chain management, and lower structural costs. Airbus, for instance, analyzes big data to determine the most fuel-efficient flight paths.

Small Data and Designed Data

In contrast to big data, "*small data*" are easily accessible datasets that can impact decisions in the present (Miglani, 2016). It typically fits within a standard spreadsheet and can be analyzed without quantum technology. Personal data – driving records and internet search histories, for example – are often small data, as are "*designed data*." Designed data are collected for a specific, predetermined purpose

(Groves, 2011). Data from surveys, questionnaires, and administrative forms are designed data. The US Census – used to count and locate all people in the country to determine federal funding – is an example. Big businesses and government have largely controlled small data; however, their lackadaisical attitude toward data security and privacy has become problematic.

Data Control

Hackers breached Equifax in 2017 and exposed the personal information, including social security numbers, of 143 million Americans. Cambridge Analytica, a former British political consulting firm, harvested millions of Facebook users' data without consent in 2018. Combined, these events (plus others) have amplified calls for data regulation and proliferated trends in personal data ownership. Vermont now requires data brokers to register with the state (Melendez, 2019). California enacted the *California Consumer Privacy Act*, allowing state residents to prevent the sale of their data (Whittaker, 2020). Hawaii, Maryland, Massachusetts, Mississippi, and New Mexico have all introduced similar legislation (Lazzarotti & Gavejian, 2019). The European Union (EU) passed the *General Data Protection Regulation (GDPR)*. The GDPR affords all EU citizens the right to opt out of having their personal data collected and the right to have their personal data deleted (Burgess, 2020). Any foreign organizations operating in the EU and collecting identifiable data from EU citizens must respect these rights (Burgess, 2020).

Moreover, more individuals are beginning to own and sell their personal data. Andrew Yang, a 2020 Democratic presidential candidate, created the Data Dividend Project, which attempts to compensate individuals for the use of their data. Similarly, Universal Basic Data Income (UBDI) and BIGtoken allow individuals to sell their data directly to advertisers. As such, companies will need to be strategic in how they acquire, leverage, and secure consumer data going forward. While the abundance of data is helping humans profit financially, it is helping computers profit intellectually, hurdling us closer toward achieving artificial superintelligence.

Machine Learning and Artificial Intelligence

The amount of computational resources being applied to AI is doubling every three and a half months (Amodei & Hernandez, 2018). Google's director of engineering, Ray Kurzweil, predicts the arrival of AI that is emotionally and intellectually indistinguishable from humans by 2029 with super-intelligent AI arriving shortly thereafter (ITU News, 2019). Rapidly advancing machine learning techniques, including approaches where AI evolves autonomously, make realizing this prediction a distinct possibility. *Machine learning systems* use algorithms to analyze big data and detect patterns, automating analytical model building (Hao, 2018; SAS, n.d.). Humans do not program machine learning systems; we train them using big data. We feed the computer data, the computer analyzes that data and then makes decisions independently based upon its analysis. As the computer consumes more data, its knowledge increases, and its decision-making improves (Tanz, 2016). Machine learning powers social media algorithms and language translation apps. Organizations are using machine learning and big data to engage in social listening, find common ground between groups, and better manage crises (Maerowitz, 2018).

Machine Learning Use Cases

Social Listening

Social listening is tracking online discourse about a brand or industry to gain insight from the public; however, it does not monitor specific marketing campaigns (Skyword, n.d.). By engaging in social listening, an organization can better understand its stakeholders and develop customized products and offers for them. Social listening can be leveraged to calculate public opinion about current events and social issues (Maerowitz, 2018), allowing a brand the opportunity to determine its customers' stance before issuing a public statement. Moreover, through social listening, an organization can determine its conversation share within a certain space or with a certain demographic, helping guide marketing strategies and resource allotment.

Common Ground

Using machine learning systems, organizations can analyze vast quantities of social media posts from opposing groups to detect overlapping patterns in language and sentiment, helping to find common ground between the groups (Maerowitz, 2018). A company that employs such a strategy could attract a new set of customers with whom it may not have previously tried to connect, thus expanding its reach, footprint, and brand.

Crisis Management

Organizations can leverage machine learning systems to track rumors online. For instance, a machine learning system can analyze the volume of tweets spreading a rumor and predict its truthfulness (Maerowitz, 2018). With such insights, a company can predict the duration and seriousness of a crisis and adjust its response accordingly.

Artificial Intelligence

Machine learning powers AI technologies. *AI* aims to give computers the ability to think and act intelligently (Newell, 1981). In theory, AI can perform tasks that necessitate human intelligence, and it responds to stimulation in ways consistent with human behavior (Shubhendu & Vijay, 2013). There are three types of AI: artificial narrow intelligence (ANI), artificial general intelligence (AGI), and artificial superintelligence (ASI).

ANI performs predetermined tasks and fuels technologies such as virtual voice assistants, navigation apps, language translation services, and online chatbots. *Chatbots* – AI programs designed to simulate human conversations (Techopedia, 2019) – are one of the most common uses of ANI today. When you chat online with a company representative, you are likely communicating with a chatbot. Chatbots have several advantages. They are cost-effective, replicable, always available, and don't require salaries (Fox et al., 2015). Chatbots allow a company to offer true 24/7 customer support, potentially improving the customer experience.

That said, ANI virtual assistants are disrupting employment. Shortly after the onset of the COVID-19 pandemic in 2020, chatbots replaced entire workforces at several call centers. At the time, Rob Thomas, senior vice president of cloud and data platform at IBM, remarked: "I really think this is a new normal–the pandemic accelerated what was going to happen anyway" (Semuels, 2020). Indeed, the chatbot market is expected to hit $9.4 billion by 2024 (Nguyen, 2020). Businesses may soon use AI to generate all print content, including social media posts and replies. The Associated Press, *The Washington Post,* and *Los Angeles Times* are all experimenting with AI bots that can both assist reporters with research and generate stories independently (Martin, 2019).

AGI, a step above ANI, can "reason, experiment, and understand" by recalling and learning from previous experiences (Brown, n.d.). We have yet to fully achieve true AGI. Once we do, though, it is likely that unless somehow constrained, AI systems will undergo an "intelligence explosion" (Muehlhauser, 2015), surpassing humans in intellectual capability and achieving ASI. *ASI* is currently a hypothetical type of AI that is self-aware and that has emotions and desires (O'Carroll, 2020). Some scholars believe unconstrained super-intelligent AI would be an existential threat to our species (Bostrom, 2014). Less debatable, perhaps, is that our interactions with virtual beings and objects will increase and become banal as XR slowly becomes our new reality.

Extended Reality

XR refers to the triad of technologies that afford users the ability to interact with the real and virtual world simultaneously by inserting digital information into the physical world, altering how we perceive and define reality (Antin, 2020).

These technologies are augmented reality (AR), mixed reality (MR), and virtual reality (VR).

Augmented Reality

AR superimposes, or overlays, digital media onto the physical world as if they coexisted, thus supplementing, or augmenting, reality (Azuma, 1997). To date, AR mostly has been used for mobile entertainment. "Pokémon Go," a mobile game wherein users view their physical surroundings through their mobile camera and capture digitally projected Pokémon characters, and Snapchat filters are prominent examples of AR.

An advantage of AR technology is that it requires minimal processing power, making it compatible with most smartphones and tablets (Wendt, 2020). Several companies are using AR to deliver the benefits of shopping in person directly to the customer. With the appropriate app and a mobile device, shoppers can instantly try on a pair of glasses (e.g., Warby Parker), a watch (e.g., Rolex), and a new shade of makeup (Sephora) from the comforts of their home.

Mixed Reality

MR anchors virtual objects in the physical world, combining real and digital elements (Marr, 2019; Intel, n.d.), changing how we interact with the physical world (Rogers, 2018). MR requires a headset, often called smart glasses, such as the Microsoft HoloLens or Magic Leap One. The principle difference between MR and AR is that users can interact with the virtual objects depicted in MR. Using smart glasses, a user can not only see a virtual plate depicted onto a real table, she can reach out and pick up the depiction, too. With AR technology, a user can only see the virtual plate.

Although still in its infancy, companies are already implementing MR solutions. The impact MR has on industry will only continue to grow as its processing power improves. Employees at the French company Renault Trucks wear Microsoft HoloLenses, which project digitized engine parts over the actual engine, to help guide them through the complicated assembly process. Reports predict that roughly 14.4 million US workers will wear smart glasses by 2025 (Rogers, 2018).

Virtual Reality

As opposed to AR and MR, VR is a completely immersive experience that blocks out the physical world. Through the use of a head-mounted display, *VR* virtually transports users to a computer-generated world with which they can interact as if it were real. Presence (the feeling of being there) and interactivity (the ability to act there) are defining characteristics of VR experiences (Sanchez-Vives & Slater, 2005).

VR is finding applications in industries such as tourism, real estate, healthcare, education, and manufacturing. The VR market is expected to reach $61.2 billion by 2027 (Grand View Research, 2020), and consulting firm Deloitte estimates that at least 52 of the Fortune 500 companies are exploring AR/VR solutions (Rogers, 2018). Wal-Mart trains all of its US employees using VR technology, thus significantly reducing travel expenses while ensuring that every employee at its nearly 5,000 stores nationwide receives the same instruction (Incao, 2018). Employees can practice using new checkout technology in a VR module before it is installed in stores, helping to ensure a seamless rollout (Incao, 2018)

Training experiences like these are often experienced individually; however, many virtual environments afford users the opportunity to engage with a variety of different virtual beings known as agents and avatars.

Virtual Beings and Multiple Selves

Agents

Virtual beings or agents – virtual representations of humans, controlled by computer algorithms – are becoming ubiquitous in retail, education, healthcare, and marketing (Fox et al., 2015). In virtual worlds and video games, agents are typically interactive characters; in the physical world, they are commonly employed in online customer service roles (Fox et al., 2015). Chatbots, which we briefly discussed above, are a type of agent. Agents are an attractive option for such roles because they are programmable, multifunctional, cost-effective, and often indistinguishable from humans (Fox et al., 2015). When users believe they are interacting with a human, they may become more easily persuaded, thus agents are often used to influence users (Fox et al., 2015), such as in advertising.

Virtual worlds beget enterprising marketing strategies (Ahn & Bailenson, 2011). Self-endorsing advertisements (SEA) display to a user a virtual doppelganger of herself, created with information and pictures gathered online, using a certain product (Ahn & Bailenson, 2011). This can unduly persuade the user to purchase the product (Ahn et al., 2017). Such practices raise many ethical questions that will need to be addressed considering that our interactions with virtual beings are likely to increase in the near future.

The importance of virtual beings aligns with the advancement of AI systems. The most effective use of ANI and AGI might be its embodiment in virtual beings taking the roles of our coworkers and friends. During the lockdowns caused by the COVID-19 pandemic in 2020, more than half a million people downloaded the AI-powered chatbot app Replika to combat loneliness.

Some users reported developing strong emotional ties to their "Replika," coming to view them as friends or romantic partners (Metz, 2020). Yet, we will also have plenty of opportunities to interact with other humans in virtual environments through the use of avatars.

Avatars

An *avatar* is a digital representation of a user that the user controls (Ahn & Bailenson, 2011). Avatars can be photorealistic or customized to reflect any gender, skin color, hair color, eye color, weight, etc. This allows a user to create and project as many different identities as she desires. Individuals creating several digital identities was a well-established behavior long before the emergence of virtual worlds. The average internet user has multiple social media accounts (Mander, 2016), often with different personas finely tuned for each platform (Zhong et al., 2017). Millions of people engage with others via their avatars on massive multiplayer online platforms (MMOP's) and in social VR.

Social VR is a 3D virtual space in which multiple, geographically separated users, each represented by an avatar, can gather and socialize in real-time as if they were face-to-face- (Perry, 2016). This is ripe territory for individuals to create "*multiple selves,*" which could impact how we come to view our identities. The *proteus effect* describes how individuals change their behavior in the virtual world based on the characteristics of their avatar (Yee & Bailenson, 2007). For instance, users given taller avatars in a virtual environment behaved more confidently when negotiating than users given shorter avatars (Yee & Bailenson, 2007). Such effects could drastically impact how organizations and individuals conduct business, especially as more companies begin to utilize collaborative virtual spaces.

The trend of users creating multiple selves is likely to accelerate as XR becomes more ubiquitous and begins to (re)define reality. Indeed, XR may soon feel more natural than physical reality. The reasons for this are twofold. First, XR technology creates and enhances virtual spaces in ways that trick our brains into believing they are real (Hu et al., 2016; Peterson et al., 2018). Second, XR technology upends the traditional affordances of our physical selves. That is, the constraints of engaging in physical spaces and the laws of physics no longer apply. These expanded affordances will challenge us to extend and evolve our identities to match our new capabilities (Van Looy, 2015).

Conclusion

Returning to reality, we have covered many topics in this chapter. To review: technological advances are drastically altering how organizations conduct business and connect and communicate with stakeholders. The Internet of Things, among other sources, is producing exorbitant amounts of organic "big data." Traditional computers lack the processing power required to analyze big data; thus, more resources are being dedicated to the development of quantum computers. The analysis of big data is fueling innovative solutions in myriad industries such as science, medicine, finance, and manufacturing. Together, quantum computing and big data are powering machine learning systems, which in turn, are giving rise to advanced AI that can teach itself and perform many of the same tasks as humans. AI technologies are making it more common for humans to interact with virtual beings at the same time that XR technologies are redefining our perception of ourselves and our definition of reality. The overall impact of these technologies on business, communication, and human behavior remains to be seen; however, it will surely be unlike anything we have ever seen (or experienced) before.

References

Ahn, S. J., & Bailenson, J. N. (2011). Self-endorsing versus other-endorsing in virtual environments. *Journal of Advertising, 40*(2), 93–106. https://doi.org/10.2753/JOA0091-3367400207

Ahn, S. J., Phua, J., & Shan, Y. (2017). Self-endorsing in digital advertisements: Using virtual selves to persuade physical selves. *Computers in Human Behavior, 71*, 110–121. https://doi-org.proxy-remote.galib.uga.edu/10.1016/j.chb.2017.01.045

Amodei, D., & Hernandez, D. (2018, May 16). AI and compute. *OpenAI.* https://openai.com/blog/ai-and-compute/

Antin, D. (2020, July 7). Extended reality is the frontier for the digital future. *Medium.* https://medium.com/predict/extended-reality-is-the-frontier-of-the-digital-future-a2c05785fc72

Azuma, R. T. (1997). A survey of augmented reality. *Presence: Teleoperators & Virtual Environments, 6*(4), 355–385. https://doi.org/10.1162/pres.1997.6.4.355

Bostrom, N. (2014). *Superintelligence: Paths, dangers, strategies.* Oxford University Press.

Bourzac, K. (2016, February 5). Intel: Chips will have to sacrifice speed gains for energy savings. *MIT Technology Review.* https://www.technologyreview.com/2016/02/05/9327/intel-chips-will-have-to-sacrifice-speed-gains-for-energy-savings/

Brassard, G., Chuang, I., Lloyd, S., & Monroe, C. (1998). Quantum computing. *Proceedings of the National Academy of Sciences of the United States of America, 95*(19), 11032–11033. https://doi.org/10.1073/pnas.95.19.11032

Brown, E. (n.d.). Building god: Why super intelligent A.I. will be the best (or last) thing we ever do. *High Existence.* https://highexistence.com/building-god-superintelligent-ai-will-best-last-thing/

Burgess, M. (2020, March 24). What is GDPR? The summary guide to GDPR compliance in the UK. *Wired UK.* https://www.wired.co.uk/article/what-is-gdpr-uk-eu-legislation-compliance-summary-fines-2018

Coombs, W. T., & Holladay, S. J. (Eds.). (2010). *The handbook of crisis communication.* Wiley-Blackwell.

DOMO. (2018). *Data never sleeps* (6th ed.). https://www.domo.com/solution/data-never-sleeps-6

Fox, J., Ahn, S. J., Janssen, J. H., Yeykelis, L., Segovia, K. Y., & Bailenson, J. N. (2015). Avatars versus agents: A meta-analysis quantifying the effect of agency on social influence. *Human-Computer Interaction, 30*(5), 401–432. https://doi.org/10.1080/07370024.2014.921494

Gartner. (n.d.). Big data. *Gartner Glossary.* https://www.gartner.com/en/information-technology/glossary/big-data

Ghose, T. (2019, June 21). Forget Moore's law – quantum computers are improving according to a spooky "doubly exponential rate." *Live Science.* https://www.livescience.com/65651-quantum-computers-get-scary-fast.html

Grand View Research (2020, June). *Virtual reality market size, share & analysis report, 2020–2027.* https://www.grandviewresearch.com/industry-analysis/virtual-reality-vr-market

Groves, R. (2011, May 31). "Designed Data" and "Organic Data." *United States Census Bureau.* https://www.census.gov/newsroom/blogs/director/2011/05/designed-data-and-organic-data.html

Hao, K. (2018, November 17). What is machine learning? *MIT Technology Review.* https://www.technologyreview.com/2018/11/17/103781/what-is-machine-learning-we-drew-you-another-flowchart/

Hartnett, K. (2019, June 18). A new law to describe quantum computing's rise? *Quanta Magazine.* https://www.quantamagazine.org/does-nevens-law-describe-quantum-computings-rise-20190618/

Hu, G., Hannan, N. B., Tearo, K., Bastos, A., & Reilly, D. (2016). Doing while thinking: Physical and cognitive engagement and immersion in mixed reality games. *Proceedings of the 2016 ACM Conference on Designing Interactive Systems,* 947–958.

Huber, A., Hannapel, H., & Nagode, F. (2014, July 2). Big data: Potentials from a risk management perspective. *Banking Hub.* https://www.bankinghub.eu/banking/finance-risk/big-data-potentials-from-a-risk-management-perspective

IBM. (n.d.). What is quantum computing? https://www.ibm.com/quantum-computing/learn/what-is-quantum-computing/

Incao, J. (2018, September 20). How VR is transforming the way we train associates. *Wal-Mart.* https://corporate.walmart.com/newsroom/innovation/20180920/how-vr-is-transforming-the-way-we-train-associates

Intel. (n.d.). Demystifying the virtual reality landscape. https://www.intel.com/content/www/us/en/tech-tips-and-tricks/virtual-reality-vs-augmented-reality.html

ITU News. (2019, May 29). "The future is better than you think:" Predictions on AI and development from Ray Kurzweil. https://news.itu.int/the-future-is-better-than-you-think-predictions-on-ai-and-development-from-ray-kurzweil/

Kopanakis, J. (2018, June 14). 5 real-world examples of how brands are using big data analytics. *Mentionlytics.* https://www.mentionlytics.com/blog/5-real-world-examples-of-how-brands-are-using-big-data-analytics/

Latha, T. A., & Lakshmi, N. N. (2016). Improving operational efficiencies using big data for financial services. *IOSR Journal of Computer Engineering, 18*(4), 75–77.

Lazzarotti, J. J., & Gavejian, J. C. (March 15, 2019). State law developments in consumer privacy. *The National Law Review.* https://www.natlawreview.com/article/state-law-developments-consumer-privacy

Maerowitz, S. (2018, February 6). 4 ways machine learning may soon solve (some of your) PR problems. *PRNews.* https://www.prnewsonline.com/heyward-machine-learning-pr

Mander, J. (2016, June 9). Internet users have average of 7 social accounts. *Global Web Index.* https://blog.globalwebindex.com/chart-of-the-day/internet-users-have-average-of-7-social-accounts/

Marr, B. (2018, May 21). How much data do we create every day? The mind-blowing stats everyone should read. *Forbes*. https://www.forbes.com/sites/bernardmarr/2018/05/21/how-much-data-do-we-create-every-day-the-mind-blowing-stats-everyone-should-read/#4d83f60f60ba

Marr, B. (2019, July 19). The important difference between virtual reality, augmented reality, and mixed reality. *Forbes*. https://www.forbes.com/sites/bernardmarr/2019/07/19/the-important-difference-between-virtual-reality-augmented-reality-and-mixed-reality/#4089116535d3

Martin, N. (2019, February 8). Did a robot write this? How AI is impacting journalism. *Forbes*. https://www.forbes.com/sites/nicolemartin1/2019/02/08/did-a-robot-write-this-how-ai-is-impacting-journalism/#f76ffc977957

Melendez, S. (2019, March 2). A landmark Vermont law nudges over 120 brokers out of the shadows. *Fast Company*. https://www.fastcompany.com/90302036/over-120-data-brokers-inch-out-of-the-shadows-under-landmark-vermont-law

Metz, C. (2020, June 16). Riding out quarantine with a chatbot friend: "I feel very connected." *The New York Times*. https://www.nytimes.com/2020/06/16/technology/chatbots-quarantine-coronavirus.html

Miglani, S. (2016, October 24). Big data and small data: What's the difference? *Dataversity*. https://www.dataversity.net/big-data-small-data/

Muehlhauser, L. (2015, November 10). *Intelligence explosion FAQ*. Machine Intelligence Research Institute. https://intelligence.org/ie-faq/9

Newell, A. (1981). A textbook that points the way. *Contemporary Psychology*, *26*(1), 50–51. https://doi-org.proxy-remote.galib.uga.edu/10.1037/019640

Nguyen, M. H. (2020, January 23). The latest market research, trends, and landscape in the growing AI chatbot industry. *Business Insider*. https://www.businessinsider.com/chatbot-market-stats-trends

O'Carroll, B. (2020, January 31). What are the 3 types of AI? A guide to narrow, general, and super artificial intelligence. *Codebots*. https://codebots.com/artificial-intelligence/the-3-types-of-ai-is-the-third-even-possible

Oracle. (n.d.). *What is big data?* https://www.oracle.com/big-data/what-is-big-data.html

Palenchar, M. J. (2009). Historical trends of risk and crisis communication. In R. L. Heath, & H. D. O'Hair (Eds.), *Handbook of risk and crisis communication* (pp. 31–52). Routledge.

Perry, T. S. (2016). Virtual reality goes social. *IEEE Spectrum*, *53*(1), 56–57. https://doi.org/10.1109/MSPEC.2016.7367470

Peterson, S. M., Furuichi, E., & Ferris, D. P. (2018). Effects of virtual reality high heights exposure during beam-walking on physiological stress and cognitive loading. *PLoS ONE*, *13*(7), 1–17. https://doi-org.proxy-remote.galib.uga.edu/10.1371/journal.pone.0200306

Rogers, S. (2018, December 4). What is mixed reality and what does it mean for enterprise? *Forbes*. https://www.forbes.com/sites/solrogers/2018/12/04/what-is-mixed-reality-and-what-does-it-mean-for-enterprise/#760eddd85df9

Sanchez-Vives, M.V., & Slater, M. (2005). Opinion: From presence to consciousness through virtual reality. *Nature Reviews Neuroscience*, *6*(4), 332–339. https://doi-org.proxy-remote.galib.uga.edu/10.1038/nrn1651

SAS. (n.d.) Machine learning: What it is and why it matters. https://www.sas.com/en_us/insights/analytics/machine-learning.html

Semuels, A. (2020, August 6). Millions of Americans have lost jobs in the pandemic-and robots and AI are replacing them faster than ever. *Time*. https://time.com/5876604/machines-jobs-coronavirus/

Shubhendu, S., & Vijay, J. (2013). Applicability of artificial intelligence in different fields of life. *International Journal of Scientific Engineering and Research, 1*(1), 28–35.

Simonite, T. (2016, May 13). Moore's law is dead, now what? *Wired.* https://www. technologyreview.com/2016/05/13/245938/moores-law-is-dead-now-what/

Skyword. (n.d.). Social listening. https://www.skyword.com/marketing-dictionary/ social-listening/

Tanz, J. (2016, May 17). Soon we won't program computers. We'll train them like dogs. *Wired.* https://www.wired.com/2016/05/the-end-of-code/

Techopedia. (2019, February 25). What is a chatbot? https://www.techopedia.com/ definition/16366/chatterbot

Van Looy, J. (2015). Online games characters, avatars, and identity. *The international encyclopedia of digital communication and society* (pp. 1–11). John Wiley & Sons, Inc.

Wendt, Z. (2020, February 14). Extended reality explained: AR, VR & mixed reality technology. *Arrow.* https://www.arrow.com/en/research-and-events/articles/ extended-reality-explained-ar-vr-and-mixed-reality-technology

Whittaker, Z. (2020, January 2). Here's where California residents can stop companies selling their data. *Tech Crunch.* https://techcrunch.com/2020/01/02/california-privacy-opt-out-data/?guccounter=1#:~:text=California's%20Consumer%20Privacy%20Act%20 (CCPA,privacy%20rules%20in%20a%20generation.

Yee, N., & Bailenson, J. (2007). The proteus effect: The effect of transformed self-representation on behavior. *Human Communication Research, 33*(3), 271–290. https://doi-org.proxy-remote.galib.uga.edu/10.1111/j.1468-2958.2007.00299.x

Zak, P. J. (2015). Why inspiring stories make us react: The neuroscience of narrative. *Cerebrum: The Dana Forum on Brain Science, 2015*(2). https://www.ncbi.nlm.nih.gov/pmc/articles/ PMC4445577/

Zhong, C., Chan, H., Karamshuk, D., Lee, D., & Sastry, N. (2017). Wearing many (social) hats: How different are your different social network personae? http://pike.psu.edu/ publications/icwsm17.pdf

15

DARK SOCIAL INFLUENCER ENGAGEMENT IN BRAND COMMUNICATION

Jason Shi-yang Lim, Claresta Si Ya Yeo, Weihui Leow, Xian Hui Ng, and Augustine Pang

Introduction

Increasingly, consumers are seeking immediate and personalized communication with businesses (Facebook, 2018) and organizations are expected to engage customers in a two-way dialogue. Engagement encapsulates "high relevance of brands to consumers and the development of an emotional connection between consumers and brands" (Rappaport, 2007, p. 138). Online engagement connotes commitment to a relationship, "personified by the website or other computer-mediated entities designed to communicate brand value" (Mollen & Wilson, 2010, p. 923).

To engage consumers, businesses are turning to social media influencers (SMIs), who have their own social networks online (Khamis et al., 2016). Growing concerns over privacy and control over online communications have led to the rise of dark social media (Madden, 2012) that facilitate communication in private channels such as WhatsApp and Facebook Messenger.

This chapter attempts to: (1) understand the role of dark social in marketing communication; (2) find out how peer-to-peer communication can enhance engagement; and (3) fill the gap in current literature by developing a dark social influencer engagement framework to help organizations engage audiences and build positive relationships before crisis.

Literature Review

The Rise of Dark Social

Dark social, accounting for 84% of sharing online (RadiumOne, 2016), refers to web traffic that cannot be attributed to a known source (Madrigal, 2012)

DOI: 10.4324/9781003043409-21

that is often from social sharing in private digital channels such as email and instant messaging. It is not measurable by analytics software (Madrigal, 2012) and brands (McMullan, 2016) because "links copied and pasted into emails or instant messages, or shared via text messages" do not contain tracking tags unless they include an Urchin Tracking Module (UTM) code (Parker, 2017).

With 63% of people preferring to share on private messaging apps (Glenday, 2019), dark social is increasingly significant in audience engagement as it provides an avenue for one-to-one interactions that are private and conversational (Wehring, 2019). Organizations thus need a targeted, personalized, and private relationship marketing strategy (Kotler et al., 2017).

Leveraging Influencers

SMIs are "independent third-party endorsers who shape audience attitude" through social media (Freberg et al., 2011, p. 1) with their personable brand of communication, which help organizations engage audiences and build trust (Papasolomou & Melanthiou, 2012). Consumers facing fatigue (Bell, 2012, p. 34) are turning to SMIs for information (Linqia, 2020) as they are viewed as credible and persuasive (Pang et al., 2016).

Many brands work with SMIs to create content and share brand stories (Weinswig, 2016). This has become a cost-efficient alternative in engaging omni-channel customers as a new platform can be expensive and paid media advertising has proven to be mostly ineffective (Devlin, 2016).

We first seek to examine the use of dark social in audience engagement:

RQ1: What role does dark social play in audience engagement?

Relationship Marketing

Commitment-Trust Theory suggests that the key to successful relationship marketing is commitment and trust (Morgan & Hunt, 1994). It encourages brands to cooperate with partners and maintain a long-term relationship, and "view potentially high-risk actions as being prudent because of the belief that their partners will not act opportunistically" (Morgan & Hunt, 1994, p. 22)

Social Exchange Theory suggests that trust is vital for companies, especially in today's digital era (Luo, 2002). Trust in social exchanges is stronger when they are reciprocal rather than negotiated, such as binding contractual agreements as "the risk of giving without reciprocity" will inculcate trustworthiness in both parties (Molm et al., 2000, p. 1422).

Customer Relationship Management focuses on understanding customers, increasing customer retention and developing relationships (Chen & Popovich, 2003).

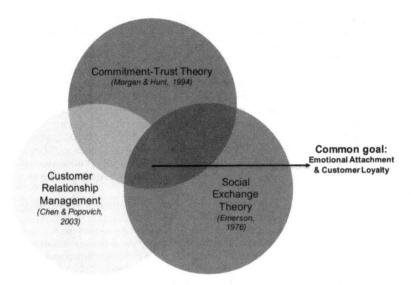

FIGURE 15.1   Relationship Marketing Theories

It is a "process of acquiring, retaining, and partnering with selective customers to create superior value for the company and the customer" through the creation of a mutually beneficial relationship (Parvatiyar & Sheth, 2001, p. 5).

All three theories focus on achieving customer loyalty and emotional attachment through consumer-brand relationship marketing (see Figure 15.1). As customers move from a transactional relationship to a true connection, organizations must deliver value to prolong this relationship (Business News Daily Editor, 2020).

Relationship Marketing Success Drivers and Factors

From these theories, we examine eight key relationship marketing success drivers (see Table 15.1).

These drivers will lead to three success factors – (1) customer trust, (2) customer commitment, and (3) customer reciprocity – resulting in seven desirable relationship marketing outcomes. Here, we focus on three outcomes desired by organizations:

1. *Stable relationship*: A desirable outcome of performance (Kumar et al., 1992), customer relationship stability is linked to commitment and manifests in the customer's low "propensity to leave" the relationship in the near future (Morgan & Hunt, 1994);

TABLE 15.1 Eight Key Relationship Marketing Success Drivers

S. No.	Drivers	Description
1	Seller expertise	"knowledge, experience, and overall competency of seller" (Palmatier, 2008). When a seller is well-informed or trustworthy, the information received is regarded as more consistent, beneficial, and convincing (Dholakia et al., 1977)
2	Relationship benefits	"time-saving, convenience, companionship and improved decision-making" can result in customer commitment, especially when compared with trust (Palmatier, 2008)
3	Shared beliefs and values	"of behaviors, goals and, policies" whether "important or unimportant, appropriate or inappropriate, and right or wrong" (Morgan & Hunt, 1994)
4	One-to-one interaction	a vital factor toward customer commitment and retention (Eckerson & Watson, 2000)
5	Communication (quality and timely) and interaction frequency	repeated interactions allow customers to gain more information, reduce ambiguity about future conduct and increase trust (Palmatier, 2008). High-quality communication leads customers to perceive organizations as knowledgeable and valuable (Peppers & Rogers, 2001)
6	Less opportunistic behavior	"the essence of opportunistic behavior is deceit-oriented violation of implicit or explicit promises about one's appropriate or required role behavior," which leads to a decline in relationship commitment as customers feel that they cannot trust the opposite party (Morgan & Hunt, 1994)
7	Cultural sensitivity	influences trust-building relationship marketing and effectiveness, especially in the international context (Bressan & Signori, 2014)
8	Gratitude	increases when customers deem the relationship marketing to be carried out is based on free will rather than a set of obligations (Emmons, 2004)

2. *Favored status*: Customers with positive relationships with brands would limit their searches for alternative options and be more resistant to the brand's price and competitors (Palmatier, 2008); and

3. *Brand advocacy*: Customers' likelihood to speak positively about the brand and recommend it to others (Palmatier, 2008), which is an indicator of customer loyalty.

Integrated Relationship Management Framework

Based on these success drivers, factors, and outcomes, we propose an Integrated Relationship Management (IRM) Framework as the main theoretical lens for this study. Figure 15.2 illustrates the three-step framework.

Through the lens of the IRM Framework, we further examine:

RQ2: What factors contribute to successful dark social marketing communication for (a) influencer and (b) non-influencer campaigns?

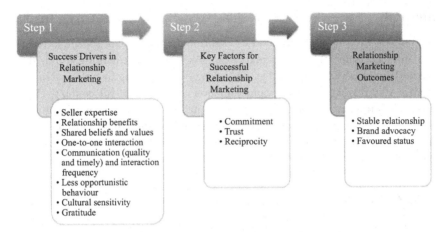

FIGURE 15.2 Integrated Relationship Management Framework

RQ3: What are the risks in dark social marketing communication for (a) influencer and (b) non-influencer campaigns?

Online Brand Community Engagement

Online brand community engagement (OBCE) is the customers' identification with the online brand community (Wirtz et al., 2013, p. 229). OBCE can help reduce the impact of a product-harm crisis (Yuan et al., 2020, p. 43) as committed customers will continue to support the brand (Tax et al., 1998, p. 72).

The New Consumer Journey

Advocacy is a brand's best source of influence and indicator of customer loyalty. This new consumer journey is reflected in the five A's model: (1) *Aware*: Customers' brand awareness; (2) *Appeal*: Customers shortlist brands they like; (3) *Ask*: Customers seek brand information; (4) *Act*: Customers make purchase decisions; and (5) *Advocate*: Customers develop brand loyalty and become advocates (Kotler et al., 2017).

These models demonstrate how relationship building and word-of-mouth communication can lead to brand commitment and advocacy. Organizations can rebound post-crisis when they have more reputation capital to spend (Coombs & Holladay, 2006).

Therefore, dark social marketing may be an effective pre-crisis strategy to build brand-customer relationships.

Method

We employ the case study method to examine the use of dark social platforms and influencers in relationship marketing. As this is an emerging trend, this method serves as a research strategy (Stoecker, 1991) enabling an empirical investigation into this "contemporary phenomenon within its real-life context" (Yin, 2003). A multiple case study approach is adopted to analyze cases with common patterns (Eisenhardt, 1991) as their findings can be considered robust and reliable (Baxter & Jack, 2008), creating a more convincing theory (Eisenhardt & Graebner, 2007).

Data Collection

Four cases of relationship marketing on dark social platforms are studied (see Table 15.2).

TABLE 15.2 Summary of Case Studies Methods

	Involving influencers		Not involving influencers	
	Successful	*Less successful*	*Successful*	*Less successful*
	Marriott International's Travel Brilliantly Campaign	Adidas's Tango Squads	Hellmann's WhatsCook Campaign	ASOS on WeChat
Platform	Snapchat	WhatsApp, Facebook Messenger	WhatsApp	WeChat
Data collection	December 2014– February 2015	July 2016–April 2017	May 2014	April 2014–May 2016
Data source	• Marriott International's social media • Marriott International website • Alexa • Google trends using search term "Marriott International" • Customer Quotient US Report 2016 • Customer Quotient UK Report 2016	• Adidas main website • Alexa • Google trends using search terms "Adidas" and "Adidas Tango Squads" • 2017 MBLM brand intimacy	• Hellmann's Brazil website • Google trends using search terms "WhatsCook" and "Hellmann's" • Warc marketing report • Unilever 2014 annual report • Agency report by CUBOCC (Hellmann's Brazil)	• ASOS's WeChat • ASOS's China website • ASOS annual report 2014, 2015, and 2016 • Baidu index using search term "ASOS"

Cases

Marriott International's Travel Brilliantly Campaign

In December 2014, Marriott partnered with four influencers in a Snapchat campaign and recorded over 24.1 million views.

Adidas's Tango Squads

Adidas formed squads of 100 to 250 youths in 15 cities worldwide through WhatsApp and Facebook Messenger in July 2016. The squads were reduced in December 2018 as it was difficult to measure engagements.

Hellmann's WhatsCook Campaign

In May 2014, Hellmann's launched a 10-day campaign on WhatsApp in Brazil to provide personalized cooking advice. They reached over 5 million people with 13,000 registrants.

ASOS on WeChat

ASOS utilized WeChat to target Chinese consumers in 2013. However, the campaign flopped, ASOS suffered losses and closed its China operations in May 2016.

Data Analysis

As primary data from dark social campaigns is not trackable to non-primary users, the cases are analyzed in detail using documentary information. Two sets of data are collected and analyzed.

Data Set 1

Organizations and influencers' online content for the campaigns are collected. Documentation of the campaigns and screenshots of the content posted by the organizations, influencers, and external parties, such as annual, brand, and campaign reports, and news articles, were collected. This set of data is used to examine the cases for the relationship marketing strategies, the use of influencers, and the campaign effectiveness.

Data Set 2

Engagement metrics (i.e., number of page views per user, bounce rate, the time users spend on the site), traffic trends (i.e., number of global internet audience that visited the site), and traffic sources (i.e., how and where audiences arrive on the campaign site) for the corporate websites are obtained through Alexa. Online search trends on related keywords, such as organization and campaign names are also tracked using Google Trends and Baidu Index. As the use of Google is limited in China, Baidu Index is used for the ASOS on WeChat case. Baidu is the leading search engine in China, handling about 80% of China's web searches (Ovide, 2016). This set of data to determine online brand awareness, interest, and engagement during the campaigns serve as proxies to assess campaign outcomes.

According to Yin (2003), the preferred analytic strategy for case study analysis is relying on theoretical propositions to guide the analysis by comparing the data to the underlying propositions. Here, the cases are qualitatively and quantitatively analyzed and matched with the IRM Framework. Data set 1 is examined for relationship marketing factors and the use of influencers on the campaigns, which are then categorized according to the success drivers in the IRM Framework. Both data sets are used to evaluate the campaign outcomes, which are mapped to the relationship marketing outcomes in the IRM Framework. The data is analyzed for patterns across all four cases to identify factors that led to the campaign's success or failure and the impact of leveraging influencers.

Findings

RQ1 asks what role does dark social play in marketing communications.

Personalization in Long-Term Relationship Building

All four case studies showed that dark social allows for private and personalized conversations. In Hellmann's campaign, chefs utilized WhatsApp to connect with participants, who remained engaged for 65 minutes, on average. The campaign was successful as it had "real conversations and connections" (Uchino, 2014, p. 22).

Marriott's *Travel Brilliantly* campaign demonstrated that dark social can, through influencers, increase brand interest. Website analytics showed a 57.7% increase in the amount of time target audiences spent on Marriott's website; justifying the campaign's success in relationship building.

However, it is important to note that this may also result in unsustainability, serving as a potential threat to the viability of dark social marketing campaigns.

Unsustainability in Dark Social Relationship Marketing

Adidas' *Tango Squad* campaign used the squads' networks to enhance customer outreach and while there were no privacy concerns, Adidas struggled in measuring the campaign's engagement success. Hellman's had to reduce the campaign to keep the number of participants under control.

ASOS's WeChat failure illustrated how the traditional one-way approach of pushing out messages was ineffective for dark social campaigns. However, leveraging influencers could mitigate this limitation. Marriott's influencers went beyond what the company alone could have achieved, based on the one-to-many engagement model. RQ1 has shown that while dark social allows organizations to better engage audiences through personalized interactions, the sustainability of the campaigns may be limited.

RQ2 asks what factors contribute to the success of dark social marketing for (a) influencer and (b) non-influencer campaigns.

Extending Reach by Leveraging Influencers

Both Marriott and Adidas used influencers to extend their reach. Marriott's influencers frequently conversed with followers on Snapchat. Similarly, Adidas' football enthusiasts co-created content and shared them with their social networks.

Increased Relevance of User-Generated Content

User-generated content (UGC) has become increasingly relevant for consumers, as seen in Hellmann's campaign. Participants shared their dish online, which went viral as it was relevant to the wider public. In Marriott's case, audience participation in decision-making led to increased engagement; it also helped them appreciate the brand's expertise and shared values.

Cultivating a Win-Win Relationship

Based on the IRM Framework, a win-win relationship is cultivated when a positive outcome is achieved through successful relationship marketing.

By providing expert cooking tips, Hellmann's offered relationship benefits that led to trust in the brand and fostered a sense of gratitude; participants shared their stories online about the campaign as a form of reciprocity. ASOS's case illustrated the need for tangible relationship benefits to attain the desired outcomes. The infrequency in providing this contributed to its failure in forging customer relationships.

Marriott allowed audiences to be part of the storytelling experience. They also witnessed Marriott's genuine care for its customers. Marriott could implement several Snapchat campaigns with the same group of influencers, who created content that suited the audience. In contrast, Hellmann's was unable to achieve this level of sustainability due to the limitations mentioned in RQ1. RQ2 illustrated that dark social campaigns leveraging influencers are successful because they extend reach to a wider audience, help organizations cultivate a win–win relationship with consumers, and facilitate UGC that is more relevant and engaging for audiences.

RQ3 asks what the risks of dark social marketing for (a) influencer and (b) non-influencer campaigns are.

Loss of Control over UGC

One of the risks in dark social is a potential loss of control over the content. For Hellmann's and Adidas, including audiences in the content creation led to less control and affected their campaign's effectiveness. However, Marriott was able to work with influencers to restrict the locations to a selected list of Marriott properties and successfully guided the narrative. Hence, it may be argued that dark social communication should be guided both at the brand and influencer levels for effective control.

Lack of Cultural Sensitivity

Cultural sensitivity is an important aspect of relationship building, especially in international relationship marketing (Bressan & Signori, 2014). Most of ASOS WeChat updates were translated promotional messages for its United Kingdom audience, making them culturally irrelevant to the Chinese audience. In contrast, Hellmann's observed locals' habits and tastes. This shows that without personalized local content, organizations fail to build trust, particularly on dark social.

Failure to Align with Audiences

Utilizing influencers may lead to a risk of not aligning with the main target audience, which was found to be key to an effective dark social campaign. While Adidas granted Tango Squad members direct access to the brand, it did not benefit the campaign's target audience – the influencers' social contacts. This resulted in low website visitor loyalty rates and brand intimacy.

Marriott strengthened its relationship with its target audience by providing benefits such as the "experience" of overseas travel via interactions with the influencer. This demonstrates the importance of relationship benefits and brand alignment with the audience in dark social marketing.

Overtly Opportunistic Behavior

The exhibition of opportunistic behavior can also hinder dark social campaigns. ASOS appeared interested only in sales targets rather than fulfilling customers' needs. In contrast, Adidas's and Marriott's use of influencers as a bridge between the organization and customers allows organizations to appear less overtly opportunistic. RQ3 outlined the potential pitfalls and risks in dark social campaigns. Organizations utilizing dark social platforms, with or without influencers, should ensure control over UGC, avoid exhibiting overly opportunistic behavior, and demonstrate sensitivity to cultural differences.

Discussion

Dark social is increasingly prevalent as an engagement platform. It allows for more natural communication as conversations are carried out in private, highlighting the importance of word-of-mouth in shaping customer attitudes and behaviors.

Influencers have become key trusted information sources in the consumer decision process. Consumers can easily research products online and reach out to their network. Therefore, UGC is a key area that communications professionals will have to pay attention to (Forbes, 2020). The IRM Framework is designed to examine how influencers affect consumers' and marketers' decisions.

Dark Social Influencer Engagement Framework

Based on insights from the case studies on the factors required for successful OBCE on dark social, we propose a Dark Social Influencer Engagement Framework to guide the use of dark social and influencers in relationship marketing and SMI strategies (see Figure 15.3). It aims to help organizations attain greater marketing communication and engagement success at the pre-crisis stage by establishing a benefit-exchange relationship championed by influencers.

The framework consists of three campaign design phases – pre-campaign, campaign, and post-campaign – that form the OBCE processes for dark social influencers and are the key factors for success. The first phase details a three-step pre-campaign planning process: (1) identifying marketing objectives; (2) identifying dark social platforms; and (3) determining dark social measurement metrics.

The second phase pertains to the implementation of a dark social influencer campaign and adapts key elements from the IRM Framework and the five A's model. Based on the IRM Framework, satisfaction of the key success drivers is essential to achieve the desired outcomes in customer brand engagement on social media.

This framework presents the customer path as a continuous loop. It looks beyond the purchase decision and toward stable relationships, favored status, and brand advocacy as the end goal. This is based on the nature of dark social influencer marketing communications observed from the case studies. The case studies start the cycle with advocacy from influencers to the target audience, driving them through the customer journey with the aim of eventually creating

A *5-Step* Campaign Design

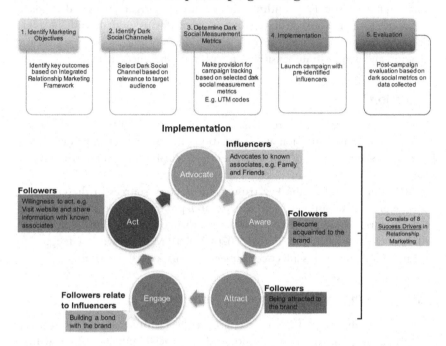

FIGURE 15.3 Dark Social Influencer Engagement Framework

advocates out of them and initiating another cycle of successful relationship management outcome with them now as influencers.

This cycle of OBCE will benefit the organization during a product-harm crisis. The community's commitment can alleviate the consequence of negative brand-related information and enhance the influence of positive brand-related information. Hence, we have renamed and repositioned the stages to create a loop between the *act* and *advocate* stages in the framework, illustrating that dark social influencer engagement begins and ends with advocacy.

The customer journey in the framework includes five stages:

1. *Advocate*: Advocate to known associates, e.g., followers, family, and friends;
2. *Aware*: Known associates become acquainted with the brand;
3. *Attract*: Known associates start to be attracted to the brand through communication materials, experiences, and reviews by influencers (who can be their friends and peers from the online community);
4. *Engage*: Known associates start to approach influencers for more information and seek their opinions and recommendations. This key process in the journey is marked by a star;

5. *Act*: Known associates build a positive relationship with the brand. Following this, they become a brand advocate through positive stakeholder engagement with the brand, which leads them back to stage 1, *Advocate*, now as influencers and the process continues.

Similar to the five A's model, this OBCE process can expand and/or narrow depending on the interests of known associates once the advocates start interacting with them. The framework also considers unknown associates, i.e., non-followers, who may have gotten to know the brand through peers or members of their online communities (who are not brand advocates).

The framework's final phase refers to post-campaign measures that evaluate the campaign's effectiveness based on data collected from metrics designed and implemented in the first two phases.

The proposed framework lays out the process of converting audiences into potential customers and, subsequently, brand advocates. The dark social and influencer marketing communication strategies are applicable as part of the organization's communication strategy toward a private and conversational approach in relationship building among its customers.

Conclusion

This exploratory study aims to shed light on how dark social platforms can be used to create communication messages that build a strong relationship with consumers. However, there is significant untapped potential in utilizing dark social to meet relationship management objectives. Hence, this study lays out a framework as a preliminary guide to help communications professionals implement a dark social influencer marketing communication campaign.

As dark social campaigns are untraceable to non-primary users, this study was limited to the use of proxies such as secondary data, analysis reports, and Alexa data on the organization's main corporate website. Another limitation of the study is that the data was drawn from 2016. Even with this methodological limitation, we argue it does not invalidate our study. We contend that the data provided a preview of the emergence of dark social, and the framework we developed provides a viable model to study the impact. For future research, scholars can look into better alternatives for analyzing dark social campaigns, including the insertion of tracking tags into web links in messages that can be shared via dark social platforms to obtain more precise data for evaluation. This study sought to analyze cases through the IRM Framework, but it would be worthwhile to examine dark social marketing communications via other pre-crisis communication theories to gain further insights into its potential in the area of marketing communications.

References

Baxter, P., & Jack, S. (2008). Qualitative case study methodology: Study design and implementation for novice researchers. *The Qualitative Report, 13*(4), 544–559. https://doi.org/10.46743/2160-3715/2008.1573

Bell, I. B. (2012). Create a buzz around your business through influence marketing: Interview with Mark W. Schaefer, author of return on influence. *Strategic Direction, 28*(9), 33–36. https://doi.org/10.1108/02580541211256549

Bressan, F., & Signori, P. (2014). Get off to a good start. International relationship marketing in emerging markets. *Procedia-Social and Behavioral Sciences, 150,* 1230–1239. https://doi.org/10.1016/j.sbspro.2014.09.139

Business News Daily Editor. (2020, February 13). Consumers have humanlike relationships with brands. https://www.businessnewsdaily.com/2821-consumers-relationships-brands.html

Chen, I. J., & Popovich, K. (2003). Understanding customer relationship management (CRM): People, process and technology. *Business Process Management Journal, 9*(5), 672–688. https://doi.org/10.1108/14637150310496758

Coombs, W. T., & Holladay, S. J. (2006). Unpacking the halo effect: Reputation and crisis management. *Journal of Communication Management, 10*(2), 123–137. https://doi.org/10.1108/13632540610664698

Devlin, K. (2016, March 30). The influencer impact on Instagram. *IBM Watson Customer Engagement.* https://www.ibm.com/blogs/watson-customer-engagement/2016/03/30/the-influencer-impact-on-instagram/

Dholakia, R. R., & Sternthal, B. (1977). Highly credible source: Persuasive facilitator of persuasive liabilities?. *Journal of Consumer Research, 3* (March), 223–232.

Eckerson, W., & Watson, H. (2000). *Harnessing customer information for strategic advantage: Technical challenges and business solutions.* The Data Warehousing Institute.

Eisenhardt, K. M. (1991). Better stories and better constructs: The case for rigor and comparative logic. *Academy of Management Review, 16*(3), 620–627. https://doi.org/10.5465/amr.1991.4279496

Eisenhardt, K. M., & Graebner, M. E. (2007). Theory building from cases: Opportunities and challenges. *Academy of Management Journal, 50*(1), 25–32. https://doi.org/10.5465/amj.2007.24160888

Emmons, R. A. (2004). The Psychology of Gratitude: An Introduction. In R. A. Emmons & M. E. McCullough (Eds.), The psychology of gratitude (pp. 3-16). Oxford University Press. https://doi.org/10.1093/acprof:oso/9780195150100.003.0001

Facebook. (2018, October 2). *3 ways messaging is transforming the path to purchase.* https://www.facebook.com/business/news/insights/3-ways-messaging-is-transforming-the-path-to-purchase

Forbes Communication Council & Rafael Schwarz (2020, September 8). *The power word-of-mouth has in marketing, and how to cultivate it.* https://www.forbes.com/sites/forbescommunicationscouncil/2020/09/08/the-power-word-ofmouth-has-in-marketing-and-how-to-cultivate-it/#5b8908c43df0

Freberg, K., Graham, K., McGaughey, K., & Freberg, L. A. (2011). Who are the social media influencers? A study of public perceptions of personality. *Public Relations Review, 37*(1), 90–92. https://doi.org/10.1016/j.pubrev.2010.11.001

Glenday, J. (2019, March 25). 63% of people prefer to share content on "dark social" channels. *The Drum.* https://www.thedrum.com/news/2019/03/25/63-people-prefer-share-content-dark-social-channels

Khamis, S., Ang, L., & Welling, R. (2016). Self-branding, "micro-celebrity" and the rise of social media influencers. *Celebrity Studies, 8*(2), 191–208. https://doi.org/10.1080/19392397.2016.1218292

Kotler, P., Kartajaya, H., & Setiawan, I. (2017). *Marketing 4.0 moving from traditional to digital.* John Wiley & Sons, Inc.

Kumar, N., Stern, L. W., & Achrol, R. S. (1992). Assessing reseller performance from the perspective of the supplier. *Journal of Marketing Research, 29*(2), 238–253. https://doi.org/10.1177/002224379202900208

Linqia. (2020). *The state of influencer marketing 2020.* https://www.linqia.com/insights/the-state-of-influencer-marketing-2020/

Luo, X. (2002). Trust production and privacy concerns on the internet: A framework based on relationship marketing and social exchange theory. *Industrial Marketing Management, 31*(2), 111–118. https://doi.org/10.1016/S0019-8501(01)00182-1

Madden, S. (2012, February 5). How companies like Amazon use big data to make you love them. *Co.Design.* https://www.fastcodesign.com/1669551/how-companies-like-amazon-use-big-data-to-make-you-love-them

Madrigal, A. C. (2012, August 12). Dark Social: We have the whole history of the web wrong. *The Atlantic.* https://www.theatlantic.com/technology/archive/2012/10/dark-social-we-have-the-whole-history-of-the-web-wrong/263523/

McMullan, C. (2016, October 17). What is "Dark Social" and why are Adidas using it?. *Digital Sport.* http://digitalsport.co/what-is-dark-social-and-why-are-adidas-using-it

Mollen, A., & Wilson, H. (2010). Engagement, telepresence and interactivity in online consumer experience: Reconciling scholastic and managerial perspectives. *Journal of Business Research, 63*(9–10), 919–925. https://doi.org/10.1016/j.jbusres.2009.05.014

Molm, L. D., Takahashi, N., & Peterson, G. (2000). Risk and trust in social exchange: An experimental test of a classical proposition. *American Journal of Sociology, 105*(5), 1396–1427. https://doi.org/10.1086/210434

Morgan, R. M., & Hunt, S. D. (1994). The commitment-trust theory of relationship marketing. *Journal of Marketing, 58*, 20–38. https://doi.org/10.1177/002224299405800302

Ovide, S. (2016, June 7). China has moved on without Google. *Bloomberg.* https://www.bloomberg.com/opinion/articles/2016-06-07/google-doesn-t-need-china-any-more-than-china-needs-it

Palmatier, R. W. (2008). *Relationship marketing.* Marketing Science Institute.

Pang, A., Yingzhi Tan, E., Song-Qi Lim, R., Yue-Ming Kwan, T., & Bhardwaj Lakhanpal, P. (2016). Building effective relations with social media influencers in Singapore. *Media Asia, 43*(1), 56–68. https://doi.org/10.1080/01296612.2016.1177962

Papasolomou, I., & Melanthiou, Y. (2012). Social media: Marketing public relations' new best friend. *Journal of Promotion Management, 18*(3), 319–328. https://doi.org/10.1080/10496491.2012.696458

Parker, S. (2017, February 7). Why your business can't ignore Dark Social. *Hootsuite.* https://blog.hootsuite.com/dark-social/

Parvatiyar, A., & Sheth, J. N. (2001). Customer relationship management: Emerging practice, process, and discipline. *Journal of Economic and Social Research, 3*(2), 1–34.

Peppers, D., & Rogers, M. (2001). *One to one B2B: Customer development strategies for the business-to-business world,* Doubleday.

RadiumOne. (2016). The dark side of mobile sharing. https://www.marketingmag.com.au/hubs-c/89-mobile-sharing-happens-via-dark-social-report/

Rappaport, S. D. (2007). Lessons from online practice: New advertising models. *Journal of Advertising Research, 47*(2), 135–141. https://doi.org/10.2501/S0021849907070158

Stoecker, R. (1991). Evaluating and rethinking the case study. *The Sociological Review, 39*(1), 88–112. https://doi.org/10.1111/j.1467-954X.1991.tb02970.x

Tax, S. S., Brown, S. W., & Chandrashekaran, M. (1998). Customer evaluations of service complaint experiences: Implications for relationship marketing. *Journal of Marketing, 62*(2), 60–76. https://doi.org/10.1177/002224299806200205

Uchino, T. (2014, September 30–October 1). Hellmann's Whatscook [Conference presentation]. SM2 Innovation Summit, New York City. https://www.mmaglobal.com/files/Tuesday_9.40_Unilever.pdf

Wehring, O. (2019, December 10). "The shift we're seeing is towards more personal and private social networks" – just-drinks speaks to Diageo's chief digital officer, Ben Sutherland – Part 1. *just-drinks.com*. https://www.just-drinks.com/interview/the-shift-were-seeing-is-towards-more-personal-and-private-social-networks-just-drinks-speaks-to-diageos-chief-digital-officer-ben-sutherland-part-i_id129450.aspx

Weinswig, D. (2016, October 5). Influencers are the new brands. *Forbes*. https://www.forbes.com/sites/deborahweinswig/2016/10/05/influencers-are-the-new-brands/#4a1de9ad7919

Wirtz, J., Ambtman, A. D., Bloemer, J., Horváth, C., Ramaseshan, B., Klundert, J. V. D., & Kandampully, J. (2013). Managing brands and customer engagement in online brand communities. *Journal of Service Management, 24*(3), 223–244. https://doi.org/10.1108/09564231311326978

Yin, R. K. (2003). *Case study research* (3rd ed.). Sage.

Yuan, D., Lin, Z., Filieri, R., Liu, R., & Zheng, M. (2020). Managing the product-harm crisis in the digital era: The role of consumer online brand community engagement. *Journal of Business Research, 115*, 38–47. https://doi.org/10.1016/j.jbusres.2020.04.044

SECTION IV

Areas of Application

SECTION IV-A

Areas of Application: Corporate

16

CORPORATE CASE CHAPTER: IT'S WAR

The New Dilemma for Corporations and Social Issues

Richard Levick

The Internet has changed everything. Power now resides in the grassroots more so than in Washington or Wall Street. Virtually every major social issue including the anti-GMO, sugar, and fracking movements, climate change, the Keystone Pipeline, #MeToo, and #BLM have been born at the grassroots and, within years, blossomed into powerful social movements forcing corporations to increasingly take sides.

How do companies maximize shareholder value while minimizing brand risk at a time when a generation demands that brands stand for *something* while at the same time GOP leaders recently announced that "woke" companies are *the* issue they can win on in 2022? How do we lead?

Brand neutrality is dead. Since the murder of George Floyd and the insurrection of January 6, everything is different. There is "no middle ground" as Merck CEO Ken Frazier and former American Express CEO Ken Chenault have forcefully articulated (Stankiewicz, March 31, 2021). Companies may not want to be pulled into politics because it's not a winning proposition – but they also cannot avoid it. Like Missourians caught between the Union and the Irregulars during the Civil War, we've become ensnared by the battle.

The Arc of History

In 2010, after *Citizens United* (Lau, December 12, 2019), the unintended consequences of the Supreme Court's split decision to find First Amendment rights in corporations also meant that companies would have First Amendment *responsibilities*. Going forward, companies would be judged not just for their brands but for their political activity. The Court majority's assumption that independent

DOI: 10.4324/9781003043409-23

spending would be transparent first proved to be incorrect but is lately becoming a transparency albatross for companies. The good government NGO Public Citizen recently identified the corporations that collectively spent $50 million funding candidates supporting voter restrictions. Popular Information – with their two-person staff – has been doing such a remarkable job tracing the issue of corporate PAC funding since before January 6, 2021 that the traditional media *follows them.* Since 2019, the Center for Political Accountability has been making formerly opaque 527 contributions public. If you fund them, you now own the consequences.

Political contributions have become the new supply chain liability. But so is your DEI, environmental footprint, labor practices, and more. Like it or not, corporations may not be the new "woke parallel government" as Senator Mitch McConnell (R- KY) has said, but they are judged by the company they keep and the things they do *outside* of what they sell.

Milton Friedman's truism, that "a firm's sole responsibility is to its shareholders," may have once been true, but how can you reconcile that to an age when brand neutrality is dead – and younger consumers expect their brands to have a purpose?

The New Rules

How does a company walk the tightrope that looks more like a Gordian knot? Here are a few rules to get you started:

1. *With apologies to Rod Serling, you have entered the perception zone.* The first casualty of war is truth; on high-tension issues such as universal suffrage, truth is not going to be a defense. The Georgia law is complex; in some ways, it extends voting hours and access, and in others, clearly targets traditional Democratic strongholds. If your company is going to weigh in on a highly controversial issue, make sure your team is interdisciplinary. If just your public affairs or legal executives are looking at it, they will miss perception issues the way your brand and communications professionals alone would miss legal issues. Silos are no longer an effective way to make decisions.

2. *As author Simon Sinek writes, "start with the why"* (Sinek, 2009). It is no longer satisfactory to be in business to maximize profits. What is your raison d'etre? Michelin sells safety, not tires. Starbucks sells a lifestyle. Apple sells creativity. Nike sells the inner athlete. Each company knows precisely why it is in business, which allows them to approach theology more than just a brand. When you read something in the Bible that you don't believe, you don't lose faith. You just carve out that one story, that parable. The same is true for brands that are disciplined enough to have an umbilical connection with their customers. Know thyself and to your customers be true.

3. *Track trends like your business life depends on it. It does.* Too many businesses look at big data like an accountant. Instead, look upon it as if you worked at the CIA. A couple of coincidences may portend a trend. Have people who understand business, politics, and the cycles of history track the news including, of course, social activity. Lots of screaming can often be ignored, while sometimes a single high-authority blogger or lawsuit can mean change is afoot.

4. *There is no Las Vegas – nothing "stays here."* What happens in Georgia can happen in Texas. What happens to a competitor can happen to you. Plan for it and view what happens to others as your laboratory. Activists look for companies domiciled in battleground states. If you are headquartered there, there is no excuse to be surprised.

5. *Don't fret calls for boycotts.* The reason the 1965–1970 grape boycott led by Cesar Chavez captured the nation's attention and changed buying habits is because of the rarity of the strategy. Today, there is a call for a national boycott nearly every hour, one of the most recent, of course, being against Major League Baseball. Calling for a boycott is a click away; acting on them takes both tremendous organizing and a public willing to be impassioned by the cause more than the inconvenience of new purchasing habits. Over the past few years, boycotts and threats of boycotts by more progressive causes seem to be more effective than those by the right. Nike did exceptionally well after calls for boycotts when it embraced Colin Kaepernick. It was no accident. They planned for it.

6. *Be genuine.* Calls for boycotts against Chick-fil-A have never had any momentum, despite their original anti-LGBTQ position. Why? Not because of the politics of it, but because they effectively explained their position as stemming from sincere religious beliefs, not bias or hatred. Audiences can parse issues and intent, given enough time and the integrity of the company.

7. *Nothing is an accident.* In 1971, Saul Alinsky wrote *Rules for Radicals* (Alinsky, 1989). While few activists today have read it, they have all stolen pages from its playbook and applied them to the Internet. There are no accidents. Have you wondered why apologies don't work as well as they used to? It's because part of the playbook is to leak damaging information *after* the apology. You need to think like activists. Be in their head. "What would I do if I were them?"

8. *Pick your issues carefully.* Companies should not become vocal on many issues. It is just another version of brand extension; the market won't support it. Be strategic about your ESG and CSR, so you have a history of investment before an issue lands at your front door. If you do comment on an issue, be deliberate and highly selective.

9. *Issues about protecting democracy and Civil Rights are sacred.* There is a scale of social issues that the general public cares about – fewer care about corporate tax cuts, more about minimum wage, and more still about the environment. Support for democracy, franchise, and diversity are at the top of the list. Treat them with reverence.

10. *DEI and PAC contributions are indivisible.* You cannot support diversity and inclusion while also supporting candidates who perpetuate voter suppression any more than you could support Members of Congress who failed to vote for presidential certification. There is no wiggle room. The murder of George Floyd and the #BLM protests are a movement – not a moment. There is no going back. DEI support and support for the universal franchise are inseparable.

The country is split but it is not as divided as you think. Large numbers of Americans support the direction the country has taken, including infrastructure, diversity, vaccinations, environmental stewardship, and other issues. Your goal is not to find a place to offend no one but to understand your corporate "tribe" – and speak to them as your partner to the future.

References

Alinsky, S. D. (1989). *Rules for radicals: A practical primer for realistic radicals.* Vintage Books.

Lau, T. (2019, December 12). Citizens united explained: The 2010 Supreme Court decision further tilted political influence toward wealthy donors and corporations. The Brennan Center for Justice. https://www.brennancenter.org/our-work/research-reports/citizens-united-explained

Sinek, S. (2009). Start with why: How great leaders inspire everyone to take action. Simonsinek.com. https://simonsinek.com/product/start-with-why/

Stankiewicz, K. (2021, March 31). "There is no middle ground" – Black CEOs urge companies to oppose restrictive voting laws. *CNBC.com.* https://www.cnbc.com/2021/03/31/ken-frazier-black-ceos-urge-firms-to-oppose-restrictive-voting-laws.html

17

SOCIAL MEDIA AND THE ROLE OF INTERNAL COMMUNICATION FOR CRISIS PREVENTION AND MANAGEMENT

Silvia Ravazzani and Alessandra Mazzei

Introduction

Internal crisis communication is a growing area of academic interest and organizational practice, intended as "the communicative interaction among managers and employees, in a private or public organisation, before, during and after an organisational or societal crisis" (Johansen et al., 2012, p. 271). The internal dimension of crises puts the accent on the crisis-related voices, reactions, and behaviors of top managers, middle managers, and employees who become both senders and receivers of crisis communication (Frandsen & Johansen, 2017; Heide & Simonsson, 2014; Mazzei et al., 2012; Strandberg & Vigsø, 2016) as well as crisis sensemakers and sensegivers (Kim, 2018; Ravazzani, 2016). All this can impact the development of and less or more successful exit from a crisis. Despite its fundamental role, the study of internal crisis communication lags behind the more established area of external crisis communication (Frandsen & Johansen, 2011; Goodman, 2018; Heide & Simonsson, 2014; Kim, 2018; Ravazzani, 2016; Strandberg & Vigsø, 2016).

The need to know more about internal crisis communication is even more pressing if we consider the mounting rise of social media where "organizations no longer have a choice about whether to integrate social media into crisis management; the only choice is how to do so" (Jin et al., 2014, p. 76). Social media has reshaped internal communication (Ewing et al., 2019) and created new challenges. Social media in fact can become triggers and accelerators of organizational crises (Coombs, 2014; Frandsen & Johansen, 2017), for example, by creating more and more possibilities for employees to engage in negative word of mouth (Austin & Jin, 2017; Lee & Suh, 2020). This requires important

DOI: 10.4324/9781003043409-24

crisis prevention work to be accomplished through internal communication. Moreover, social media plays a pivotal role in the management of crises where, for example, different social media platforms can be used by organizations internally for crisis information sharing and collective sensemaking, and externally for encouraging employees to become influential advocates (Mazzei et al., 2019b; Opitz et al., 2018). Nonetheless, research focusing on how internal communication and social media have become intertwined in times of crisis is notably scarce.

It is against this backdrop that this chapter intends to advance research on internal crisis communication, looking in particular at the growing role and impact of social media. To do so, first, the chapter deals with crisis prevention by illustrating the drivers leading employees to perform appropriate or inappropriate communication behaviors (ECBs) and the role of social media policies (SMPs) to turn employees into advocates and not adversaries of the organization on social media. Second, the chapter delves into crisis management by considering the role and uses of internal and external social media in crisis situations and presenting the results from a qualitative study carried out in the context of the 2020 COVID-19 pandemic. The chapter ends with reflections on how social media can both enhance and complicate internal crisis communication and implications for practice.

Internal Communication for Crisis Prevention on Social Media

This section investigates the role of internal communication for crisis prevention by looking in particular at crises deriving from inappropriate behaviors enacted by employees on social media. When on social media, voluntarily (mostly anonymously) or involuntarily, employees can break laws, e.g., on property rights; violate ethical norms, such as transparency and honesty; or damage the company's reputation by spreading negative messages (Krishna & Kim, 2015; Mazzei & Butera, 2016; Rokka et al., 2014).

Employees can spread online brand-related messages via personal social media accounts and anonymous outlets (Ravazzani & Mazzei, 2018; Rokka et al., 2014), becoming advocates or adversaries of their company (Opitz et al., 2018). Damage to reputation caused by employee attacks on social media is higher compared to that caused by consumer complaints (Opitz et al., 2018).

Therefore, a company should pay attention to all possible strategies capable of preventing inappropriate critical behaviors of employees on social media. In the following, we first discuss the drivers for employee communication behaviors in general and in crisis situations specifically. Second, we illustrate the role of SMPs conceived as part of internal communication strategies to prevent inappropriate ECBs in online outlets.

The Drivers of ECBs: A Holistic and Enabling View of the Process

ECBs stem from a complex process including several steps: from contextual organizational conditions to employee cognitive-emotional states, employee attitudes, employee behavioral intentions, and employee behaviors (Mazzei & Ravazzani, 2015). This holistic view suggests that it is not possible to obtain desirable ECBs by means of prescriptions and control, but indirectly through the management of the organizational contextual conditions that foster employee cognitive-emotional states, attitudes, behavioral intentions, and final behaviors. An enabling approach is the most appropriate, i.e., based on internal communication conditions that promote voluntary and discretionary ECBs in favor of the company (Mazzei & Ravazzani, 2017).

Employee engagement triggers appropriate ECBs (Kang & Sung, 2017; Ruck et al., 2017), whereas employee disengagement is linked to the expression of dissent outside of the organization (Kassing, 2011). There are three main managerial levers affecting the organizational contextual conditions affecting ECBs (Mazzei et al., 2019a): the kind of relational approach with employees, ranging from hierarchical to inclusive; the human resources management approach, ranging from accommodative to developmental; and the organizational justice climate, ranging from unfair to fair.

But what about ECBs specifically in crisis situations? Three factors have proved playing a fundamental role, as detailed in the following.

Relationship Quality as a Foundation for Appropriate ECBs during Corporate Crises

The qualitative case study of a multinational company (Mazzei et al., 2012) shows that the good quality of relationships between a company and its employees results in appropriate ECBs while decreasing the occurrence of inappropriate communication actions. The studied company experienced a major accident in one of its plants, leading to the death of a young blue collar. Its employees, far from blaming the company for the accident, acted as company advocates when reporting the unfortunate episode to the news media.

This study shows how continuous, transparent, and consistent internal communication together with the company's actions and multiple managerial practices toward work safety had cultivated quality relationships with employees that positively impacted ECBs in crisis situations. A corporate policy that is preventive rather than curative contributes to building strong positive relationships between an organization and its employees, and eventually prevents negative affective and behavioral reactions both on social media and in any other kind of communication situation when a crisis occurs.

Perceived Authenticity and Employee Empowerment to Increase Employee Positive Megaphoning during Corporate Crises

Another study investigated the impact of perceived authenticity of organizational behaviors and employee empowerment, next to the already discussed factor of relationship quality, on employee megaphoning during crises (Mazzei et al., 2019b). An organization is perceived as authentic when it shows truthfulness, transparency, and consistency in its behaviors. Empowerment is a process of psychological state manifested in meaning, competence, self-determination, and impact. Megaphoning is the likelihood of employees' voluntary information forwarding or information sharing about organizational strengths (accomplishments) or weaknesses (problems), therefore it can be positive or negative (Kim & Rhee, 2011).

The study was based on a survey administered to 306 employees working full-time in a semiconductor company experiencing a corporate crisis, which also generated negative media coverage. Results suggest that both the organizational authentic behaviors and the degree of employee empowerment increased the occurrence of positive megaphoning while reducing the intentions to enact negative megaphoning. Furthermore, a significant mediation impact of the organization-employee relationship on ECBs related to the crisis was found.

SMPs to Prevent Negative ECBs on Social Media

As mentioned in the introduction, social media today represents one of the most important arenas for crisis generation and management. An increasing number of companies therefore have been developing guidelines and codes of conduct to support employees in their use of social media, the so-called SMPs (Mazzei & Butera, 2016). SMPs are issued to prevent the risks of inappropriate behavior of employees on social media from causing damage to the company. However, an internal SMP could also boost online ECBs that strengthen reputation and increase positive dialogue with stakeholders. Used as an internal communication tool, an SMP can help employees avoid the above-described risks and encourage them to actively contribute to reputation building and advocacy efforts in crisis situations.

A qualitative content analysis of the internal SMPs of 25 companies belonging to the 2015 Fortune 500 ranking investigated their SMPs' objectives and approaches. The study examined whether the objective was risk prevention or stakeholder dialogue for corporate advocacy; and whether the approach taken to govern employee online behaviors was mainly based on prescriptions and prohibitions or on the enablement of discretionary and voluntary ECBs on social media.

Results show that 25 of the studied SMPs aim at preventing legal risks; 24 ethical and reputational risks too; and 13 productivity and security risks additionally. Only 13 SMPs seem to embrace the importance of social media for strengthening reputation and stakeholder relationships. Some companies set forth a series of measures aimed at encouraging the adoption of consistent online ECBs. Among these, eight companies created an explicit link between their SMPs and the corporate values. Nineteen include suggestions for improving employees' online communications skills, and 14 mention counseling services. Only three SMPs include specific social media training targeted to all employees. Finally, 15 SMPs specify negative consequences for employees who communicate online inappropriately, i.e., personal legal responsibility in case, e.g., an employee violates privacy statements. Seventeen SMPs refer to various forms of organizational sanctions, from suspension to dismissal. But this can be risky because SMPs that prescribe and punish can also provoke resistance and cynicism.

On the whole, the analysis shows that many companies, even those with the best performance, are missing out on an important opportunity. On the one hand, they simply enact SMPs to prevent corporate risks, but do not take the opportunity to encourage employees to enact voluntary advocacy efforts. On the other hand, they seek to rule the online behavior of employees mainly through threatening negative consequences and sanctions. SMPs should be rather exploited as part of crisis prevention and integrated with the internal communication strategy to be effective in enhancing consistent and authentic ECBs on social media.

Internal Communication for Crisis Management on Social Media

Internal communication is equally important for managing crises while they are occurring. Social media can play a pivotal role in these communicative processes. Yet, there is an open debate around whether employee social-mediated crisis communication represents an opportunity or a threat to organizations (Opitz et al., 2018). In the following, we shortly frame internal and external social media in relation to internal crisis communication and then exemplify their possible role and uses through a qualitative study carried out in the context of the COVID-19 pandemic.

Internal and External Social Media to Support Internal Crisis Communication

Literature focused on *internal social media* highlights that the transformations brought about through the incorporation of social media in organizations are greater than simply adding an additional channel (Huang et al., 2013). Internal social media deeply impacts the scope and frequency of horizontal, upward, multivocal, co-produced, and participatory communication (Madsen, 2018; Treem & Leonardi, 2013). Being a rich, dialogical, and humanized communication channel driving employee engagement (Ewing et al., 2019), in crisis situations, internal social media enriches internal crisis communication in such new ways, supporting typical communicative processes such as (Frandsen & Johansen, 2017; Mazzei & Ravazzani, 2011, 2013; Strandberg & Vigsø, 2016): sharing crisis information or instructions across the organization; upholding employee motivation and engagement; providing space for internal disclosure and sensemaking; guiding employee communication behaviors; as well as handling internal interpretations of false information, rumors, and crisis response strategies applied in external crisis communication.

In the context of crises, *external social media* can function as an additional leverage for managing employee storytelling and supportive behaviors in view of all stakeholders, which contributes to safeguarding corporate trust and reputation (Ewing et al., 2019). Organizations have the opportunity to mobilize employees communicatively and benefit from their characteristics of highly credible organizational advocates (Opitz et al., 2018; Rokka et al., 2014). Opitz et al. (2018) have demonstrated that employee adversary messages on social media can seriously damage organizations while also suggesting that employees may be employed as advocates when involved in the official crisis communication strategy.

On the whole, research so far has just started rooting out the specific role and uses of social media in internal crisis communication. So how in practice can internal and external social media be leveraged in support of internal communication during a crisis?

Leveraging Internal and External Social Media for Employee Crisis Sensemaking and Storytelling: Learnings from the COVID-19 Pandemic in Italy

To answer this question, we present key insights from a very recent study carried out at the beginning of the COVID-19 pandemic in Italy to collect the immediate perceptions and experiences of internal communication managers.[1] The crisis commenced at the end of February 2020 and rapidly led to serious preventive and containing measures including a lockdown of public offices and spaces (http://www.salute.gov.it/portale/nuovocoronavirus/homeNuovoCoronavirus.jsp?lingua=english) and the largest national experimentation of smart-working solutions to protect employees, their families, and society at large. In the first half of April 2020, we conducted two focus group interviews with fourteen organizations; and ten interviews (one video interview and nine email interviews) between mid-April and early May 2020. After offering an overview of internal crisis communication's general role and objectives, we focus on the role and uses of internal and external social media.

According to interviewees, internal crisis communication played a pivotal role in supporting managers and employees in their efforts to cope with the sudden crisis situation. One interviewee described internal communication "playing a virtuous circular role: from being the 'final point' of connection with colleagues to being the 'new starting point' after listening to them." In collaboration with the top management and Human Resources and Information Technology, internal communication rapidly revised priorities and implemented ad hoc instruments and initiatives. In the words of one interviewee: "on the one hand we felt the need to re-focus internal communication objectives and priorities on the basis of the changed conditions, while on the other continuing along the path taken towards listening and engaging colleagues."

The interviewees highlighted the following key internal crisis communication objectives:

- supporting employees through continuous and pragmatic information and training (e.g., on safety measures, smart-working practices, business decisions);
- reassuring employees while also reducing physical and psychological distance through optimistic and empathic communication, building also a larger sense of unity and pride in the country and its resilient capacities;
- listening to employees' needs and expectations through two-way communications, also to improve internal crisis communication strategy.

In order to meet such objectives, the organizations under study leveraged a variety of digital instruments that were either newly introduced or further strengthened: SMS, instant messaging, Intranet, and internal social media. In most cases, for the first time, digital internal (crisis) communication took precedence over more traditional tools in order to reach and engage employees, especially the majority working from home. As explained by one interviewee, "in conditions where you cannot turn to paper, you have to invent completely new roads (...), a new internal communication approach completely different from routine." Dedicated mobile apps were also created for employees working on site and not having access to a computer.

Internal social media was described as central for sharing timely crisis information, for supporting employees emotionally and practically, and for soliciting internal sensemaking and storytelling. In terms of content, internal social media platforms were widely used to share newsletters, booklets, top management video messages, technical and educational videos, or audio podcasts; but also entertainment content, personal stories, photos, and solidarity messages among employees themselves. Interviewees highlighted a surprising rise in the use of these platforms by employees: e.g., "interactions in internal social media tripled" and "user-generated content represents the majority of the content published."

While not having internal social media as such, some organizations heavily relied on the corporate Intranet where special sections were created for collecting news on the pandemic, communicating corporate initiatives and external communication campaigns (e.g., donations to hospitals, employee volunteering), and gathering employee needs, questions, and stories through initiatives labeled, e.g., #stayincontactwithyourcompany. In the experience of the internal communication managers involved, the Intranet and internal social media in those few weeks have seen a quick evolution from being simple collectors of corporate resources and work-related conversations to becoming a truly human "digital workplace."

External social media was described as fundamental too in the accounts of the interviewees. First of all, internal communication managers themselves used external social media to share internal initiatives and stories. For example, one interviewee shared on LinkedIn accounts of how internal communication was managed in their organization to "tell the behind the scenes of what has happened in these weeks (...), (accounts that) are worth because they sanction the key landmarks of internal crisis communication (...) and give it a shape through words and voice." Other organizations launched internal communication campaigns encouraging employees themselves to share selfies, photographs, and positive messages on social media. An example was the opening of a Spotify channel gathering internal testimonies as "a way to leave a trace, an emotional relief valve, to tell the story of the accomplishments" of employees and "to channel spontaneous communication (...) to the outside world, to the media." Thus, external social media platforms were employed as vehicles for employee crisis storytelling, crossing the organizational boundaries and creating emotional closeness between employees and families, friends, and external stakeholders in general. On the negative side, in the experience of a few both internal and external social media were used for voicing dissent about the perceived unequal treatment between smart-working employees and those on the field.

On the whole, our findings underline that internal and external social media were extensively used for effective crisis management and communication in this particular emergency context, and more intensively than in previous crises. Interviewees even indicated that, in their prospective intentions, this sudden evolution and intense use of digital and multimedia tools for internal communication are not anymore to be seen as temporary and emergency-bound, but will certainly continue to remain crucial for internal communication also in the post-emergency as a sign of "new human and professional relationships based on quality and true sharing" and of the organization being always "close" to and "in constant conversation" with its managers and employees. To conclude, in the words of one interviewee, "these have always been the guiding principles for internal communication ... the COVID-19 crisis has heightened awareness among all of the relevant roles of internal communication."

Summing up Reflections

This chapter has clarified the pressing need for internal communication to embrace and manage effectively social media, internally and/or externally, before and/or during a crisis. Social media appears to be deeply interwoven with organizations and the way they enact and undergo communication, especially considering that employees are active sensemakers and sensegivers in crisis situations (Frandsen & Johansen, 2011; Kim, 2018; Mazzei et al., 2012; Ravazzani, 2016) as well as impactful stakeholders and communicators in a crisis (Opitz et al., 2018) who may either cause social media crises with inappropriate behaviors or participate as supportive or damaging voices in already ongoing crises. Therefore, effective and cognizant use of social media for crisis prevention and management is a priority for internal communication that cannot wait anymore and demands supplementary scholarly attention.

On the practical side, organizations are advised to be more sensible to the risks posed by negative ECBs as well as to the opportunities offered by appropriate ECBs, in particular when employees act as authentic and credible ambassadors in crisis situations. For this reason, an enabling and empowering approach should guide the creation of SMPs and other internal communication initiatives for crisis prevention, to be capitalized in crisis situations by integrating employee voices in official crisis communication responses. So in the context of crisis management too, organizations should not overlook the power of social media since they may facilitate a more humanized and participatory internal crisis communication supporting employee sensemaking and resilient response to crises, as well as more effective and choral external crisis communication.

Note

1 This study was conducted by the Centre for Employee Relations and Communication (CERC) @Università IULM. It was supported by the Working Group Employee Communication (WG_EC) @CERC, Università IULM, editions 2018–2020 and 2020–2022, and by the Department of Business LECB "Carlo A. Ricciardi" @ Università IULM. CERC company partners for WG_EC 2018–2020 and 2020–2022 are: Campari Group, Coopselios, Cromology Italia, E.ON, Eni, Ferrero, Gruppo Unipol, LFoundry, MM, Sanofi, Saras, Sella, Snam, Takeda, Unicoop Firenze, Vodafone Italia, and Whirlpool EMEA.

References

Austin, L., & Jin, Y. (2017). Social media and crisis communication. Explicating the social-mediated crisis communication model. In A. Dudo, & L. Kahlo (Eds.), *Strategic communication. New agendas in communication* (pp. 163–186). Routledge.

Coombs, W. T. (2014). *Ongoing crisis communication: Planning, managing, and responding.* SAGE.

Ewing, M., Men, L. R., & O'Neil, J. (2019). Using social media to engage employees: Insights from internal communication managers. *International Journal of Strategic Communication, 13*(2), 110–132. https://doi.org/10.1080/1553118X.2019.1575830

Frandsen, F., & Johansen, W. (2011). The study of internal crisis communication: Towards an integrative framework. *Corporate Communications: An International Journal, 16*(4), 347–361. https://doi.org/10.1108/13563281111186977

Frandsen, F., & Johansen, W. (2017). *Organizational crisis communication.* SAGE.

Goodman, M. B. (2018). Communicating strategic change: The continuum of reputation, issues management, and crisis management is built on a positive corporate culture. In L. Austin, & Y. Jin (Eds.), *Social media and crisis communication* (pp. 41–56). Routledge.

Heide, M., & Simonsson, C. (2014). Developing internal crisis communication. New roles and practices of communication professionals. *Corporate Communications: An International Journal, 19*(2), 128–146. https://doi.org/10.1108/CCIJ-09-2012-0063

Huang, J., Baptista, J., & Galliers, R. D. (2013). Reconceptualizing rhetorical practices in organizations: The impact of social media on internal communications. *Information & Management, 50*(2–3), 112–124. https://doi.org/10.1016/j.im.2012.11.003

Jin, Y., Liu, B., & Austin, L. (2014). Examining the role of social media in effective crisis management: The effects of crisis origin, information form, and source on publics' crisis responses. *Communication Research, 41*(1), 74–94. https://doi.org/10.1177/0093650211423918

Johansen, W., Aggerholm, H. K., & Frandsen, F. (2012). Entering new territory: A study of internal crisis management and crisis communication in organizations. *Public Relations Review, 38*(2), 270–279. https://doi.org/10.1016/j.pubrev.2011.11.008

Kang, M., & Sung, M. (2017). How symmetrical employee communication leads to employee engagement and positive employee communication behaviors. *Journal of Communication Management, 21*(1), 82–102. https://doi.org/10.1108/JCOM-04-2016-0026

Kassing, J. W. (2011). *Dissent in organizations.* Polity Press.

Kim, Y. (2018). Enhancing employee communication behaviors for sensemaking and sensegiving in crisis situations. Strategic management approach for effective internal crisis communication. *Journal of Communication Management, 22*(4), 451–475. https://doi.org/10.1108/JCOM-03-2018-0025

Kim, J. N., & Rhee, Y. (2011). Strategic thinking about employee communication behaviour (ECB) in public relations: Testing the models of megaphoning and scouting effects in Korea. *Journal of Public Relations Research, 23*(3), 243–268. https://doi.org/10.1080/1062726X.2011.582204

Krishna, A., & Kim, S. (2015). Confessions of an angry employee: The dark side of de-identified "confessions" on Facebook. *Public Relations Review, 41*(3), 404–41. https://doi.org/10.1016/j.pubrev.2015.03.001

Lee, S. B., & Suh, T. (2020). Internal audience strikes back from the outside: Emotionally exhausted employees' negative word-of-mouth as the active brand-oriented deviance. *Journal of Product & Brand Management.* https://doi.org/10.1108/JPBM-02-2019-2239

Madsen, T. M. (2018). Participatory communication on internal social media – A dream or reality?: Findings from two exploratory studies of coworkers as communicators. *Corporate Communications: An International Journal, 23*(4), 614–628. https://doi.org/10.1108/CCIJ-04-2018-0039

Mazzei, A., & Butera, A. (2016). Brand consistent behavior of employees on social media: The role of social media governance and policies. *Mercati & Competitività, The Journal of the Italian Society of Marketing, 4*, 85–106. https://doi.org/10.3280/MC2016-004006

Mazzei, A., Butera, A., & Quaratino, L. (2019a). Employee communication for engaging workplaces. *Journal of Business Strategy, 40*(6), 23–32. https://doi.org/10.1108/JBS-03-2019-0053

Mazzei, A., Kim, J.-N., & Dell'Oro, C. (2012). Strategic value of employee relationships and communicative actions: Overcoming corporate crisis with quality internal communication. *International Journal of Strategic Communication, 6*(1), 31–34. https://doi.org/10.1080/1553118X.2011.634869

Mazzei, A., Kim, J.-N., Togna, G., Lee, Y., & Lovari, A. (2019b). Employees as advocates or adversaries during a corporate crisis. The role of perceived organizational authenticity and employee empowerment. *Sinergie Italian Journal of Management, 37*(2), 195–212. https://doi.org/10.7433/s109.2019.10

Mazzei, A., & Ravazzani, S. (2011). Manager-employee communication during a crisis: The missing link. *Corporate Communications: An International Journal, 16*(3), 243–254. https://doi.org/10.1108/13563281111156899

Mazzei, A., & Ravazzani, S. (2013). Employee communicative actions and companies' communication strategies to mitigate the negative effects of crises. In G. Gonçalves, I. Somerville, & A. Melo (Eds.), *Organisational and strategic communication research: European perspectives* (pp. 47–67). Livros LabCom.

Mazzei, A., & Ravazzani, S. (2015). A holistic model of behavioural branding: The role of employee behaviours and internal branding. *Micro & Macro Marketing, 24*(2), 239–262. https://doi.org/10.1431/80828

Mazzei, A., & Ravazzani, S. (2017). Internal branding and employee brand consistent behaviours: The role of enablement-oriented communication. *Mercati & Competitività. The Journal of the Italian Society of Marketing, 1*, 121–139. https://doi.org/10.3280/MC2017-001007

Opitz, M., Chaudhri, V., & Wang, Y. (2018). Employee social-mediated crisis communication as opportunity or threat? *Corporate Communications: An International Journal, 23*(1), 66–83. https://doi.org/10.1108/CCIJ-07-2017-0069

Ravazzani, S. (2016). Exploring internal crisis communication in multicultural environments: A study among Danish managers. *Corporate Communications: An International Journal, 21*(1), 73–88. https://doi.org/10.1108/CCIJ-02-2015-0011

Ravazzani, S., & Mazzei, A. (2018). Employee anonymous online dissent: Dynamics and ethical challenges for employees, targeted organisations, online outlets and audiences. *Business Ethics Quarterly, 28*(2), 175–201. https://doi.org/10.1017/beq.2017.29

Rokka, J., Karlsson, K., & Tienari, J. (2014). Balancing acts: Managing employees and reputation in social media. *Journal of Marketing Management, 30*(7/8), 802–827.

Ruck, K., Welch, M., & Menara, B. (2017). Employee voice: An antecedent to organisational engagement? *Public Relations Review, 43*(5), 904–914. https://doi.org/10.1016/j.pubrev.2017.04.008

Strandberg, J. M., & Vigsø, O. (2016). Internal crisis communication: An employee perspective on narrative, culture, and sensemaking. *Corporate Communications: An International Journal, 21*(1), 89–102. https://doi.org/10.1108/CCIJ-11-2014-0083

Treem, J. W., & Leonardi, P. M. (2013). Social media use in organizations: Exploring the affordances of visibility, editability, persistence, and association. *Annals of the International Communication Association, 36*(1), 143–189. https://doi.org/10.1080/23808985.2013.11679130

18

FACTORS INFLUENCING CRISIS ARENA CROSSOVERS

The Apple iPhone #ChargeGate Case

Mark Badham, Matias Lievonen,
and Vilma Luoma-aho

Introduction

This chapter addresses crisis situations from an external communication perspective. We build on the conceptualization of arenas in corporate communication literature (Coombs & Holladay, 2014; Frandsen & Johansen, 2010,
2016; Luoma-aho & Juholin, 2017; Luoma-aho & Vos, 2010; Vos et al., 2014)
to introduce *crisis arenas* as dynamic online communicative spaces where stakeholders participate in the formation and expression of mostly negative assessments about issues and which contribute to the social construction and spread
of crises. We take a stakeholder-centered approach to crisis communication
(Fraustino & Liu, 2018) to explore how stakeholders' assessments about organizations and their products communicated online influence the progression of a
crisis within and across arenas. We adopt Coombs' (2007b) definition of a crisis:
"the perception of an event that threatens important expectancies of stakeholders and can seriously impact an organization's performance and generate
negative outcomes" (pp. 2–3). This definition incorporates the idea that a crisis emerges when stakeholders participate communicatively within and across
one or more arenas to complain about a problem perceived to be caused by or
related to an organization.

This chapter contributes to crisis-as-process research (Coombs, 2007b; Fink,
1986; Pang et al., 2014) by shedding light on how a crisis formed in one arena
can cross over synchronously or asynchronously to other arenas, leading to rapid
progression and expansion of a crisis in social media. The Crisis Arena Crossover
(CAC) framework developed in this chapter is based on the following four propositions. First, the predominance of negative engagement in arenas forms crisis

DOI: 10.4324/9781003043409-25

arenas. Second, a crisis dominating one arena may cross over to another arena to form a new crisis arena. Third, the predominance of negative engagement will likely lead to arena crossover. Finally, arena crossover is more likely when there are one or more of these factors in two or more arenas: the issue being discussed is popular, similar, and clearly identifiable as a problem, stakeholder connectors are present, and the organization, as a stakeholder in the problem, remains largely silent.

We examine Apple iPhone's 2018 #ChargeGate case as an illustrative example to explore these four propositions. This case reveals key factors that influenced the formation of multiple crisis arenas and the crossover between them. The CAC framework offers crisis communication managers an analytical tool with which to monitor and manage the development of crisis arenas and their spread through social media.

Literature Review

Arenas for Issues and Crises

The concept of *arenas* that has emerged within corporate communication research (Coombs & Holladay, 2014; Frandsen & Johansen, 2010, 2016; Luoma-aho & Vos, 2010; Luoma-aho et al., 2013; Raupp, 2019) points to offline and online places where stakeholders meet for the purpose of interacting with one another and with entities, such as organizations, that are directly or indirectly the target of their discussion. Luoma-aho and colleagues introduce *issue arenas* as real or virtual spaces in online media environments where topics of shared interests are debated by stakeholders and organizations (Luoma-aho & Vos, 2010; Luoma-aho et al., 2013; Vos et al., 2014). In this chapter, we refer to an issue as "a point of contention between two or more parties" (Coombs et al., 2019, p. 33), which can also refer to stakeholder perceptions of problems that may directly or indirectly implicate an organization and its products. Frandsen and Johansen (2010, 2016) apply the *arena* concept to the study of crisis communication to define a rhetorical arena as a space that opens during a crisis and where different stakeholders, including the news media, offer a multivocality of perspectives through which stakeholders interpret an organizational problem. Coombs and Holladay (2014) extend the idea of *rhetorical arenas* to explain how they can be fragmented into sub-arenas where a crisis is discussed. They refer to *sub-arenas* as forums for expression or "spaces" where publics may express and hear ideas about a crisis.

We build on these theories about arenas to define a *crisis arena* as a dynamic online communicative space where stakeholders participate in the formation and expression of mostly negative assessments about an issue that often affects and/or is affected by an organization. Here we make two observations. First, a crisis arena contributes to the social construction and spread of a crisis. Second, issue arenas are linked to crisis arenas; just as issues and crises share a dynamic relationship (i.e., an issue can progress into a crisis and a crisis can regress into an issue status), issue arenas can transition into crisis arenas and vice versa. We contend that an issue arena is a space specialized by the themes or topics that define the issue and a crisis arena is a space specialized by the themes or topics that define the crisis. Because arenas are bounded and defined by issue or crisis themes, a simple way to identify an arena is to look for hashtags and other social markers linked to a theme and around which an arena can exist, morph and expand online.

Negative Engagement Enables Crisis Arenas

We argue that stakeholder sentiment within arenas, ranging between positive and negative assessments about an issue and/or organization, contributes to the formation of a crisis arena. Crisis emotions literature (Choi & Lin, 2009; Jin, 2010; Weiner, 1986) has shown that the emotional needs of stakeholders are particularly high during a crisis (Perse et al., 2002). Opinions about organizations that contain emotional content increase the likelihood that they will be shared and disseminated further (Berger & Milkman, 2012). Emotionally charged opinions tend to propagate rapidly in social networks through emotional contagion, which refers to the convergence of one person's emotional state with others' emotional states (Hatfield et al., 1994).

We examine how negative engagement (Lievonen et al., 2018) influences the spread of crises across arenas in the online environment. We contend that stakeholder debates taking place in arenas may merge into and create crisis arenas when negative engagement overtakes positive engagement. In general, we identify negative engagement in arenas as overwhelming communication of negative assessments about an organization and positive engagement as overwhelming communication of positive assessments. We acknowledge that a crisis may emerge and dissipate within an already existing arena, such as when negative engagement begins to dominate that arena and later die out again. In this situation, we would identify the arena as a crisis arena during the period in which negative engagement prevails. While we contend that issue arenas contain both positive and negative engagement in roughly equal measures and that these valence levels fluctuate, they transition into crisis arenas when dominated by negative engagement. Issues can develop into organizational crises primarily when they become more oppositional toward an organization. Accordingly, we put forward the following initial proposition:

> Proposition 1: A crisis arena is identified by the existence of predominantly negative engagement.

Crisis Arena Crossovers

Crisis communication and issues management research have offered some observations of how an issue and a crisis can build and spread across social media (e.g., Jin et al., 2014; Pang et al., 2014). For example, Coombs and Holladay (2012) contend that the trajectory of a crisis is a function of the amount and valence of crisis messages in both traditional news media and social media (p. 211). The concept of issue contagion (e.g., Coombs, 2002) offers some understanding of how an issue can rapidly spread from person to person, much like a virus. We apply the issue contagion concept to the CAC framework to shed light not only on how an issue can rapidly develop into a crisis, but also how a crisis can quickly spread across multiple arenas. While Coombs introduced the idea of a *crossover* to describe how an issue can spread from social media to traditional/legacy news media or vice versa (Coombs & Holladay, 2012, p. 211), we extend this crossover concept to the way an issue and/or a crisis can jump from arena to arena.

Crises often are the result of controversial issues that emerge in social media and travel rapidly through large social networks (Yang & Saffer, 2019). Emotions are a key factor here. Coombs (2014) argues that in a crisis communication process, stakeholder responses, including their emotions, can affect the trajectory of crisis development and shape the outcome of crisis communication. In their study examining how social disapproval spreads online, Wang et al. (2021) found that social media contributes to a greater velocity of opinions, emotionality, and communality.

Nevertheless, crisis communication research has not sufficiently considered how a crisis can spread from one media or channel to another media or channel or from one arena to another arena. Given the porous nature of arenas (i.e., they may dynamically morph and share the same stakeholders and issues under discussion), we offer the following proposition:

> Proposition 2: A crisis dominating one arena may synchronously or asynchronously cross over to another arena to form a new crisis arena.

Building on these first two propositions, we also contend:

> Proposition 3: When negative engagement dominates an arena (i.e., forming a crisis arena), it is more likely to cross over to another arena, thus potentially forming another crisis arena.

Other Factors Contributing to Crisis Arena Crossover

In our final proposition, we point out five other factors contributing to CACs. Figure 18.1 illustrates all six factors in the CAC framework. Though one factor alone is enough to cause a crossover from a crisis arena to another arena, the more factors are present, the more likely crossover will occur, leading to new crisis arenas.

Crisis Arena Crossover (CAC) framework

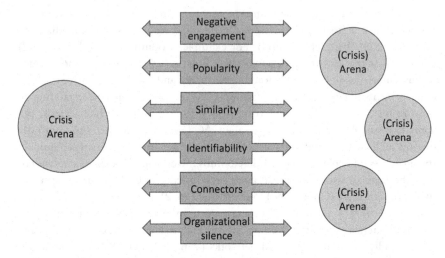

FIGURE 18.1 Factors Influencing Crisis Arena Crossover

Popularity

In our CAC framework, *popularity* refers to a combination of the salience of a problem and the amount of discussion related to it. It also relates to how many people engage in discussions about the problem in the (crisis) arenas. Coombs and Holladay (2012) draw on the observation made by Crable and Vibbert (1985) that issues gain strength when they attract a lot of attention, to argue that the amount of crisis-related messages in social media is an indicator of a crisis trajectory (Coombs and Holladay, 2012, p. 411).

Similarity

If arenas share a similar problem being discussed by arena participants, a crisis developing in one arena may cross over to other arenas. In other words, arenas that share similar issues or crisis themes are more likely to see a crisis crossover between them.

Identifiability

Identifiability refers to stakeholders' personal acknowledgment of an issue, such as through their own encounters with the problem. For example, arena participants with similar experiences of a faulty product can create discussion around that issue in multiple arenas simultaneously and this is conducive to CAC.

Stakeholder Connectors

While there are various types of stakeholders who participate in arenas, some stakeholders act as connectors who spread an issue or crisis within and across arenas. These connectors not only communicate their viewpoints about a crisis within an arena, thus inflaming a crisis in that arena, they also introduce and promote new crisis information within other arenas. In this way, they play a vital linking role between arenas, thus contributing to CAC.

Organizational Silence

When an organization does not adequately engage in arena discussions, where the organization is a stakeholder in the problem being discussed, especially in a developing crisis situation, this can escalate a crisis and manifest negative engagement crossover in multiple arenas. If the organization cannot provide sufficient responses during the crisis build-up, it will likely generate more negative engagement around an issue.

Thus, we offer the following proposition:

> Proposition 4: Crisis arena crossover is more likely when there are one or more of the following factors in two or more arenas: the issue being discussed is popular, similar and clearly identifiable as a problem, stakeholder connectors are present, and the organization, as a stakeholder in the problem, remains largely silent.

Case Study: Apple iPhone #ChargeGate

Introduction

The Apple iPhone #ChargeGate case illustrates how an issue can quickly turn into a crisis while spreading across multiple online arenas. Three days after Apple launched its iPhone XS model on September 21, 2018, XS customers began complaining in Apple's Support Communities (ASC) discussion forum (discussions.apple.com) that there was a problem: the phone did not charge in sleeping mode. Specifically, these complaints dominated the "iPhone XS Max lightning port charging issue" conversation within that forum. An ASC forum participant who was also an Unbox Therapy YouTube channel viewer, wrote to the host of the channel, Lewis Hilsenteger, asking him to try to get Apple to fix the problem. Subsequently, on September 29, Unbox Therapy released a video titled "The iPhone XS Has A Serious Problem..." (see Unbox Therapy, 2018a). The hashtag #ChargeGate was included in the description. This video went viral (to date, there are 9 million views and almost 70,000 comments). So did the hashtag #ChargeGate on Instagram and Twitter.

TABLE 18.1 Progression of Key 2018 #ChargeGate Crisis Events

Apple launches iPhone XS	Complaints begin in Apple support community	Video posted in unbox therapy YouTube channel	#ChargeGate begins trending on Twitter and Instagram	BBC, Business Insider, The Guardian	Apple Hub announces upcoming iOS update to fix #ChargeGate problem	Daily Mail report; Apple launches iOS update to fix the problem
September 21, 2018	September 24	September 29	September 29	October 1	October 2	October 8

Within a few days, legacy news media like the *BBC* (in its Technology News section), *The Guardian* and *Business Insider* began reporting the problem and referred to #ChargeGate. The *Daily Mail* ran a story about #ChargeGate on October 8 and its readers contributed to a discussion about the problem in the comments section linked to the news report. That same day, 18 days after the launch of the iPhone XS, Apple released a new iOS update (iOS 12.0.1) designed to fix the problem. By then, damage to Apple's online reputation had been done. (The sequence of these events can be seen in Table 18.1.)

Negative Engagement Shaping #ChargeGate Crisis Arenas

Next, we address the first proposition as it relates to this case:

A crisis arena is identified by the existence of predominantly negative engagement.

From September 29 onward, Unbox Therapy became overwhelmed with negative engagement related to #ChargeGate and targeted at Apple. In other words, negative engagement dominated the discussion. Accordingly, we identify this channel as a crisis arena within the period of overwhelming negative engagement over the iPhone XS charging problem. We also identify the following as crisis arenas because of predominant negative engagement within those arenas for a period of time: the ASC forum (specifically the "iPhone XS Max lightning port charging issue" conversation within that forum), a discussion forum centered around a news report about #ChargeGate by The *Daily Mail*, and the #ChargeGate discussion on Twitter and Instagram.

#ChargeGate Crisis Arena Crossovers

Next, we address the second and third propositions:

A crisis dominating one arena may synchronously or asynchronously cross over to another arena to form a new crisis arena.

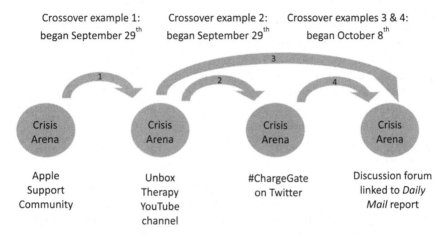

FIGURE 18.2 Apple iPhone #ChargeGate Crisis Arena Crossovers

When negative engagement dominates an arena (i.e., forming a crisis arena), it is more likely to cross over to another arena, thus potentially forming another crisis arena.

Here we illustrate each CAC in sequential order in this case (see Figure 18.2). Originally, the negative engagement process began on September 24 in the ASC forum. When negative engagement overwhelmed this arena, it became a crisis arena. The crisis in this arena began crossing over to the Unbox Therapy arena on September 29 when an ASC forum participant communicated the XS problem to Hilsenteger, thus linking these two arenas with the #ChargeGate theme. This demonstrates the first CAC in this case.

A second crisis crossover was between Unbox Therapy and the #ChargeGate arena on Twitter. Unbox Therapy's video was launched on September 29 and it quickly became viral. That same day #ChargeGate began trending on Twitter. Negative engagement rapidly dominated this arena, thus demonstrating how the #ChargeGate crisis spread from the Unbox Therapy arena to the #ChargeGate arena on Twitter.

A third and fourth CAC took place between the Unbox Therapy arena, the #ChargeGate arena on Twitter, and the discussion forum arena linked to the *Daily Mail* news report. On October 8, the *Daily Mail* published a news report about #ChargeGate. The journalist had seen the Unbox Therapy video and #ChargeGate trending on Twitter. The story referred to how Unbox Therapy had confirmed the charging problem (see Belam, 2018; Villas-Boas, 2018). Readers voiced their opinions in the comments section of this report and negative engagement began to dominate this arena. This demonstrates the crisis crossover between the Unbox Therapy and *Daily Mail* arenas and between the Twitter #ChargeGate and *Daily Mail* arenas.

Other Factors Contributing to Crisis Arena Crossover

We now address the fourth and final proposition:

> *Crisis arena crossover is more likely when there are one or more of the following factors in two or more arenas: the issue is popular, similar, and clearly identifiable as a problem, stakeholder connectors are present, and the organization, as a stakeholder in the problem, remains largely silent.*

Popularity

The iPhone XS charging problem was a popular trending issue in the ASC arena largely because this arena is dedicated to problems associated with Apple issues. Thus the amount of #ChargeGate messages was high. Likewise, with 12 million subscribers at that time, it is not surprising that Unbox Therapy attracted a lot of attention to the issue. The *Daily Mail* arena only attracted ten comments, which suggests this was not necessarily a popular issue in this arena.

Similarity

Discussions in the Unbox Therapy and ASC arenas focused on similar themes related to technology, which contributed to CAC. Discussions on the #ChargeGate arenas on Twitter and Instagram are specifically targeted to the iPhone XS charging problem and thus share similar themes with Unbox Therapy and ASC arenas. As a news outlet, the *Daily Mail* covers a wide variety of issues, which is why news media arenas tend to contribute to a wide spectrum of arena crossovers.

Identifiability

In this case, most participants of the ASC, Unbox Therapy, and Twitter #ChargeGate arenas shared personal experiences of the XS charging problem, commented on others' experiences, and demanded Apple's response.

Connectors

In this case, Unbox Therapy's Hilsenteger and the iPhone XS customer commenting in the ASC arena were *connectors* linking the ASC crisis arena, the Unbox Therapy crisis arena, and subsequently the #ChargeGate crisis arena on Twitter. Thus, both Hilsenteger and this XS customer were instrumental in causing the #ChargeGate crisis to cross over between at least three arenas. A third connector was the *Daily Mail* journalist who linked the discussion arena centered around the news story with both the Twitter #ChargeGate and Unbox Therapy crisis arenas.

Organizational Silence

At the time of the video release in the Unbox Therapy channel, Apple had not released any official statement regarding the charging problem. Although Apple released a software update that eventually fixed the issue, the corporation gave no explanation about the problem or what was actually changed in the software update to fix the problem (Independent, 2018). Apple is well-known for its lack of communication and not keeping its customers informed (Gorman, 2019).

Conclusion

CACs pose emerging challenges for crisis communication managers. The speed with which an issue can develop into a crisis and then jump across multiple arenas should be a concern to all corporate communication practitioners. High levels of negative engagement dominating and crossing over crisis arenas tend to rapidly attract large numbers of peripheral stakeholders into these arenas' orbits, empowering their growth in size and intensity. If not properly managed, they can be especially damaging to organizational reputation.

The CAC framework provides practitioners with an analytical tool with which to gain some foresight and strategic understanding of CACs to help them deal with organizational crises in the online environment. In particular, we propose that crisis managers actively identify and monitor issue and crisis arenas and the factors that influence CACs.

Limitations and Future Research

Future research could further develop this CAC framework in a number of ways. In this chapter, we mostly focused on the macro-level of analysis of crisis communication, in particular the way a crisis progresses as it spills over from one arena to another. However, there is a need for future research to explore the more micro-level process in which a crisis develops within an individual arena, such as the way arena participants debate crisis information before it spills over to another arena. For example, building on our first proposition, future crisis communication studies could contribute to more clarity in the dynamic and fluid relationship between issue arenas and crisis arenas in social media, including how an issue being debated in an issue arena may transition into a crisis played out in a crisis arena, thus exposing the potential for progression of online arena crises affecting organizations.

References

Belam, M. (2018, October 1). IPhone XS and XS Max: "ChargeGate" sees some devices fail to charge. *The Guardian*. https://www.theguardian.com/technology/2018/oct/01/iphone-xs-and-xs-max-chargegate-sees-some-devices-fail-to-charge

Berger, J., & K. Milkman, L. (2012). What makes online content viral? *Journal of Marketing Research, 49*(2), 192–205. https://doi.org/0.1509/jmr.10.0353

Choi, Y., & Lin, Y. H. (2009). Consumer responses to Mattel product recalls posted on online bulletin boards: Exploring two types of emotion. *Journal of Public Relations Research, 21*(2), 198–207. https://doi.org/10.1080/10627260802557506

Coombs, T. W. (2002). Assessing online issue threats: Issue contagions and their effect on issue prioritisation. *Journal of Public Affairs, 2*(4), 215–229. https://doi.org/10.1002/pa.115

Coombs, T. W. (2014). State of crisis communication: Evidence and the bleeding edge. *Research Journal of the Institute for Public Relations, 1*(1). https://prjournal.instituteforpr.org/wp-content/uploads/CoombsFinalWES-1.pdf

Coombs, W. T. (2007b). *Ongoing crisis communication: Planning, managing, and responding* (2nd ed.). Sage.

Coombs, W. T., & Holladay, S. J. (2012). The paracrisis: The challenges created by publicly managing crisis prevention. *Public Relations Review, 38*, 408–415. https://doi.org/10.1016/j.pubrev.2012.04.004

Coombs, W. T., & Holladay, S. J. (2014). How publics react to crisis communication efforts comparing crisis response reactions across sub-arenas. *Journal of Communication Management, 18*(1), 40–57. https://doi.org/0.1108/JCOM-03-2013-0015

Coombs, W. T., Holladay, S. J., & Tachkova, E. (2019). Crisis communication, risk communication, and issues management. In E. Brunner (Ed.), *Public relations theory: Application and understanding* (pp. 31–47). Wiley-Blackwell.

Crable, R. E., & Vibbert, S. L. (1985). Managing issues and influencing public policy. *Public Relations Review, 11*, 3–16. https://doi.org/10.1016/S0363-8111(82)80114-8

Fink, S. (1986). *Crisis management: Planning for the inevitable*. AMACOM.

Frandsen, F., & Johansen, W. (2010). Apologizing in a globalizing world: Crisis communication and apologetic ethics. *Corporate Communications: An International Journal, 15*(4), 350–364. https://doi.org/10.1108/13563281011085475

Frandsen, F., & Johansen, W. (2016). Crisis communication research in Northern Europe. In A. Schwarz, M. W. Seeger, & C. Auer (Eds.), *The handbook of international crisis communication research* (pp. 373–383). John Wiley & Sons.

Fraustino, J. D., & Liu, B. F. (2018). Foundations and frameworks: Audience-oriented approaches and considerations. In L. Austin, & Y. Jin (Eds.), *Social media and crisis communication* (pp. 129—40). Routledge.

Gorman, E. (2019, January 30). Is Apple's communication strategy the real bug? *Lewis*. https://www.teamlewis.com/uk/magazine/is-apples-communication-strategy-the-real-bug/

Hatfield, E., Cacioppo, J. T., & Rapson, R. L. (1994). *Emotional contagion*. Cambridge University Press.

Independent. (2018, October 3). IPhone XS "ChargeGate": Apple reveals fix for handsets that have major charging problem. https://www.independent.co.uk/life-style/gadgets-and-tech/news/iphone-xs-chargegate-not-charging-ios-12-problem-not-working-download-fix-a8566986.html

Jin, Y. (2010). Making sense sensibly in crisis communication: How publics' crisis appraisals influence their negative emotions, coping strategy preferences, and crisis response acceptance. *Communication Research, 37*(4), 522–552. https://doi.org/10.1177/0093650210368256

Jin, Y., Liu, B. F., & Austin, L. L. (2014). Examining the role of social media in effective crisis management: The effects of crisis origin, information form, and source on publics' crisis responses. *Communication Research, 41*(1), 74–94. https://doi.org/10.1177=0093 650211423918

Lievonen, M., Luoma-aho, V., & Bowden, J. (2018). Negative engagement. In K. Johnston, & M. Taylor (Eds.), *Handbook of communication engagement* (pp. 531–548). Wiley Blackwell.

Luoma-aho, V., & Juholin, E. (2017). *Mitattava viestintä.* ProComma Academic.

Luoma-aho, V., Tirkkonen, P., & Vos, M. (2013). Monitoring the issue arenas of the swine-flu discussion. *Journal of Communication Management, 17*(3), 239–251. https://doi.org/10.1108/JCOM-11-2010-0069

Luoma-aho, V., & Vos, M. (2010). Towards a more dynamic stakeholder model: Acknowledging multiple issue arenas. *Corporate Communications: An International Journal, 15*(3), 315–331. https://doi.org/10.1108/13563281011068159

Pang, A., Hassan, A., & Chong, A. C.Y. (2014). Negotiating crisis in the social media environment: Evolution of crises online, gaining credibility offline. *Corporate Communications: An International Journal, 19*(1), 96–118. https://doi.org/10.1108/CCIJ-09-2012-0064

Perse, E., Signorielli, N., Courtright, J., Samter, W., Caplan, S., Lambe, J., & Cai, X. (2002). Public perceptions of media functions at the beginning of the war on terrorism. In B. S. Greenberg (Ed.), *Communication and terrorism* (pp. 39–52). Hampton.

Raupp, J. (2019). Crisis communication in the rhetorical arena. *Public Relations Review, 45*(4), 1–12. https://doi.org/10.1016/j.pubrev.2019.04.002

Unbox Therapy. (2018a, September 29). *The iPhone XS has a serious problem…* [Video file]. https://www.youtube.com/watch?v=J_lRJuQtBmc

Unbox Therapy. (2018b, October 10). *Apple responds to chargegate.* [Video file]. https://www.youtube.com/watch?v=I_gyYjKMN50

Villas-Boas, A. (2018, October 1). Some iPhone XS owners are reporting that their new iPhones have problems charging. *Business Insider.* https://www.businessinsider.com/apple-iphone-xs-not-charging-chargegate-2018-10?r=US&IR=T

Vos, M., Schoemaker, H., & Luoma-aho, V. (2014). Setting the agenda for research on issue arenas. *Corporate Communication: An International Journal, 19*(2), 200–215. https://doi.org/10.1108/CCIJ-08-2012-0055

Weiner, B. (1986). *An attributional theory of motivation and emotion.* Springer.

Yang, A., & Saffer, A. J. (2019). Embracing a network perspective in the network society: The dawn of a new paradigm in strategic public relations. *Public Relations Review, 45*(4), 1–11. https://doi.org/10.1016/j.pubrev.2019.101843

Wang, X., Reger, R. K., & Pfarrer, M. (2021). Faster, hotter, and more linked in: Managing social disapproval in the social media era. *Academy of Management Review.* https://doi.org/10.5465/amr.2017.0375

Areas of Application: Nonprofit

19

NONPROFIT CASE CHAPTER: PETA'S CRISIS HISTORY

A Case Study

Logan White

History

People for the Ethical Treatment of Animals (PETA) is a young nonprofit, founded 40 years ago in 1980. Over the past four decades, PETA has established itself as the world's largest nonprofit animal rights group and the most audacious group of protesters. Its primary goals include stopping animal abuse in laboratory research, the food industry, the fashion world, and entertainment (Kort, 2017).

Co-founders Ingrid Newkirk and Alex Pacheco built PETA upon philosopher, Peter Singer's, radical definition of animal rights in which he directly compares animal exploitation to racism and sexism (Newkirk, n.d.).

Newkirk, currently 70 years old and serving as PETA's president, has been under extreme scrutiny herself. InfluenceWatch describes her as "notoriously anti-humanity." Newkirk stands adamantly behind the aggressive protesting tactics of PETA, estimating she has been arrested herself 40 to 50 times (Sizemore, 2001).

InfluenceWatch describes PETA's tactics as "extremist" and "...designed for the principal purpose of attracting mainstream press attention." From disturbing public performances to insensitive advertisements, PETA utilizes shock value to garner media attention and name recognition.

Contributions

Despite its militant tactics of persuasion, PETA has made great strides in the fight for animal rights that often go unrecognized. Designers BCBG, Guess, and Rebecca Minkoff banned the use of fur in their products, Pepsi and Coca-Cola

DOI: 10.4324/9781003043409-27

stopped animal product testing, Tesla switched to vegan interiors, and General Motors discontinued animal crash testing (PETA). PETA reached these milestones in the past two years alone.

Most notably, PETA spent thirty-six years, almost equivalent to the nonprofit's entire existence, protesting Ringling Brothers and Barnham & Bailey Circus, which was documented chaining, beating, and electrocuting its animals. Largely due to PETA's consistent protesting and exposition, the circus finally shut down in 2017 (Allen, 2017). This is one of the greatest accomplishments of PETA, yet accomplishments like this are not heavily publicized. If they are, they are rarely accredited to PETA.

In contrast, PETA's offensive communications go viral. This does skew the perception of its fight against animal abuse. However, this could also demonstrate PETA's lack of concern about reputation, only about producing results.

Alarming Euthanasia Rates

PETA experienced its most detrimental public controversy of the decade in 2014, when two employees euthanized Maya, the Zarate family's chihuahua. When called to a mobile home in Accomack County, Virginia, Victoria Carey and Jennifer Wood removed Maya from the Zarate's property and euthanized her. Not only did this violate the mandatory five-day waiting period before euthanizing an animal, but the public also questioned why PETA would put down a healthy dog in the first place (*The Guardian*, 2017).

The Zarate family sought $7 million compensation in a lawsuit, the basis of their case exposing the alarming rates at which PETA euthanizes animals (*The Guardian*, 2017). In 2016, PETA euthanized 1,400 of 2,000, or 70%, of the animals in its Norfolk, Virginia shelter. This rate climbed to 72% in 2018 (Llorente, 2017).

PETA fired the two employees and settled the lawsuit in 2017 for $49,000, plus a $2,000 donation to the SPCA in Maya's honor (*The Guardian,* 2017). However, the public still questioned how PETA could destroy animals at this magnitude, while constantly criticizing others. PETA has also publicly stated its controversial belief that it is more humane to euthanize an animal than to cage it while awaiting an unlikely adoption (Winerip, 2013). Thus, it quickly became the public opinion that "PETA kills animals."

Plant Based News asked Newkirk about these alarming statistics, and she explained that PETA is not an animal shelter; it is an animal activist group (Newkirk, 2018). Adoptions are not PETA's specialty, hence the low adoption rate. PETA also offers free euthanasia for families that cannot afford the service for ill pets, heavily skewing the statistics. Furthermore, the animals PETA is given are often in terrible condition from abuse or neglect and must be euthanized.

"It's nice for people who've never worked in a shelter to have this idealistic view that every animal can be saved," said PETA's vice president of cruelty investigation, Daphna Nachminovitch. "They don't see what awful physical and emotional pain these poor dogs and cats suffer" (Winerip, 2013).

Animal activist, Nathan Winograd, defended PETA, stating that no-kill shelters have the "luxury" to refuse euthanization because they turn away the dying animals that PETA puts down humanely (Llorente, 2017). Professor of religion and animal rights, Paul Waldau affirmed that if PETA is receiving animals in the worst conditions, its euthanasia rates will inevitably be much higher than those rescuing the "the golden retrievers of life." However, Waldau recognized the validity of concerns that PETA could be euthanizing less (Markoe, 2015).

While PETA had explanations for much of this controversy, its past radical behaviors prompted the public to distrust its statements. Regardless of the truth, public opinion and perception are incredibly strong forces with the power to adversely affect PETA's animal rights efforts.

Disturbing Veganism Campaign

PETA's advertising campaigns have earned a reputation in public relations history; some as thought-provoking, others as offensive. The consistent use of nudity, gore, and sensitive political topics attracts massive media attention, although predominantly negative. From shocking comparisons of the American Kennel Club to the Klu Klux Klan in 2009, of the poultry industry to the Holocaust in 2016, and of cows in the dairy industry to victims of sexual assault in 2018, there seems to be no boundary PETA is not willing to push (Peirano, 2018).

In January 2019, PETA executed one of its most disturbing veganism campaigns in Sydney, Australia, featuring a fake barbecued dog on a grill surrounded by vegetables. The stunt was meant to promote veganism and demonstrate society's belief that eating certain animals is acceptable, but eating others is unnatural. Passing kids were disturbed, and some were drawn to tears after seeing the setup (Shakhnazarova, 2019).

PETA outreach liaison, Emily Rice, told the *New York Post*, "It's always mixed, it can be confronting to challenge what people think of as normal…but if we manage to plant some seeds and start a conversation about speciesism then that's a good thing" (Graham & Wolfe, 2019).

These campaigns further affirm PETA's goal of bringing as much awareness to its cause as possible. If shock value and negative reactions bring in the most attention, then this strategy could be more valuable than being "liked" by the public.

PETA vs. Irwin

Steve Irwin, also known as "The Crocodile Hunter," was a beloved Australian TV personality and wildlife conservationist. He spent his life advocating for animals and educating on the importance of protecting wildlife. His show on Animal Planet, *The Crocodile Hunter*, followed Irwin into various habitats as he got up close and personal with wild animals. Irwin reached over 500 million people worldwide, educating them about animals they may have previously feared and misunderstood.

At only 44 years old, Irwin was fatally stabbed by the barb of a stingray while filming a documentary in 2006. His unexpected death shocked the public and made headlines across the globe.

On February 22, 2019, what would have been Irwin's fifty-seventh birthday, Google honored the late wildlife activist by featuring him in that day's "Google Doodle" displayed on the search engine's home page. When Google tweeted announcing the tribute, PETA responded with this accusation:

> *"#SteveIrwin was killed while harassing a ray; he dangled his baby while feeding a crocodile & wrestled wild animals who were minding their own business. Today's #GoogleDoodle sends a dangerous, fawning message. Wild animals are entitled to be left alone in their natural habitats."*

PETA's response was viewed as disrespectful and defamatory, heavily implying that Irwin's death was warranted. After receiving over 40,000 negative responses via Twitter alone, PETA released two follow-up tweets defending its previous statement, rather than apologizing to the Irwin family as the public demanded (Bechtel, 2019).

PETA's blatant disregard for the conservation legacy that Steve Irwin left outraged the public. However, it is necessary to examine the controversies that surrounded Irwin during his lifetime. On January 2, 2004, a video surfaced of Irwin bringing his son, Robert, into a crocodile enclosure during one of his shows. This is the incident described in PETA's tweet as "dangling his baby while feeding a crocodile." Irwin insisted that he was in control of the situation and Robert needed to grow up being exposed to crocodiles (Bunting, 2004).

Prominent conservationist, Anneka Svenska, admitted that Irwin did have a difficult time understanding that animals need space. "But at the time he was doing it, it inspired loads and loads of children to go on and work with animals" (BBC News, 2019). Today Irwin's methods would be inappropriate, however, this does not negate the fact that he inspired millions to advocate for wildlife, a mission that PETA says it supports as well.

This is yet another example of organizational misdeed, releasing defensive statements rather than admitting fault. The incident damaged PETA's reputation as an advocate for animals. People questioned if PETA is effective in its mission to end animal suffering, as it seemed in this instance to place more importance on placing blame than making an impact. Twitter users even began to dig up PETA's 2014 euthanasia scandal once again.

Conclusion

PETA does not effectively address controversies or admit fault. Regardless of opinion on certain issues, its exploitation of sensitive topics affects its reputation and credibility, which may also negatively impact the likelihood of people publicly supporting and donating.

However, PETA's radicalism has facilitated actual results and improvements. When assessing PETA's communication strategy, it is important to weigh how important a "likeable" persona should be when the more abrasive strategies are producing desired changes. Being the most publicly adored organization has never been PETA's goal, but it should be concerned when messaging strategies cause its motives to be questioned.

References

Allen, E. (2017). These are all the good things that happened for animals in 2017. *The Independent*. https://www.independent.co.uk/voices/animal-rights-sentience-peta-abattoirs-dolphins-faux-fur-vegan-fashion-a8134536.html

BBC News. (2019). Steve Irwin: How should the crocodile hunter be remembered? https://www.bbc.com/news/newsbeat-47343688

Bechtel, W. (2019). PETA gets blasted for defaming "the crocodile hunter" Steve Irwin. *Drovers*. https://www.drovers.com/article/peta-gets-blasted-defaming-crocodile-hunter-steve-irwin

Bunting, C. (2004). Outrage as Australian "crocodile hunter" dangles his baby son near reptile's jaws. *The Independent*. https://www.independent.co.uk/news/world/australasia/outrage-as-australian-crocodile-hunter-dangles-his-baby-son-near-reptiles-jaws-74696.html

Graham, B., & Wolfe, N. (2019). PETA sparks outrage by barbecuing "Dog" in Mall. *New York Post*. https://nypost.com/2019/01/24/peta-sparks-outrage-by-barbecuing-dog-in-mall/

Influence Watch. People for the Ethical Treatment of Animals (PETA). https://www.influencewatch.org/non-profit/people-for-the-ethical-treatment-of-animals-peta/

Kort, E. D. (2017). People for the Ethical Treatment of Animals (PETA). *Encyclopedia Britannica*. https://www.britannica.com/topic/People-for-the-Ethical-Treatment-of-Animals

Llorente, E. (2017). PETA Shelter was a "slaughterhouse" group claims. *Fox News*. https://www.foxnews.com/us/peta-shelter-was-a-slaughterhouse-group-claims

Markoe, L. (2015). At PETA's shelter, most animals are put down. PETA calls them mercy killings. *The Washington Post*. https://www.washingtonpost.com/national/religion/at-petas-shelter-most-animals-are-put-down-peta-calls-them-mercy-killings/2015/03/12/e84e9af2-c8fa-11e4-bea5-b893e7ac3fb3_story.html

Newkirk, I. (2018). PETA's founder on euthanasia, sea world & vegan activism. Plant Based News. https://www.youtube.com/watch?v=u1pScFMeH2c

Newkirk, I. What as animal liberation? Philosopher Peter Singer's groundbreaking work turns 40. *PETA*. https://www.peta.org/about-peta/learn-about-peta/ingrid-newkirk/animal-liberation/

Peirano, J. (2018). PETA's most shocking campaigns of all time. *Showbiz CheatSheet*. https://www.cheatsheet.com/culture/petas-most-shocking-campaigns-of-all-time-including-a-donald-trump-inspired-ad.html/

Peta. PETA's victories and accomplishments. https://www.peta.org/about-peta/victories/

RT. (2019). Peta faces Twitter wrath for slamming Steve Irwin on deceased star's birthday. https://www.rt.com/news/452246-peta-steve-irwin-twitter-backlash/

The Guardian. (2017). Peta says sorry for taking girl's Pet Chihuahua and putting it down. https://www.theguardian.com/us-news/2017/aug/17/peta-sorry-for-taking-girls-dog-putting-it-down

Shakhnazarova, N. (2019). Hot dog Peta slammed for sick stunt barbecuing a "Dog" in Sydney street leaving young kids in tears. *The Sun*. https://www.thesun.co.uk/news/8268674/peta-slammed-for-sick-stunt-barbecuing-a-dog-in-sydney-street-leaving-young-kids-in-tears/

Sizemore, B. (2001). Animals rights group faulted as "cult-like" and abusive. *The Baltimore Sun*. https://www.baltimoresun.com/news/bs-xpm-2001-01-18-0101180005-story.html

Winerip, M. (2013). PETA finds itself on receiving end of others' anger. *The New York Times*. https://www.nytimes.com/2013/07/07/us/peta-finds-itself-on-receiving-end-of-others-anger.html

20

PHILANTHROPIC CRISIS COMMUNICATION

Brooke W. McKeever and Minhee Choi

Think of the last time you donated to or volunteered for a nonprofit organization... What made you donate money or goods, or what compelled you to volunteer your time and talents?

Was it because you knew someone involved with or affected by the issue? Was it because you recognized a problem and just wanted to do something about it? Was it because you believed in an idea or felt empathy, concern, anger, or some other emotion about a cause or an injustice in the world?

Responses to this question vary, of course, but most people who get involved in philanthropic efforts with nonprofit organizations do so for one or more of those reasons, which are based on relationships, trust, and communication. When a nonprofit organization has a crisis, trust is broken (or at least questioned as details of the crisis come to light), and such damage can hurt the brand of a nonprofit as much if not more so than other entities.

The Nature of Philanthropic Organizations

One of the *key features of being nonprofit* is that these organizations are voluntary and noncoercive (Frumkin, 2002). This means that nonprofits rely on volunteers to donate their hard-earned money or goods or their time and talents to support the mission of the organization. Without this support, most nonprofit organizations would cease to exist.

Another key feature of a nonprofit organization, of course, is that they have no profits to distribute to stakeholders (Frumkin, 2002). Most of the funding that nonprofits amass go back into the mission of the organization – whether that is to support medical research or treatment, to take care of animals that may

DOI: 10.4324/9781003043409-28

not have homes, to clothe or house people who are in need, to support advocacy work related to social injustices, or myriad other causes. Nonprofits do not answer to shareholders, like a publicly traded company. However, nonprofits have numerous other individuals who have a stake in the organization (more on that in a moment).

The third key feature of nonprofits is that they operate without simple, clear lines of ownership or accountability (Frumkin, 2002). This means nonprofits vary tremendously in terms of size, organization, structure, daily operations, and more. These differences make it hard to generalize for all nonprofits, but the commonalities mentioned here make the industry similar enough to make comparisons, especially when it comes to crisis communication.

Related to these key *differences*, another noticeable feature for those who have worked for nonprofit organizations is that philanthropic organizations have numerous stakeholders watching and listening to what the organization does, and this includes on social media. First and foremost, there are the constituents or members served by the organization. Depending on the organization, this could be cancer patients or people with other illnesses, it could be the homeless population or people facing food insecurity, it could be families and prospective adopters of animals, it could be members of a nonprofit art museum or other type of arts organization. There is variety in this group alone, of course, but nonprofits also rely on the following types of stakeholders: donors, volunteers, board members, government entities and policymakers, corporate sponsors or partners, their own employees, the media, and more. Communicating to and with this many stakeholders can be challenging to say the least, and of course, there is never a more trying time to communicate than during a crisis.

As noted, some key features that are part of the nature of being nonprofit make these organizations different than corporate or government entities. However, there are also many *similarities* in terms of communicating on behalf of a nonprofit, particularly during a crisis. First, nonprofits rely on visibility and awareness, just like any other type of organization. While a crisis can make a nonprofit more visible for a time, it is generally not in a positive way, and nonprofits rely on positive perceptions and attitudes among their stakeholders just like other organizations. While they do not have profits to distribute to shareholders, nonprofits are responsible for meeting certain fundraising goals, and without meeting such goals, a service the nonprofit provides could cease to exist. Because nonprofits are voluntary and rely so heavily on the kindness of donors and volunteers, trust, relationship building, and communication are key.

Being a philanthropic organization brings about many *opportunities*, of course – and many of the best nonprofit organizations are adept at building relationships with multiple constituencies, but it also brings about *challenges*. There is an increased number of nonprofits in recent decades in the U.S., as many public needs previously fulfilled by government entities are now (since the late 1980s/ early 1990s) provided by nonprofit organizations (Boris & Steuerle, 2006; Hall, 2006). Because nonprofits are dependent upon individuals for donations, the sustainability of the organizations is also dependent upon economic circumstances. And because there are so many nonprofits now, and economic circumstances vary from year to year, the industry can be competitive as many causes and organizations are vying for the same limited number of resources (donors and volunteers).

So, what works in terms of communicating with nonprofit stakeholders? Like many forms of communication these days, storytelling is important (McKeever, 2015). And, of course, that *storytelling* must be based on authenticity and trust. Philanthropic organizations, in particular, have some incredible stories to tell and many of them do it very well, especially now with the frequency and technological advances available through social media.

Shareable content is also key, particularly on social media. Remember the ice bucket challenge? The ALS ice bucket challenge started in the summer of 2014 and has been called the world's largest global social media phenomenon (The ALS Association, 2017). Millions of people uploaded videos of themselves pouring buckets of ice water on themselves, while challenging friends to do the same and/or to make donations to the nonprofit, Amyotrophic Lateral Sclerosis (ALS, also known as Lou Gehrig's disease) Association (ALSA). Within about two weeks of the challenge starting on social media, the ALSA reported 146,000 new donors, and the organization received more than $115 million in donations by the end of that year (Pressgrove et al., 2018).

One of the things that made this challenge work was that it involved people calling on people they know, and it provided a *call to action*. Those are two important factors in fundraising and philanthropic success. For more than 50 years, 70 percent or more of all giving in the U.S. has been done by individuals (Giving USA Foundation, 2019). While corporations can be important stakeholders and donors to nonprofit organizations, individual donors and volunteers are the most important stakeholder groups, and as we all know, many of these individuals are on social media.

Research, Theories, and Models Related to Philanthropic Communication

With the rise in the number of nonprofit organizations in recent decades, research on what works in terms of nonprofit public relations and communicating during a crisis and/or on social media has increased in recent years, too (Sisco et al., 2013). Theories and models help explain why these organizations succeed or fail in certain situations and help us understand how to replicate some successes or avoid certain mistakes or crises in the future.

For example, the *Technology Acceptance Model* (TAM) was created to measure the publics' attitudes toward and acceptance of new technologies. Text messaging has been used in the public relations domain for crisis communication alerts, but in recent years, it has also been used for fundraising following a crisis (Weberling & Waters, 2012). The "Text for Haiti" campaign has been one of the most successful text-based fundraising campaigns in recent years, benefiting the American Red Cross following an earthquake that devastated Haiti in 2010. To help support relief efforts in Haiti, the American Red Cross mobilized a fundraising campaign. By texting the word "Haiti" to the number "90999," individuals were able to make a $10 donation to the "Text for Haiti" campaign. Through this campaign, more than $32 million was raised through mobile donations (American Red Cross, 2010).

TAM proposes that perceived usefulness and perceived ease of use of a technology or platform influences our attitudes toward using it, which leads to our intentions to use and actual use of the technology or platform (see Figure 1 in Weberling & Waters, 2012). Through an online survey of previous American Red Cross donors, donors to the "Text for Haiti" campaign had more favorable attitudes than those who did not donate via text messaging (Weberling & Waters, 2012). This supports the idea that people need to feel comfortable with a technology to want to use it, and in terms of communicating during or after a crisis, it is important for nonprofit organizations to know where their stakeholders are on social media and to communicate accordingly. While new platforms are emerging all the time to help us communicate, nonprofits do not necessarily need to be on all of them to communicate effectively. Knowing your audience is key in any communication situation, and the same is true for philanthropic organizations communicating during or after a crisis. This is especially important for nonprofits, which likely have limited resources for communication.

The *Theory of Situational Support* (TSS) (McKeever et al., 2016) is another model that helps explain nonprofit fundraising, advocacy, and other forms of organizational support. This model blends variables from the situational theory of problem solving and the theory of reasoned action to predict communicative and behavioral intentions to support nonprofit organizations by taking actions such as communicating about an organization on social media or participating in fundraising events such as Relay for Life benefiting the American Cancer Society. Through multiple studies, the theory has been found to predict such actions on the part of individuals. While this theory has not been used in the context of crisis communication, knowing which variables predict communicative and behavioral support is important for understanding what might make people continue to or cease to support an organization during or following a crisis.

For example, in TSS, problem recognition, constraint recognition, involvement, attitudes, and subjective norms all influence information activity and behavioral intentions (see Figure 1 in McKeever et al., 2016). In this model, subjective norms refer to what one believes "important others" (friends, family, etc.) in their lives are doing or find acceptable. The idea behind subjective norms is that most people will do what others in their life are doing or want them to do. We see this variable highlighted in philanthropic communication whenever an organization highlights how many people in a community have donated already, which tends to make more people donate or otherwise get involved. Following a crisis, one way nonprofit organizations are able to help communities recover or bounce back is through fundraising, which often involves social media. Knowing the factors that influence individuals' communication about and participation in such efforts can help nonprofit organizations be successful in such instances.

A third model that may be useful for understanding philanthropic organizations and communication with various stakeholders focuses on *Nonprofit Relationship Management* (Pressgrove & McKeever, 2016). Research in this area focuses on the concept of stewardship, which consists of multiple relationship cultivation strategies that nonprofits use to build trust, satisfaction, and commitment between stakeholders and the organization. Stewardship consists of responsibility, which means acting in a socially responsible way; reporting, which consists of conveying information that demonstrates accountability; relationship nurturing, which refers to initiating and participating in dialogues and other acts with various stakeholders; and reciprocity, which includes recognizing stakeholders and showing regard for their philanthropic contributions.

If and when stewardship is practiced by organizations, it often leads to positive affect or feelings of trust, commitment, and satisfaction with an organization. This, in turn, can lead to loyalty, which can lead to continued intentions to support a nonprofit organization (see Figure 1 in Pressgrove & McKeever, 2016). Of course, when stewardship is not practiced well by an organization, or when other factors along the way get damaged – such as trust in the case of a crisis that may be the fault of the philanthropic organization – nonprofits run the risk of losing support from important stakeholders, including donors and volunteers.

Examples of Nonprofits in Crisis

Many nonprofits face crises, often because of decisions made coupled with the way these decisions are communicated. In 2012, Susan G. Komen for the Cure cut off funding to Planned Parenthood because of political pressure. Komen had been providing funding for mammograms provided through Planned Parenthood clinics, but some stakeholders did not like being linked to the organization because of its association with abortion. There was an uproar on social media in response, which caused Komen to reverse its decision after only three days, but the nonprofit suffered long-term damage to its brand. According to the *Los Angeles Times*, Komen lost $77 million or 22 percent of its income in the following fiscal year (Friedenthal, 2018).

Komen could have prevented this type of crisis by doing some research first, before making such a big and controversial decision. Surveying stakeholders such as donors, employees, and volunteers could have prevented the organization from de-funding Planned Parenthood altogether, which could have prevented the ensuing crisis. Alternatively, if Komen had done some research and decided this was the best course of action, they could have predicted the social media uproar and had a plan in place for how to respond to the criticism they received and defend their decision. Like any organization, having a plan in place for dealing with a crisis is key – and those plans should include social media communication and response strategies.

This isn't the first time Komen faced controversy for its partnerships or organizational decisions. In 2010, the nonprofit partnered with Kentucky Fried Chicken (KFC) for a promotion called "Buckets for the Cure." For every pink bucket of chicken KFC sold, the company was going to donate 50 cents to Komen. Critics quickly pounced on Komen for this partnership. People were angry about the promotion of fried foods that contribute to obesity, which has been linked to an increased risk of breast cancer. The news and criticism went viral, and Komen's public relations team remained silent – across Twitter, Facebook, the organization's website, and in the media. Eventually, the organization responded, defending the partnership by stating that it was able to reach a new demographic by working with KFC. In both this instance and the one two years later with Planned Parenthood, it became clear that Komen needed not only proactive communications planning but better plans in place to deal with crises and how to reactively communicate on social media and elsewhere with various stakeholder publics (Crisco, 2013).

One of the biggest animal rights organizations in the U.S., People for the Ethical Treatment of Animals (PETA) and one of South Korea's most prominent animal rights groups, Coexistence of Animal Rights on Earth (CARE) have had euthanasia scandals that were forms of crises for the organizations. PETA has been a strong proponent of euthanasia, arguing that euthanasia policies are mercy killings. PETA's euthanasia practices have been controversial and have gotten the group into legal trouble. For example, in 2007, two PETA employees were acquitted of animal cruelty after leaving dead animals in dumpsters in a shopping center in North Carolina. Admitting employees' wrongdoings during the trial, PETA was clear about its euthanasia policy. Although euthanasia is one of the main criticisms PETA faces, the group has always had a very strong and consistent stance toward the issue (King, 2017).

In a related example in South Korea, several CARE employees accused the director, Park So-yeon, of euthanizing rescued dogs for years, while promoting the group's "no kill" shelter. Park is the key figure of the group for her dedicated dog rescuing campaigns through mass media and her own social media channel. Although Park apologized on CARE's social media saying, "some animals were given up under extreme circumstances," CARE employees held a press conference condemning Park. She had to face negative media coverage and public criticism. Many donors cut their funding and the director was accused of violating animal protection laws (Kwon, 2019).

Both organizations faced criticism with euthanasia practices as prominent animal rights groups. While PETA admitted their staff's wrongdoings and expressed the group's strong stance toward euthanasia collectively and consistently, CARE employees criticized the director and the group showed two conflicting stances through different media channels. These cases show three important takeaways regarding nonprofit and crisis communication. First, because mission is the core focus for nonprofit organizations, any issues violating an organization's mission puts a nonprofit in crisis (Sisco, 2012). Second, in any type of crisis management, having one consistent voice as a group is important (Coombs, 2010). Considering that each nonprofit organization's mission can be interpreted differently, and each stakeholder may have different views of a crisis, having a clear and consistent stance and communicating that stance through various media is important. Although a group's stance may not be agreed upon and accepted by all stakeholders, the group should do its best to reach out to stakeholders to communicate consistently and clearly.

Finally, regarding crisis management and social media, while Park had been using her personal social media account for various campaign promotions, she posted the apology statement to the organization's social media account. Although other CARE employees accused Park, and the euthanasia was solely Park's decision, her actions actually led to a significant decrease in donations to the organization, and the employees faced enormous criticism, too. This example shows the importance of platform or channel choice as something to be considered in crisis communication. Some organizations manage multiple social media accounts, and of course, leaders and employees within an organization may also have their own accounts where they sometimes communicate about their work. If an organization has various social media accounts, it needs to consider "who is the messenger?" and provide a consistent voice in creating content and engaging in dialogue. Doing so will help organizations decide which channel to use to communicate with stakeholders with clarity and consistency during a crisis.

Advocacy and Activism as They Relate
to Philanthropic Crisis Communication

As the public has been increasingly active on various social justice issues, advocacy and activism have grown as a theme in corporate communication as well as in public relations research, news, and nonprofit communication. Advocacy and activism are often carried out through or highlighted on social media. Advocacy and activism have been defined in various ways. Although the terms have been used interchangeably, this section will provide some distinctions between advocacy and activism based on academic literature.

One definition of advocacy is "any attempt to influence the decisions of an institutional elite on behalf of a collective interest" (Jenkins, 1987, p. 297). In a broader definition, advocacy is those "activities aimed at influencing the social and civic agenda and at gaining access to the arena where decisions that affect the social and civil life are made" (Schmid et al., 2008, p. 582). Meanwhile, activism is defined as "the use of direct and often vigorous action in order to challenge oppressive power relations or ideologies" (Ophélie, 2016, pp. 757–758). Activism has also been referred to as, "an individual's developed, relatively stable, yet changeable propensity to engage in various collective, social-political, problem-solving behaviors spanning a range from low-risk, passive, and institutionalized acts to high-risk, active, and unconventional behaviors" (Corning & Myers, 2002, p. 704). Although both advocacy and activism involve collective actions to bring about change related to an issue, cause, or organization, advocacy focuses on influencing and amplifying, while activism has been described as more dedicated action and execution (Lewis, 2018).

Online or digital advocacy and activism have made these concepts more visible on social media. Public relations scholars have long been interested in identifying factors influencing people's communication behaviors. One factor that influences people in terms of speaking out on social media is emotion, and one such emotion is anger. The Anger Activism Model (AAM) explains that anger is a predictor of individuals' commitment to fix a problem (Turner, 2007). For example, in recent years, anger has provided motivation for donating. After the 2016 presidential election, civil and human rights organizations experienced an increase in "rage donations" from individuals who support political and social causes the new administration opposed (Chapman, 2018). When people get involved, they often try to engage others in similar collective actions, and this outreach is often done on social media.

In another example involving a nonprofit, Greenpeace uploaded a video condemning Nestle about buying palm oil from suppliers who destroyed rainforest homes of orangutans in Indonesia. Nestle asked YouTube to pull the clip down, arguing copyright infringement. Greenpeace moved the video to a different platform. Nestle faced enormous backlash on social media. Removing the clip from YouTube enraged the public, and this resulted in even more active spread of the video on social media (Armstrong, 2010). While this case is often cited as an example of failed social media use by Nestle, it could also be seen as a "win" for Greenpeace, which is a nonprofit organization. This case also shows the importance of social media as a venue for organizations – and their supporters or detractors – to engage in advocacy and activism. Not all philanthropic organizations participate in advocacy and activism, of course, but for those that do, social media is an important component. And any nonprofit could become the focus of public advocacy or activism – or a crisis – all of which become more visible via social media.

Chapter Summary

In this chapter, we discussed the nature of nonprofit organizations, including some similarities and differences in philanthropic communication. Next, we highlighted three theories or models that may be helpful in explaining how and why stakeholders support nonprofit organizations and why those same organizations may lose support during a crisis. Then we provided examples of nonprofit organizations that faced crises and discussed the mis-steps and ways the organizations could have responded better during these crises. Finally, we discussed the importance of advocacy and activism to nonprofit organizations, and how these concepts can be involved in crises and crisis communication, especially on social media. We hope the lessons learned in this chapter are useful to students, practitioners, and scholars interested in nonprofit organizations, social media, and crisis communication.

References

The ALS Association. (2017). ALS ice bucket challenge – FAQ. http://www.alsa.org/about-us/ice-bucket-challenge-faq.html

American Red Cross. (2010). Haiti earthquake one-month progress report. http://www.redcross.org/haiti

Armstrong, P. (2010, March 20). Greenpeace, Nestle in battle over Kit Kat viral. *CNN.* https://www.cnn.com/2010/WORLD/asiapcf/03/19/indonesia.rainforests.orangutan.nestle/index.html

Boris, E. T., & Steuerle, C. E. (2006). Scope and dimensions of the nonprofit sector. In W.W. Powell, & R. Steinberg (Eds.), *The nonprofit sector: A research handbook.* Yale University Press.

Chapman, G. (2018, November 22). Time to make the donates! *The New York Times.* https://www.nytimes.com/2018/11/22/style/donation-panic-giving-tuesday.html

Coombs, W.T. (2010). Parameters for crisis communication. In W.T. Coombs, & S.J. Holladay (Eds.), *The handbook of crisis communication* (pp. 65–90). Blackwell.

Corning, A. F., & Myers, D. J. (2002). Individual orientation toward engagement in social action. *Political Psychology*, *23*(4), 703–729. https://doi.org/10.1111/0162-895x.00304

Crisco, L. B. (2013). Pink politics: How Komen's Planned Parenthood communications response unraveled the pink ribbon. https://page.org/study_competitions/2013-case-study-competition

Friedenthal, A. (2018, May 16). What's your nonprofit social media crisis response plan? https://www.softwareadvice.com/resources/nonprofit-social-media-crisis-response/

Frumkin, P. (2002). *On being nonprofit: A conceptual and policy primer.* Harvard University Press.

Giving USA Foundation. (2019). Giving USA 2019: The annual report on philanthropy for the year 2019. https://givingusa.org/giving-usa-2019-americans-gave-427-71-billion-to-charity-in-2018-amid-complex-year-for-charitable-giving/

Hall, P. D. (2006). A historical overview of philanthropy, voluntary associations, and nonprofit organizations in the U.S., 1600–2000. In W. W. Powell, & R. Steinberg (Eds.), *The nonprofit sector: A research handbook* (pp. 32–65). Yale University Press.

Jenkins, J. C. (1987). Nonprofit organizations and policy advocacy. In W. W. Powell (Ed.), *The nonprofit sector* (pp. 296–318). Yale University Press.

King, L. (2017, Jan 25). Lawyers face off in PETA workers' trial in North Carolina. *The Virginian-Pilot.* https://www.pilotonline.com/news/crime/article_6c039fc3-1f37-5171-b49a-9ed73dd3cdf7.html

Kwon, J. (2019, Jan 17). Head of S Korean dog charity secretly euthanized hundreds of animals. *CNN.* https://www.cnn.com/2019/01/17/asia/south-korea-dog-care-euthanasia-intl/index.html

Lewis, E. (2018). What's the difference between an advocate and an activist? Have you been mislabeling? https://theblog.adobe.com/whats-difference-advocate-activist-mislabeling/

McKeever, B. W. (2015, December). What to watch for in 2016 and beyond: Nonprofit trends. *PRSay: The Voice of Public Relations.* https://prsay.prsa.org/2016/01/28/prin2016-what-to-watch-for-in-2016-and-beyond-nonprofit-trends/

McKeever, B. W., Pressgrove, G., McKeever, R., & Zheng, Y. (2016). Toward a theory of situational support: A model for exploring fundraising, advocacy and organizational support. *Public Relations Review*, *42*(1), 219–222.

Ophélie, V. (2016). (Extra)ordinary activism: Veganism and the shaping of hemeratopias. *International Journal of Sociology and Social Policy*, *36*(11/12), 756–773. https://doi.org/10.1108/IJSSP-12-2015-0137

Pressgrove, G. N., & McKeever, B. W. (2016). Nonprofit relationship management: Extending the organization-public relationship to loyalty and behaviors. *Journal of Public Relations Research*, *28*(3–4), 193–211. https://doi.org/10.1080/1062726x.2016.1233106

Pressgrove, G. N., McKeever, B. W., & Jang, S. (2018). What's contagious? Exploring the reasons why content goes viral on Twitter. *International Journal of Nonprofit and Voluntary Sector Marketing*, *23*(1), 1–8. https://doi.org/10.1002/nvsm.1586

Schmid, H., Bar, M., & Nirel, R. (2008). Advocacy activities in nonprofit human service organizations: Implications for policy. *Nonprofit and Voluntary Sector Quarterly*, *37*(4), 581–602. https://doi.org/10.1177/0899764007312666

Sisco, H. F. (2012). Nonprofit in crisis: An examination of the applicability of situational crisis communication theory. *Journal of Public Relations Research*, *24*(1), 1–17. https://doi.org/10.1080/1062726x.2011.582207

Sisco, H. F., Pressgrove, G., & Collins, E. L. (2013). Paralleling the practice: An analysis of the scholarly literature in nonprofit public relations. *Journal of Public Relations Research, 25*(4), 282–306. https://doi.org/10.1080/1062726x.2013.806869

Turner, M. M. (2007). Using emotion in risk communication: The anger activism model. *Public Relations Review, 33*(2), 114–119. https://doi.org/10.1016/j.pubrev.2006.11.013

Weberling, B., & Waters, R. D. (2012). Gauging the public's preparedness for mobile public relations: The "Text for Haiti" campaign. *Public Relations Review, 38*(1), 51–55. https://doi.org/10.1016/j.pubrev.2011.11.005

21

ADVANCING RESEARCH ON CRISIS COMMUNICATION AND RELIGION

Jordan Morehouse and Cylor Spaulding

All types of organizations will likely encounter at least one crisis during their existence. Those that respond appropriately are more apt to survive the crisis and regain the trust of stakeholders. Multiple factors must be considered when determining an effective crisis response, including the type of organization facing the crisis, the location, and the demographics and psychographics of stakeholders. A crisis is perceptual and is occurring if stakeholders believe it is, thus the perceptions of stakeholders are important to understand for both acknowledging the crisis and understanding how to appropriately address it (Coombs, 2019).

One factor in understanding stakeholder perceptions is to recognize their religious perspectives. A person's faith may impact their determination that a crisis is occurring, and it may help determine whether the stakeholders accept and agree with an organization's response to a crisis. Understanding the context of religion is important to gaining a full comprehension of crisis communications since there are unique considerations to account for when working with religious publics. Depending on the type of crisis and the stakeholders involved, there may be numerous factors that could exacerbate a crisis if they are not considered (Spaulding, 2018).

Crisis communication is a thriving body of scholarship with theoretical variety and applied outcomes that are more important than ever. However, there is a key limitation in this body of scholarship. Namely, scholars tend to focus on similar types of crises from similar types of organizations. The lack of focus on crises with a religious component and crises that occur within religious organizations presents a notable gap in the literature, which ultimately constrains theory building and scholars' ability to assist practitioners in helping organizations and publics recover from crises. Given how pervasive religion is throughout the

DOI: 10.4324/9781003043409-29

world (Hackett & McClendon, 2017; Tamir et al., 2020), it is problematic that religion is overlooked when determining the motivations and needs of stakeholders during a crisis.

To synthesize and understand research on religious organizations and crises, this chapter features an in-depth review of existing research on crises within religious organizations and crises with a religious component to examine the theoretical frameworks previous scholars have applied to religious crises and outcomes of their research. This chapter starts with an examination of the multiple approaches scholars have taken to analyze crises within the Catholic Church and evangelical Christian churches, followed by a discussion on religiously charged crises affecting non-religious organizations. This chapter concludes with a discussion on the future of research on religious crises, particularly in terms of social media, and recommendations on the direction of this area of scholarship.

Religious Institutions and Crisis Communication

Crisis communication emerged as an area of literature that sought to help organizations recover from crises and study the process of their recovery efforts. When crises occur, organizations' reputations are at risk, trust from stakeholders is damaged, and other financial consequences can occur (Coombs, 2019). The current section discusses research that focuses on how religious organizations managed crises before turning to a discussion on crises with religious elements.

Catholic Church Sexual Abuse Crisis

Much of the literature on crisis communication and religious organizations focuses on the Catholic Church's sexual abuse crisis (Barth, 2010; Boys, 2009; Dixon, 2004; Kauffman, 2008; Maier, 2005; Maier & Crist, 2017; Mancini & Shields, 2014; Morehouse, 2020; Rezendes, 2002). The Catholic sexual abuse crisis occurred when reporters from the *Boston Globe* published accounts detailing decades of sexual abuse of minors by religious leaders within the Catholic Church and described the Catholic Church's failure to hold pedophiliac leaders accountable for their actions (Rezendes, 2002). In response to the crisis, the Catholic Church hosted press conferences, created committees, issued Church-commissioned reports, and implemented new charters and policies (Barth, 2010; Catholic Church Child Sexual Abuse Scandal, 2019). In subsequent research, scholars argue the Catholic Church continued to mismanage the crisis and post-crisis communication (Barth, 2010).

Scholars largely analyze the rhetorical tools and tactics the Catholic Church utilized following the sexual abuse revelation (Dixon, 2004; Kauffman, 2008). The focus on rhetorical tools utilized by the Catholic Church is not a new area of scholarship (Blaney, 2001; Cali, 1998; Dixon, 2004); however, analyzing the *crisis* rhetoric of the Catholic Church is a limited area of research.

Assessing crisis and post-crisis messages reveals unique insights that are otherwise lost when examining non-crisis communication. For instance, Dixon (2004) examined the post-crisis responses of Pope John Paul II and American Cardinals to analyze pastoral power and the balance between orthodoxy and individualism. Through the study, Dixon (2004) determined the religious leaders aimed to flex their authority over congregants while simultaneously trying to silence critics, as opposed to admitting wrongdoing or repairing the Church's image.

Additionally, Kauffman (2008) examined Archbishop Cardinal Bernard Law's image restoration strategies during a press conference and Q&A session after the conference. The Cardinal utilized the following image restoration strategies in order: mortification, defeasibility, bolstering, and corrective action (Kauffman, 2008). Despite utilizing image restoration strategies and receiving positive media coverage as a result, Kauffman (2008) argued the Cardinal's messages did little to improve the relationship with the victims of the crisis. Kauffman (2008) posited the failure to repair the Cardinal's image (and subsequently the Catholic Church's image) results from a lack of trust with the Cardinal, the offensiveness of the crisis, and victims' relationship with the Cardinal prior to the crisis. While Dixon's (2004) and Kauffman's (2008) results suggest contrasting strategies from the Catholic Church, their approach of analyzing post-crisis messages from the offending organization has been mirrored frequently within research on the Catholic sexual abuse crisis, and crisis communication research overall.

On the other hand, another group of scholars approached the Catholic sexual abuse crisis from a different angle. Specifically, Boys (2009) and Morehouse (2020) examined the post-crisis communication of stakeholder-formed organizations created as a result of the crisis. Stakeholder-formed organizations are defined as, "non-profit organizations, activist groups, or other groups that are created by stakeholders of the offending organization as a response to a crisis" (Morehouse, 2020, p. 244).

While the two studies share similarities regarding topics, Boys (2009) and Morehouse (2020) approached the subject in differing ways. Boys (2009) examined the crisis response strategies of two stakeholder-formed organizations by content analyzing press releases and statements from 2002 to 2005 to determine their crisis goals. Boys (2009) determined Voice of the Faithful (VOTF) aimed to gain legitimacy with the Catholic Church, whereas Survivors Network of those Abused by Priests (SNAP) sought to end abuse within the Catholic Church through their post-crisis communication. Morehouse (2020) furthered this approach in their study on another stakeholder-formed organization, Leadership Roundtable. Results reveal Leadership Roundtable utilized discourse of renewal to help the Catholic Church as an institution, Catholic leaders, *and* Catholic believers recover from the crisis. The focus on stakeholder-formed organizations is a disruption from the traditional method of examining messages from offending organizations during and after a crisis occurs.

A final group of scholars examined the Catholic Church's crisis from a variety of approaches. Mancini and Shields (2014) employed a media cultivation framework and surveyed the general public and Catholic believers to assess the degree to which media coverage impacted confidence in the Church. Results suggest more media exposure positively influenced Catholic believers' perceptions of the Church and their confidence in the Church's ability to prevent a similar crisis from occurring in the future. Additionally, scholars like Barth (2010) and Maier (2005) provided key lessons learned from the mismanaged Catholic sexual abuse crisis to inform others who might manage similar crises in the future. Lessons include advice like cultivating "relationships characterized by openness, attentiveness, and responsiveness" (Maier, 2005, p. 224), and accepting the burden of higher expectations placed on some organizations by stakeholders and society (Barth, 2010).

Conversely, Maier and Crist (2017) examined the crisis communication strategies of the Catholic Church using a unique framework. Maier and Crist (2017) utilized a phenomenological philosophy to situate the crisis as a "wicked crisis" that requires a specific type of post-crisis response strategy: responsive witness. Responsive witness is defined as "consciously turning toward the pain and complexities the crisis continues to reveal, even if these revelations mean deepening the sense of confusion" (p. 171). To utilize this strategy, Maier and Crist (2017) suggest organizational and religious leaders employ communication "that articulates, with brutal clarity, what has occurred, why it occurred, why it is still occurring, and what the stakes truly are for American Catholics" (p. 171). The responsive witness approach requires organizational leaders to "give everything, even to the point of martyrdom," which echoes the sentiments of Boys' (2009) and Morehouse's (2020) approach to a public-centric approach to post-crisis communication (Maier & Crist, 2017, p. 172).

While the Catholic Church's crisis is considered one of the more widely researched crises in religious crisis communication scholarship, literature on crises within religious organizations and institutions is still scarce. Some have described the Catholic Church as a hotbed of crises in the 21st century; however, the Catholic Church is not the only religious organization at the center of scholarly investigation.

Crises within Evangelical Christian Churches

Similar to research on crises within the Catholic Church, scholars have examined crises in other Christian denominations through a variety of theories and approaches (Courtright & Hearit, 2002; Legg, 2009; Spaulding, 2018).

Courtright and Hearit (2002) utilized the apologia framework to examine the crisis response of the Christian and Missionary Alliance (C&MA) denomination. Courtright and Hearit (2002) focused on the religious organization's communication of guilt in C&MA's post-crisis communication, including crisis reports, letters, commissions, and denomination-led events. To elaborate on the institutions handling of guilt, the authors contrasted the treatment of guilt from corporations to this religious organization and noted that corporations tend to "'isolate' guilt in the person of the chief executive officer or a few employees, it is remarkable that this does not occur in [C&MA] denomination's corporate response" (p. 354). Courtright and Hearit (2002) uncovered a novel treatment of guilt, one that does not assign victimage and goes beyond mortification by having multiple leaders within the organization apologize and accept responsibility for the crisis.

Legg (2009) also analyzed image repair strategies and post-crisis rhetoric in their examination of Jimmy Swaggart's crisis involving sex workers and the unacceptance of religious institutional punishment. Legg (2009) examined the stages of Swaggart's crisis through the stage theory framework and assessed the post-crisis rhetoric Swaggart utilized to repair his image. Swaggart utilized three image repair strategies in the first crisis (i.e., violation of moral standards), including mortification, provocation, and bolstering (Legg, 2009). Additionally, Swaggart implemented four image repair strategies in the second crisis (i.e., violating disciplinary action), including minimization, transcendence, attacking his accusers, and denial. Legg (2009) included an analysis of which crisis was more devastating to the reputation and organization Swaggart had built and concluded Swaggart's continued use of sex workers was "an irrecoverable situation" (p. 248).

Scholars have furthered this area of scholarship by examining crises with the Situational Crisis Communication Theory (SCCT) framework (Coombs, 2019). Spaulding (2018) examined the post-crisis communication strategies of four evangelical Christian leaders through SCCT. Spaulding (2018) analyzed news coverage and pastors' post-crisis statements to examine how evangelical leaders responded to and recovered from same-sex sex scandals. The pastors utilized various post-crisis communication strategies, including attacking the accuser, denial, excuse, ingratiation, and apology. The recovery strategies were complicated for certain pastors because some crises were based on rumors as opposed to evidence of crises (Spaulding, 2018). Thus, while most pastors utilized the recommended crisis response strategy according to SCCT, some failed to recover and were removed from their positions (Spaulding, 2018).

Crises with Religious Elements

With the majority of the world following a faith (Hackett & McClendon, 2017), religious belief has the potential to exert significant influence on stakeholders. Many activities, from entertainment to politics, can be influenced to some degree by faith practices within a given country. It is beneficial for an organization to thoroughly understand how to interact with audiences of different religions and what their needs and concerns are in relation to the organization's products and services. Failure to gain this understanding can lead to crises for an organization both from the members of the given faith and the general public if it perceives the organization as being insensitive.

The examination of religious crises affecting non-religious organizations represents another gap in the scholarship, and these crises are not accounted for in many crisis theories. While many incidents involving religious beliefs can be made to fit in crisis categories, they may not account for specific violations of religious beliefs. For example, SCCT does not provide guidance with regard to a crisis of a spiritual nature. Similarly, Benoit's (2020) Image Repair Theory does not have specific categories that account for complicated concerns related to spiritual harm and a violation of religious beliefs.

While research in the area of crisis communication is robust, it is lacking in terms of examining religious factors affecting crises in non-religious organizations. There are numerous incidents of companies experiencing paracrises with a religious angle, but many of these do not develop into full crises, and they have not been widely discussed in academic literature. A paracrisis is a crisis warning sign that can turn into a crisis if it is not addressed, and they often occur publicly, particularly on social media (Coombs, 2019). Activism by religious groups can be a visible cause of paracrises (Dodd, 2016), and in the United States, these can be seen in the form of boycotts from conservative Christian groups.

Issues management is also a critical aspect of crisis communication, as it identifies issues external to the organization with the goal of preventing them from becoming crises. In a religious context, many issues are related to moralistic concepts that religious groups or institutions feel an organization is violating. Jacques (2013) discussed the example of the activist organization Australian Christian Lobby (ACL) objecting to ads promoting safe sex that included a gay couple embracing, and the response of the advertising companies. The ACL and its supporters objected to the ads because they claimed they promoted gay sex and the "sexualisation of children through exposure to condom use" (Jaques, 2013, p. 55). When the concerns were voiced to the two advertising companies who hosted the ads on their billboards, one chose to remove the ad, resulting in a larger counter protest from the organization behind the ads, forcing the company to repost it (Jaques, 2013). In this case, the issue was exacerbated by the counter protest, and provides an example of a case where religious beliefs contradict public sentiment.

Also related to issues management, Jaques (2015) noted that issues frequently arise when multinational corporations from western, largely Christian countries move into areas where other religions are more dominant. Additionally, these companies may also be moving into countries where religion is closely aligned with government and politics, which can further complicate crises. In particular, they cited the case of porcine DNA being found in Cadbury chocolate bars in Malaysia, which would violate Islamic dietary practices (Jaques, 2015). The company handled the crisis on a regional level, so the response team would be familiar with the concerns and able to address them in a way appropriate to the religious and cultural sensitivities. This case is also illustrative of the potential for religious crises in one country to impact organizations in other countries as well. Jacques (2015) noted that as a result of the issue in Malaysia, Saudi Arabia, another Muslim-majority country, announced that it would begin testing Cadbury products for porcine DNA.

According to Coombs (2019), issues or risks not identified and addressed will likely escalate into crisis. Some organizations have either not recognized issues relating to religion, or have purposefully ignored them or spurred controversy. One crisis that has been extensively examined by academics is that of Danish newspaper *Jyllands-Posten's* publishing of 12 cartoons of the prophet Muhammed, which was seen as blasphemy by many Muslims (Gaither & Curtin, 2007). This crisis escalated dramatically and became a "mega-crisis" that affected other Danish companies operating in Muslim-majority countries (Frandsen & Johansen, 2010). The Danish dairy company, Arla, was particularly affected when Saudi Arabian media and religious leaders called for boycotts of Danish products (Gaither & Curtin, 2007). While the newspaper that initiated the crisis faced some backlash in Denmark, the larger impact of the crisis was felt by multinational Danish companies, and Arla had a difficult time speaking to stakeholders inside and outside of the Muslim community simultaneously. Frandsen and Johansen (2010) pointed out that following the SCCT response strategies alone would not adequately address this crisis, since the organization was initially seen as a victim in Denmark, but attempts to ingratiate itself to Arab audiences angered Danish stakeholders.

The cartoon crisis also affected companies in New Zealand when a paper there reprinted the cartoons. Unlike Arla, New Zealand companies exporting to Muslim-majority countries could anticipate the crisis and prepare (Knight et al., 2009). Dairy company Fonterra was particularly vulnerable to the crisis since it operated visibly in the Middle East. The company was proactive in issuing statements and allowing its regional representatives to handle the issue on a local level, and the New Zealand government publicly stated it did not condone the publishing of the cartoons (Knight et al., 2009). Unlike Arla, Fonterra and the New Zealand government were able to balance stakeholder interests by emphasizing the idea that the company had nothing to do with and did not condone publishing the cartoons, which stopped short of condemning free speech (Knight et al., 2009). Again, in this case, a multinational corporation had to navigate concerns related to faith, but it was saved by being able to recognize warning signs and leave its response to more regional contacts.

The examples discussed in this section are illustrative of how crisis communication needs to account for concerns related to issues of faith, and this should be an area of further study for scholars. Understanding the implications of faith can help organizations identify potential threats and issues earlier and help them communicate relevant information to audiences.

Directions for Future Research

This chapter identified gaps in current research on crisis communication and religion through an in-depth review of research on crisis within religious organizations, as well as crises with a religious component. Next, this chapter will discuss directions for future research.

Inclusion of Social Media

Research on religious crises does not consider how crises play out on social media, crises that occur on social media, and how crises spread on social media. Three of the four categories Liu and Fraustino (2014) identify in their report on crisis communication theories are represented in research on crisis communication and religion; however, research considering the context in which crises occur and are shared on social media are markedly absent from scholarship.

While this body of research is limited in size and depth, the exclusion of social media in studies on crises and religion is nonetheless problematic. Studies like Perreault and Perreault (2019) are bridging this gap with their examination into social media and visual rhetoric with crises involving religious celebrities; however, additional research examining how social media platforms influence the practice of crisis communication is needed to bolster theory building and understanding of religious crises. The first recommendation for future research concerning crisis communication and religion is to increase the focus on how crises occur, spread, and play out on social media. Bridging this gap in scholarship will assist in strengthening our understanding regarding how religious organizations and publics respond to crises.

The Impact of Identity

The second limitation focuses on the impact of stakeholder identity. Scholars have not considered the impact of religious identity and religiosity when evaluating stakeholders' perceptions of the crisis, crisis response strategies, image, or reputation of the offending organization. Of the scholars who have incorporated elements of identity, religious identity is revealed to be an influential factor for both victims and publics of the offending organization (Jaques, 2015; Morehouse, 2020). Overlooking stakeholders' identities or ignoring the context in which crises occur limits our understanding of the values violated by the crisis and the work organizations have to do to recover. Acknowledging and investigating the multiple identities stakeholders have – including religious identity and religiosity – as well as the impact of those identities will strengthen crisis communication theory by enabling researchers to examine additional influential factors in the crisis response and recovery process.

Prioritizing Publics

The final limitation centers on publics. Publics are largely a secondary focus of crisis communication research, with scholars prioritizing the survival and recovery of organizations. Research on crises within religious organizations and crises with a religious component highlight the need to prioritize publics over organizations, or equally to organizations, in the crisis communication and recovery process (Maier & Crist, 2017). Future research should explore publics' perceptions to a sacrificial crisis response strategy, which communicates organizations are prioritizing the well-being of publics over the well-being of organizations when a crisis occurs. Examining the sacrificial crisis response strategy would refocus the purpose of crisis communication from the survival of organizations to the flourishing of publics.

While organizations benefit from understanding the ethical and moralistic implications initiatives can have for religious stakeholders, existing literature notes that non-religious organizations often struggle with speaking with secular and religious publics simultaneously. In some cases, the publics' needs clash, which forces organizations to choose who to accommodate. In other cases, organizations do not distinguish religious publics from others, leaving their needs unmet. To benefit the industry, future research should focus on the unique communication needs of adherents of different faiths beyond Christian faiths. Additionally, future research should examine how organizations can successfully operate in countries with different religions and how to craft messages that resonate with the faithful. Understanding faith audiences should be a continued area of focus for professional development for practitioners.

References

Barth, T. (2010). Crisis management in the Catholic Church: Lessons for public administrators. *Public Administration Review*, *70*(5), 780–791. https://doi.org/10.1111/j.1540-6210.2010.02205.x

Benoit, W. L. (2020). Image repair theory. In F. Frandsen, & W. Johansen (Eds.), *Crisis communication* (pp. 105–120). Walter de Gruyter Inc.

Blaney, J. R. (2001). Restoring the juridical image: Apologia for Ex Corde Ecclesiae. *Journal of Communication & Religion*, *24*(1), 94–109.

Boys, S. (2009). Inter-organizational crisis communication: Exploring source and stakeholder communication in the Roman Catholic clergy sex abuse case. In R. L. Heath, E. L. Toth, & D. Waymer (Eds.), *Rhetorical and critical approaches to public relations* (pp. 290–300). Routledge.

Cali, D. D. (1998). The posture of presumption in John Paul II's Veritatis Splendor. *Journal of Communication & Religion, 21*(1), 47–66.

Catholic Church Child Sexual Abuse Scandal. (2019, February 26). https://web.archive.org/web/20200208094242/https://www.bbc.com/news/world-44209971

Coombs, W. T. (2019). *Ongoing crisis communication: Planning, managing, and responding* (5th ed.). Sage Publications.

Courtright, J. L., & Hearit, K. M. (2002). The good organization speaking well: A paradigm case for religious institutional crisis management. *Public Relations Review, 28*(4), 347–360. https://doi.org/10.1016/S0363-8111(02)00166-2

Dixon, M. A. (2004). Silencing the lambs: The Catholic Church's response to the 2002 sexual abuse scandal. *Journal of Communication & Religion, 27*(1), 63–86.

Dodd, M. D. (2016, Aug. 4–7). Conceptualizing parasocial interactions for activism. In B. St. John III (chair), *Beyond products and services: Institutional parasocial engagement with publics and implications for social responsibility.* Paper presented at the Association for Education in Journalism and Mass Communication Conference, Minneapolis, MN.

Frandsen, F., & Johansen, W. (2010). Crisis communication, complexity and the cartoon affair: A case study. In W. T. Coombs, & S. J. Holladay (Eds.), *The handbook of crisis communication* (pp. 425–448). Wiley Blackwell.

Gaither, T. K., & Curtin, P. A. (2007). Examining the heuristic value of models of international public relations practice: A case study of the Arla foods crisis. *Journal of Public Relations Research, 20*(1), 115–137. https://doi.org/10.1080/10627260701727051

Hackett, C., & McClendon, D. (2017, April 5). Christians remain the world's largest religious group, but they are declining in Europe. https://www.pewresearch.org/fact-tank/2017/04/05/christians-remain-worlds-largest-religious-group-but-they-are-declining-in-europe/

Jaques, T. (2013). Ensnared in a gay health controversy: A comparative study in responding to issue activism. *Journal of Public Affairs, 13*(1), 53–60. https://doi.org/10.1002/pa.1442

Jaques, T. (2015). Cadbury and pig DNA: When issue management intersects with religion. *Corporate Communications: An International Journal, 20*(4), 468–482. https://doi.org/10.1108/CCIJ-10-2014-0066

Kauffman, J. (2008). When sorry is not enough: Archbishop Cardinal Bernard Law's image restoration strategies in the statement on sexual abuse of minors by clergy. *Public Relations Review, 34*(3), 258–262. https://doi.org/10.1016/j.pubrev.2008.03.001

Knight, J. G., Mitchell, B. S., & Gao, H. (2009). Riding out the Muhammad cartoons crisis: Contrasting strategies and outcomes. *Long Range Planning, 42*, 6–22. https://doi.org/10.1016/j.lrp.2008.11.002

Legg, K. L. (2009). Religious celebrity: An analysis of image repair discourse. *Journal of Public Relations Research, 21*(2), 240–250. https://doi.org/10.1080/10627260802557621

Liu, B. F., & Fraustino, J. D. (2014). Beyond image repair: Suggestions for crisis communication theory development. *Public Relations Review, 40*(3), 543–546. https://doi.org/10.1016/j.pubrev.2014.04.004

Maier, C. T. (2005). Weathering the storm: Hauser's vernacular voices, public relations and the Roman Catholic Church's sexual abuse scandal. *Public Relations Review, 31*(2), 219–227. https://doi.org/10.1016/j.pubrev.2005.02.017

Maier, C., & Crist, J. R. (2017). From "wicked crisis" to responsive witness: Jean-Luc Marion and the American Roman Catholic sexual-abuse scandal. *Southern Communication Journal*, *82*(3), 164–174. https://doi.org/10.1080/1041794X.2017.1315453

Mancini, C., & Shields, R. T. (2014). Notes on a (sex crime) scandal: The impact of media coverage of sexual abuse in the Catholic Church on public opinion. *Journal of Criminal Justice*, *42*(2), 221–232. https://doi.org/10.1016/j.jcrimjus.2013.06.006

Morehouse, J. (2020). Stakeholder-formed organizations and crisis communication: Analyzing discourse of renewal with a non-offending organization. *Journal of International Crisis and Risk Communication Research*, *3*(2), 243–274. https://doi.org/10.30658/jicrcr.3.2.5

Perreault, M. F., & Perreault, G. (2019). Symbolic convergence in the 2015 Duggar scandal crisis communication. *Journal of Media and Religion*, *18*(3), 85–97. https://doi.org/10.10 80/15348423.2019.1678945

Rezendes, M. (2002, January 06). Church allowed abuse by priest for years. *The Boston Globe*. October 02, 2020. https://www.bostonglobe.com/news/special-reports/2002/01/06/church-allowed-abuse-priest-for-years/cSHfGkTIrAT25qKGvBuDNM/story.html

Spaulding, C. (2018). Evangelical Christian crisis responses to same-sex sex scandals. *Journal of Media and Religion*, *17*(1), 28–40. https://doi.org/10.1080/15348423.2018.1463717

Tamir, C., Connaughton, A., & Salazar, A. M. (2020, July 20). The global god divide. https://www.pewresearch.org/global/2020/07/20/the-global-god-divide/

Areas of Application: Health and Political

22

HEALTH CASE CHAPTER

Influencer Crisis Communication During the COVID-19 Pandemic: @KatieMCrenshaw

Marilyn Broggi

When the COVID-19 pandemic reached the U.S., the Centers for Disease Control and Prevention (CDC) encouraged widespread social distancing and quarantine practices in an effort to slow the rapid spread of the deadly virus ("Social Distancing," 2020). Social media influencers (SMIs), highly followed individuals who usually post niche content to promote brands, effectively leveraged their reach to spread information about social distancing (Desaulniers, 2020). A small line of crisis communication research to date using the Social Mediated Crisis Communication model (SMCC) has examined SMIs for causing damage to organizations (Austin et al., 2012; Ewing & Lambert, 2019; Sng et al., 2019). SMIs, however, have not been studied as a source of health crisis information.

SMIs provided a roadmap to social distancing for their unique followers in line with the Health Belief Model (HBM). HBM posits health behavior change is likely when an individual: (1) perceives a health risk is severe, (2) recognizes they are susceptible, (3) perceives benefits from reducing risky behavior, and (4) believes barriers associated with behavior change are low (Rosenstock, 1966). HBM has primarily been applied in health risk communication contexts, but it has recently been used to examine the response to a coronavirus (MERS-CoV) megacrisis in Saudi Arabia. Findings showed those who perceived higher benefits and lower barriers to engage in preventative behaviors were more likely to follow the governmental campaign's recommendations (Alsulaiman & Rentner, 2018). Unlike a government source, SMIs can demonstrate specific ways their niche following can combat a health crisis.

This chapter examines how a widely followed millennial mom SMI, @ KatieMCrenshaw, leveraged Instagram's features in line with the HBM (Meet

DOI: 10.4324/9781003043409-31

Our Speakers, 2020). She showed her 83k followers how to social distance with children, and she also held her audience accountable for adhering to social distancing guidelines by using follower engagement strategies. Crenshaw created an Instagram community devoted to staying at home by coordinating efforts with 15 other SMIs. Her content worked to foster strong parasocial, or one-sided, relationships with followers, which promotes commitment (Seo et al., 2019). The following is an overview of content she posted on her main Instagram feed, which are traditional posts that appear on followers' feeds and her homepage. The progression of her content falls in line with HBM:

1. *First, Crenshaw addressed the severity of COVID-19 on March 15:*
   She used a photo of her children playing together (see Figure 22.1 by Katie Crenshaw). Using a long-form caption, she first acknowledged the shock

FIGURE 22.1 Photo 1 Posted by Katie Crenshaw

and implications of COVID-19 globally. She reminded her followers, "We have each other...We are NOT alone." She ends her caption with one word to reinforce the central theme of her entire post: "Together."

2. *The following day, she engaged with her followers about their susceptibility to outcomes associated with the virus:*
   In her caption, she addresses her followers collectively as "fam," which is short for family. She asks two questions to prompt followers to comment on their susceptibility to the effects of the virus: "What has all of this meant for you/your family so far?" and "What is making you anxious?" Respondents described the stresses of COVID-19 including job loss and childcare struggles. Crenshaw replied to comments by acknowledging her followers' concerns and offering words of encouragement.

3. *She then gathered a social media community together to both create and illuminate the benefits of social distancing:*
   In March 20 post, she used photos of yoga poses and a graphic to introduce the hashtag "#CreativeAtHomeChallenge" started by her and 15 influencer friends. Hashtags organize user-generated content by gathering all posts labeled with the hashtag together for easy reference, and social media "challenges" give users a call to action to complete and post about using a hashtag. She cited the purpose of the 30-day challenge as being, "If we have to be stuck at home, let's have fun with it." Each day for 30 days, she and the other influencers encouraged their followers to post a photo matching a specific theme of staying home that day. On March 21, the theme was "front yard," and Crenshaw posted photos of her family in their front yard with the hashtag #CreativeAtHomeChallenge (see Figure 22.2 by Katie Crenshaw). The caption listed "10 things [they] experienced in an hour in the front yard," including activities like "listening to [their] wind chimes" and "collecting mulch."

4. *She posted casual and interactive content aimed at reducing barriers to social distancing for her unique audience of moms:*

In addition to traditional posts on her main feed, Crenshaw used Instagram's Story feature to deliver more casual, interactive social distancing content. This content reduced barriers specific to moms implementing social distancing measures. Instagram Stories are temporary posts, expiring after 24 hours, that are viewed in an automatic slideshow format. This feature also enables the user to conduct an interactive livestream with followers, called Instagram Live. After Crenshaw's social distancing Stories expired, she organized and pinned the content to her account homepage through a feature called Story Highlights for extended visibility.

She used Instagram Live to host a COVID-19 support group session for her followers. This gathered moms together, while also setting an example of how to practice social distancing. The session brought followers free, real-time support and accountability to the palms of their hands.

katiemcrenshaw ✓   •••

FIGURE 22.2 Photo 2 Posted by Katie Crenshaw

Crenshaw made an Instagram Story Highlight titled "COVID-19 Info" to compile content to make social distancing easier for moms. The Highlight is linked to a Google Document with a "Giant list of ideas for being at home with kids." A few ideas on the list were "try stop motion animation with play-dough," "write a story cooperatively," and "have an Olympics with a bunch of [funny] events." Crenshaw's Highlight also included graphics of a grocery list and healthy food plan detailing how to prepare for one week of feeding a family entirely at home. Another graphic on the "COVID Info" Highlight outlined a schedule appropriate for a toddler who is inside all day. The graphic also listed ideas for learning and playtime activities. Crenshaw's Instagram Story Highlight content aimed to reduce barriers to social distancing for moms. Crenshaw is just one of many influencers in the U.S. who effectively used their reach to combat the spread of COVID-19 (Desaulniers, 2020).

Insights

- Crisis communicators should look to the HBM when seeking effective behavior change from their audiences during a health crisis.
- Crisis communicators should equip SMIs with the information needed to make accurate posts.
- SMIs should provide practical ways to implement the crisis response recommendations and foster a community committed to adhering to crisis response guidelines.
- Researchers should consider examining SMI followers' parasocial relationships with SMIs using the Social-Mediated Crisis Communication model. It is not known how this could drive audiences' information seeking behavior during a health crisis.
- Future research should examine consumers' responses to SMIs sharing health crisis information, especially as it pertains to source credibility and celebrity endorsement effectiveness.

References

Alsulaiman, S. A., & Rentner, T. L. (2018). The health belief model and preventive measures: A study of the Ministry of Health Campaign on coronavirus in Saudi Arabia. *Journal of International Crisis and Risk Communication Research*, 1(1), 27–56. https://doi.org/10.30658/jicrcr.1.1.3

Austin, L., Liu, B. F., & Jin, Y. (2012). How audiences seek out crisis information: Exploring the social-mediated crisis communication model. *Journal of Applied Communication Research*, 40(2), 188–207. https://doi.org/10.1080/00909882.2012.654498

Desaulniers, S. (2020, April 10). How Instagram influencers are trying to slow the spread of the coronavirus. *CNBC*. https://www.cnbc.com/2020/04/10/coronavirus-instagram-influencers-try-to-slow-covid-19-spread.html

Ewing, M. & Lambert, C. (2019). Listening In: Fostering Influencer Relationships to Manage Fake News. *Public Relations Journal*, 12(4). https://prjournal.instituteforpr.org/wp-content/uploads/Listening-In-Updated-090519.pdf

Meet Our Speakers (2020). *Mom Congress*. https://www.mom-congress.com/2020-speakers

Rosenstock, I. M. (1966). Why people use health services. *Milbank Memorial Fund Quarterly*, 44, 94–127. https://doi.org/10.1111/j.1468-0009.2005.00425.x

Seo, Y., Primovic, M., & Jin, Y. (2019). Social media strategies for overcoming stakeholder social media fatigue: A Trialogue approach. *Journal of Business Strategy* (special issue on *Transformation of Strategy*), 40(6), 40–48. https://doi.org/10.1108/JBS-04-2019-0071

Sng, K., Au, T. Y., & Pang, A. (2019). Social media influencers as a crisis risk in strategic communication: Impact of indiscretions on professional endorsements. *International Journal of Strategic Communication*, 13(4), 301–320. https://doi.org/10.1080/1553118X.2019.1618305

Social Distancing (2020, July 15). *Centers for Disease Control and Prevention*. https://www.cdc.gov/coronavirus/2019-ncov/prevent-getting-sick/social-distancing.html

23

OPPORTUNITIES FOR INSTRUCTIONAL CRISIS COMMUNICATION THROUGH SOCIAL MEDIA

Communicating Self-Protective Actions for Food Safety during the COVID-19 Pandemic

Rodrigo Soares, Silvia Dumitrescu, Tamika Sims, Timothy L. Sellnow, Deanna D. Sellnow, and Matthew W. Seeger

Health-related crises, particularly pandemics, create considerable uncertainty and fear. Addressing the resulting confusion requires strategic instructional communication that promotes cognitive, affective, and behavioral learning. More specifically, the primary objective is to promote evidence-driven self-protective actions to reduce risk. During the first months of the COVID-19 crisis in the United States, considerable confusion emerged among publics about food safety and potential package contamination. Using the IDEA model (internalizing risk, distributing messages, explaining risks, and articulating action steps), we analyze the communication efforts of the International Food Information Council (IFIC) through social media to provide accurate, evidence-based instructional messages to consumers about the risk of contracting COVID-19 through food and packaging.

For three decades, IFIC has pursued its mission to communicate science-based information on health, nutrition, and food safety to diverse publics. To achieve their mission, IFIC's in-house experts are continuously available to help media counter dis- and mis-information. Although IFIC-produced messages about COVID-19 have appeared on CNN, Business Insider, and WebMD, their greatest reach is through social media. IFIC's social media channels consist of over 500,000 followers (@foodinsight on Facebook, Twitter, and Instagram)

DOI: 10.4324/9781003043409-32

and more than 3.5 million consumers visit the IFIC website (https://foodinsight. org/) annually.

Our chapter begins with references to existing literature that provide a context for IFIC's response to the COVID-19 crisis. Next, we provide detailed reflections from our IFIC authors about their communication objectives, strategies, and reactions during the crisis. We then examine IFIC's outreach through Twitter. We end with conclusions and practical recommendations.

Instructional Crisis Communication

Research shows that people turn to social media for information and instruction during periods of crisis and risk (e.g., Spence et al., 2016; Anderson & Vogels, 2020) and doing so more and more with the proliferation of smartphone technology (Niles et al., 2019). During a crisis, publics need quick and easy access to actionable instructions based on "accurate facts and reasonable interpretations of those facts upon which an individual should rely in making reason-based decisions" (Gerwin, 2012, p. 630). In fact, government agencies have been using social media to respond to global pandemics for more than a decade (Smith, 2009) and social media alerts are particularly effective in helping publics avoid "unsafe consumption" during food crisis events (Mou & Lin, 2014, p. 595).

Although the use of Twitter to reach disparate publics regarding risk and crisis events is growing exponentially, it does have limitations based on maximum character parameters (Lachlan et al., 2014). For example, Meadows et al. (2019) found that short Twitter messages served as a platform for sharing opinions rather than comprehensive informative during the 2015 California Measles outbreak. Nevertheless, more than 70% of U.S. residents searched online for information during the height of the COVID-19 global pandemic (Pew Research Center, 2020). Moreover, given the increase in 24/7 accessibility to social media via smartphones and IFIC's established Twitter following, examination of the messages shared as a form of instructional communication during the COVID-19 pandemic is warranted.

A growing body of research confirms that effective instructional communication regarding risk and crisis must be developed and delivered in ways that achieve outcomes focused on three learning domains (Bloom, 1956; Dewey, 1938; Krathwohl et al., 1973;Simpson, 1972). To achieve effective learning, such communication must motivate receivers to pay attention to and remember the information. Some strategies for doing so include demonstrating personal relevance and potential impact. In other words, such messages must address questions regarding the degree to which the receivers and those they care about are affected. Effective messages achieve cognitive learning when the information is both accurate and translated in ways that make it intelligible to the intended audience (Wensing et al., 2010). Finally, instructional communication achieves behavioral learning and efficacy when consumers believe they can and do perform desired actions.

The IDEA model was created as an easy-to-understand-and-apply framework for designing such messages (Sellnow & Sellnow, 2019). The utility of the model for message creation and delivery has been confirmed in myriad studies focused on effective instructional risk and crisis communication (e.g., D. D. Sellnow et al., 2017, 2019; T. L. Sellnow et al., 2017, 2019; Sellnow-Richmond et al., 2018). IDEA is essentially an acronym representing each of the four dimensions of the model. "I" stands for internalization. Messages must appeal to emotions in ways that motivate listeners to attend to and remember. The "D" represents distribution. Messages must be delivered through multiple communication channels and by a variety of sources to reach disparate publics. "E" denotes explanation. Messages must be accurate and based on data, as well as translated for intelligibility among disparate audiences. Finally, "A" is for action. Messages must offer specific action steps to prepare for and respond to an event in ways that are appropriately tailored to risk type and receiver norms.

Methods

The blend of communication researchers and practitioners on the team employed a mixed-methods approach for this study. Specifically, the IFIC professionals provide a case study that generates a rich context for understanding the organization's communication goals, strategies, and reflections. The academic researchers facilitated a theoretically grounded thematic analysis of a segment of IFIC's tweets during an acute period of the crisis when uncertainty was high.

More specifically, the thematic analysis examines IFIC's tweets according to the IDEA model categories of internalization, explanation, and action. (Distribution was not analyzed thematically since all messages in the data set were shared via Twitter.) We captured all IFIC tweets between March 11, 2020, the day the World Health Organization declared COVID-19 a worldwide pandemic, and July 20, 2020. We chose these dates because they represent a period of intensified threat and tremendous uncertainty about the nature of COVID-19. Over this period, IFIC shared 156 tweets referencing COVID-19. The unit of analysis was tweet content and links to additional information were not included. Doing so ensured the analysis was limited to messages created by IFIC. Three coders analyzed the tweets. To maintain objectivity, none were directly affiliated with IFIC. As mentioned earlier, an etic approach was used to evaluate the tweets, using "conceptual categories provided by our disciplinary knowledge and theory" (Lindlof & Taylor, 2011, p. 95) – in this case, the IDEA model. Following the thematic coding recommendations of Boyatzis (1998), all three coders had an extensive knowledge of the IDEA model, Twitter, and IFIC. Coders familiarized themselves with the Tweets independently before discussing how to categorize them into themes and subthemes. Any disagreements were resolved by reaching a consensus through discussion. Some individual tweets were coded in more than one category. Thus, some tweets were assigned to multiple categories. The team conducted member checks with IFIC practitioners to verify the contextual accuracy of our interpretation (Lindlof & Taylor, 2011).

Reflections from IFIC

The COVID-19 pandemic presented a unique opportunity for IFIC experts to explain the intricacies of an evolving crisis in ways that empowered them to make informed choices while shopping for food. They did so by providing evidence-based information in a simple and accessible way.

How Social Media Was Used Strategically to Get Messages Out during the Pandemic

IFIC leveraged the expertise of an in-house virologist, Tamika Sims, PhD, to serve as a spokesperson regarding safe food handling, social distancing, and handwashing pertaining to grocery stores and restaurants, as well as ranging from in-store shopping and in-house dining to curbside pickup and delivery.

Twitter was the platform used most for engaged dialogue with scientists, journalists, healthcare professionals, and the public. Twitter was also used to amplify IFIC information shared via traditional media. Our social presence in social media events also afforded an opportunity to partner with notable influencers such as Headspace, Cornell University's Food Safety Department, the Academy of Nutrition and Dietetics, and the United Nations' Food and Agriculture Organization.

Commonly asked questions included (listed in the order of frequency of occurrence from March to July 2020):

1. Are grocery or restaurant foods safe?
2. Are packaged foods safer to consume than those that are not (fresh produce, deli items, etc.)?
3. What are some safety measures I can take while I shop for groceries?
4. Are my groceries unsafe due to shoppers potentially transferring the coronavirus to products?
5. Should I wipe my groceries down with cleaning products to disinfect them, or leave them outside for three days to eliminate any live virus that could be on the surface?
6. Is getting groceries or restaurant food delivery safe?
7. Are stores having a shortage of food and other shelf items because national supplies are low?

8. What are some safety measures I can take while I dine outside of my home or host a gathering?

In the following section, the thematic analysis of IFIC's tweets using the IDEA model reveals how these questions and issues were addressed.

Thematic Analysis of IFIC's COVID-19 Twitter Activity

Figure 23.1 summarizes IFIC's allocation of twitter messages across the three categories of internalization, explanation, and action. The narrative discussion of each category includes an overview of the content and representative examples of IFIC's tweets.

Internalization

Most of the IFIC tweets emphasizing internalization did so in conjunction with proposing specific actions. Early tweets (e.g., Memorial Day weekend instructions) confirmed the need to social distance in order to reduce personal risk (IFIC, 2020c). Beyond endorsing these widely prescribed actions, Tweets dedicated to internalization focused primarily on acknowledging the concerns publics had about the safety of their food, challenges for storing food during a pandemic, and maintaining high immunity through good nutrition.

IFIC referenced its own survey research to affirm that most consumers remained confident in the food supply. In a June 29, 2020 tweet, IFIC wrote, despite the pandemic, "nearly 7 in 10 consumers (67%) are at least somewhat confident in the safety of the U.S. #food supply" (IFIC, 2020d). By contrast,

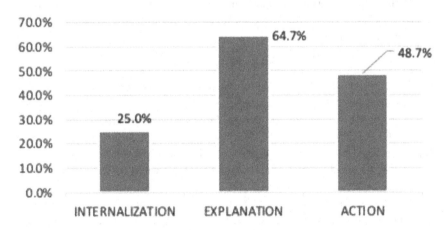

FIGURE 23.1 Distribution of Tweets using IDEA Model Categories

IFIC also acknowledged lingering concerns about eating food prepared outside the home. For example, a July 7, 2020 tweet explained, "When asked about their concerns in the context of #pandemic, nearly half (48%) of consumers were at least somewhat concerned about #food prepared outside the home." Sharing these statistics helped consumers place their concerns and fears in the context of a broad sample of other American consumers.

IFIC also confirmed that consumers were not alone in their challenges with storing food and their concerns about maintaining good nutrition. IFIC also acknowledged consumer frustration about shopping less frequently. As illustrated in this April 20, 2020 Tweet, internalization was often combined with action: "picking items with long shelf lives: frozen and canned foods and packaged foods like pasta, oats and rice" (IFIC, 2020). Similarly, IFIC confirmed that consumers can improve their immunity through good nutrition. For example, IFIC tweeted on July 14, 2020, "#VitaminD supports immune #health and is found in fatty fish, eggs, milk and milk products and some fruit juices" (IFIC, 2020e).

Explanation

Explanation was the most prevalent of the elements in the IFIC Tweets, although the information shared was far from comprehensive. For example, rather than explaining the nature of COVID-19 in the tweet, a link directed viewers to another website. Although Twitter's character limitations prohibit lengthy explanations, the medium does allow for robust explanations by embedding multimedia content that can offer considerable detail (Molyneux & Mourão, 2019). IFIC offered links to extended explanations that could be found on its own website, foodinsight.org. Links to other organizations were also referenced (e.g., USDA, U.S. Surgeon General, Centers for Disease Control and Prevention, U.S. Food and Drug Administration, Harvard University, World Cancer Research Fund). Explanation content focused almost exclusively on food safety/packaging, the food supply, and nutrition.

In March, IFIC tweeted that "CDCgov and other food safety agencies all agree that there is *no* evidence to support transmission of #COVID19 associated with #food" (IFIC, 2020). IFIC also addressed risks associated with ordering groceries for delivery or consuming food prepared at a restaurant or deli. For example, IFIC's March 28 tweet, "How safe is it to order food delivery during#COVID? We have your #foodsafety questions answered." IFIC provided a series of links to its foodinsight.org site and a link to a recommendation from CDC to check to make sure cooked food delivered to one's home is at a safe temperature before consuming (IFIC, 2020).

IFIC also addressed consumer concerns about whether to sanitize packaged food and produce from grocery stores. For example, in an April 16 tweet combining explanation with action, IFIC tweeted, "We do not advise sanitizing food packages before opening them, opt for washing your hands thoroughly before and after touching food packages" (IFIC, 2020). This tweet was consistent with IFIC's transcending explanation that standard food safety principles such as frequent hand washing, proper food storage, and cooking to acceptable temperatures were effective means of managing the food-related risk of COVID-19.

IFIC also offered explanations about the flexibility of the U.S. food supply and maintaining nutrition during the pandemic. In an April 23 tweet, IFIC addressed the resilience of the food supply by asserting, "What happens to the food supply during a #pandemic? Everything from farms to warehouses have to quickly adjust" (IFIC, 2020). This tweet included links to agriculture source exemplars in responding to the challenges of the pandemic. True to its mission, IFIC continued to explain the importance of nutrition throughout the pandemic. These tweets included both reinforcement and clarification. For example, IFIC reinforced its long-standing objective to promote nutrition at all times by tweeting, "According to our #research, 43% of consumers report that they consider their eating habits to be healthier than they were a few months ago." IFIC also offered clarification to counter tips from others the agency believed were invalid. For example, IFIC tweeted, "No, the elderberry syrup and protein powders that you're seeing ads for do not have strong evidence-or often, any evidence at all-to back up their claims related to #immune." Overall, the explanatory messages tweeted by IFIC emphasized the value of evidence-based research in comprehending the true risks associated with COID-19.

Action

Regarding action steps, earlier tweets emphasized safe at-home food preparation. Later tweets also recommended actions related to eating at restaurants and celebrating on July 4. As mentioned earlier, IFIC emphasized maintaining good nutrition and standard food safety practices, as detailed on its website, for reducing the risk of contracting COVID-19 through mishandling food. IFIC also countered misinformation on food safety. For example, the agency cautioned consumers to avoid bleach when washing fruits and vegetables. In this March 26 tweet, IFIC (2020a) commented, "If you're concerned about your fruits and vegetables, don't wash them with bleach. Opt for cooking them, or washing thoroughly with warm water." IFIC's website includes details on how and why rinsing in warm water is the best option to minimize the risk of contamination through mishandling fruits and vegetables. IFIC also cautioned consumers against over-buying during the pandemic. For example, in this April 26 tweet, they wrote, "By not overbuying, we can all do our part to waste less #food while ensuring that everyone has access to the food they need during this difficult time" (IFIC, 2020b).

As states began reopening in-house dining options, IFIC addressed the risk by encouraging "delivery or takeout, but if not, opt for outside spaces (patio seating), be mindful if servers are wearing masks, limit contact with other patrons and wash your hands before eating" (June 11, 2020). IFIC also recognized the risks for consumers hosting or attending July 4 holiday events. IFIC tweeted, "Hosting a gathering for the #4thofJuly? Follow these tips for hosting during a #pandemic." Readers were then directed to IFIC's website for a detailed explanation on how to safely prepare and share food at a small gathering. For example, readers were told to host the event outside, keep the gathering small, ask guests to bring their own food and beverages, and use standard food safety practices such as washing hands, keeping fruits and vegetables separate from meat products, cook foods to recommended temperatures, and chill foods before and soon after serving.

Conclusions and Implications

As suggested by previous research, consumers had many questions about health and safety during the COVID-19 pandemic. Many of them focused on safety and dependability of the U.S. food system. IFIC had already established foodinsight.org as a reliable source of information and continuously monitored media coverage of food-related issues during COVID-19. The next section provides conclusions and implications based on the personal observations of IFIC communication specialists and academic researchers.

IFIC Professional Reflections: Pros and Cons in Using Social Media

Social media allowed our team to send timely messages on food safety as advice from regulatory and public health authorities evolved all the time. The platforms facilitated outreach to large audiences in real-time to add our science-based messaging to the conversation. We were also able to establish relationships with new influencers and work with reputable organizations to be able to balance the dialogue and help translate the science for the public.

At the beginning of the COVID-19 outbreak, people needed foundational information about how the virus spread from person to person and how to protect themselves. During this early period, we focused on clarifying that coronavirus was not a foodborne illness. By late spring, people were asking about the safest way to shop for food, have food delivered, and gaps in the food supply chain. As businesses started to reopen in the U.S. (early June 2020), people expressed interest in safety issues when dining out and participating in small gatherings. Social media allowed us to pivot and upgrade our advice quickly based on the most in-demand information at the time.

Conversely, our use of social media also had negative implications. Information is only shared in short messages, which sometimes prevents a full explanation of a complex issue. While we encourage people to visit our website to read comprehensive articles that give more in-depth information, not everyone does it. This means important information that could empower people to make informed decisions might never reach them.

Perhaps most concerning was the exponential spread of fake news. Self-proclaimed experts, meme creators, and attention-seeking individuals gain an audience easily via social channels and can spread misinformation fast, far, and wide.

Lastly, the lack of participation by prominent scientists and public health professionals in social media conversations contributed to an imbalanced dialogue among credible voices sharing scientific messages. The same can be said about not contributing to the conversation when it was needed. Topics constantly change and evolve in both traditional and social media, but speed and timeliness are particularly important for the latter.

Academic Researcher Reflections: Practical Applications and Theoretical Contributions

Effective instructional communication is essential for protecting individuals during the acute phase of crises. In pandemics, the acute phase lingers far longer than in most other crisis types (e.g., floods, fires, hurricanes, earthquakes). As a prolonged crisis, the COVID19 required IFIC to continuously monitor the situation and adapt its messages as the crisis evolved. Previous research has not examined communication during the acute phase of a prolonged crisis of this nature. This analysis suggests that instructional processes must be nimble enough to adjust to the changing needs of those at risk and also consistent enough to provide viewers with a trustworthy set of guidelines for safety and protection. Future research should take note of the agile nature of instructional communication to adapt to the changing needs of publics during crises with extended acute phases. Comprehending these changing needs might be well informed by recent research on the role dialogue can play, particularly through digital platforms, in accurately comprehending the concerns and needs of audiences at risk. Taylor and Kent (2007), for example, argue that organizations can adapt their digital presence to create two-way interaction with publics that meets the standards of dialogue. Organizations and agencies that engage in dialogue during crises enhance their capacity to accurately comprehend and respond to the concerns of their audiences.

This study also reveals a link between a well-established, often-visited website and Twitter. Twitter only affords limited discussion of who is at risk, of what, and with what options for self-protection. In fact, previous research noted only minimal applications of Twitter during the most acute phases of such crises as hurricanes (Spence et al., 2015). IFIC, however, was able to provide actionable information by embedding content from its website, foodinsight.org, into tweets about COVID-19. This option was particularly fitting for IFIC because many of the procedures needed for the standard practice of food safety were essential for avoiding the spread of COVID-19 through food preparation. IFIC already had a loyal audience and access to considerable information. This combination enabled them to fully capitalize on Twitter's affordances.

To date, instructional risk and crisis communication research has focused primarily on providing warning messages (Mileti & Peek, 2000) and instructions for minimizing the potential harm of a crisis (Sellnow & Sellnow, 2019). The IFIC communication professionals convincingly argue for developing guidelines for how instructional messages can effectively counter misinformation. Future research should consider the capacity for instructional communication to counter mis- and dis- information spread through rumors, as well as manipulating scientific information with the intent of misleading publics.

This analysis is limited in that we only analyzed tweets by IFIC during the first four months of the COVID-19 crisis in the U.S. We see value in this focus, however, because the first four months generated tremendous uncertainty about food supply safety and IFIC relied on Twitter over other forms of social media, there is an inherent limitation regarding generalizability.

COVID-19 placed unprecedented burdens on consumers and caused a great deal of anxiety among disparate publics. Although individuals could survive without many of the COVID-19 restrictions, everyone needed food. The essential nature of food made information about its access and safe preparation paramount. IFIC recognized this need and dedicated considerable time and resources to answering the most pressing questions from consumers about the threat of COVID-19 to their daily food consumption. The evidence-based instructions IFIC provided throughout the initial phase of the crisis illustrate the value in addressing relevance and impact for diverse populations. IFIC's well-established website and its deft use of Twitter serve as examples for other organizations seeking to serve their stakeholders during crises.

References

Anderson, M., & Vogels, E. A. (2020, March 31). Americans turn to technology during COVID-19 outbreak: Say an outage would be a problem. Pew Research Center. https://www.pewresearch.org/fact-tank/2020/03/31/americans-turn-to-technology-during-covid-19-outbreak-say-an-outage-would-be-a-problem/

Bloom, B. S. (1956). *Taxonomy of educational objectives: Handbook I: The cognitive domain.* David McKay.

Boyatzis, R. E. (1998). *Transforming qualitative information: Thematic analysis and code development.* Sage.

Dewey, J. (1938). *Experience and education.* University of Chicago Press.

Gerwin, L. E. (2012). The challenge of providing the public with actionable information during a pandemic. *The Journal of Law, Medicine & Ethics, 40,* 630–654. http://dx.doi. org/10.1111/j.1748-720X.2012.00695.x

IFIC [@FoodInsight]. (2020a, March 26). If you are concerned about your fruits and vegetables, don't wash them with bleach. Opt for cooking them, or washing them thoroughly with warm water- https://bit.ly/2x92Jl8 #COVID19 #foodsafety. [Tweet; attached image and link]. Twitter. https://twitter.com/FoodInsight/status/1243161289897189378?s=20

IFIC [@FoodInsight]. (2020b, April 26). By not overbuying, we can all do our part to waste less #food while ensuring that everyone has access to the food they need during this difficult time- [Tweet; attached image and link]. Twitter. https://twitter.com/FoodInsight/status/1254472820958146561?s=20

IFIC [@FoodInsight]. (2020c, May 24). Hosting a "socially distant" barbecue this #MemorialDayWeekend? Don't forget these #foodsafety tips. [Tweet; attached image]. Twitter. https://twitter.com/FoodInsight/status/1264717075936956416?s=20

IFIC [@FoodInsight]. (2020d, June 29). Despite the #pandemic, nearly 7 in 10 consumers (67%) are at least somewhat confident in the safety of the U.S. #food supply, according to our research. [Tweet; attached image and link]. Twitter. https://twitter.com/FoodInsight/status/1277730826726375434?s=20

IFIC [@FoodInsight]. (2020e, July 14). #VitaminD suports immune #health and is found in fatty fish, eggs, milk and milk products and some fruit juices.. [Tweet; attached image and link]. Twitter. https://twitter.com/FoodInsight/status/1283166649563189249?s=20

Krathwohl, D. R., Bloom, B. S., & Bertram, B. M. (1973). *Taxonomy of educational objectives, the classification of educational goals, Handbook II: Affective domain.* David McKay.

Lachlan, K. A., Spence, P. R., Lin, X., Najarian, K. M., & Greco, M. D. (2014). Twitter use during a weather event: Comparing content associated with localized and nonlocalized hashtags. *Communication Studies, 65*(5), 519–534. https://doi.org/10.1027/1864-1105/a000037

Lindlof, T. R., & Taylor, B. C. (2011). *Qualitative communication research methods* (3rd ed.). Sage.

Meadows, C. W., Meadows, C. Z., Tang, L., & Liu, W. (2019). Unraveling public health crises across stages: Understanding Twitter emotions and message types during the California measles outbreak. *Communication Studies, 70*(4), 453–469. http://dx.doi.org/10.1080/10510974.2019.1582546

Mileti, D. S., & Peek, L. (2000). The social psychology of public response to warnings of a nuclear power plant accident. *Journal of Hazardous Materials, 75,* 181–194. http://dx.doi. org/10.1016/S0304-3894(00)00179-5

Molyneux, L., & Mourão, R. R. (2019). Political journalists' normalization of Twitter: Interaction and new affordances. *Journalism Studies, 20*(2), 248–266. http://dx.doi.org/10.1080/1461670X.2017.1370978

Mou, Y., & Lin, C. A. (2014). Communicating food safety via the social media: The role of knowledge and emotions on risk perception and prevention. *Science Communication, 36,* 593–616. http://dx.doi.org/10.1177/1075547014549480

Niles, M. T., Emery, B. F., Reagan, A. J., Dodds, P. S., & Danforth, C. M. (2019). Social media usage patterns during natural hazards. *PloS One, 14*(2), e0210484. http://dx.doi. org/10.1371/journal.pone.0210484

Pew Research Center. (2020). Most Americans have used email and messaging services to connect with others during the COVID-19 outbreak, while one-in-four have used video calling for work [data set]. Pew Research Center. https://www.pewresearch.org/fact-tank/2020/03/31/americans-turn-to-technology-during-covid-19-outbreak-say-an-outage-would-be-a-problem/ft_2020-03-31_techcovid_01/

Sellnow, D. D., Johansson, B., Sellnow, T. L., & Lane, D. R. (2019). Toward a global understanding of the effects of the IDEA model for designing instructional risk and crisis messages: A food contamination experiment in Sweden. *Journal of Contingencies and Crisis Management, 27*, 102–115. http://dx.doi.org/10.1111/1468-5973.12234

Sellnow, D. D., Lane, D. R., Sellnow, T. L., & Littlefield, R. S. (2017). The IDEA model as a best practice for effective instructional risk and crisis communication. *Communication Studies, 68*, 552–567. http://dx.doi.org/10.1080/10510974.2017.1375535

Sellnow, T. L., Parker, J. S., Sellnow, D. D., Littlefield, R. R., Helsel, E. M., Getchell, M. C., Smith, J. M., & Merrill, S. C. (2017). Improving biosecurity through instructional crisis communication: Lessons learned from the PEDv outbreak. *Journal of Applied Communications, 101*(4). https://doi.org/10.4148/1051-0834.1298

Sellnow, D. D., & Sellnow, T. L. (2019). The IDEA model of effective instructional risk and crisis communication by emergency managers and other key spokespersons. *Journal of Emergency Management, 17*(1), 67–78. https://doi.org/10.5055/jem.2019.0399

Sellnow, T. L., Sellnow, D. D., Helsel, E. M., Martin, J., & Parker, J. S. (2019). Crisis communication in response to rapidly emerging diseases in the agriculture industry: Porcine epidemic diarrhea virus as a cases study. *Journal of Risk Research, 22*(7), 897–908. https://doi.org/10.1080/13669877.2017.1422787

Sellnow-Richmond, D. D., George, A. M., & Sellnow, D. D. (2018). An IDEA model analysis of instructional risk communication in the time of Ebola. *Journal of International Crisis and Risk Communication Research, 1*(1), 135–165. http://dx.doi.org/10.30658/jicrcr.1.1.7

Simpson, E. J. (1972). *The classification of educational objectives in the psychomotor domain.* Gryphon House.

Smith, S. (2009, December 11). New media spread the word on H1N1: Twitter, YouTube messages aimed at public. *Boston Globe.* http://archive.boston.com/news/health/articles/2009/12/11/new_media_spread_the_word_on_h1n1/

Spence, P. R., Lachlan, K. A., Lin, X., & del Greco, M. (2015). Variability in Twitter content across the stages of a natural disaster: Implications for crisis communication. *Communication Quarterly, 63*(2), 171–186. http://dx.doi.org/10.1080/01463373.2015.1012219

Spence, P. R., Sellnow-Richmond, D., Sellnow, T. L., & Lachlan, K. A. (2016). Social media and corporate reputation during crises: The viability of video-sharing websites for providing counter-messaging to traditional broadcast news. *Journal of Applied Communication Research, 44*, 199–215. http://dx.doi.org/10.1080/00909882.2016.1192289

Taylor, M., & Kent, M. L. (2007). Taxonomy of mediated crisis responses. *Public Relations Review, 33*(2), 140–146. http://dx.doi.org/10.1016/j.pubrev.2006.11.017

Wensing, M., Bosch, M., & Grol, R. (2010). Developing and selecting interventions for translating knowledge to action. *CMAJ, 182*(2), E85–E88. https://doi.org/10.1503/cmaj.081233

24

POLITICAL CASE CHAPTER: POLITICAL PIVOT

Framing the COVID-19 #GoVAXMaryland Campaign in Social Media

Heather Davis Epkins

> "We made increased engagement from the social media platforms our top priority for reaching out, informing, and hearing from Marylanders. With over 3.2 million impressions and 45,000 followers [from just our eight offices among scores of other agencies[i]], we look forward to connecting even more of our citizens to needed resources statewide and advancing the Hogan administration's outreach and support mission to all Marylanders in 2021 and beyond."
>
> – Patrick J. Lally, Executive Director,
> Governor's Coordinating Offices
> (Maryland Governor's Coordinating Offices, January 13, 2021)

During a crisis, social media use increases (Pew Internet & American Life Project, 2006), and social media interactions can equate the power and influence of a human relationship (Reeves & Nass, 1996). Government communications can act as a catalyst for change in human behavior (Fearn-Banks, 2011), including health crisis response (Rosenstock, 1966). Social media is one tool government communicators utilize to engage with citizens – especially constituents who may be underrepresented or uneasily reached (Bertot et al., 2012). Educating people through social media platforms helped reduce the mental health consequences of the COVID-19 pandemic and ultimately aided in managing the global health crisis (Abbas et al., 2021).

However, while social media addressed emotional isolation; unfortunately, these channels also carried the risk of misinformation, fragmentation, overwhelm, and in some cases were associated with increasing the spread of COVID-19 through the ability to organize off-line events (Kong et al., 2021).

DOI: 10.4324/9781003043409-33

In some ways, social media became as hazardous as the virus itself. The Governor's Coordinating Offices (GCO) communications team quickly realized that their social media channels were the socially distanced tool of choice to share critical health crisis information, but that these channels were dynamic, so the urgency for communication clarity, coordination, and accuracy was top of mind.

Messaging supported public health communications best practices (Austin et al., 2012) such as communicating with one voice; funneling audiences toward other accurate, trusted social media outlets; building trust with underserved communities; and equipping targeted audiences and social media influencers to amplify the rapid and timely messaging coming from the central Office of Maryland Governor Larry Hogan. Under Governor Hogan's direction, Maryland is considered a national leader in the effective handling of the COVID-19 pandemic (Dottle & Tartar, 2021; Maul et al., 2021; Siemaszko, 2020).

Governor's Coordinating Offices

The Governor's Coordinating Offices (GCO) are a group of eight offices – located separately from the main Governor's Office – unified by Maryland Governor Larry Hogan to organize a shared services business model that would reduce taxpayer costs and connect Marylanders with needed resources statewide. Each office has a specific mission and target audience. At the beginning of the COVID-19 pandemic, these offices included: Governor's Office of Crime Prevention, Youth, and Victim Services, Governor's Office of Community Initiatives, Governor's Office on Service and Volunteerism, Governor's Office of the Deaf and Hard of Hearing, Governor's Office of Small, Minority and Women Business Affairs, Volunteer Maryland, Banneker-Douglass Museum, and the Governor's Office of Performance Improvement. The GCO has a communications director, and each office employs a public information officer (PIO); this group works as a team to communicate to constituents across Maryland using multiple communication channels.

Framing

Framing theory describes the process of content selection and exclusion, highlighting certain aspects over others to communicate a particular point of view. A frame can socially construct meaning via "organizing principles that are socially shared and persistent over time, that work symbolically to meaningfully structure the social world" (Reese, 2001, p. 11). Specifically, framing uses the selection of some aspects of a perceived reality, making them more salient to the audience with an outcome that can help promote a certain problem definition, causal interpretation, moral evaluation, and/or treatment recommendation for the topic (Entman, 1993, p. 52). Overall, framing is exercising the power to control and shape a message (Entman, 2004; Goffman, 1974) and can impact audience understanding and subsequent choices (Pfau et al., 2004).

Researchers Fairhurst and Sarr (1996) argue that political communicators often add a value judgment that might not be otherwise apparent by using positive or negative language to frame a topic. They further propose that communicators can use metaphor, stories, tradition, slogans, jargon, catchphrases, artifacts, and contrast as techniques to frame the message. Four of these techniques will be detailed in this case study including: artifacts (using a visual object with intrinsic value holding more meaning than the object itself), slogans/catchphrases (to make the message memorable and relatable); stories (to use narrative in a vivid and memorable way), and metaphor (to frame an idea as a comparison to something else).

Case Study

As part of its broader communications strategy, the GCO pledges to utilize social media to align messaging with the governor to amplify one voice; utilize one point of contact to streamline flow; ensure a chain of approvals to provide accuracy; direct users to trusted sources only; support sister office messaging; and post truthfully, early, and often to create a drumbeat of consistent communication. The "coordinating" offices mission is to collaborate and connect relevant offices, agencies, and citizens with resources to serve and protect Marylanders. To accomplish this during the COVID-19 pandemic, GCO PIOs (along with all PIOs) were thrust onto the front lines in a daily grind to ensure consistency, frequency, and accuracy of highly sensitive, life-changing information.

As the GCO PIO team walked out of the physical building that second week in March of 2020 as the state government began working from home, members hit the ground running to meet an urgent, new demand coming from the citizens served by each office. From day one of the pandemic, the Governor's Office of the Deaf and Hard of Hearing worked to ensure access for 1.2 million Deaf and hard of hearing Marylanders by securing qualified emergency American Sign Language interpreters for all of the governor's press conferences, and utilizing social media to ensure ongoing access with a repository of more than 100 videos and lists of pertinent resources.

Many other shifts and new routines came about including: the creation of our own version of a real-time war room to ensure a unified voice. This is where the team also discussed media inquiries; handling a new slew of FOIAs; prepping internal experts for media and community inquiries; building "hot lists" of reporters and third-party surrogates who could deftly address false information and promote relevant information; checking rumors; attending weekly calls with the 24 county-level PIOs and other knowledgeable stakeholders; ramping up content on the governor's new Marylanders Serving Marylanders webpage;

brainstorming with colleagues on how to best reach targeted audiences – including our internal audiences – and pivoting to communicate the latest research and breaking news across 16 social media channels.

GCO PIOs immediately forged a new framing routine for original social media content. All messages and images needed to avoid: imagery of people touching, closely spaced, or without masks; alarmist rhetoric and insensitive or untimely language; and otherwise normal communications for April Fool's Day and other light-hearted observances, hashtags, captions, content, and collateral. Likewise, offices were asked to frame messages using positive language, to follow a layered approval process checked against trusted sources, and utilize a unified hashtag – #MarylandStrong. Each office was assigned a day of the week for specific COVID-19 messaging so at least one GCO social media channel carried the governor's message every day.

PIOs ramped up social content to postpone (and later cancel) upcoming in-person events, reflect the governor's near daily messaging, amplify trusted medical voices, promote timely and trusted COVID-19 news addressing common questions about vaccine safety and hesitancy, and raise internal and external awareness about measures to protect people from COVID-19. The team filtered information needing translation from the complex to the relatable, and sought to use engaging visuals and content intended to evoke the response needed to keep everyone safe. In addition, PIOs worked to rebrand all social media and forward facing communications to align with what all state agencies were asked to use: "Be a Hero – Stay at Home." Messaging promoted social distancing, and later, mask-wearing.

Proactively, the GCO team reached out to new reporters covering the COVID crisis to offer comments based on their targeted mission and grant releases, and also connected off-topic media inquiries with the proper state experts and agencies to ensure the public received accurate and up to date information. GCO staff participated in the governor's new Vaccine Equity Taskforce, so the team sought to use social media to reach new audiences, including a deeper dive into ethnic communities across Maryland with messaging pertaining to vaccine hesitancy and racial disparities.

The team also worked to promote tangential topics directly impacted by the pandemic, such as the alarming rise of child abuse and domestic violence through the creation of PSAs that ran on local TV and radio stations. GCO social media also promoted these PSAs and shared information stemming from these and other alarming trends like the rise of opioid use, unemployment, and adverse childhood experiences. At the same time, PIOs gained a bit of respite to thank front-line heroes promote the work of community volunteers, and make pleas for more volunteers for various needs. PIOs sometimes coordinated and daily reposted timely health-related communications from agencies like Planning, Labor, Aging, Veterans, Emergency Management, and others.

In addition, the Governor's Office of Performance Improvement tracked GCO social media analytics to help PIOs understand the demographics and timing needs of their target audiences.

Social media rebranded numerous times through the pandemic. After "Be a Hero – Stay at Home," the "Masks on Maryland" campaign ran for the remainder of 2020 and into 2021. Once COVID-19 vaccines became available in early 2021, messaging again pivoted to "GoVAXMaryland" to focus on the importance, distribution, and availability of vaccines. This particular time frame was tricky because the demand for vaccines outweighed supply, so the focus of social media centered on the state's plan to launch mass vaccination sites, often answering citizens' and local officials' frustration and confusion. Once vaccine supply caught up, messaging morphed to the "Vaccine Equity Taskforce" to address vaccine hesitancy and then through campaigns such as "VAXCASH," and the "Shottery" to advertise the entrance of the Maryland Lottery as part of a larger vaccination incentive program.

In addition, each office utilized social media to field incoming messages and frame public health information for their specific audience using various framing techniques to include stories, slogans and catchphrases, artifacts, and metaphors (Fairhurst & Sarr, 1996).

First, all offices utilized the framing technique of *stories* to show imagery of various trusted community leaders receiving a vaccine, asking Marylanders to get vaccinated, and showing the malevolence of front-line workers and volunteers to inspire service and unity. Under the Governor's Office of Community Initiatives (GOCI), social media was used to leverage the stories and powerful voices from the eight ethnic commissions to reach underserved communities, show visuals from vaccine-related events held in these communities, and detail the work of the governor's Vaccine Equity Task Force. In addition, social media showed mobile vaccine clinics for gatherings of the Deaf, Asian, Hispanic, Native American, and African American communities inside local community halls and places of worship to address the inherent cultural barriers preventing some communities from getting a COVID-19 vaccine. A unit of GOCI, Volunteer Maryland detailed the supporting role of AmeriCorps members serving on the front line to keep Marylanders safe.

The stories technique also worked to promote 1,000 socially distanced community events distributing hundreds of thousands of crucial PPE items to those in need; awarding $200 million in grants; facilitating 15,000 volunteers serving 50,000 volunteer hours; launching COVID-19 workgroups; serving more than 20,000 small businesses; assisting more than 130,000 crime victims and the law enforcement and nonprofit organizations who support them; pivoting essential resources for easy, online access; and spearheading innovative collaboration across state agencies to address the needs arising from the COVID-19 pandemic.

Second, the GCO also used the framing technique of *slogans and catchphrases* such as "Let's End COVID, Maryland" and "Vaccines save lives, and so can you." Anecdotally, GCO staff learned that these phrases evoked an emotional response from the audience, persuading them to action. For example, the Governor's Office on Small Business, Minority & Women Affairs caught attention by using catchphrases to couch difficult information regarding the impact on small businesses to share emergency loan information, unemployment resources, and procurement opportunities.

Third, the framing technique of the *artifact* was used. For example, social media carried a visual of a Native American Indian Chief donning a traditional wardrobe with an intrinsic cultural value, acting as meaningful symbols for this ethnic group with the chief asking others to get vaccinated. A unit of GOCI, the Banneker Douglass Museum engaged their audience by showing visuals of African Americans using masks, social distancing, and receiving vaccines.

Finally, the Governor's Office on Crime Prevention, Youth, and Victim Services long utilized the hashtag #ASaferMD to communicate efforts to address crime. During the COVID-19 pandemic, this office used the *metaphor* technique to reframe the hashtag to encourage their audience to get vaccinated for "A Safer Maryland." The Governor's Office on Service & Volunteerism utilized the metaphor to reframe their #iServeMD hashtag as a call to action on social media and a vehicle to drive Marylanders to the newly built "Marylanders Serving Marylanders" section of the governor's new #MarylandersUnite webpage. This page listed the latest social media from the governor, urgent volunteer opportunities, translations of COVID-19 health documents in the top 5 non-English languages for Maryland, and crucial resources "by agency" across the state.

Social media was quickly elevated as the main tool for the GCO PIO team to engage in COVID-19 crisis communications, and was a vehicle to forge new relationships with citizens that will continue even after the pandemic and beyond.

Note

1 Inserted note by chapter author

References

Abbas, J., Wang, D., Su, Z., & Ziapour, A. (2021). The role of social media in the advent of the COVID-19 pandemic: Crisis management, mental health challenges and implications. *Risk Management and Healthcare Policy, 14*, 1917–1932.

Austin, L., Fisher Liu, B., & Jin, Y. (2012). How audiences seek out crisis information: Exploring the social-mediated crisis communication model. *Journal of Applied Communication Research, 40*(2), 188–207.

Bertot, J. C., Jaeger, P. T., & Hansen, D. (2012). The impact of policies on government social media usage: Issues, challenges, and recommendations. *Government Information Quarterly, 29*, 30–40.

Dottle, R., & Tartar, A. (2021, June 16). Fifth state has vaccinated half of Black or Hispanic people this week: Covid-19 tracker. Tracking Covid vaccines by race: Black and Hispanic rates lower than White and Asian. *Bloomberg.* bloomberg.com.

Entman, R. M. (1993). Framing: Toward clarification of a fractured paradigm. *Journal of Communication, 43*, 51–58.

Entman, R. M. (2004). *Projections of power: Framing news, public opinion, and U.S. foreign policy.* University of Chicago Press.

Fairhurst, G., & Sarr, R. (1996). *The art of framing.* Jossey-Bass.

Fearn-Banks, K. (2011). *Crisis communications: A casebook approach.* Routledge.

Goffman, E. (1974). *Frame analysis: An essay on the organization of experience.* Harper and Row.

Kong, J. D., Tekwa, E. W., & Gignoux-Wolfsohn, S. A. (2021). Social, economic, and environmental factors influencing the basic reproduction number of COVID-19 across countries. *PLoS ONE, 16*(6), e0252373. https://doi.org/10.1371/journal.pone.0252373

Maryland Governor's Coordinating Offices. (2021, January 13). Governor's Coordinating Offices releases 2020 impact report: Millions of Marylanders provided PPE, crucial COVID-19 resources. https://goci.maryland.gov/2021/01/13/governors-coordinating-offices-releases-2020-impact-report/

Maul, A., Reddy, K., & Joshi, M. (2021, April 23). Vaccine equity index shows reduction in Maryland Covid-19 vaccination disparity in less than two months. *NEJM Catalyst.* https://catalyst.nejm.org/doi/full/10.1056/CAT.21.0126

Pew Internet & American Life Project (2006, November 20). The Internet as a resource for news and information about science. *Pew Research Center.* https://www.pewresearch.org/internet/2006/11/20/pew-internet-project-and-the-exploratorium-find-that-the-internet-is-a-pervasive-research-tool-for-science-news-and-information-use-of-online-science-resources-is-linked-to-better-attitudes-about-scie/

Pfau, M., Haigh, M., Gettle, M., Donnelly, M., Scott, G., Warr, D., & Wittenberg, E. (2004). Embedding journalists in military combat units: Impact on newspaper story frames and tone. *Journalism & Mass Communication Quarterly, 81*, 74–88.

Reese, S. (2001). Framing public life: A bridging model for media research. In S. Reese, O. Gandy, & A. Grant (Eds.), *Framing public life* (pp. 7–31). Erlbaum

Reeves, B., & Nass, C. (1996). *The media equation: How people treat computers, television, and new media like real people and places.* Cambridge University Press.

Rosenstock, I. M. (1966). Why people use health services. *Milbank Memorial Fund Quarterly, 44*, 94–127.

Siemaszko, C. (2020, March 22). Maryland Gov. Larry Hogan emerges as a leader in early action on coronavirus. *NBC.* https://www.nbcnews.com/news/usnews/maryland-gov-larry-hogan-emerges-leader-early-action-coronavirus-n1164256

25

NAVIGATING POLITICAL SCANDAL AND REPUTATION CRISIS IN SOCIAL MEDIA

Joseph Watson, Jr. and James D. Firth

Introduction

In the span of a decade, social media use in politics and public affairs has gone from a novelty to an essential tool of public officials, candidates, corporations, and nonprofit organizations. The first White House and congressional social media accounts were established in 2009 during the administration of President Barack Obama (Schulman, 2016). Today, Twitter, Facebook, Instagram, and YouTube accounts, among others, are not only ubiquitous but have become required communications tools for these organizations. These social media platforms allow organizations to communicate directly with voters, supporters, and customers, permitting them to circumvent traditional media.

Social media accounts are critical tools for branding, as well as reputation management in public affairs. Candidates and public affairs officials are increasingly focused on establishing a brand identity (Siegel, 2017). To this end, social media accounts afford them an opportunity to do so with key audiences for public affairs. Public affairs audiences are highly engaged on social media platforms and how candidates, officials, and organizations utilize them is an increasingly significant expression of their brand identities. Beyond facilitating the establishment of brand identities for newly formed campaigns and organizations, social media expressions must also be consistent with established brand identities for already well-established public affairs brands.

For established, as well as fledgling brands, social media has also emerged as a useful means of managing organizations' reputations. Social media analytic tools allow brands to track mentions, positive and negative, as well as trends. Monitoring these trends and patterns in brand mentions is a critical tool for

DOI: 10.4324/9781003043409-34

modern brands. Whereas in the past, brands might have to wait for earnings to lag, a rankings decrease, or a crisis to tell them something is amiss, today's brands can see these things coming nearly in real time by tracking trends in their social media analytics.

Risks

Unfortunately, as with most things, these powerful social media tools come with a price for public affairs actors. Social media exposes public affairs practitioners to a variety of risks, including heightened scrutiny of messaging and an accelerated news cycle, among other risks. Perhaps the most prevalent risk for even the savviest public affairs communicator in the social media space is the level of scrutiny applied to their organizations. Social media exposes them to review of their messaging by the general public that was once only seen by members of the media and insiders. This has the potential to subject them to criticism for inconsistency or in more extreme cases hypocrisy and insensitivity.

Political Polarization

Of special consideration for public affairs communications practitioners is the current trend toward political polarization. Political polarization is at an all-time high in the United States (Jones, 2020). In a few places, this is more evident than in social media. Some research suggests that social media may even contribute to political extremism (Hong & Kim, 2016). Regardless of whether social media drives political polarization or is merely symptomatic of polarization that is already present in our society, its impact on how organizations interested in public affairs navigate issues and campaigns is unmistakable.

Just as America's major political parties are engaged in a never-ending battle for political and electoral supremacy, so too are its adherents. Organizations that weigh in on contested public affairs matters in this polarized environment must expect that they will draw swift opposition from some segment of the political spectrum. They may also garner some support from opposing segments, but in social media, opposition is usually more reliable than support.

Partisan Lens

Feeding into this political polarization is the partisan lens through which social media audiences tend to view issues, individuals, and organizations. Today's communicators face a social media landscape in which its participants increasingly view the world in partisan terms. Contributing to this is that social media permits audiences to create echo chambers in which their preexisting views are reinforced rather than challenged. Social media audiences are able to follow individuals, organizations, and media outlets that reflect these views. So, for example, even when partisan audiences are presented with the same news events, this information is filtered in such a manner that they may draw totally different conclusions about it.

Public affairs practitioners have to be cognizant of the partisan lens through which audiences view the world if they hope to successfully navigate this terrain for their campaigns or other initiatives. In some circumstances, particularly, political campaigns for elective office, it may make sense to play into these partisan narratives. This is useful because for both new and established candidates, it is important to ensure the support of the partisan political base to bolster the odds of electoral success. For communicators working with organizations that are promoting an issue and that are not necessarily hardcore partisans, it may be more important to chart a path amidst these stormy partisan waters in such a manner as to avoid drawing partisan rancor to their cause. This is often much easier said than done, which is a lesson swiftly learned by those who inadvertently find themselves in the midst of a political firestorm.

Political Scandal

When organizations find themselves in the midst of a crisis born from social media or extending into that context, these opportunities and risks that the medium offers are heightened. The public officials and candidates for elective office in the midst of a political scandal confront operational risks from managing social media accounts, exposure to trolls and bots, as well as public confusion regarding the parties responsible for its management. Organizations face similar, but distinct, risks in a crisis. Organizations that are not accustomed to regular engagement in public affairs find themselves in uncharted waters when learning to navigate these issues in a crisis. They may be exposed to unusually high levels of social media pressure and face the prospect of lasting damage to their brands.

Management of social media assets is important under the best of circumstances and is even more imperative during a crisis. Organizations must establish clear lines of responsibility for social media messaging if they are not already in place. Messaging must be consistent between social media platforms, as well as an organization's other communications outlets such as media relations and internal communications, for example. It is well-established that inconsistent messaging across these platforms can expose organizations to heightened reputational risk and may even yield a crisis if one is not already underway. The absence of coordinated messaging and clear lines of responsibility for social media will exacerbate a scandal.

Another social media risk enures from its very operation. The mere presence of a candidate or an organization in this space exposes them to the aforementioned scrutiny of their messaging as well as their brands themselves. In

Christopher Nolan's film, *The Dark Knight,* Michael Caine portraying Alfred Pennyworth remarks that "some men just want to watch the world burn." The existence of social media trolls who seem to exist to fan the flames of conflict in social media would appear to prove this supposition. Trolls can inject even more accelerant into an already volatile crisis that is roiling in a turbulent partisan environment. Adding even more chaos to mix are bots. Bots maybe even more incendious as they may be agents of foreign states seeking to undermine our very institutions. While they may not have natural enmity to a given campaign or organization, these entities may serve as convenient targets of opportunity and further embroil an organization in the midst of a political scandal or crisis.

Case Studies

An examination of two political scandals can assist in bringing to light some of the challenges that public officials in particular face in the social media context. Consider the case of Virginia Governor Ralph Northam. This case demonstrates how partisan views can accelerate a public affairs communications crisis in social media. On February 1, 2019, a right-wing political website, Big League Politics, published images taken from Northam's page in his medical school yearbook that included a photo of two individuals, one in blackface and another in Ku Klux Klan hood and robes. The reaction on social media, as well as from the traditional media, and other public officials, both Republican and his fellow Democratic colleagues, was immediate and not surprisingly severe. There were almost immediate bipartisan calls for his resignation and his communications team was with little doubt caught unaware. However, Northam apologized the same day stating:

> "Earlier today, a website published a photograph of me from my 1984 medical school yearbook in a costume that is clearly racist and offensive. I am deeply sorry for the decision I made to appear as I did in this photo and for the hurt that decision caused then and now. This behavior is not in keeping with who I am today and the values I have fought for throughout my career in the military, in medicine, and in public service. But I want to be clear, I understand how this decision shakes Virginians' faith in that commitment. I recognize that it will take time and serious effort to heal the damage this conduct has caused. I am ready to do that important work. The first step is to offer my sincerest apology and to state my absolute commitment to living up to the expectations Virginians set for me when they elected me to be their Governor."
>
> (Mirshahi, 2019)

Northam made some adjustments to his initial explanation of what he had done in the past and was able to weather the storm, thanks in part to his swift communications response. Interestingly, the publication of the yearbook photo came on the heels of controversial statements that Northam had made regarding abortion, demonstrating how even political figures who wade into these controversial issues can face public relations consequences from them (Mark, 2019). In the aftermath of the publication of the blackface and KKK photographs and his subsequent apology, a Washington Post-Schar School poll posed the question, "Considering everything, do you think Northam should step down as governor of Virginia or not?" Given the nature of the controversy, one might expect African Americans would largely support resignation. However, 58% of African Americans polled opposed resignation, a figure that is virtually identical to the percentage of Democrats opposed to resignation – 57%. This is in contrast to 56% of Republicans who believed that he should in fact resign. A contemporaneous Quinnipiac University poll produced similar results with 56% of black voters opposing resignation and 57% of Democrats opposing resignation. In that poll, a majority of Republicans, 60% believed that he should resign. The fact that Northam had such strong support among both Democrats and black voters, a key Democratic constituency, was a significant factor in his ability to survive the crisis.

U.S. Senator Ted Cruz, a Republican from Texas, found himself in the midst of a mini-political scandal that is highly emblematic of the social media age. On September 12, 2017, it was reported that Senator Cruz liked an explicit Twitter video clip featuring Cory Chase, a pornographic actress (O'Keefe & Selk, 2017). This incident was covered by print and broadcast outlets including CNN and *The Washington Post*, among others (Diaz 2017). While in hindsight, this seems like simply fodder for humor, in reality, it posed a serious issue for a conservative Republican focused on family issues. Ultimately, Cruz addressed the issue on camera in an interview with CNN reporter Dana Bash and attributed it to a staffer's "honest mistake." This also again begs the question of who is responsible for a public official's social media account. Is it the individual in question or can and should it be delegated to staff? There are pluses and minuses to both approaches. Having the official manage it themselves or appear to manage gives the official and the accounts an air of greater authenticity and relatability to followers and audiences, which is beneficial. However, as the Cruz incident demonstrates, all of that may be lost if you need to deny responsibility for the content or online behavior.

Reputation Crisis

Public officials and political candidates are not the only public affairs players that face challenges in crises in a social media context. Corporations and nonprofits advocating on public policy issues face similar challenges. To make matters worse, not all such organizations are as savvy or competent in navigating public affairs social media as their political counterparts may be. Beyond similar challenges associated with inconsistent messaging and lack of clarity in roles and responsibilities for social media amidst a public affairs crisis, these organizations also face brand risk associated with their public affairs engagement itself. The brand risk that these organizations are exposed to in social media may be more long-lasting than a news or an election cycle for a political candidate.

Case Studies

Two case studies involving corporations underscore the challenges that these organizations face when they intentionally or inadvertently wade into public affairs debates and find themselves in the midst of a social media crisis. For those organizations, crises that touch on particularly divisive public policy issues such as abortion or gun control can prove difficult for even the most seasoned corporate communications executives to manage. In February 2018, in the wake of the Parkland High School shooting, social media calls to boycott the National Rifle Association's corporate partners trended on Twitter. In response to these calls, United Airlines and Delta Airlines announced that they would cut ties to the organization. Delta issued the following statement:

"Delta informed the National Rifle Association Saturday that the airline will end its contract for discounted fares for travel to the association's 2018 annual meeting. The company requested that the NRA remove Delta's information from its meeting website.

Delta's decision reflects the airline's neutral status in the current national debate over gun control amid recent school shootings. Out of respect for our customers and employees on both sides, Delta has taken this action to refrain from entering this debate and focus on its business. Delta continues to support the 2nd Amendment.

This was not the first time Delta has withdrawn support over a politically and emotionally charged issue. Last year, Delta withdrew its sponsorship of a theater that staged a graphic interpretation of "Julius Caesar" depicting the assassination of President Trump. Delta supports all of its customers but will not support organizations on any side of any highly charged political issue that divides our nation."

(Galluccio, 2018)

In the wake of this statement, Georgia-based Delta Airlines faced a backlash led by Republican gubernatorial candidates who chided the company for not supporting Second Amendment rights. This ultimately led the state legislature to abandon plans to consider favorable tax legislation for the airlines during the 2018 legislative session in Atlanta.

Sometimes brands themselves may draw negative attention on social media platforms. Consider the case of Quaker Oats' now-defunct Aunt Jemima brand. Quaker Oats Aunt Jemima brand is used to market pancake mix and syrup, among other items, and features prominently on its package a black woman's image, with a former slave originally portraying the character at events after its establishment in 1889. The brand's imagery was frequently decried as racist over the years, but it endured nonetheless, even making efforts to modernize the depiction in the 1980s (Hsu, 2020). In June 2020, in the midst of Black Lives Matter protests in communities across the United States, the 131-year-old brand that had endured media scrutiny and political recriminations for more than a century was laid low, by a 42-second long video on TikTok. In the video, the history of the brand is recounted quickly culminating in the video's subject noting that "black lives matter, even over breakfast" while pouring the pancake mix in the sink. This video was widely shared on a variety of social media platforms. Social media posts renewed calls for Quaker Oats to retire the brand and the company ultimately acquiesced. On June 17, 2020, Quaker Oats issued a press release containing the following statement attributed to Kristin Kroepfl, Vice President and Chief Marketing Officer, Quaker Foods North America:

> As we work to make progress toward racial equality through several initiatives, we also must take a hard look at our portfolio of brands and ensure they reflect our values and meet our consumers' expectations. We recognize Aunt Jemima's origins are based on a racial stereotype. While work has been done over the years to update the brand in a manner intended to be appropriate and respectful, we realize those changes are not enough. We acknowledge the brand has not progressed enough to appropriately reflect the confidence, warmth and dignity that we would like it to stand for today. We are starting by removing the image and changing the name. We will continue the conversation by gathering diverse perspectives from both our organization and the Black community to further evolve the brand and make it one everyone can be proud to have in their pantry.

Perhaps most striking about Quaker Oats decision to end the Aunt Jemima brand under a cloud of negative media coverage and social media traffic is that the brand contemplated doing so two years prior, but ultimately deferred a decision citing challenges related to the controversy surrounding parent company PepsiCo's controversial Kendall Jenner ad. The decision to defer painful or difficult decisions can often expose companies to the wrath of social media audiences as illustrated by the Aunt Jemima case study. Unlike the prior era of more stable traditional media coverage, the oftentimes lightning-fast pace and momentum of public affairs controversies in social media require swift and decisive action.

Conclusion

There are several key takeaways and lessons learned that can be gleaned from an examination of these challenges. First, it is imperative to build an appropriate infrastructure for managing social media crises in the public affairs context. This infrastructure should include the use of appropriate analytics, notably as a means of monitoring trends, positive or negative in the space. It is also very important to establish clear lines of responsibility for social media. This helps to ensure message consistency, the absence of which may yield a crisis in and of itself. This can also give a party the ability to quickly identify responsibility for problematic social media conduct on the brand's social media accounts and assets.

Beyond these table stakes best practices, organizations engaged in public affairs should also consider incorporating third-party advocacy, including, but not limited to, the use of surrogates and coalitions to amplify their messaging in social media and ensure that they always have some friends or supporters there. Sometimes, it may make more sense for these third parties to lead the vanguard on challenging issues to minimize the exposure of a public official, corporation, or nonprofit. Finally, the establishment of a long-term reputation management program can help organizations endure even unforeseen crises in the midst of a political scandal or reputation crisis. Ultimately, public officials and non-public brands are often in this space for the long term and having these tools can help them maintain their brands well into the future. Without adopting these best practices, brands engaged in public affairs will likely have a turbulent experience enduring crises in social media.

References

Diaz, D. (2017). Cruz blames 'staffing issue' for porn video 'liked' on his Twitter account. *CNN. com*. https://www.cnn.com/2017/09/12/politics/ted-cruz-twitter/index.html

Galluccio, B. (2018, February 26). Georgia senate blocks Delta tax break after company cuts ties with NRA. *KCJB*. https://kcjb910.iheart.com/featured/political-junkie/content/2018-02-26-georgia-senate-blocks-delta-tax-break-after-company-cuts-ties-with-nra/

Hong, S., & Kim, S. H. (2016). Political polarization on Twitter: Implications for the use of social media in digital governments. *Government Information Quarterly, 33*(4), 777–782. https://doi.org/10.1016/j.giq.2016.04.007

Hsu, T. (2020, June 17). Aunt Jemima brand to change name and image over "racial stereotype." *The New York Times*. https://www.nytimes.com/2020/06/17/business/aunt-jemima-racial-stereotype.html

Jones, J. M. (2020, January 21). Trump third year sets new standard for party polarization. *Gallup.* https://news.gallup.com/poll/283910/trump-third-year-sets-new-standard-party-polarization.aspx

Mark, M. (2019, February 3). The tip about the racist photo in Gov. Ralph Northam's yearbook reportedly came from an ex-classmate angry about his abortion comments. *BusinessInsider.com.* https://www.businessinsider.com/ralph-northam-racist-yearbook-photo-tip-concerned-citizen-2019-2

Mirshahi, D. (2019, February 4). Gov. Northam addresses "clearly racist and offensive" yearbook photo. *WRIC.* https://www.wric.com/news/virginia-news/gov-northam-addresses-clearly-racist-and-offensive-yearbook-photo/

O'Keefe, E., & Selk, A. (2017, September 13). After @tedcruz liked a porn tweet, Sen. Ted Cruz blamed it on a staffer's "honest mistake." *The Washington Post.* https://www.washingtonpost.com/news/powerpost/wp/2017/09/12/after-tedcruz-liked-a-porn-tweet-sen-ted-cruz-blamed-a-staffing-issue/

Schulman, K. (2016, October 31). The digital transition: How the presidential transition works in the social media age. *The White House Blog.* https://obamawhitehouse.archives.gov/blog/2016/10/31/digital-transition-how-presidential-transition-works-social-media-age

Siegel, B. (2017, June 13). The dos and don'ts of branding a candidate. *Campaigns & Elections.* https://www.campaignsandelections.com/campaign-insider/the-dos-and-don-ts-of-branding-a-candidate

26

iSCOTLAND

Crises, the Integrated Model of Activism, and Twitter

Audra Diers-Lawson

> Twitter isn't really about changing people's minds who aren't already favourable to independence – the algorithms manipulate what we see to create a bubble, so we see the messages and the types of messages that agree with us, so Twitter can create and empower the community.
>
> – An Influencer's View

Across Europe there are several nations facing active independence movements. However, the Scottish independence movement (Yes) is unique because it is politically powerful, despite losing a referendum on independence in 2014. For example, in 2020, approximately four weeks of consecutive polling placed support for Yes substantially over 50% (Curtis, 2020). This stands in comparison to 2014 when the first independence referendum was held – at the highest point ahead of the failed referendum polling showed a statistical tie (Dahlgreen, 2014) between Yes and No in Scotland. What has changed in the United Kingdom (UK) to tip the scales? Two crises have emerged that seem to be persuading Scots that independence may be a better option than remaining in the union. First, in 2016 the UK voted to leave the European Union (EU); however, in Scotland every voting area (councils) voted to remain in the EU (BBC, 2016). Second, the COVID-19 pandemic has highlighted Scotland's ability to manage its affairs as well and if not better than England. For example, pandemic leadership approval ratings of Scotland's First Minister Nicola Sturgeon through the pandemic have been consistently higher compared to British Prime Minister Boris Johnson's, with one polling expert remarking that the foundations of the union itself look weak at this point (Webster, 2020).

DOI: 10.4324/9781003043409-35

Scotland's socio-political environment is also complex because of a negative UK media environment for Yes supporters (Dekavalla, 2016; Morisi, 2016) and the existence of a robust social media environment supporting independence (Lachlan & Levy, 2016). Therefore, the aims of this chapter are to better understand the influence that crisis can have on political movements and the role that social media can play in a complex media and political environment.

Contextualizing the Scottish Independence Question

Mackay's (2015) analysis of the 2014 independence campaign argues that to fully unpack the political arguments, it is important to understand the contextual demands of the political campaign and place it within a specific cultural context. Though Scotland has been an identifiable polity since around 850, the UK was formed when the Acts of Union in 1707 formally unified England (which already included Wales and Ireland) with Scotland as "equal" partners. In Mullen's (2014) legal reflection on the 2014 referendum and its implications, he points out that Scotland has always retained distinct political, legal, and educational autonomy within the union, which was institutionalized with the establishment of the Scottish parliament in 1999 and the formal devolution of many domestic matters like education, health, and social services (Solly, 2020).

The Stability of the United Kingdom

In his analysis of whether the union will survive, Mullen (2014) identifies three litmus tests for the viability of it. First, whether people's identity is British and/or Scottish is vitally important. Second, continued support for "society" through public programs is necessary to maintain the union's viability. Third, from a Scottish view, the health of the union is only preserved if there are more benefits than disadvantages. Initially, Brexit constitutes a crisis for Scots because the fear of being outside of the EU was one of the critical reasons that many Scottish residents voted to remain in the union in 2014; essentially with Brexit Scotland voted twice to remain in the EU (Ross, 2019). Moreover, COVID-19 might highlight differences between Scottish and UK governments to tip the balance in the evaluation of the advantages and disadvantages of union membership.

Not Just Fake News

An analysis of media framing in the 2014 referendum suggests the battle for independence was not the social welfare and social justice that the SNP wanted (Mooney & Scott, 2015); rather it was dominated by the UK narrative because the media framed it as a strategic game to be played and about issues of economics and governance. Media outlets focused on shared "British" identity, whether

Scotland should be *allowed* the right of self-determination, and portrayed the vote as a difficult or undesirable "divorce." Coupled with findings suggesting when there was asymmetry in risk assessments between independence and remaining in the UK, concerns about personal economic situations also swayed voters to reject independence (Morisi, 2016). However, the media's framing of the 2014 referendum may well contribute to a pro-independence interpretation of the Brexit and COVID-19 crises in 2021 and beyond.

Social Media Activism Is More Than Slacktivism

Though Lachlan and Levy (2016) found social media is becoming increasingly important during political campaigns and referenda and a central feature in the Scottish independence debate, others suggest that social media may not be the best places for referendum deliberation (Quinlan et al., 2015). Viewing social media as a platform for meaningful deliberation of political topics is probably the wrong way to frame its function in political campaigns. Increasingly research suggests that rather than social media engagement being illustrative of "slacktivism" – making a lot of noise but has little impact –there are significant relationships between engagement online about politics, political information seeking, and offline political action – including voting (Brennan, 2018; Greijdanus et al., 2020; Karamat & Farooq, 2016; Štětka & Mazák, 2014; Tupper, 2014; Velasquez & LaRose, 2015). Data suggests rather than engaging political opponents, social media may best function to develop communities contributing to offline political efficacy and action (Greijdanus et al., 2020; Karamat & Farooq, 2016). UK-based research suggests that social media consumption can help to mobilize offline activism and political participation (Leyva, 2017).

Integrative Model of Activism on Contentious Issues

Though there is a preponderance of evidence suggesting that social media activism is more than mere slacktivism, there remains a paucity of research explaining what drives people to online activism and how that might relate to offline activism. However, Chon and Park's (2020) research, testing the integrative model of activism on contentious issues, provided explanations of the driving forces of activism in the context of the Black Lives Matter (BLM) movement. They found four factors that drive social media activism – a hostile media perception, affective injustice, social media efficacy, and situational motivation in problem solving.

Crises as Contentious Issues for Situational Motivation

In their model, Chon and Park (2020) examine contentious issues for the BLM movement like gun ownership and police abuse of power; however, they do not consider specific crises as a trigger point for coalescing and focusing engagement about contentious issues. Yet the authors also indirectly discuss triggers like protests over the deaths of black men caused by white police officers, suggesting the model would benefit from expansion to explicitly consider the role of crises, social media, and activism. Crises have three characteristics that can trigger activism – they are inherently public, activate many potential stakeholders, and pose a risk to traditional relationships between institutions and public stakeholders (Diers-Lawson, 2020). In their study of three Mexican social and political movements, Sandoval-Almazan and Gil-Garcia (2014) specifically found that cyberactivism needed more than an enduring and negative situation; it required a triggering event to heighten the flow of information during political events or social disruptions. Therefore, directly exploring crises as triggers for activism represents a contribution to the model.

Applying the Integrative Model of Activism to the Yes Movement

To better understand the influence that crisis can have on political movements and social media's role in these complex media and political environments, this chapter applies and revises the integrative model of activism. This provides the opportunity to better understand the Yes movement, a powerful independence and political movement, and meet the chapter's objectives.

Method

Chon and Park (2020) used questionnaires to demonstrate the robustness of the model; however, their research drew together disparate bodies of research to produce something new. To continue to evaluate and develop the integrated activism framework, applying different methodologies to interrogate the appropriateness of the connections drawn affords a greater opportunity to evaluate the model.

In-depth interviews of Yes supporters were conducted (N = 23). This involved one-on-one interviews conducted via email (N = 3) as well as over the phone and Skype (N = 20). Respondents (both via email and live discussions) were prompted with broad themes including their interest and involvement in the Yes movement, reflections on the role of Twitter in the Yes movement, contentiousness within the Yes movement online and views of pro-union supporters on Twitter, reflections on Brexit and COVID-19 on the Yes movement. The depth interviews yielded nearly 32 hours of discussion to produce thematic saturation after ten interviews with additional interviews conducted to ensure saturation (Abraham et al., 2018; Daymon & Holloway, 2011).

Most participants (N = 20) presently live in Scotland; three grew up in Scotland but currently live outside of Scotland. Fifteen self-identified as SNP members, six self-identified as members of the new Independence for Scotland (ISP) party or the Green party, and the remaining participants did not self-identify their party membership. Participants included a variety of professional backgrounds including laborers, public servants, political activists/politicians, former military, communications specialists, and professionals in industries like oil and gas or technology. This diversity of backgrounds is important because the consistency of attitude and experience emerging from these data suggest a common cultural and political experience of being a Scottish Yes supporter and social media user.

Data Analysis

Interviews were transcribed and data analyzed from a grounded theory perspective employing Strauss and Corbin's (1990) constant comparative method approach to analyzing the data with a focus on coding the data throughout (Richards & Morse, 2012). This method focuses on analyzing data using three coding processes together: (1) *open coding* to identify critical themes emerging from each interview were identified as a way to compare, conceptualize, and categorize the data; (2) *axial coding* was used to interrogate the conditions, context, and interaction of attitudes emerging within the categories; and (3) *selective coding* was used to match the emergent themes in the axial coding process to components of the integrated model of activism. Emergent themes were discussed with known Yes supporters outside of the study for cultural accuracy and relevance.

Hostile Media Perceptions

Chon and Park (2020) found that hostile media perceptions represent people's perception of bias in news coverage of issues coupled with the belief that the media is negatively affecting the situation. In Scotland's case, this is a measurable phenomenon, as Mooney and Scott's (2015) findings demonstrate on the media framing of the 2014 Independence Referendum. It is also a common point of discussion amongst Yes supporters on Twitter itself.

When asked their views of media coverage of independence, three critical themes emerged from the participants: biased outlets, an anti-independence media spin, and a negative framing of Scotland. Participants consistently referred to mainstream media sources (MSM) as *biased*; for example, one noted, "I personally don't think our media is that fair or independent ... it's very difficult to understand what's happening unless you read across different publications."

More directly, participants consistently articulated the view that the MSM has an *anti-independence spin* citing newspapers as well as television and radio broadcasters. One of the more important points made by several participants was a concern about how people who relied on legacy media could get information could make an informed decision about Scottish independence. Beyond merely being pro-union, the hostile media perception also includes a belief that Scotland is negatively framed in the MSM. For example, one participant pointed to a BBC Scotland morning news report from June 2020 where Scotland had its second day of no COVID-19 deaths while England's deaths were still over 100 and the lead story was how the economic upturn in Scotland was slower than in England stating, "And that was just a typical spin of 'let's find something to knock the Scottish government for.'"

Affective Injustice

The negativity about Scotland is something that came up as a central point of discussion throughout the interviews. Chon and Park (2020) found that it is an essential factor predicting social media activism because it describes a context in which a deep sense of unfairness exists at a group level of deprivation. Comments related to affective injustice produced three distinctive themes. The first major theme was *talking down Scotland*. This referred to the denigration of Scotland and Scots including historic denigration with several participants reflecting on different moments in Scottish history, with one participant noting that the "Scottish cringe is real" because Scots are often taught that their culture is relegated to history, thus not modern. Another way the talking down Scotland theme emerged was how it manifested itself into a Scottish lack of confidence:

> I think for most of my life, that message of too wee, too poor, too stupid to go your own way, I think has been the message. And I think most Scots have that innate kind of a loathing of their own confidence.

The lack of confidence was also discussed as participants highlighted that Scottish dependency on England is pervasive. Participants made comments like, "it's silly and emotive to say that we have been downtrodden for years," but would highlight different examples of dependency or that being Scottish is second best.

The second perception of affective injustice participants identified was *discrimination*. Discrimination was discussed in the context of English exceptionalism with references to "Just get rid of Scotland" "like we're a cancer to get rid of." Also, discrimination was discussed as an element of Scottish cultural reductionism and the "promulgation of the myth of the Scotsman who turns up in London drunk, nuts the barman, and gets arrested." In a British context, if the participants questioned these, it would be brushed aside as "just banter." One participant reflected on his experience in the British military and the "abuse that I would take, the name-calling and physical abuse just because of where you come from that's seen as banter." Multiple participants reported examples of direct discrimination where senior English managers were heard saying they would rather employ English workers than Scots.

The final affective injustice theme that emerged from the participants' that the relationship between Scotland and England was "the last bastion of colonialism." In many cases, participants referred to a democratic deficiency because of the sheer population differences between Scotland and England, stating that what England voted for was what all four nations had to live with. They also referred to an argument that has been used over the years to try to dissuade former colonies from seeking independence that Scotland was "Too wee, too poor, and too stupid" to be able to be independent.

Crisis as Problem Recognition

Though there are many aspects of problem recognition relevant to Scottish independence like participants' views of the union, politics, the 2014 referendum, the meaning of independence, and the importance of gaining confidence emerging from the interviews, most of these relate to participants' long-standing criticisms of the union. However, most participants believe that Brexit and COVID-19 have meaningfully changed the prospects for independence.

Though Brexit is not viewed as a crisis universally in the UK, in Scotland it is with most participants identifying four reasons that it may be a trigger for independence.

- Brexit will damage Scotland's economy, Scots value EU membership.
- Scotland's interests have been ignored in the Brexit negotiations.
- Brexit demonstrates the democracy deficit between England and Scotland as a simple population issue.
- England and Scotland have different priorities.

One participant noted, "I think it [Brexit] solidified the fact that we don't get what we vote for...and the differences between Scotland and England." Participants identified that Brexit demonstrates the comparative disadvantage of the union building the case for independence (Mullen, 2014).

Participants' reflections on the COVID-19 pandemic identify it as a collective confidence builder, demonstrating that Scotland will do at least as well if not better on its own as if it is in the union. Participants identified three reasons they believed this was true. First, the pandemic has materially shown Scotland's competence at self-governance, characterizing it as imperfect but adaptive, humane, and well-reasoned. One of the points highlighted was the confidence that the daily briefings from Nicola Sturgeon had in providing clear guidance, explaining the situation, and responding to media questions and criticisms. Second, participants believe the Scottish government is trustworthy. Because of the daily briefings during the lockdown, participants noted that people were able to see unfiltered and unframed information about the Scottish government's performance and that "Nicola has played a blinder" by simply being competent.

The third reason that participants believed that the pandemic has influenced those who never supported independence is the "shambolic handling [of the pandemic] by Boris Johnson and his cabinet which has highlighted the union isn't the best way forward." The juxtaposition of the Scottish competence in responding to the crisis compared to the overall British incompetence is something that participants believe is helping to build support for Yes both online and offline.

There was one exception that reflects an engrained negative attitude – from a participant who is a passionate lifelong Yes supporter:

> I think once it has cleared up [COVID-19] and disappeared everything will just go back to normal; everything will just go back to the way it was. Which is me being negative and Scottish.

Social Media Efficacy and Activism

Given the perceived hostile media environment, affective injustice, and the impact of Brexit and COVID-19, from a Yes perspective, the question is how to avoid the pessimistic outcome articulated by the participant. Chon and Park (2020) found that while hostile media perceptions and affective injustice would spur both online and offline activism, that in order to generate social media activism, people must believe engagement on social media will lead to a positive outcome.

Participants reflected on both Twitter and social media, articulating a consistent belief that social media is serving as a part of a political movement. Most expressed a general sentiment something like: "Twitter and Facebook have a place in independence and Scottish politics…" and three distinctive functions emerged – informational, relational, and activist. This suggests functions social media can serve may be more important than the efficacy beliefs Chon and Park (2020) found. First, participants suggest Twitter serves an information-sharing function, "for the majority of ordinary Twitter users…it is a source of quick information" suggesting they believed they could find more fair and balanced information shared on Twitter than in the MSM. Participants also argued that social media is a tool for managing MSM hostility toward Yes. In fact, they view

Twitter activism as a method to directly challenge the talking points repeated across the MSM by sharing more credible information.

Participants also described relational and community building function for Twitter by identifying its importance as the opening quotation to this chapter and also included reflections like, "Twitter has been invaluable to me – I have made so many new friends, but the most important thing is I have learned so much about the fight for Scottish independence."

Finally, participants argued that online engagement, movement promotion, and support for offline activism are opportunities for social media activism to contribute to political change. The influencers I spoke with believed they had a responsibility to ensure the information they shared was accurate and not inflammatory because they knew that it was being shared with each of their relatively large audiences. Similarly, when non-influencers discussed engagement, they talked about it as looking at sources for credible information sources they could really read and share. Defining engagement as information sharing was about driving the language and conversations to counter negativity about Scotland and build a positive case for independence. Participants argued that social media activism directly supported the Yes movement. Respondents acknowledge that they may not sway hard-line No voters, but that for soft-no's there is a meaningful opportunity to represent the movement suggesting, "it [Twitter] opens up avenues for conversations and ultimately people will be won over by a conversation." Additionally, participants suggested a belief that online and offline activism are connected, "The more information that gets out there and the more informed people are, it tentacles out into the community" and with a cautious optimism that when the next vote for independence occurs, good information will tip the scales.

Social Media Activism Risks

However, participants acknowledged two internal risks associated with social media activism including speaking into the proverbial echo chamber indicating a "danger we only communicate with those we agree with." They also expressed concerns about creating toxicity within the movement because issues can be picked up by social media advocates and amplified, which in many participants' views could weaken the case for independence.

Participants also identified two external risks emerging from social media activism – trolling and doxxing, with participants remarking that "Twitter is a bit like Marmite; it can be very good or absolutely shockingly bad" because of the way that people can be "piled on" (i.e., trolling) for saying something controversial. One participant described being trolled as "soul-destroying" but also laughed and commented that she had learned to pick her battles better. In a less humorous way, participants reflected on being doxx'ed – where their identities had been outed. For example, one of the influencers discussed a feature story in the *Daily Mail* (a British tabloid) in 2014 where he and several other online activists were targeted and labeled as "cybernats" and "nationalists" (i.e., fascist). The article listed the organizations that each of these people worked for to "create hassle for them in their workplaces."

Going Online, Offline, and Back Again

One of the consistent themes that participants discussed was the convergence of their online and offline experiences. Participants acknowledged that they did not or could not participate as fully in person; however, most discussed how either their online activities led them to offline activism including creating new independence parties, attending marches, knocking on doors both during the 2014 independence campaign and/or during the more recent elections for both the UK and Scottish parliaments. A few also noted that their offline activities also led them online to keep engaged with the movement even when there were no upcoming elections or during the pandemic lockdown. Thus, instead of being a unidirectional flow from online activism to offline engagement, as Chon and Park (2020) suggest, participants consistently talked about the online and offline going hand-in-hand that it suggests a bi-directional flow, where activism reinforced activism, no matter the "platform."

Conclusions and Applications

The case of Scottish independence affords an opportunity to better understand complex interactions between political movements, the media, and crises to better identify the potential functions that social media can serve in enduring political movements. This chapter demonstrates a symbiotic relationship between online and offline political advocacy heightened once crises emerge. Beyond refining "contentious issues" as crises, this chapter also builds on previous research about the role social media plays in political movements identifying informational, community building, and activist functions that it serves. These data also demonstrate a bi-directional influence of online and offline activism, further refining Chon and Park's (2020) model. Finally, these data also reveal both internal and external risks associated with online activism as well, which may factor into how movement supporters use Twitter to engage with movements.

In the case of Scottish independence, these data demonstrate the importance of trigger events to push a political objective and provide a deeper explanation as to why the 2014 independence referendum did not pass – historic and enduring perceptions of affective injustice do not necessarily lead to political change; specific triggers seem necessary to overcome the inertia of the status quo.

References

Abraham, E. M., Asor, V., Torviawu, F., Yeboah, H., & Laryea, F. (2018). Public perception of corporate social responsibility of AngloGold Ashanti in Obuasi Municipality, Ghana. *Social Responsibility Journal, 14*(3), 485–500. https://doi.org/10.1108/SRJ-08-2016-0149

BBC (Producer). (2016, August 24, 2020). Results. *EU Referendum*. https://www.bbc.co.uk/news/politics/eu_referendum/results

Brennan, G. (2018). How digital media reshapes political activism: Mass protests, social mobilization, and civic engagement. *Geopolitics, History, and International Relations, 10*(2), 76–81. https://doi.org/10.22381/GHIR102201810

Chon, M.-G., & Park, H. (2020). Social media activism in the digital age: Testing an integrative model of activism on contentious issues. *Journalism & Mass Communication Quarterly, 97*(1), 72–97. https://doi.org/10.1177/1077699019835896

Curtis, C. (Producer). (2020, August 24, 2020). Scottish independence: Yes leads by 53% to 47%. https://yougov.co.uk/topics/politics/articles-reports/2020/08/12/scottish-independence-yes-leads-53-47

Dahlgreen, W. (Producer). (2014, August 24, 2020). "Yes" campaign lead at 2 in Scottish Referendum. https://yougov.co.uk/topics/politics/articles-reports/2014/09/06/latest-scottish-referendum-poll-yes-lead

Daymon, C., & Holloway, I. (2011). *Qualitative research methods in public relations and marketing communications* (2nd ed.). Routledge.

Dekavalla, M. (2016). Framing referendum campaigns: The 2014 Scottish independence referendum in the press. *Media, Culture & Society, 38*(6), 793–810. https://doi.org/10.1177/0163443715620929

Diers-Lawson, A. (2020). *Crisis communication: Managing stakeholder relationships*. Routledge.

Greijdanus, H., de Matos Fernandes, C. A., Turner-Zwinkels, F., Honari, A., Roos, C. A., Rosenbusch, H., & Postmes, T. (2020). The psychology of online activism and social movements: Relations between online and offline collective action. *Current Opinion in Psychology, 35*, 49–54. https://doi.org/10.1016/j.copsyc.2020.03.003

Karamat, A., & Farooq, A. (2016). Emerging role of social media in political activism: Perceptions and practices. *South Asian Studies (1026-678X), 31*(1), 381–396.

Lachlan, K. A., & Levy, D. R. (2016). BIRGing, CORFing, and Twitter activity following a political referendum: Examining social media activity concerning the 2014 Scottish independence vote. *Communication Research Reports, 33*(3), 217–222. https://doi.org/10.1080/08824096.2016.1186625

Leyva, R. (2017). Exploring UK millennials' social media consumption patterns and participation in elections, activism, and "slacktivism." *Social Science Computer Review, 35*(4), 462–479. https://doi.org/10.1177/0894439316655738

Mackay, R. R. (2015). Multimodal legitimation: Selling Scottish independence. *Discourse & Society, 26*(3), 323–348. https://doi.org/10.1177/0957926514564737

Mooney, G., & Scott, G. (2015). The 2014 Scottish independence debate: Questions of social welfare and social justice. *Journal of Poverty and Social Justice, 23*(1), 5–16. https://doi.org/10.1332/175982715X14231434073599

Morisi, D. (2016). Voting under uncertainty: The effect of information in the Scottish independence referendum. *Journal of Elections, Public Opinion and Parties, 26*(3), 354–372. https://doi.org/10.1080/17457289.2016.1178648

Mullen, T. (2014). The Scottish independence referendum 2014. *Journal of Law and Society, 41*(4), 627–640. https://doi.org/10.1111/j.1467-6478.2014.00688.x

Quinlan, S., Shephard, M., & Paterson, L. (2015). Online discussion and the 2014 Scottish independence referendum: Flaming keyboards or forums for deliberation? *Electoral Studies, 38*, 192–205. https://doi.org/10.1016/j.electstud.2015.02.009

Richards, L., & Morse, J. M. (2012). *Readme first for a user's guide to qualitative methods*. Sage.

Ross, E. (2019). Is Brexit worth Scotland's independence?. *The Atlantic*. https://www.theatlantic.com/international/archive/2019/08/scottish-independence-and-brexit/595234/

Sandoval-Almazan, R., & Gil-Garcia, J. R. (2014). Towards cyberactivism 2.0? Understanding the use of social media and other information technologies for political activism and social movements. *Government Information Quarterly, 31*(3), 365–378. https://doi.org/10.1016/j.giq.2013.10.016

Štětka, V., & Mazák, J. (2014). Whither slacktivism? Political engagement and social media use in the 2013 Czech Parliamentary elections. *Cyberpsychology: Journal of Psychosocial Research on Cyberspace, 8*(3). https://doi.org/10.5817/CP2014-3-7

Strauss, A., & Corbin, J. (1990). *Basics of qualitative research: Grounded theory procedures and techniques*. Sage.

Solly, M. (2020). A not-so-brief history of Scottish independence. In *Smithsonian Magazine* (30 January, 2020 ed., pp. online).

Tupper, J. (2014). Social media and the idle no more movement: Citizenship, activism and dissent in Canada. *Journal of Social Science Education, 13*(4), 87–94. https://doi.org/10.2390/jsse-v13-i4-1354

Velasquez, A., & LaRose, R. (2015). Youth collective activism through social media: The role of collective efficacy. *New Media & Society, 17*(6), 899–918. https://doi.org/10.1177/1461444813518391

Webster, L. (2020). Nicola Sturgeon's approval rating soars in new YouGov survey. *The National*. https://www.thenational.scot/news/18645237.nicola-sturgeons-approval-rating-soars-new-yougov-survey/

Areas of Application: Sport

27

SPORT CASE CHAPTER: A CRISIS OF COOL

Baseball's Race against Time

Vince Benigni and Lance Porter

In 1997, pro sports reached epic popularity through an unlikely convergence of dynasty and diversity. Michael Jordan captured the fifth of his six NBA titles, Tiger Woods won the Masters at age 21 by a record 12 strokes, and Derek Jeter was in the midst of a five-year run that yielded four World Series crowns.

Meanwhile, another Rushmorian Black superstar emerged. Seattle's Ken ("The Kid") Griffey Jr. glistened the diamond with a gliding gait and a signature swing to become the unquestioned face of baseball (Cortes, 2016). Griffey's childlike smile and backward-facing cap brought a coolness to a sport long fraught with Neanderthalic norms and, more viscerally, … a lack of color.

"Junior" was featured in the sport's groundbreaking videogames while fronting Nike's iconic Swingman product line. He made television ("The Fresh Prince of Bel-Air") and movie ("Little Big League") cameos, giving baseball a vibrant new face (Carig, 2020).

However – just as the sport was flexing its entrepreneurial muscle – Griffey's rising star (as the reigning American League's Most Valuable Player) was eclipsed by fellow sluggers Mark McGwire and Sammy Sosa, whose home run chase in 1998 enraptured a fan base still stewing from a 1994 Major League Baseball (MLB) season-ending player strike. However, the duo's association with anabolic steroid usage would eventually spark a Congressional investigation and a public outcry from which the sport has never fully recovered.

While the NBA and NFL have lit up the 2000s, baseball has lost its cool, and its color. Black American presence in the major-league game has cratered, from nearly 30 percent in the 1970s (Everding, 2007) to fewer than 8 percent today (Nightengale, 2020). Until MLB fully employs its political and socially

DOI: 10.4324/9781003043409-37

communicative platforms to examine the foundations enabling institutional racism in the sport, this trend will continue.

While Patrick Mahomes and LeBron James are the progressive, colorful faces of American sport, baseball's culture is rooted in the past. Black baseball stars such as Mookie Betts lack the Q-rating of superstars in other sports (Stone, 2021). Baseball won't return to our national conscience until it embraces youth and urban culture and displaces the roots of White privilege (Glover, 2007). The "old-school" norms of the sport, long seen among Whites as its charm, are oppressive barriers to emerging audiences in an increasingly globalized sports world.

Sport is the ultimate stage for performativity and self-expression ... incentivized in other pro sports but demonized in baseball (Cortes, 2016). Sailes (1996) attributes basketball's popularity to its association with personal empowerment, displayed through individual expression. Performance orientations of the Black athlete stem from the distinctive stylings of folk heroes such as Julius Erving, Michael Jordan, and Magic Johnson (Glover, 2007; Sailes, 1996), who represented a cutting-edge excitement rooted in urban playgrounds while bringing a crossover racial popularity to the NBA (Boyd & Shropshire, 2000).

Newman and Rosen (2014) analyzed Black baseball and its racial and economic consciousness through the lens of race leader W.E.B. DuBois, who espoused a disruptive philosophy in urging African-Americans to develop their identity (in the authors' case, as an accepted entertainment enterprise). This counters theories of non-combative assimilation proffered by Booker T. Washington (Newman & Rosen, 2014), the blueprint for Jackie Robinson's integration of MLB in 1947.

The trope of the quiet black male (Gaston, 1986) is being challenged by more combative and expressive Black baseball players such as Tim Anderson. The Chicago White Sox star – who frequently addresses social justice issues on Twitter and Instagram – is "White America's nightmare in cleats...representative of that generation's confidence, hip-hop entrenched culture, freedom of expression, trash-talking, world-changing and anti-establishment vibe." (Gamble, 2019; pp. 2, 4).

Baseball is expensive and repetitious, requiring a significant financial commitment that excludes a significant minority population, causing an occupational segregation effect (Sack et al., 2005). A Black child must live in a White town where baseball is prominent (Apstein, 2020). Furthermore, while major college football and basketball programs are fully funded, college baseball teams must distribute 11.7 scholarships among 35 players, offering less help to players from historically repressed groups. Consequently, only about four percent of NCAA players are Black (Apstein, 2020).

Essayist Gerald Early notes that Blacks stray from baseball because it lacks a firm place in their culture (Everding, 2007), not because of a deficit of agency. Baseball's appeals to nostalgia and tradition harken to eras painful to people of color (Everding, 2007). Former manager and current MLB consultant Jerry

Manuel (who is Black) recommends forming an African-American team to reconnect with the young Black athlete (Rhoden, 2018).

MLB debuted its Diversity Fellowship Program in 2017 to include women and people of color in its league and team offices. In 2020, Commissioner Rob Manfred brought two African-Americans (including one female) into its previously all-White MLB's executive office (Apstein, 2020). In 2021, Manfred moved the MLB All-Star Game from Atlanta in light of a Georgia bill perceived to restrict voting access to minority populations.

Such gestures only matter if that momentum permeates the game's underlying culture. Griffey touts social media as an ideal outlet for youth players to send videos (to MLB and scouting networks) of them playing multiple positions, asking for advice, tracking their growth (Nightengale, 2021). The climb is steep, given that MLB has roughly 6 million Instagram followers, well behind the NFL's 16 million and the NBA's 44 million (Moran, 2020).

While technological and traditional touchpoints targeted at Black youth may kindle incremental interest in the sport, baseball should turn to sports' merchants of cool to forge more immediate immersion. Will it go the Kaepernickian way of the NFL, shunning the concerns of the Black community? Or will it follow the lead of Nike, acknowledging such concerns and embracing its culture while increasing the value of its brand by $6 billion (Beer, 2019)?

In 2021, LeBron James (followed by 82 million on Instagram and 50 million on Twitter) wore Griffey-inspired LeBron 15 Nike teal-and-black sneakers. Now the shoe is on the other foot. MLB should follow LeBron's lead with regard to social and cultural consciousness.

It's what the cool kids are doing.

References

Apstein, S. (2020, July 17). Why baseball is losing Black America. *Sports Illustrated.* https://bit.ly/3unQd9N

Beer, J. (2019). One year later, what did we learn from Nike's blockbuster Colin Kaepernick ad? *Fast Company.* https://bit.ly/3cyCtTs

Boyd, T., & Shropshire, K. L. (2000). *Basketball Jones: America above the rim.* NYU Press.

Carig, M. (2020, April 2). Solving the mystery within Ken Griffey Jr. Presents Major League Baseball. *The Athletic.* https://bit.ly/3wcwCef

Cortes, R. (2016, July 25). There's never been anyone quite like Ken Griffey Jr. *The Undefeated.* https://bit.ly/3ubkoR4

Everding, G. (2007, April 12). Blacks aren't playing baseball simply because "they don't want to" says Gerald Early. *The Source.* https://bit.ly/3sCXKRu

Gamble, J. R. (2019, April 29). Tim Anderson is White America's nightmare in cleats. *The Shadow League.* https://bit.ly/3sBIYdz

Gaston, J. C. (1986). The destruction of the young black male: The impact of popular culture and organized sports. *Journal of Black Studies, 16*(4), 369–384. https://doi.org/10.1177/002193478601600402

Glover, T. D. (2007). Ugly on the diamonds: An examination of white privilege in youth baseball. *Leisure Sciences, 29*, 195–208. https://doi.org/10.1080/01490400601160895

Moran, E. (2020, January 28). Baseball tries to boost its social media efforts. *Front Office Sports*. https://bit.ly/3m6thbS

Newman, R. J., & Rosen, J. N. (2014). *Black baseball, black business: Race enterprise and the fate of the segregated dollar*. University Press of Mississippi.

Nightengale, B. (2021, February 25). Ken Griffey Jr. wants to help diversify Major League Baseball, get the sport "back where it belongs." *USA Today*. https://bit.ly/3sEKPOR

Rhoden, W. C. (2018, October 26). A radical idea to solve the lack of African-American players in baseball. *The Undefeated*. https://bit.ly/2QTb3iL

Sack, A. L., Singh, P., & Thiel, R. (2005). Occupational segregation on the playing field: The case of Major League Baseball. *Journal of Sport Management, 19*, 300–318. https://doi.org/10.1123/jsm.19.3.300

Sailes, G. A. (1996). An examination of basketball performance orientations among African American males. *Journal of African American Men, 1*, 37–46. https://doi.org/10.1007/BF02733918

Stone, L. (2021, January 30). Can Mariners Hall of Famer Ken Griffey Jr. help make baseball cool again? *The Seattle Times*. https://bit.ly/3czRa8x

28

RECOGNIZING THEIR POWER

How Athletes Have Utilized Social Media to Influence Crisis Communication Decisions During COVID-19

Natalie Brown-Devlin and Hayoung Sally Lim

On March 12, 2020, the National Basketball Association canceled the remainder of their season after Utah Jazz players Rudy Gobert and Donovan Mitchell tested positive for COVID-19 (Aschburner, 2020). Other leagues, including Major League Baseball, Major League Soccer, and the National Hockey League, followed. As both COVID-19 infection and death rates continued to climb in the United States, discussions regarding how National Collegiate Athletic Association (NCAA) fall sports and the National Football League (NFL) could safely compete received ample media attention. Organizational decision-makers, including League Commissioners, University Athletic Directors, the NCAA President and Board of Directors, and others, were tasked with deciding whether the season could be played safely, and if so, had to determine how teams could preserve revenue while maintaining player/personnel safety.

Fueled by COVID-19 health concerns, NFL and NCAA players quickly articulated their desire to play the 2020 season; however, they wanted assurance that safety would be prioritized. While NFL athletes are unionized through the NFL Players Association (NFLPA), NCAA athletes are not. The NFLPA and the NFL entered into a Collective Bargaining Agreement (CBA) after negotiating issues such as player safety. Conversely, NCAA athletes often have little influence pertaining to organizational decisions, making it more difficult to ensure that their concerns are fully considered (Thibault et al., 2010).

In this chapter, we analyze how internal stakeholders (i.e., players) utilized their personal social media accounts to influence organizational decision-making during the COVID-19 pandemic. First, this chapter discusses the role of internal stakeholders within the scope of crisis communication before reviewing the role of social media during sports-related crises. Next, we analyzed two athlete-led

DOI: 10.4324/9781003043409-38

social media campaigns that sought to influence their Leagues' decisions regarding COVID-19 procedures: (1) NFL Athletes' #WeWantToPlay campaign, and (2) NCAA Athletes' #WeAreUnited and #WeWantToPlay campaigns. Lastly, we discuss the implications of these campaigns and their influence on crisis management.

Internal Crisis Communication

Internal communication occurs in response to the success or failure of a major organizational change or crisis (Barrett, 2002). During a crisis, the quality and the quantity of internal communication influence the trust and involvement of internal stakeholders (e.g., employees, sports team players). Thus far, crisis communication research has primarily focused on the reputation repair strategies organizations deliver to external stakeholders (i.e., customers, media, other organizations). However, research is needed to unpack how new media environments influence internal communication where external/internal stakeholders and organizations are freely interactive (Frandsen & Johansen, 2011).

By examining the relationships among an organization and its various stakeholder groups, stakeholder theory suggests that stakeholders "identify with an organization, what it provides, and what it says about itself" (Smudde & Courtright, 2011, p. 138). Organizations must identify various stakeholder relationships, ranging from employees, sponsors, fans, community members, or the media. Ulmer (2001) warns that neglecting certain stakeholder group needs can produce severe consequences for an organization, particularly in crises that involve potential health risks.

Organizational crises are not solely ignited by accusations from external stakeholders (customers, media); rather, internal stakeholders also discuss organizational issues. Thus, internal stakeholders can initiate crisis communication, engaging external stakeholders and the organization. Indeed, crisis communication scholars have examined whether employee social-mediated crisis communication provides more organizational opportunities or threats, particularly on social media (Opitz et al., 2018). When a *New York Times* (*NYT*) article condemned Amazon for its workplace culture (Kantor & Streitfeld, 2015), Amazon employee Nick Ciubotariu posted a lengthy response refuting the LinkedIn article. Ciubotariu responded before Amazon, subsequently receiving attention from the media and Amazon's CEO (Titcomb, 2015). Employees are uniquely positioned during a crisis, as they are closer to the organization and the crisis than other stakeholders (Helm, 2011). Yet, they may also be viewed distinctly from their organization (Dreher, 2014; van Zoonen & van der Meer, 2015).

Employees are not often blamed for organizational crises; yet, researchers have suggested unique, psychological dimensions offer credibility to their engagement in crisis communication. Thibault et al. (2010) advocated for the

"increased democratization of sport organizations" by highlighting the importance of "[involving] the voices of all organizational actors, including athletes"
(p. 7). The authors argued that organizations must allow athletes to elect representatives with voting abilities to create accountability and give athletes a role in
organizational decisions. While customers are likely to listen to employees and
perceive their statements as credible, it is logical to assume that sports fans would
similarly attend to players' stances during a crisis. Athletes maintain considerable
influence to engage fans in their communication. This internal (sports players)
to external (sports fans) communication has received widespread media attention
provides an interesting, yet under-researched, dynamic in crisis communication.

Organizations, Athletes, and Fans on Social Media

Ample scholarship has examined the intersection of sport and social media, portraying social media as a virtual sports bar gathering of teams/organizations, fans,
and athletes. Pegoraro (2010) identified Twitter, in particular, as an influential tool
allowing for fan/athlete interaction. For sports organizations, interacting with fans
on social media can increase fans' levels of team identification (Meng et al., 2015).
A key sports communication concept, team identification extends social identity
theory by measuring fans' commitment to a team and the degree to which a team's
actions are regarded as personally relevant (Wann, 2006). Within crisis communication, highly identified fans consider themselves personally vexed by crises that
befall a team/athlete with which they identify (Brown-Devlin, 2018).

Scholars have often examined how sports organizations and athletes have
utilized social media websites to engage in reputation repair (Hambrick et al.,
2015). Moreover, research has identified that sports fans respond online to ongoing crises, and often, will engage in traditional reputation repair strategies on
behalf of their preferred teams/athletes (Brown & Billings, 2013; Brown et al.,
2015; MacPherson & Kerr, 2019; Sanderson, 2013). During a crisis, both internal (i.e., athletes, coaches, league officials) and external stakeholders' (i.e., fans)
social media comments can "ultimately influence the emotions experienced by
their followers and, in turn, influence the view of the organization and its crisis
communication efforts" (Brummette & Sisco, 2015, p. 5). Koerber and Zabara
(2017) noted the buffering role of fans during a crisis, as they come "between
the crisis and the team's or athlete's reputation and image, limiting damage"
(p. 194). Conversely, there are risks associated with fan involvement during a crisis, as well. Sanderson and colleagues (2016) outlined how Twitter users hijacked
a Florida State University campaign called "Ask Jameis," which was intended
to provide fan/athlete interactions featuring their starting quarterback. Instead,
negative comments flooded the social media hashtag, alerting sporting organizations that "public relations practices via social media [could] morph into narratives that frame the organization unfavorably" (Sanderson et al., 2016, p. 36).

As such, organizations embroiled in a crisis must engage in proper social listening techniques and enact social media policies for employees to properly manage their online reputation. While sports organizations have long recognized the potential influence an athlete's Twitter account could wield over their organization's reputation (Pegoraro, 2010), scholarship has not yet examined how that power could galvanize online fan reactions to influence internal, organizational decisions.

Case Study 1: NFL Athletes and #WeWantToPlay

On July 7, 2020, NFL preseason training camps drew near, and NFLPA President JC Tretter released a statement expressing concern regarding a lack of communicated COVID-19 health and safety protocols for players and teams. The Association held a conference call with 50 influential players the following week, presenting a united response while demanding "daily testing, no preseason games, and a 'ramp up' period [for physical activities during practices]" (ESPN.com news services, 2020). On July 18, the NFL announced the dates on which training camp would begin.

The following day, several high-profile players utilized their personal social media accounts to directly respond to the league, communicating their desire to *safely* play the 2020 season with the hashtag #WeWantToPlay. The coordinated social media campaign was orchestrated by Miami Dolphins cornerback Byron Jones and included several athletes with large social networks, including Drew Brees, Myles Garret, and DeAndre Hopkins. The players proclaimed that the 2020 season would not happen without proper NFL-mandated health protocols. Houston Texan JJ Watt outlined their full list of demands.

Interestingly, some players spoke directly to the fans in their tweets. Todd Gurley II tweeted, "You want to watch football this year? Us players need to remain healthy in order to make that happen. The @NFL needs to do their part in order to bring football back safely in 2020. #WeWantToPlay." Fans, indeed, responded, helping the hashtag to trend on Twitter. While some disparaged the effort, others urged NFL actions that would preserve the season. One user tweeted, "I find it funny that you have a ton of #NFL players voicing concerns both during meetings and on Twitter yet the @ nfl and @nflcommish have no released any sort of statement. Answer your players. #WeWantToPlay #wewantaseason." Another user tweeted, "I love all these NFL players asking the league for safety protocols. And the #WeWantToPlay initiative. All I can say as a fan is #WeWantYouToPlay. #NFL #NFLP."

The next day, the NFL and NFLPA reached an agreement on testing protocols. On July 24, the two sides also agreed to eliminate preseason games and schedule a ramp-up period for team practices.

Case Study 2: NCAA Football Athletes' #WeAreUnited and #WeWantToPlay

During summer 2020, as college football athletes returned to campus for practices and regularly scheduled workouts, key internal decision-makers from Power Five conferences, such as league commissioners, university athletic directors, and head coaches, began focusing on how fall sports should proceed. In this instance, college football players, an oftentimes excluded and exploited internal stakeholder during such operational decision-making (Thibault et al., 2010) formulated a social media strategy that was reminiscent of the earlier NFL campaign. The athletes used Twitter and other forms of online communication to incite public pressure from external stakeholders (i.e., fans and social media users) to obtain a metaphorical seat at the table for discussions pertaining to COVID-19 safety protocols and the decisions about whether seasons should be played at all.

On August 2, a group of Pac-12 players published an article in *The Player's Tribune,* outlining a series of demands that, if were not met and "guaranteed in writing," would lead to players "[opting]-out of Pac-12 fall camp and game participation" (Players of the Pac-12, 2020). Their demands included increased COVID-19 testing and safety protocols, plans to protect all sports from a budgetary perspective, plans to prompt an end to racial injustice in college sports and society, and plans for economic freedom and equity (including pay for athletes, providing medical expense coverage, and an ability to monetize their image/ likeness). The article featured the hashtag #WeAreUnited to unite messaging around their demands. Many athletes tweeted the article from their personal social media accounts, spurring discussion among key external stakeholders in the sports media and their respective fanbases. The #WeAreUnited players met with California Governor Gavin Newsom and Pac-12 Commissioner Larry Scott to discuss their concerns, obtain support for their initiative, and request a potential executive order that would provide oversight, especially for COVID-19 safety protocols (Russo, 2020). Additionally, players from the Big Ten conference utilized the hashtag #BigTenUnited and released a similar list of demands, although they did not threaten player boycotts, opting, instead, for dialogue with league leadership (Peter & Schad, 2020). The players' movement contributed to progress, resulting in daily antigen testing in the Pac-12 and prompting guaranteed scholarship protection for athletes who opted out of the season due to health concerns (Sallee, 2020).

However, despite progress with testing, concerns for possible spikes in COVID-19 cases once university students returned to their respective campuses (Burke, 2020) prompted some schools to quickly shift to completely online instruction and seemingly reignited concerns pertaining to fall collegiate sports. On August 8, the Mid-American Conference (MAC) became the first college conference to cancel the 2020 football season (Russo, 2020). Shortly after, the Big Ten, a Power Five conference, announced that affiliated teams could not yet hold full-contact practices, signaling hesitancy concerning the 2020 season. The next day, players from Power Five conferences, including Clemson University's Trevor Lawrence, started the #WeWantToPlay movement, which was dedicated to ensuring that the 2020 football season would be played. However, on August 10, two influential Power Five conferences, the Big Ten and the Pac-12, officially postponed the 2020 football season due to COVID-19 concerns. Players from other conferences continued to fuel the #WeWantToPlay movement on social media, hoping to prevent the remaining conferences from canceling the season. Players received influential support from other internal stakeholders, such as many head coaches and athletic directors. Their hashtag and social media messages also provoked external stakeholders, including fans and even politicians, to tweet support for the players' movement. This unified messaging from league internal stakeholders and resulting viral social media posts from external stakeholders seemingly helped prevent the remaining Power Five conferences from canceling or postponing their seasons. The SEC, ACC, and Big-12 conferences officially kicked off their 2020 seasons in September.

Simultaneously, Big-10 and Pac-12 players once again united to send a message to decision-makers, utilizing the #WeWantToPlay hashtag to persuade the conferences to reconsider the season postponement. Ohio State Quarterback Justin Fields garnered over 300,000 signatures via an online petition before restarting the #WeWantToPlay hashtag (Hass-Hill, 2020). On September 16, the Big Ten reversed their earlier cancellation, and on September 24, the Pac-12 announced that they, too, would play the 2020 football season.

Implications for Crisis Management and Internal Stakeholder Best Practices

These cases provide notable examples of internal stakeholders revolutionizing the crisis management decision-making process by wielding power afforded to them by social media. Anderson (2020) noted that "athletes are starting to realize and wield the power they have over coaches, university officials, and even boosters and fans and are speaking out as a collective more than ever before due to social media" (para. 8). Previous scholarship evidenced how social media has empowered highly identified fans to comment on team/athlete crises (Brown et al., 2015). Yet, social media has not simply shifted power to fans alone. Rather, social media has seemingly led to the internal democratization of power advocated for by Thibault et al. (2010) pertaining to the formulation of organizational responses by further empowering coaches and athletes, as well. In both aforementioned cases, athletes ensured that their concerns would be heard by engaging in strategic online communication, utilizing their own social media accounts to bypass traditional gatekeepers (i.e., team communication officials), and speaking directly to key external stakeholders (i.e., fans). *USA Today* noted that these acts seemed to signal that athletes were "[raising] their collective voices to address these issues like rarely before, fueled by health concerns stemming from the COVID-19 pandemic and a belief that unity can lead to structural change" (Peter & Schad, 2020, para. 3).

In this instance, sport might be signaling a notable shift in the crisis management process that could also extend to other industries. Recent academic research outlined the importance and influence of brand identification (Ma, 2020; Kuenzel & Halliday, 2008) during corporate crises. Ma (2020) determined that consumers who were highly identified with a brand in crisis perceived brands more positively, as response strategies were more effective with this audience. Furthermore, Kim et al. (2001) found a positive relationship between brand identification and positive word-of-mouth. As such, whether in a sport or corporate context, fans comprise a crucial audience whose social media posts possess the potential to influence an organization's reputation. As noted by Aula (2011), stakeholders control the manner in which "reputational meanings are born and disseminated" online (p. 28), as "an organization's reputation is built on the stories formed by stakeholders and spread within networks" (p. 30).

However, scholarship has yet to fully explore how organizations or individuals can fully influence or predict social media users' reactions during a crisis. In the context of sport, fan online response has varied widely from uniting for organizational support (Brown & Billings, 2013) to aggressive and abusive online behavior (Sanderson, 2013). Furthermore, the unstructured, interactive nature of social media affords external stakeholders the ability to potentially transform and reclaim control of a crisis narrative (Chewning, 2015). Thus, crisis managers must approach their social media response quite carefully during a crisis. However, as the cases above have shown, it is not simply the internal crisis managers that have realized the potential impact that fan online conversations possess. Rather, additional internal stakeholders such as athletes, themselves, seem to have recognized the power afforded by social media and have demonstrated a willingness to utilize that power to activate those with higher levels of brand identification in hopes of influencing critical organizational decisions.

The two case studies provided examples of best practices for internal stakeholders who wish to utilize social media to influence organizational decisions. First, internal stakeholders must organize a collective group who share similar concerns. For the NFL players, this group already existed through the NFLPA, who claimed to help the player-led initiative with ensuring that their claims were fact based. This role fulfilled two of Seeger's (2006) crisis communication best practices by being honest and working with a credible source (Young & Flowers, 2012). Pac-12 athletes organized themselves by initially starting the #WeAreUnited movement. College players from all Power 5 conferences formed an unofficial College Football Players Association in hopes of eventually unionizing (Blackwell, 2020). In both instances, by forming a collective group, athletes had bargaining power by threatening season boycotts (and resulting revenue losses) if their safety concerns were not met.

Next, stakeholders should remain consistent by using a single, unique hashtag that communicates their message. For the NFL players, #WeWantToPlay communicated that their demands were rooted in a desire for player safety rather than complaints of simply not wanting to play. For the NCAA Athletes' message of #WeWantToPlay, they followed the existing blueprint of the NFL players and communicated a similar desire for their seasons to continue. Yet, in the case of #WeAreUnited/#BigTenUnited, the use of similar, simultaneous hashtags works against the intended, embedded message of unity, particularly when one organization (#WeAreUnited) was threatening a season boycott and the other (#BigTenUnited) was not. Also, the close timeline of the formation of #WeAreUnited and #WeWantToPlay likely confused the players' overall goals. While the #WeAreUnited campaign did not receive their demands beyond the COVID-19 protections, it seemed that players' desire to play the 2020 season usurped the remaining outlined issues.

Next, stakeholders should utilize those with large social networks to share a consistent message that describes their objectives at a coordinated time. In the case of the NFL, a majority of players tweeted midday on July 19. With a sudden influx of tweets that contained a similar hashtag, sports media and fans quickly took notice, causing the hashtag to trend. NCAA athletes, many of whom also boast substantial social followings, used a similar strategy of tweeting collectively. Posts should communicate the organization's message succinctly and other online platforms can be used to provide more details of demands. For instance, #WeStandUnited utilized *The Players' Tribune* to publish a detailed list that provided more rationale for their demands and concerns. For the NFL's #WeWantToPlay, Houston Texan JJ Watt used screenshots of his iPhone Notes app to further explain their concerns.

For both NCAA and NFL athletes, most tweets included emotionally framed persuasive arguments that highlighted players' reasons for their COVID-19 concerns. NFL Player Russell Wilson disclosed that his safety concerns were rooted in the fact that his wife was pregnant, and Austin Corbett revealed he had battled severe asthma since he was two. These messages humanized their requests, providing a stark contrast to a larger, bureaucratic organization such as the NFL or NCAA and inspiring empathy from fans. This tactic seemed crucial for winning public support and galvanizing social media users to support their initiatives.

Conclusion

Professional and collegiate football players collectively employed the influence of their social networks to mandate health and safety protocols during the COVID-19 pandemic. Thus, these cases provided a unique lens through which to examine how social media has democratized power and internal decision-making during crisis management. By uniting around a common cause, internal stakeholders usurped their typical roles in operational decision-making by activating external stakeholders (i.e., fans) on social media to ensure that their concerns were heard. Future research should examine whether similar events could happen in other corporate contexts.

References

Anderson, G. (2020, July 2). On the offensive and in the lead. *Inside Higher Ed.* https://www.insidehighered.com/news/2020/07/02/athletes-push-and-achieve-social-justice-goals

Aschburner, S. (2020, March 12). Coronavirus pandemic causes NBA to suspend season after player tests positive. *NBA.com.* https://www.nba.com/article/2020/03/11/coronavirus-pandemic-causes-nba-suspend-season

Aula, P. (2011). Meshworked reputation: Publicists' views on the reputational impacts of online communication. *Public Relations Review, 37*, 28–36. https://doi.org/10.1016/j.pubrev.2010.09.008

Barrett, D. J. (2002). Change communication: Using strategic employee communication to facilitate major change. *Corporate Communications: An International Journal, 7*(4), 219–231. https://doi.org/10.1108/13563280210449804

Blackwell, J. (2020, September 29). Najee Harris discusses #WeWantToPlay movement, preparations for Texas A&M. *Sports Illustrated.* https://www.si.com/college/alabama/bamacentral/najee-harris-discusses-we-want-to-play-movement-texas-am-blackwell

Brown, N. A., & Billings, A. C. (2013). Sports fans as crisis communicators on social media websites. *Public Relations Review, 39*, 74–81. https://doi.org/10.1016/j.pubrev.2012.09.012

Brown, N. A., Brown, K. A., & Billings, A. C. (2015). "May no act of ours bring shame": Fan-enacted crisis communication surrounding the Penn State sex abuse scandal. *Communication & Sport, 3*(3), 288–311. https://doi.org/10.1177%2F2167479513514387

Brown-Devlin, N. (2018). Experimentally examining crisis management in sporting organizations. In A.C. Billings, W.T. Coombs, & K.A. Brown (Eds.), *Reputational challenges in sport* (pp. 41–55). Routledge.

Brummette, J., & Sisco, H. F. (2015). Using Twitter as a means of coping with emotions and uncontrollable crises. *Public Relations Review, 41*(1), 89–96. https://doi.org/10.1016/j.pubrev.2014.10.009

Burke, L. (2020, August 26). Cases spike at universities nationally. *Inside Higher Ed.* https://www.insidehighered.com/news/2020/08/26/cases-spike-universities-nationally

Chewning, L.V. (2015). Multiple voices and multiple media: Co-constructing BP's crisis response. *Public Relations Review, 41*(1), 72–79. https://doi.org/10.1016/j.pubrev.2014.10.012

Dreher, S. (2014). Social media and the world of work: A strategic approach to employee's participation in social media. *Corporate Communications: An International Journal, 19*(4), 344–356. https://doi.org/10.1108/CCIJ-10-2013-0087

ESPN.com News Services (2020, July 19). Players blitz NFL with tweets about safe return. *ABC News*. https://abcnews.go.com/Sports/players-blitz-nfl-tweets-safe-return/story?id=71868694

Frandsen, F., & Johansen, W. (2011). The study of internal crisis communication: Towards an integrative framework. *Corporate Communications: An International Journal, 16*(4), 347–361. https://doi.org/10.1108/13563281111186977

Hambrick, M. E., Frederick, E. L., & Sanderson, J. (2015). From yellow to blue: Exploring Lance Armstrong's image repair strategies across traditional and social media. *Communication & Sport, 3*(2), 196–218. https://doi.org/10.1177%2F2167479513506982

Hass-Hill, C. (2020, September 13). Justin Fields reignites #wewanttoplay campaign ahead of possible Big Ten decision on season. *Eleven Warriors*. https://www.elevenwarriors.com/ohio-state-football/2020/09/116496/justin-fields-reignites-wewanttoplay-campaign-ahead-of-possible-big-ten-decision-on-season

Helm, S. (2011). Employees' awareness of their impact on corporate reputation. *Journal of Business Research, 64*(7), 657–663. https://doi.org/10.1016/j.jbusres.2010.09.001

Kantor, J., & Streitfeld, D. (2015, August 7). Inside Amazon: Wrestling big ideas in a bruising workplace. *The New York Times*. www.nytimes.com/2015/08/16/technology/inside-amazon-wrestling-big-ideas-in-a-bruising-workplace.html?_r=0

Kim, C. K., Han, D., & Park, S. B. (2001). The effect of brand personality and brand identification on brand loyalty: Applying the theory of social identification. *Japanese Psychological Research, 43*(4), 195–206. https://doi.org/10.1111/1468-5884.00177

Koerber, D., & Zabara, N. (2017). Preventing damage: The psychology of crisis communication buffers in organized sports. *Public Relations Review, 43*(1), 193–200. https://doi.org/10.1016/j.pubrev.2016.12.002

Kuenzel, S., & Halliday, S. V. (2008). Investigating antecedents and consequences of brand identification. *Journal of Product & Brand Management, 43*(4), 195–206. https://doi.org/10.1108/10610420810896059

Ma, L. (2020). How the interplay of consumer-brand identification and crisis influences the effectiveness of corporate responses strategies. *International Journal of Business Communication*. https://doi.org/10.1177%2F2329488419898222

MacPherson, E., & Kerr, G. (2019). Sport fans' responses on social media to professional athletes' norm violations. *International Journal of Sport and Exercise Psychology, 19*(1), 1–18. https://doi.org/10.1080/1612197X.2019.1623283

Meng, M. D., Stavros, C., & Westberg, K. (2015). Engaging fans through social media: Implications for team identification. *Sport, Business and Management: An International Journal, 5*(3), 199–217. https://doi.org/10.1108/SBM-06-2013-0013

Opitz, M., Chaudhri, V., & Wang, Y. (2018). Employee social-mediated crisis communication as opportunity or threat? *Corporate Communications: An International Journal, 23*(1), 66–83. https://doi.org/10.1108/CCIJ-07-2017-0069

Pegoraro, A. (2010). Look who's talking—athletes on Twitter: A case study. *International Journal of Sport Communication, 3*(4), 501–514. https://doi.org/10.1123/ijsc.3.4.501

Peter, J., & Schad, T. (2020, August 6). From #WeAreUnited to COVID-19 whistleblowing, college athletes are raising their voices like rarely before. *USA Today*. https://www.usatoday.com/story/sports/ncaaf/2020/08/06/weareunited-covid-19-whistleblowing-college-athletes-speak-out/3299442001/

Players of the Pac-12. (2020, August 2). #WeAreUnited. *The Players' Tribune*. https://www.theplayerstribune.com/en-us/articles/pac-12-players-covid-19-statement-football-season

Russo, R. D. (2020, September 3). "Game-changer": Rapid, daily virus testing coming to Pac-12. *AP News.* https://apnews.com/article/27aec6fdee725dabe1d9c01d1c7f477a

Sallee, B. (2020, August 11). What Pac-12, Big Ten schools are offering players; Pac-12 athletes still have concerns. *CBSSports.com.* https://www.cbssports.com/college-football/news/what-pac-12-big-ten-schools-are-offering-players-pac-12-athletes-still-have-concerns/

Sanderson, J. (2013). From loving the hero to despising the villain: Sports fans, *Facebook, and social identity threats. Mass Communication and Society, 16*(4), 487–509. https://doi.org/10.1080/15205436.2012.730650

Sanderson, J., Barnes, K., Williamson, C., & Kian, E. T. (2016). "How could anyone have predicted that #AskJameis would go horribly wrong?" public relations, social media, and hashtag hijacking. *Public Relations Review, 42*(1), 31–37. https://doi.org/10.1016/j.pubrev.2015.11.005

Seeger, M. W. (2006). Best practices in crisis communication: An expert panel process. *Journal of Applied Communication Research, 34*(3), 232–244. https://doi.org/10.1080/00909880600769944

Smudde, P. M., & Courtright, J. L. (2011). A holistic approach to stakeholder management: A rhetorical foundation. *Public Relations Review, 37*(2), 137–144. https://doi.org/10.1016/j.pubrev.2011.01.008

Thibault, L., Kihl, L., & Babiak, K. (2010). Democratization and governance in international sport: Addressing issues with athlete involvement in organizational policy. *International Journal of Sport Policy and Politics, 2*(3), 275–302. https://doi.org/10.1080/19406940.2010.507211

Titcomb, J. (2015, August 17). Jeff Bezos says he doesn't recognise "soulless and dystopian" portrayal of Amazon. *The Telegraph.* www.telegraph.co.uk/technology/amazon/11806849/Jeff-Bezos-says-he-doesnt-recognise-soulless-and-dystopian-portrayal-of-Amazon.html

Ulmer, R. R. (2001). Effective crisis management through established stakeholder relationships: Malden Mills as a case study. *Management Communication Quarterly, 14*(4), 590–615. https://doi.org/10.1177%2F0893318901144003

van Zoonen, W., & van der Meer, T. (2015). The importance of source and credibility perception in times of crisis: Crisis communication in a socially mediated era. *Journal of Public Relations Research, 27*(5), 371–388. https://doi.org/10.1080/1062726X.2015.1062382

Wann, D. L. (2006). The causes and consequences of sport team identification. In A. A. Raney, & J. Bryant (Eds.), *Handbook of sports and media* (pp. 331–352). Lawrence Erlbaum.

Young, C. L., & Flowers, A. (2012). Fight viral with viral: A case study of Domino's Pizza's crisis communication strategies. *Case Studies in Strategic Communication, 1*, 93–106. https://citeseerx.ist.psu.edu/viewdoc/download?doi=10.1.1.1060.7178&rep=rep1&type=pdf.

29

RALLYING THE FANS

Fanship-Driven Sport Crisis Communication on Social Media

Jennifer L. Harker and W. Timothy Coombs

The rhetorical arena theory (RAT) enlightened our view of crisis communication by noting there are multiple crisis voices that emerge throughout a crisis situation – a multi-vocal approach to crisis communication. RAT holds that a rhetorical arena forms around a crisis when various entities begin to talk about a crisis. These voices might work in concert with one another or contradict one another. What is important in the multi-vocal approach is that there can be other salient crisis voices that shape the crisis communication process beyond the traditional emphasis of a crisis manager representing the organization in crisis (Frandsen & Johansen, 2010, 2017). For instance, when an organization recalls a defective product, other crisis voices might include government agencies and consumers affected by the harmful product. RAT provides a framework for considering the multiple voices that might emerge and matter during a crisis (Frandsen & Johansen, 2017). RAT seems to have been designed for understanding sport crisis communication, too. Researchers have found that fans eagerly add their voices when a crisis involves a sport-related entity they support (e.g., Brown & Billings, 2013). Social media platforms provide easy access to the rhetorical arenas allowing a variety of crisis voices to emerge. Sport fans are active users of these social media platforms providing additional impetus to their entering rhetorical arenas and adding their voices to the mix of crisis messages. Moreover, fans are a unique contextual factor that helps to differentiate sport crises from organizational crises (Coombs, 2018). Hence, there is a need to understand how fans utilize social media sites to insert themselves into sport crisis communication efforts.

This chapter will discuss the nuanced examinations into sports fans' behavior and sport-related crisis response on social media sites. We provide an overview

DOI: 10.4324/9781003043409-39

of how the application of the theoretical frameworks rooted in psychology, sociology, and communication define our understanding of fan engagement and socially mediated sport-related crises and how all these matters commingle to motivate sports fans to engage in rhetorical self-defense on behalf of their beloved sport entity. We conclude with recommendations and best practices for researchers and practitioners.

Theoretical Overview 2012–2020

This chapter is constructed by an overview of published scholarship within the subfield of sport-related crisis communication that focuses on social media discourse. The research covers only the past decade because sport-related crisis scholarship that included fan reactions on social media did not appear in the 25 communication, media, sociology, marketing, and sport journals* we reviewed until 2012; therefore, this investigation reviews published scholarship from 2012 until 2020.

In short, when social media was the artifact researched in sport-related crisis communication research, Twitter was far and above the most popular platform studied, with Facebook (mostly specific Facebook groups) a distant second. Other online platforms included blogs, comments on news articles, and YouTube videos and commentary. One thing most of this research has in common is the offered recommendation that mass communicators must evolve from the traditional one-way outward communication model and embrace dialogue and engagement with fans across online sub-arenas (Brown et al., 2015; Coombs & Holladay, 2014; Sipocz & Coche, 2019). But this is an oversimplification of the RAT phenomenon as it is related to sport crisis.

Theoretical application aids in the breakdown of what is happening and why, and there are four theories most often applied in sport communication research at the intersection of crisis and social media. The four theories are social identity theory (Tajfel & Turner, 1986, 1979), image repair theory (Benoit, 2015), situational crisis communication theory (Coombs, 1995; Coombs & Holladay, 2002), and uses and gratification. Image repair theory and situational crisis communication theory are used as theoretical frameworks to categorize crises and analyze the rhetorical self-defense offered by fans to remediate crises. These two theories will be discussed more in the crisis types and rhetorical strategies overview that comes later in this chapter. This overview includes a concentration on uses and gratifications theory and the foundational concepts of social identity and fan identification to break down what is happening and why.

Uses and Gratification Theory and Parasocial Interaction

The uses and gratification theory is a media effects theory that posits consumers purposefully interact with media to fulfill any one or more of five specific needs:

cognitive needs, affective needs, personal integrative needs, social integrative needs, and tension-free needs. This theoretical framework has a natural application to not only social media but also to sport consumption, as gratification is an assumed sought-after outcome of social media use and of sport consumption. Researchers have applied this particular theory to social media and sport to investigate Twitter followers of the Canadian Football League (Gibbs et al., 2014), how FIFA used Twitter to interact and engage with Twitter followers (Winand et al., 2019), and the gatekeeping aspects of sports media Twitter use when covering the Olympics (Sipocz & Coche, 2019), to name a few. Several of these studies also include in-depth discussions relating parasocial interactions to exercising sport fandom on social media (Jensen et al., 2014). Parasocial interactions are not true social interactions because the relationship is one-sided but fans perceive an interaction, and to them, a relationship exists even though true interactions are lacking. Fans consume messages and fans feel a sense of intimacy from these parasocial interactions and perceived relationships (Coombs & Holladay, 2015; Schramm & Hartmann, 2008). Parasocial relationships are a gratification of social media use and can help to further facilitate fan identification and a shared sense of identity with a favored sport entity.

Social Identity, Sport Fans, and Fan Identification

The theoretical framework most aptly applied to sport crisis communication via social media, however, is social identity theory (SIT). Social identity provides a foundation for understanding fan identification and fan behavior. All three concepts are critical to appreciating why fans are a unique contextual aspect for sport-related crisis communication.

Social Identity Theory

SIT (Tajfel & Turner, 1986, 1979) is rooted in the act of "self-made social classifications" (Brown et al., 2015), where individuals participate in the act of connecting or distancing themselves from what the individual perceives as a favorable in-group or a comparative out-group. SIT research has theorized that a person's self-concept links with other, broader group memberships to aid in image management and self-esteem (Cialdini et al., 1976). An individual's identification with social groups shift and change and even overlap throughout one's lifetime, especially if that identification is challenged with any negative or dissonance-causing event (Tajfel & Turner, 1979). An individual who is threatened by a negative perception will work toward differentiating one's self from the negatively perceived group. This process also allows the individual to connect with a group that feels superior to other groups. Social comparison is therefore an internalized, ongoing dissonance battle.

These components of SIT get even more complicated when applying the theory to sport because sports fans are known to become highly identified with their favorite teams or engage in parasocial relationships with their favorite athletes. So, in some ways, the threatened negativity that comes with losing a game could result in a fair-weather fan shrinking away from acts of overt fandom while the die-hard fan remains engaged (Wann & Branscombe, 1990). The overall payoff for sports fans is obviously the win, and when a sports fan's team wins, they can differentiate themselves from the losing team's fans and flex group superiority. This superiority over others is the lure of sports and the basis of fan behavior, which is discussed in a moment, but first, we must understand how identification manifests and then triggers behavior.

Sport Identification

Sport fandom and sport fanship are two forms of sport identification that vary in intensity and result in emotional and behavioral outcomes, as well as a calibrating component of crisis perceptions (Harker, 2018b). Fandom is operationalized as a broad, social identification with and among other fans. Fanship is an individual-rooted identification operationalized as a scaled continuum of intensity from being a fair-weathered fan to being an overt, die-hard fan. Fanship is measured and discussed most often in the sport communication literature as team identification (Wann & Branscombe, 1990). Sport crisis researchers hypothesize that a sport fan's likelihood to engage in remediation attempts is calibrated by that sports fans' amount of team identification (Brown & Billings, 2013; Harker 2019b). So, the more die-hard or identified a fan, the more likely they are to engage in remediation strategies on behalf of their team. Harker (2018a) even hypothesized that fans are so driven by social identity and the need for differentiation that when threatened by a crisis-related image threat the need for superiority increases. As a result, sport-related crisis perceptions are alarmingly linked to sport rivalry (Harker, 2019a, 2019b, 2018a).

Fan Behavior

Cialdini and coauthors (1976) were among the first to document the flex of sports fans wearing team logo apparel the Monday following a Saturday collegiate gridiron win. The researchers named this image management strategy basking in reflective glory (BIRGing).

Rivalry communication is best defined as "blasting" (Cialdini & Richardson, 1980). Blasting is the overt exchange of discordant communication, or the verbal battle exchanged between fans of rival sports teams. This banter is exchanged among sports fans within individuals' online and offline social networks (Harker & Jensen, 2020). Such exchanges offer the perfect example of an identified sports fan flexing superiority over other sports fans when socially comparing and differentiating one's winning favorite team over its losing rival. This joy at another's adversity is called schadenfreude. Blasting and schadenfreude have in recent years become integrated into sport communication research as acts of rivalry communication. Countless studies have noted that the more identified a fan, the more likely the fan is to blast rivals following a game win (Harker & Jensen, 2020; Sanderson, 2014).

Moving beyond wins and losses of games, however, these same feelings and communicated behaviors also can be applied to image threats and acts of image management in response to sport-related crises (Harker, 2018a, 2019a, 2019b). These rivalry concepts are applicable because highly identified fans will work to protect a beloved sport entity's reputation in an effort to protect one's own reputation. (Kruse, 1981; Wann & Branscombe, 1990). Therefore, the characteristics that make up social identification: an internalization of belonging, in-group attribute assessment, out-group comparisons or differentiation, and superiority maintenance; are all linked here and combine to spur the sports fan into remediation action. These behaviors have implications for how fans react to a sport crisis.

The Emergence of Sport Crisis Communication

As aforementioned, the other two most applied theoretical frameworks to fan response on social media sites to sport-related crises are image repair theory (IRT) and situational crisis communication theory (SCCT). Both theories offer an array of crisis remediation strategies to apply in response to certain types of crises. IRT is primarily descriptive. It offers a list of crisis responses and case analyses involve identifying which crisis responses were used in the case coupled with an evaluation of the effectiveness of those strategies. SCCT is prescriptive and identities when specific crisis response strategies should be more or less effective. SCCT holds that the optimal crisis response, one that benefits both stakeholders and the organization in crisis, is contingent upon the nature of the crisis situation. Attributions of crisis responsibility are at the center of SCCT's assessment of the crisis situation (Coombs, 1995, 2007a; Coombs & Holladay, 2002).

This is an oversimplification of these two theories so let's first take a step back to understand the crisis sensemaking process before discussing fan-enacted crisis remediation strategies. Stakeholders first work to attribute responsibility for a crisis (Coombs, 2007b). This is where blame placement occurs. Some fans are so highly identified that placing blame on their beloved sports entity would cause great dissonance. Differentiation becomes complicated here, so reshaping the in-group to be more positively viewed becomes necessary, and it is here that fans enact crisis remediation attempts on social networking sites. Crisis remediation is one of the trends emerging from the sport crisis communication research.

Crisis Communication and Remediation Strategies

Researchers over the past decade have examined an array of sport-related crises: cheating scandals, performing enhancing drug use, domestic assault, and sexual assault. The strategies applied by fans on social media sites have included a vast array but a couple of strategies are regularly applied and stand out as an emerging trend captured by the concept of crisis remediation. For example, Sanderson and colleagues (2016) explored the use of negative sentiment expressed by fans on social media in response to sport-related crises. Stakeholder sentiment was examined through the use of a negatively valanced hashtag that expressed the public reaction to St. Louis Rams players' social activism in response to the Michael Brown shooting in 2014. A "Boycott the St. Louis Rams" Facebook page was created and the Twitter hashtag #BoycottRams was utilized to discuss the situation online. Relatedly, Brown and colleagues (2015), in a separate study, noted that fans turned against Penn State University and instead showed support of Coach Joe Paterno, even though Paterno allegedly concealed facts regarding Jerry Sandusky sexually assaulting boys while serving as an assistant coach at Penn State. Fans in this study were documented to have expressed the remediation strategies of ingratiation, reminder, scapegoat, and victimization in response to the scandal. The researchers concluded that IRT, which is based upon apologia, a political apologetic rhetorical self-defense theory (Ware & Linkugel, 1973), is better suited for athlete-level rhetorical self-defense and SCCT is best suited for organizational-level crises, as the Penn State scandal was assumed to be categorized.

Researchers also have documented that sport identification varies across levels of a sport organization and this additionally calibrates perceptions of crises. For example, Harker (2018a) noted sport identification levels were associated with crisis perception the strongest at the team level, meaning the more highly identified, the less negatively the crises were perceived. Harker concluded that stakeholders attribute responsibility at all levels of sport entities: the league, team, and athlete levels. Fortunato (2017) specified the importance of dichotomizing organizational-level crises from athlete-level crises when he researched how sponsors reacted to the FIFA corruption scandal. Fortunato noted that the use of corrective action coupled with the crisis not involving athletes or point-of-play concerns saved FIFA from financial repercussions of the league-level crisis. Still though, as countless researchers have noted, continued crises without appropriate corrective action will begin to wear down such crisis buffers (Harker, 2018b).

Back to the topic of remediation strategies, ingratiation and rallying appear to be the two most frequently applied strategies that have emerged among fans on social media (Brown & Billings, 2013; Brown et al., 2015; Frederick & Pegoraro, 2018; Sanderson, 2013). Brown and Billings (2013) defined ingratiation as "spokesperson praises the organization's stakeholders for their actions of support." The addition of a new strategy that falls outside of IRT and SCCT is rallying (Frederick & Pegoraro, 2018; Sanderson, 2013). Frederick and Pegoraro (2018) investigated the University of Louisville's applied remediation strategies on the University of Louisville Facebook page that included the strategies of reducing offensiveness, bolstering, and transcendence when the university was navigating the alleged collegiate recruits bribery scandal. The researchers noted that rallying was a clear and distinct image repair strategy that emerged. However, this study was an examination of organizational crisis remediation approaches and not of those offered or initiated by fans. Sanderson's (2013) study was a review of fan responses, though, and he too had noted rallying was occurring alongside the other strategies of stigmatizing, victimization, intimidation, and degradation.

Coping and Emotional Expression in Response to Crisis

Brown and Billings (2013) describe fan remediation strategies on social media as fan coping. Social media users, in the heat of the moment, can express their feelings in real-time. As news breaks regarding a crisis, stakeholders join the conversation and shape and reshape the rhetorical response. A good example of emotion-driven fan response can be found in a recent publication by Meadows and Meadows (2020), in which they examine tweets following Larry Nassar's sentencing. Through the exploration of emotions and attribution of blame, the authors concluded that people used social media to cope with the crisis in emotional, cognitive, and conative coping manners. Such "emotional contagion," as is often witnessed on social media, can mimic the fan behavior blasting, and in this particular study, the three dominant emotions included anger, disgust, and joy, which are components of schadenfreude.

Meadows and Meadows (2020) concluded that public sentiment should be monitored across platforms, which is what Coombs and Holladay (2014) have argued because stakeholders, through the use of social media, are also crisis communicators. Moreover, the rhetorical arena can be composed of sub-arenas: "spaces where crisis publics may express and hear ideas about the crisis" (Coombs & Holladay, 2014, p. 41). Different social media platforms can be sub-arenas and the crisis communication can vary in these different sub-arenas. Hence, crisis managers must monitor sub-arenas to understand how people are reacting to their crisis communication efforts and not rely upon aggregated data that combines the various sub-arenas. The aggregated data could hide potential liabilities or assets emerging within specific sub-arenas. Stakeholder perceptions can shape a crisis and the echo chambers that occur on social media sites are fertile ground for a minor faux pas to spiral into a full-blown crisis.

Paracrises and Fans: Not Crises but Still a Concern

As social media emerged as a factor within crisis communication, a definitional problem emerged. Practitioners and academics began using the term "social media crisis" to refer to crises that emerged on social media sites. The problem was two-fold. First, nearly all crises now involve social media to some degree, making the term too vague. Second, not all of the situations identified as social media crises could be considered actual crises. Oftentimes, these were just a bad day or a customer service problem. Coombs and Holladay (2012) developed the concept of paracrisis to clarify the difference between real crises and what many were terming social media crises. A paracrisis is defined as "a publicly visible crisis threat that charges an organization with irresponsible or unethical behavior" (p. 409). While not a crisis, there can be strong pressure to react to the situation; an organization must manage a crisis risk publicly and there is the possibility the crisis risk could escalate into a crisis (Coombs, 2017). The effects of paracrises are primarily reputational damage and rarely exist as an operational threat (Coombs, 2019).

The paracrisis has been expanded to include a variety of crisis risks that an organization must manage in public (Chen, 2019). Paracrises can form rhetorical arenas and stakeholders, or fans, actively participate in the conversation. Such participation can determine whether or not the paracrises inflict reputational damage. Fans might counter the claims the organization acted irresponsibly, thereby protecting the organization's reputation (and thus their own). More research is needed to explore the role of fans in sport-related paracrises because fans who so highly identify with sport sometimes perceive sport-related crises positively rather than negatively. Positive crisis perceptions may seem counter to traditional crisis communication research, but in sport, this phenomenon should be considered. In a traditional organizational crisis, stakeholders would not typically have feelings of schadenfreude, but in sport, this does occur (Harker 2018a; Harker & Jensen, 2020). Take, for example, the Deflategate scandal when Tom Brady faced suspension for several games. The rival fans of the New England Patriots celebrated his absence and took great joy in Patriots fans' adversity. Sport-related crisis perceptions are dependent upon an individual's perspective of the crisis or how a person might identify with an entity involved in the crisis (Harker, 2019a, 2019b).

Practical Implications and Recommendations

Social media offers sports fans a place for virtual social interaction (Smith et al., 2019). Teams use social media to build brand identity and seek fan support (Watkins, 2014), athletes become social influencers and market sponsors on social media (Hambrick & Mahoney, 2011), and sports fans use social media to discuss sporting events, share game outcomes and highlights (Smith & Smith, 2012), build community (Sanderson & Cheong, 2010), interact with athletes (Kassing & Sanderson, 2010), and of course, fans use social media to discuss and help remediate sport-related reputational crises (e.g., Brown & Billings, 2013).

For Social Media Practitioners

According to Gibbs and coauthors (2014), Twitter is most often examined to explore news-related factors and Facebook is examined for social-related factors (p. 191). Nearly 80 percent of sports fans reported checking Twitter several times a day (Gibbs et al., 2014), so it is recommended that news and messages are regularly shared via Twitter during a crisis. Sports fans, in particular, are trained for this type of engagement as they engage in sporting events via live game updates on social media, especially when viewing the game is not accessible. Therefore, practitioners should make announcements or provide updates on Twitter first (and use an anchoring hashtag for monitoring purposes when doing so), and then other social networking sites should follow.

What not to do is often just as important as what to do. One thing that has been made clear is that a crisis can become worse if the sport entity uses competing remediation strategies on social media from those used on other media mediums. Two examples of this are Richie Incognito and the Miami Dolphins' bullying scandal (Schmittel & Hull, 2015) and Lance Armstrong's doping scandal (Hambrick et al., 2015). In both cases, athletes applied divergent self-defense strategies on traditional media from those offered on social media. Hambrick and coauthors (2015) warned, "Athletes who display multifaceted image repair strategies can embolden identification and attachment with followers, but can further divide with such competing media narratives." Consistency with crisis messages is among the earliest pieces of crisis communication advice (Coombs, 2019).

For Sport Communication and Social Media Researchers

It is important that researchers understand the vast array of predictor variables at play when a fan engages in online crisis communication. Predictor variables include any array of identification components. The current fan behavior literature remains blurred by combining the psychological underpinnings and the sociological outcomes of fan behavior, but ongoing rivalry research is aiding in further defining this dichotomy (Harker & Jensen, 2020). Also, data collection across social media sites is recommended to help build this body of research, especially as uses and gratifications might apply to social media sites in varying ways.

Conclusion

Through a review of the relevant literature, this chapter has explored how fans, social media, and crisis interact to create a unique rhetorical arena for crisis managers and researchers. Fans are active on social media and eager to add their voices when a (para)crisis emerges. The fans seek to help their beloved sports organization through crisis remediation strategies. Identification built over time and facilitated through parasocial interactions are key motivating factors for fan behavior and fan crisis remediation. Lessons gained from understanding past fan crisis remediation attempts help not only those involved with sport-related crises but these lessons also have the potential to be extended to understanding other stakeholders with strong parasocial or other individuals, organizational or social identification. Research has just begun to unpack the unique dynamic of fans, social media, and crises. Thus far, the results are promising for illuminating sport crisis communication and offering insight into the broader research and practice of crisis communication in general.

References

Benoit, W. L. (2015). *Accounts, excuses, and apologies: Image repair theory and research* (2nd ed.). State University of New York Press.

Brown, N. A., & Billings, A. C. (2013). Sports fans as crisis communicators on social media websites. *Public Relations Review, 39*(1), 74–81. https://doi.org/10.1016/j.pubrev. 2012.09.012

Brown, N. A., Brown, K. A., & Billings, A. C. (2015). "May no act of ours bring shame": Fan-enacted crisis communication surrounding the Penn State sex abuse scandal. *Communication & Sport, 3*(3), 288–311. https://doi.org/10.1177%2F2167479513514387

Chen, F. (2019). *Understanding paracrisis communication: Towards developing a framework of paracrisis typology and organizational response strategies.* Texas A&M University. http://hdl.handle. net/1969.1/186574

Cialdini, R. B., Borden, R. J., Thorne, A., Walker, M. R., Freeman, S., & Sloan, L. R. (1976). Basking in reflected glory: Three (football) field studies. *Journal of Personality and Social Psychology, 34*(3), 366–375. http://dx.doi.org/10.1037/0022-3514.34.3.366

Cialdini, R. B., & Richardson, K. D. (1980). Two indirect tactics of image management: Basking and blasting. *Journal of Personality and Social Psychology, 39*(3), 406–415. http:// dx.doi.org/10.1037/0022-3514.39.3.406

Coombs, W. T. (1995). Choosing the right words: The development of guidelines for the selection of the "appropriate" crisis-response strategies. *Management Communication Quarterly, 8*(4), 447–474. http://dx.doi.org/10.1177/0893318995008004003

Coombs, W. T. (2007a). Protecting organization reputations during a crisis: The development and application of situational crisis communication theory. *Corporate Reputation Review, 10*(3), 163–176. https://doi.org/10.1057/palgrave.crr.1550049

Coombs, W. T. (2007b). Attribution theory as a guide for post-crisis communication research. *Public Relations Review, 33*(2), 135–139. http://dx.doi.org/10.1016/j.pubrev.2006.11.016

Coombs, W. T. (2017). Revisiting situational crisis communication theory: The influences of social media on crisis communication theory and practice. In L. Austin, & Y. Jin (Eds.), *Social media and crisis communication* (pp. 21–38). Routledge.

Coombs, W. T. (2018). Athlete reputational crises: One point for linking. In A. Billings, W. T. Coombs, & K. Brown (Eds.), *Reputational challenges in sport: Theory and application* (pp. 13–24). Routledge.

Coombs, W. T. (2019). *Ongoing crisis communication: Planning, managing, and responding* (5th ed.). Sage.

Coombs, W. T., & Holladay, S. J. (2002). Helping crisis managers protect reputational assets: Initial tests of the situational crisis communication theory. *Management Communication Quarterly, 16*(2), 165–186. http://dx.doi.org/10.1177/089331802237233

Coombs, W. T., & Holladay, J. S. (2012). The paracrisis: The challenges created by publicly managing crisis prevention. *Public Relations Review, 38*(3), 408–415. https://doi.org/10.1016/j.pubrev.2012.04.004

Coombs, W. T., & Holladay, S. J. (2014). How publics react to crisis communication efforts: Comparing crisis response reactions across sub-arenas. *Journal of Communication Management, 18*(1), 40–57. https://doi.org/10.1108/JCOM-03-2013-0015

Coombs, W. T., & Holladay, S. J. (2015). Public relations' "relationship identity" in research: Enlightenment or illusion. *Public Relations Review, 41*(5), 689–695. https://doi.org/10.1016/j.pubrev.2013.12.008

Fortunato, J. A. (2017). The FIFA crisis: Examining sponsor response options. *Journal of Contingencies and Crisis Management, 25*(2), 68–78. https://doi.org/10.1111/1468-5973.12125

Frandsen, F., & Johansen, W. (2010). Crisis communication, complexity, and the cartoon affair: A case study. In W. T. Coombs, & S. J. Holladay (Eds.), *The handbook of crisis communication* (pp. 425–448). Wiley-Blackwell.

Frandsen, F., & Johansen, W. (2017). *Organizational crisis communication*. Sage.

Frederick, E., & Pegoraro, A. (2018). Scandal in college basketball: A case study of image repair via Facebook. *International Journal of Sport Communication, 11*(3), 414–429. https://doi.org/10.1123/ijsc.2018-0076

Gibbs, C., O'Reilly, N., & Brunette, M. (2014). Professional team sport and Twitter: Gratifications sought and obtained by followers. *International Journal of Sport Communication, 7*(2), 188–213. https://doi.org/10.1123/IJSC.2014-0005

Hambrick, M. E., Frederick, E. L., & Sanderson, J. (2015). From yellow to blue: Exploring Lance Armstrong's image repair strategies across traditional and social media. *Communication & Sport, 3*(2), 196–218. https://doi.org/10.1177%2F2167479513506982

Hambrick, M. E., & Mahoney, T. Q. (2011). "It's incredible–trust me": Exploring the role of celebrity athletes as marketers in online social networks. *International Journal of Sport Management and Marketing, 10*(3–4), 161–179. https://doi.org/10.1504/IJSMM.2011.044794

Harker, J. L. (2018a). Crisis Perceptions, Fan Behaviors, and Egocentric Discussion Networks: An Investigation into the Impervious Nature of NFL Crises. [doctoral dissertation, University of North Carolina at Chapel Hill]. https://doi.org/10.17615/p1cd-nd94

Harker, J. L. (2018b). Knee-jerk policymaking in crisis response: A fumbled play by the NFL. In Billings, A. C., Coombs, W. T. & Brown, K. A. (Eds.), *Reputational challenges in sport: Theory and application*. Routledge.

Harker, J. L. (2019a). Let's talk sports: An egocentric discussion network analysis regarding NFL crisis perceptions. *Communication & Sport.* https://doi.org/10.1177/2167479519875970

Harker, J. L. (2019b). Identification and crisis: An exploration into the influence of sports identification on stakeholder perceptions of sports-related crisis. *Journal of Sports Media,* 14(1), 171–199. https://www.muse.jhu.edu/article/735262

Harker, J. L., & Jensen, J. A. (2020). Adding insult to rivalry: Exploring the discord communicated between rivals. *International Journal of Sports Marketing and Sponsorship.* https://doi.org/10.1108/IJSMS-12-2019-0141

Jensen, J. A., Ervin, S. M., & Dittmore, S. W. (2014). Exploring the factors affecting popularity in social media: A case study of FBS football coaches. *International Journal of Sport Communication,* 7, 261–278. https://doi.org/10.1123/IJSC.2014-0008

Kassing, J. W., & Sanderson, J. (2010). Fan-athlete interaction and Twitter tweeting through the Giro: A case study. *International Journal of Sport Communication,* 3(4), 113–128. https://doi.org/10.1123/ijsc.3.1.113

Kruse, N. W. (1981). Apologia in team sport. *Quarterly Journal of Speech,* 67(3), 270–283. http://dx.doi.org/10.1080/00335638109383572

Meadows, C. Z., & Meadows, C. W. III (2020). He will never walk outside of a prison again: An examination of Twitter users' responses to the Larry Nassar case. *Communication & Sport,* 8(2), 188–214. https://doi.org/10.1177%2F2167479519825620

Sanderson, J. (2013). From loving the hero to despising the villain: Sports fans, Facebook, and social identity threats. *Mass Communication and Society,* 16(4), 487–509. https://doi.org/10.1080/15205436.2012.730650

Sanderson, J. (2014). Shaping, driving, engaging, and influencing in 140 characters: Exploring Twitter's role in a labor dispute. *Qualitative Research Reports in Communication,* 15(1), 43–50. https://doi.org/10.1080/17459435.2014.955591

Sanderson, J., Barnes, K., Williamson, C., & Kian, E. T. (2016). "How could anyone have predicted that #AskJameis would go horribly wrong?" public relations, social media, and hashtag hijacking. *Public Relations Review,* 42(1), 31–37. https://doi.org/10.1016/j.pubrev.2015.11.005

Sanderson, J., & Cheong, P. H. (2010). Tweeting prayers and communicating grief over Michael Jackson online. *Bulletin of Science Technology Society,* 30(5), 328–340. https://doi.org/10.1177/0270467610380010

Schmittel, A., & Hull, K. (2015). "Shit got cray cray #MYBAD": An examination of the image-repair discourse of Richie Incognito during the Miami Dolphins' bullying scandal. *Journal of Sports Media,* 10(2), 115–137. https://doi.org/10.1353/jsm.2015.0009

Schramm, H., & Hartmann, T. (2008). The PSI-process scales. A new measure to assess the intensity and breadth of parasocial processes. *Communications,* 33(4), 385–401. https://doi.org/10.1515/COMM.2008.025

Sipocz, D., & Coche, R. (2019). Tweetkeeping NBC's Rio Olympics. *Ohio Communication Journal,* 57, 91–104.

Smith, L. R., Pegoraro, A., & Cruikshank, S. A. (2019). Tweet, retweet, favorite: The impact of Twitter use on enjoyment and sports viewing. *Journal of Broadcasting & Electronic Media,* 63(1), 94–110. https://doi.org/10.1080/08838151.2019.1568805

Smith, L. R., & Smith, K. D. (2012). Identity in Twitter's hashtag culture: A sport-media-consumption case study. *International Journal of Sport Communication,* 5(4), 539–557. https://doi.org/10.1123/ijsc.5.4.539

Tajfel, H., & Turner, J. C. (1979). An integrative theory of intergroup conflict. *Social Psychology of Intergroup Relations,* 33(47), 74.

Tajfel, H., & Turner, J. C. (1986). The social identity theory of inter group behavior. In Worchel S., & Austin, W. G. (Eds.). *Psychology of intergroup relations*. Nelson.

Wann, D. L., & Branscombe, N. R. (1990). Die-hard and fair-weather fans: Effects of identification on BIRGing and CORFing tendencies. *Journal of Sport and Social Issues, 14*(2), 103–117. https://doi.org/10.1177%2F019372359001400203

Ware, B. L., & Linkugel, W. A. (1973). They spoke in defense of themselves: On the generic criticism of apologia. *Quarterly Journal of Speech, 59*(3), 273–283. http://dx.doi.org/10.1080/00335637309383176

Watkins, B. (2014). An integrated approach to sports branding: Examining the influence of social media on brand outcomes. *International Journal of Integrated Marketing Communications, 6*(2), 20–30.

Winand, M., Belot, M., Merten, S., & Kolyperas, D. (2019). International Sport Federations' social media communication: A content analysis of FIFA's Twitter account. *International Journal of Sport Communication, 12*(2), 1–25. https://doi.org/10.1123/ijsc.2018-0173

Areas of Application: Disaster

30

DISASTER CASE CHAPTER: SILENCE IS NOT GOLDEN

Social Media Lessons from Puerto Rico

Rebecca Fuller Beeler

As Hurricane Laura approached Puerto Rico in August 2020, Puerto Rico's State Agency for Emergency Management and Disaster Administration tweeted evacuation plans and flash flood warnings and retweeted information from the National Weather Service, the Puerto Rico Seismic Network, and U.S. Coast Guard leaders. The consistent and frequent social media activity during Hurricane Laura was in marked contrast to that around the arrival of Hurricane Maria in September 2017, when the Puerto Rican government was largely silent on social media. In a country of heavy social media users, the absence of preparation and evacuation messages by the Puerto Rican government in 2017 stood in stark contrast to the recommendations by the Department of Homeland Security for social media use.

Social Media and Disasters

Social media can play an important role before, during, and after disasters. Social media can be used by non-government agencies and government agencies to engage in communication with the community, to gather information during a disaster, and to influence decision making by gathering real-time information (Pond, 2016; U.S. Department of Homeland Security, 2013). Twitter, in particular, has been used for disaster-related messaging in five categories: information, media sharing, help and fundraising, direct experience, and discussion and reaction (Pond, 2013). The U.S. Department of Homeland Security (2013) produced a guide to using social media during emergencies,

DOI: 10.4324/9781003043409-41

which outlined strategies for agencies and highlighted innovative uses, including:

- When an earthquake shook Christchurch, New Zealand, in 2011, community members and relief agencies used social media to identify posts providing actionable information, distributing critical information to the public, and coordinating and publicizing humanitarian efforts.
- A 2011 earthquake in Virginia led to the use of social media as the official source of information and method of contacting friends and family members when cellular networks were overwhelmed.
- In 2012, the City of New Orleans, along with other agencies, used social media and consistent hashtags to provide clear alerts and warnings, monitor social media conversations and correct misinformation, and respond directly to inquiries from the public.

Social media use by Puerto Rico's population is increasingly prevalent. In 2017, 2.2 million people in Puerto Rico were active social media users, representing 60% of the population (Kemp, 2017). While Instagram, Twitter, YouTube, and Snapchat were in use on the island, Facebook was the predominant social media platform (Kemp, 2017). By 2020, 72% of Puerto Rico's population regularly used social media. Facebook continued to be the dominant platform, but other platforms (e.g., Twitter and Snapchat) had greater use than in previous years (Kemp, 2020).

Hurricane Maria in Puerto Rico

When Hurricane Maria made landfall on September 20, 2017, it left the island without power and communication with the outside world. While social media can be used by government and relief agencies to issue preparedness messages, share shelter locations and aid stations, and catalog damage and needs, this was not the case in Puerto Rico. The government was largely silent and relief agencies used social media more to showcase the help they were offering and to solicit donations than to link survivors with resources.

Puerto Rico's government agencies and leading officials used social media sparingly. Governor Ricardo Rossello's Facebook (@rrossello) and Twitter (@RicardoRossello) accounts were silent immediately before and during landfall. Puerto Rico's State Agency for Emergency Management and Disaster Administration used Facebook (@NMEADpr) to share status updates, evacuation plans, and press briefings. However, the Twitter account (@NMEADpr) was used heavily for photo opportunities of Governor Rossello meeting with officials, visiting various sites around the country, and meeting with disaster response officials. The account was not used for guidance on when and where to find help or how to cope with the damage caused by Hurricane Maria.

Some relief agencies used social media to share updates on services, connect individuals with their loved ones, appeal for donations, highlight their service to the island, and advocate for government action. With acknowledgment of the heavy use of Facebook by Puerto Rico's residents, The Salvation Army (@SalvationArmyPR), the Puerto Rico Chapter of the American Red Cross (@CruzRojaPR), and Direct Relief (@DirectRelief) used Facebook exclusively or in conjunction with Twitter. However, since these agencies are more response agencies than preparedness agencies, their activities on social media were primarily after Hurricane Maria made landfall and in the following months – making the void left by limited government activity more apparent.

Beyond institutional use of social media to promote donations or to showcase service to those affected by the disaster, social media was used following Hurricane Maria as a means of activism and human interaction. Although the "Columbia Journalism Review," "The Guardian," and "Frontline," among others, have questioned whether the media devoted enough attention to Hurricane Maria, some journalists turned to Twitter to drive focus toward the slow relief efforts and needs of the residents of Puerto Rico (Pinchin, 2019; Ramirez de Arellano, 2017; Vernon, 2018). CBS News correspondent David Begnaud took to Twitter to make sure the public learned about the mishandling of relief supplies (Vernon, 2018). Individuals turned to social media to share photos and videos revealing the storm's impact on the island (Stone, 2017). Other individuals published diaries of their experiences on social media, sent direct messages to reach out to family and friends, and offered help to one another through the #MeUnoAyudar campaign on Twitter (Chansky, 2019; Rodriguez-Diaz, 2018; Stone, 2017). This social media use, while unofficial, was a consistent source of information and updates, albeit through the lens of individuals in the middle of the storm.

Lessons Learned

Turmoil in Puerto Rico has continued since the arrival of Hurricane Maria, which may push the development of effective disaster communications and enhanced social media strategy far down the list of things Puerto Rico's leaders and citizens will need to focus on. At the time Hurricane Maria made landfall, Puerto Rico was facing a debt crisis and political turmoil that has not waned in the following years (Einbinder, 2018; Pinchin, 2019). A month after the hurricane, Puerto Rico's residents were still facing power outages, water shortages, blocked roads, and inhabitable homes (Einbinder, 2018; Pinchin, 2019). In the months after Hurricane Maria, FEMA was under fire for the response in Puerto

Rico, and two years later, Puerto Rico's governor faced public outcry leading to his resignation (Pinchin, 2019).

The 2017 hurricane season saw Hurricanes Harvey, Irma, and Maria strike Puerto Rico. Lessons learned about effective communication following one storm could have been implemented during the next storm. However, the cumulative effect of storms taxes a community's resources and leaves hindsight with a better perspective (Einbinder, 2018). After multiple storms made landfall, some relief supplies were scarce and available supplies and federal workers were slow to arrive – Puerto Rico received fewer meals, water, tarps, and federal workers on a slower schedule than Florida and Texas, where Hurricanes Irma and Harvey made landfall, respectively (Einbinder, 2018).

In 2018, a FEMA report acknowledged that the agency had mishandled the response by failing to adequately prepare for the hurricane season and to stage supplies on the island (Schwartz, 2018). Clearly, Puerto Rico faced challenges beyond whether social media was used to communicate. The use of social media in the days and weeks before and after a disaster cannot be an organization's only communication strategy. In the case of Hurricane Maria, a week after the hurricane, 1360 of the island's 1600 cell towers were down, affecting people's ability to use the Internet and access social media (Ramirez de Arellano, 2017). So, while social media may not be the only tool, it can be an effective tool for sharing real-time information, mobilizing residents, and providing consistent updates.

References

Chansky, R. A. (2019). Auto/biography after disaster: The year in Puerto Rico. *Biography: An Interdisciplinary Quarterly, 42*(1), 124–131. https://doi.org/10.1353/bo.2019.0019

Einbinder, N. (2018, May 1). How the response to Hurricane Maria compared to Harvey and Irma. *Frontline.* https://www.pbs.org/wgbh/frontline/article/how-the-response-to-hurricane-maria-compared-to-harvey-and-irma/

Kemp, S. (2017, February 1). Digital 2017: Puerto Rico. *DataReportal.* https://datareportal.com/reports/digital-2017-puerto-rico

Kemp, S. (2020, February 18). Digital 2020: Puerto Rico. *DataReportal.* https://datareportal.com/reports/digital-2020-puerto-rico

Pinchin, K. (2019, August 2). How Hurricane Maria fueled Puerto Rico's resistance. *Frontline.* https://www.pbs.org/wgbh/frontline/article/how-hurricane-maria-fueled-puerto-ricos-resistance/

Pond, P. (2016). The space between us: Twitter and crisis communication. *International Journal of Disaster Resilience in the Built Environment, 7*(1), 40–48. https://doi.org/10.1108.IJDRBE-08-2013-0030

Ramirez de Arellano, S. (2017, September 26). Puerto Rico is on the brink of a humanitarian crisis. Where is the media? *The Guardian.* www.theguardian.com

Rodriguez-Diaz, C. E. (2018). Maria in Puerto Rico: Natural disaster in a colonial archipelago. *The American Journal of Public Health, 1,* 30–32. https://doi.org/10.2105/AJPH.2017.304198

Schwartz, E. (2018, July 13). FEMA report acknowledges failures in Puerto Rico disaster response. *Frontline*. https://www.pbs.org/wgbh/frontline/article/fema-report-acknowledges-failures-in-puerto-rico-disaster-response/

Stone, B. (2017, September 20). Social media captures Hurricane Maria's devastating damage to Puerto Rico. *Daily Dot*. https://www.dailydot.com/

U.S. Department of Homeland Security, Science and Technology Directorate, System Assessment and Validation for Emergency Responders. (2013). Innovative uses of social media in emergency management. https://www.dhs.gov/sites/default/files/publications/Social-Media-EM_0913-508_0.pdf

Vernon, P. (2018, September 25). As "the media" neglected Puerto Rico, some reporters made it their mission. *Columbia Journalism Review*. https://www.cjr.org/united_states_project/puerto-rico-begnaud-santiago.php

31

NATURAL DISASTER PREPAREDNESS, RESPONSE, AND RECOVERY CRISIS COMMUNICATION

Wenlin Liu and Lan Ni

Introduction

In recent years, government and disaster management agencies have increasingly incorporated social media in crisis and disaster communication. The adoption of social media in the public sector is first catalyzed by the Obama administration's *Open Government Initiative* (Obama, 2009). Public expectations further drive government agencies' social media activity during emergencies, as citizens increasingly turn to social media for real-time disaster information (Jin et al., 2014). These public expectations range from providing timely disaster updates, debunking rumors and misinformation to communicating accountability and leadership during emergencies (Neely & Collins, 2018). Under this backdrop, accumulating scholarly work and practitioner insights have focused on how government and disaster management agencies use social media at various stages of a disaster (e.g., Graham et al., 2015; Liu et al., 2018, 2020). Some literature focuses on the content of those messages, such as how government agencies employ various crisis response strategies when communicating with the public (e.g., Liu et al., 2018; Wukich, 2016), whereas others examine how social media is used for building and negotiating relationships (e.g., Hong et al., 2012; Liu & Xu, 2019).

Government use of social media for disaster management has also significantly evolved over the past few years. While earlier work critiques that public agencies predominantly use social media as a tool to disseminate one-way information (Roshan et al., 2016), more recent evidence suggests that dialogic communication and citizen engagement practices are gradually incorporated (Liu et al., 2020). The rapid growth of research on this topic thus calls for an

DOI: 10.4324/9781003043409-42

updated review of relevant work, with the goals to better inform scholars and practitioners aiming to leverage social media for effective crisis management.

This chapter provides a synthesized review of public agencies' social media use for disaster management and mitigation. The chapter starts by outlining the needs and communication priorities specific to each disaster management stage, identifying three primary functions that social media fulfills in the process of disaster preparedness, response, and recovery. To further illustrate these functions, we present a brief content analysis of tweets from government and emergency management organizations during Hurricane Harvey in 2017. Theoretical insights and practical recommendations for crisis managers are provided in conclusion.

Disaster Management across Various Stages: Goals and Priorities

In this chapter, we adopt Liu et al.'s (2016) definition of disaster communication as "information creation, seeking, and/or sharing among individuals, organizations, and the media surrounding an event involving largely damaging violations of publics' expectations" (p. 628). One major challenge in disaster management is the lack of shared information and integration among a multi-party emergency management team, where high uncertainty and limited information may result in broken communication and the loss in the form of human life and property damage (e.g., Bharosa et al., 2010). This challenge is exacerbated by the fact that not all involved agencies are fully aware of the role or status of service from other organizations. Therefore, these emergency response agencies not only need to maintain good relationships with one another, but to enhance knowledge of (a) their different partner entities where coordination and cooperation are required, and (b) the community members whose participation in disaster response is needed to help protect themselves from the disasters.

These overall challenges manifest themselves differently in different stages of disaster management. Borrowing the commonly used three-staged categorization of crisis communication (pre-crisis, crisis, and post-crisis, Coombs & Holladay, 2002), we classify disaster management into the three stages of disaster preparedness, disaster response, and disaster recovery. In all three phases, information provision, inter-agency coordination and mobilization, and community building are crucial, although the focus and strategies may differ at each stage.

Disaster Preparedness

When preparing for future disasters, it is critical to engage in community building to overcome the overall challenges identified earlier. Building relationships with various stakeholders is needed before a disaster, so that inter-agency coordination and mobilization are even possible when the disaster occurs. Disaster preparedness can significantly benefit from a "creation of meaningful partnerships that respond to the concerns and needs of community members for information and to bring collective wisdom and judgment to bear on that problem" (Heath & O'Hair, 2010, p. 7). Regarding the community partnership, an infrastructural approach assumes that scientifically derived information and emergency response protocols need to be discussed collectively so that community members can deliberate on facts, express concerns, and form appropriate risk perceptions. A community approach (Springston & Lariscy, 2010) not only has the potential of "achieving goals that are beyond the reach of individuals" but also surpasses the "efforts by state or national agencies/organizations that often lack the local knowledge and support that a community-level coalition can achieve" (p. 547).

Disaster Response

When responding to disasters, it is crucial to provide accurate and timely information. Information and communication among various actors are key to emergency management. Research has identified four types of communicators and patterns through a crisis communication matrix (Reuter & Kaufhold, 2018). They include (1) citizens to citizens (C2C), which involves self-coordination and help; (2) authorities to citizens (A2C), which involves crisis communication and public alerting through sharing information; (3) citizens to authorities (C2A), which requires the integration of citizen-generated content and information sharing; and (4) authorities to authorities (A2A), which refers to inter- and intra-organizational crisis management.

The multi-domain and multi-directional information flows ensure resilience in emergency management because the effectiveness of information sharing will not be completely destroyed even if one element in the whole network dysfunctions. In fact, when examining information sharing during crisis management in hierarchical versus network teams, Schraagen et al. (2010) found that compared to the hierarchical teams, network teams were overall faster and more accurate in sharing knowledge in complex scenarios.

Disaster Recovery

Successful disaster recovery helps strengthen community resilience. In this stage, it is again essential to engage in community building and empowerment. Waldman et al. (2018) more explicitly advocate for including citizens in emergency management. They argue that this is becoming "indispensable" as citizens are "increasingly presenting their labor and resources as assets to be drawn on in emergency and post-emergency situations" (p. 394). Diverse groups of citizens, community members, and voluntary organizations work as volunteers in emergency management, and they are becoming increasingly important in emergency response and recovery because they play the role of "brokers" to help emergency management agencies "access and manage community-based networks of voluntary resources" (p. 394). As a result, many disaster management organizations employ a range of formal and informal methods to engage community members in dialogues and make such collaboration sustainable during disaster recovery (McComas et al., 2010).

Functions of Social Media for Government Crisis Communication

Research suggests that the specific social media functions sought by an organization may vary depending on the internal and external environment (Oliveira & Welch, 2013). In the context of disaster management, as each phase of a crisis calls for different communication goals and priorities as outlined above, it is plausible to assume that public organizations may use social media for various purposes. A typology of government social media use for crisis management is thus helpful in mapping the different motivations that shape public agencies' crisis communication on social media. Below, we summarize three primary functions of social media use for government disaster communication from existing literature.

Information Updates and Provision

Social media provides public agencies the platforms to directly make announcements and offer crisis updates, which is critical to fulfilling public needs for accurate, timely crisis information and reducing uncertainty at various stages of a crisis (Houston et al., 2015). Regardless of organizational sectors, information provision is often the foundation of effective organizational crisis responses (Coombs, 2007).

Several characteristics of social media have made them a preferred tool for broadcasting crisis information. First, social media enables rapid message diffusion. Compared to traditional offline media, social media is more efficient in broadcasting organizational updates through large-scale and decentralized networks (Sutton et al., 2014). Second, from the citizens' side, social media platforms are increasingly used as a tool for emergency information seeking. Although various information sources are available nowadays, Freberg et al. (2013) reported that the public still most frequently referred to government sources (e.g., CDC) in their online discussion of crises.

In addition, rumors and misinformation have further reinforced the important role of public agencies in providing information. Studies have shown that refutation and warning are two effective strategies to control the spread of rumors on social media (Ozturk et al., 2015). In terms of the sources that can best dispel misinformation, van der Meer and Jin (2020) found that government agency sources were in general more successful in improving citizens' belief accuracy compared to other information sources such as social peers. Therefore, providing credible information and clarifying misinformation are the two sides of one coin in terms of providing information on social media.

Inter-Agency Coordination and Relationship Building

Crises such as natural disasters propel government and emergency management agencies to seek tangible (e.g., donations and volunteers) and intangible (e.g., information) resources from the greater community that they serve, and an organization's ability to mobilize resources depends heavily on relations built with various stakeholders (Barringer & Harrison, 2000). For example, Doerfel et al. (2013) found that inter-organizational networks among disaster-struck organizations were important mechanisms to mobilize resources and foster post-disaster resilience after Hurricane Katrina. In addition, cross-sector inter-organizational relationships between government and nonprofit or business sectors, such as in the form of corporate disaster aids or government-nonprofit partnerships, are also important for disaster relief and post-disaster recovery (Simo & Bies, 2007).

Different from offline collaboration networks, the interorganizational networks mediated by social media tend to be constituted by a set of loosely connected actors. Such a network may overlap with direct contact, collaboration, and various forms of resource exchange relationships offline (Taylor & Doerfel, 2003). Liu and Xu (2019) examined such stakeholder networks on Twitter during Hurricane Harvey, conceptualizing public agencies' Twitter mention behaviors as a strategic act for relationship building. The study identified a diverse group of social actors – ranging from citizens, activist groups, civil society organizations to businesses – that were actively mobilized by public agencies to facilitate the management of the disaster.

Community Building

Other than physical damage, the psychological and emotional toll of crises can be tremendous on the affected community. To help cope with such strains, community members may frequently turn to social media to seek social support and express emotions (Meadows et al., 2019). Social media thus can help create a sense of community in disasters. As Taylor et al.'s (2012) study suggested, social media like Facebook served as the "broker" between community members and government information sources, and they helped promote a sense of connectedness and acted as "psychological first aid" especially in the early stages of a disaster (p. 20).

From the standpoint of public agencies, providing emotional support and boosting community morale can facilitate disaster preparedness and response in several ways. First, empathetic and supportive government leadership is helpful in enhancing public trust and cooperative behaviors (Kock et al., 2019), both of which are essential for effective disaster mitigation. Second, cultivating collective identity and solidarity is instrumental in organizing community-wide collective action. Relevant research found that place-based identity was effective in bringing diverse community members together and acting on joint causes (Liu et al., 2018). A strong sense of community also contributes to community resilience, the capacity of a community to bounce back from adverse conditions such as natural disasters (Sonn & Fisher, 1998).

Government agencies increasingly recognize the importance of building community through the use of social media, and empirical work documents the positive relationship between such community-building efforts and higher public engagement outcomes. For example, Liu et al.'s (2020) study of government agencies' disaster communication on Facebook found that the messages praising stakeholders and emphasizing community solidarity were more likely to be endorsed by community members through the use of "like."

A Case Analysis of Government Social Media Message Types During a Natural Disaster

To apply the government social media use typology proposed above in a recent disaster communication context, the following reports a content analysis of government and EM agencies' tweets during different phases of Hurricane Harvey, which struck coastal Texas from August 25 to early September 2017. The following three stages were identified based on the progression of the disaster: the disaster preparation stage between 8/17/2017 and 8/21/2017, when Harvey developed from a tropical storm into a category four hurricane; the disaster response stage between 8/25/2017 and 9/1/2017, during which immediate disaster relief activities took place; and the disaster recovery stage between 9/2/2017 and 9/8/2017, a week after the major flooding.

We identified a total of 67 local government and EM agencies in the disaster-impacted regions and further collected their public tweets via Twitter's API. A total of 8,672 original tweets were content analyzed between the selected time period. In applying the coding framework, several tweets unrelated to the hurricane were identified and removed. The initial codebook was modified several times to improve reliability. At the last round of reliability check, two coders coded 1,000 tweets together and achieved a Krippendorff's alpha of 0.75 for message themes. The coders then discussed coding discrepancies to achieve 100% agreements on all mutually coded tweets.

TABLE 31.1 Nine Types of Government and EM Social Media Messages during Hurricane Harvey

	Information provision
1. Public information	Tweets that directly presented disaster or relief-related information.
2. Response to information request	Direct replies that provided information as requested by citizens.
3. Press release	Tweets that directed information to media organizations.
4. Clarification	Tweets that clarified misinformation.
5. Mediating	Tweets that served to connect residents to resources, playing the role of "information broker."
	Inter-agency coordination and relationship building
1. Action mobilization	Tweets that called for participation, donation, and mobilization of resources.
2. Appreciation and alliance	Tweets that communicated alliance, solidarity, and gratitude toward stakeholders.
	Community building
1. Assurance	Tweets that expressed comfort and social support.
2. Storytelling	Tweets that shared experience from or told stories about community members.

To explore different types of disaster messages, we used an inductive approach and identified the following nine themes that respectively represented the three functions of government social media use (see Table 31.1).

Across all three crisis stages, public information was the most prevalent theme (61%), and the majority of the tweets of this theme were intended for providing disaster or relief-related information, updates, advisory, and tips. The prominence of this theme, however, decreased over time, dropping to 55% during disaster and 50% post disaster (see Figure 31.1). The next prevalent theme was mediating or brokering, defined as the type of tweets intended to connect Twitter users to third-party information or other resources. It was the second most used theme in the pre-disaster (19%) and the disaster stage (17%), but it became far less prominent in the post-disaster stage (8%). The theme of press release, used exclusively for targeting media organizations to shape media agenda, was relatively absent in the pre- (<1%) and disaster stage (1%) but rose in great salience in the post-disaster stage (17%). The theme of responding to requested information was used the most during the disaster (4%) than before or after the disaster. Finally, given misinformation was rampant, the theme of clarification was critical in a natural disaster communication context, which appeared most frequently during and after the disaster (5%).

In terms of the function of resource mobilization and relationship building, the theme of appreciation, used for showing solidarity and gratitude toward stakeholders, rose from 6% in the pre-disaster stage to 10% during the disaster,

Themes across Stages

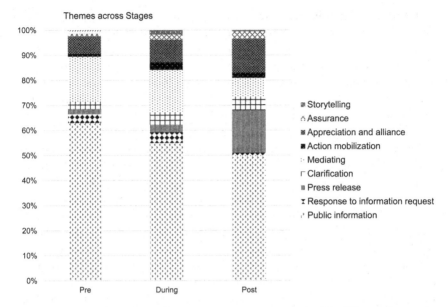

Legend:
- Storytelling
- Assurance
- Appreciation and alliance
- Action mobilization
- Mediating
- Clarification
- Press release
- Response to information request
- Public information

FIGURE 31.1 The Percentage of Government Tweets From the Nine Theme Categories Across the Three Stages of Hurricane Harvey

topping at 14% in the post-disaster stage. The theme of action and mobilization was little used in the pre-disaster stage. Its highest occurrence was observed during and after the disaster (2~3%).

Finally, the theme of assurance, used to offer emotional support for the public, only made up a relatively small percentage of all tweets, and this type of tweet was frequently used in the post-disaster stage (3%) than the other two phases. The theme of storytelling, similarly, was used more frequently only at the post-disaster stage (2%).

Conclusion

This chapter reviews recent literature on social media for public agency crisis communication and proposes a three-domain framework to understand how government and disaster management agencies use social media in the process of disaster preparedness, response, and recovery: information provision, interagency coordination and mobilization, and community building. The content analysis of government tweets has generally supported our proposed framework, identifying distinctive themes associated with the three major functions. Further, these functions are used with varying degrees across different stages of the disaster, reflective of the unique communication goals and priorities as outlined earlier in the chapter.

There are several directions for future work to further test and expand the three-function typology of social media use. First, it is worth examining if crisis type – natural disasters versus man-made disasters, for example – may lead to different patterns of government social media use. Crisis communication scholars have long noted how crisis type serves an important context and informs the development of effective response strategies (e.g., Coombs & Holladay, 2002). The current typology can be further validated via applications across different crisis types.

Second, the effects of the three social media functions from the reception side need more in-depth research. Ultimately, the use of social media is intended to achieve crisis management goals such as improving individuals' disaster-coping preparedness, efficacy, or community resilience (Houston et al., 2015). Establishing the empirical link between the specific type of social media use and disaster management outcomes can better inform how different functions should be strategically managed and prioritized across various stages of a disaster.

Last but not least, while the case analysis indeed supports our general framework, there are a few patterns that need to be addressed to better improve disaster communication. For instance, social media use for community building identified in the data is somewhat limited. The two major strategies of assurance and storytelling, while useful in comforting the community and managing their emotional needs, have not effectively tapped into the potential of the community in *actively* coping with the disaster. Much research in community-based approach and public participation (e.g., Heath & O'Hair, 2010; McComas et al., 2010) has emphasized the role of community building in proactively empowering communities in disasters and emergencies. In other words, community members should not be considered only as individuals to be helped (and comforted), but more importantly, as partners that can work with the government together in disaster response. Social media has the potential to drastically increase such participatory disaster coping behaviors. More research is needed to fully understand the utilities as well as limitations of social media use for disaster management.

References

Barringer, B. R., & Harrison, J. S. (2000). Walking a tightrope: Creating value through interorganizational relationships. *Journal of Management*, *26*(3), 367–403. https://doi.org/10.1016/S0149-2063(00)00046-5

Bharosa, N., Lee, J., & Janssen, M. (2010). Challenges and obstacles in sharing and coordinating information during multi-agency disaster response: Propositions from field exercises. *Information Systems Frontiers*, *12*(1), 49–65. https://doi.org/10.1007/s10796-009-9174-z

Coombs, W. T. (2007). Protecting organization reputations during a crisis: The development and application of situational crisis communication theory. *Corporate Reputation Review*, *10*(3), 163–176. https://doi.org/10.1057/palgrave.crr.1550049

Coombs, W. T., & Holladay, S. J. (2002). Helping crisis managers protect reputational assets: Initial tests of the situational crisis communication theory. *Management Communication Quarterly, 16*(2), 165–186. https://doi.org/10.1177/089331802237233

Doerfel, M. L., Chewning, L. V., & Lai, C. H. (2013). The evolution of networks and the resilience of interorganizational relationships after disaster. *Communication Monographs, 80*(4), 533–559. https://doi.org/10.1080/03637751.2013.828157

Freberg, K., Palenchar, M. J., & Veil, S. R. (2013). Managing and sharing H1N1 crisis information using social media bookmarking services. *Public Relations Review, 39*(3), 178–184. https://doi.org/10.1016/j.pubrev.2013.02.007

Graham, M. W., Avery, E. J., & Park, S. (2015). The role of social media in local government crisis communications. *Public Relations Review, 41*(3), 386–394. https://doi.org/10.1016/j.pubrev.2015.02.001

Heath, R. L., & O'Hair, H. D. (Eds.). (2010). *Handbook of risk and crisis communication.* Routledge.

Hong, H., Park, H., Lee, Y., & Park, J. (2012). Public segmentation and government–public relationship building: A cluster analysis of publics in the United States and 19 European countries. *Journal of Public Relations Research, 24*(1), 37–68. https://doi.org/10.1080/1062726X.2012.626135

Houston, J. B., Hawthorne, J., Perreault, M. F., Park, E. H., Goldstein Hode, M., Halliwell, M. R., & Griffith, S. A. (2015). Social media and disasters: A functional framework for social media use in disaster planning, response, and research. *Disasters, 39*(1), 1–22. https://doi.org/10.1111/disa.12092

Jin, Y., Liu, B. F., & Austin, L. L. (2014). Examining the role of social media in effective crisis management: The effects of crisis origin, information form, and source on publics' crisis responses. *Communication Research, 41*(1), 74–94. https://doi.org/10.1177/0093650211423918

Kock, N., Mayfield, M., Mayfield, J., Sexton, S., & De La Garza, L. M. (2019). Empathetic leadership: How leader emotional support and understanding influences follower performance. *Journal of Leadership & Organizational Studies, 26*(2), 217–236. https://doi.org/10.1177/1548051818806290

Liu, B. F., Fraustino, J. D., & Jin, Y. (2016). Social media use during disasters: How information form and source influence intended behavioral responses. *Communication Research, 43*(5), 626–646. https://doi.org/10.1177/0093650214565917

Liu, W., Lai, C. H., & Xu, W. W. (2018). Tweeting about emergency: A semantic network analysis of government organizations' social media messaging during Hurricane Harvey. *Public Relations Review, 44*(5), 807–819. https://doi.org/10.1016/j.pubrev.2018.10.009

Liu, W., Son, M., Wenzel, A., An, Z., Zhao Martin, N., Nah, S., & Ball-Rokeach, S. (2018). Bridging mechanisms in multiethnic communities: Place-based communication, neighborhood belonging, and intergroup relations. *Journal of International and Intercultural Communication, 11*(1), 58–80. https://doi.org/10.1080/17513057.2017.1384506

Liu, W., & Xu, W. W. (2019). Tweeting to (selectively) engage: How government agencies target stakeholders on Twitter during Hurricane Harvey. *International Journal of Communication, 13*, 4917–4939.

Liu, W., Xu, W. W., & Tsai, J. Y. J. (2020). Developing a multi-level organization-public dialogic communication framework to assess social media-mediated disaster communication and engagement outcomes. *Public Relations Review, 46*(4), 101949. https://doi.org/10.1016/j.pubrev.2020.101949

McComas, K. A., Arvai, J., & Besley, J. C. (2010). Linking public participation and decision making through risk communication. In R. L. Heath, & H. D. O'Hair (Eds.), *Handbook of risk and crisis communication* (pp. 364–385). Routledge.

Meadows, C. W., Meadows, C. Z., Tang, L., & Liu, W. (2019). Unraveling public health crises across stages: Understanding Twitter emotions and message types during the California measles outbreak. *Communication Studies, 70*(4), 453–469. https://doi.org/10.1080/10510974.2019.1582546

Neely, S. R., & Collins, M. (2018). Social media and crisis communications: A survey of local governments in Florida. *Journal of Homeland Security and Emergency Management, 15*(1), 1–13. https://doi.org/10.1515/jhsem-2016-0067

Obama, B. (2009). Transparency and open government: memorandum for the heads of executive departments and agencies. *Whitehouse Blog.* http://www.whitehouse.gov/the_press_office/TransparencyandOpenGovernment/

Oliveira, G. H. M., & Welch, E. W. (2013). Social media use in local government: Linkage of technology, task, and organizational context. *Government Information Quarterly, 30*(4), 397–405. https://doi.org/10.1016/j.giq.2013.05.019

Ozturk, P., Li, H., & Sakamoto, Y. (2015, January). Combating rumor spread on social media: The effectiveness of refutation and warning. In *2015 48th Hawaii International Conference on System Sciences* (pp. 2406–2414). IEEE.

Reuter, C., & Kaufhold, M. A. (2018). Fifteen years of social media in emergencies: A retrospective review and future directions for crisis informatics. *Journal of Contingencies and Crisis Management, 26(1),* 41–57. https://doi.org/10.1111/1468-5973.12196

Roshan, M., Warren, M., & Carr, R. (2016). Understanding the use of social media by organisations for crisis communication. *Computers in Human Behavior, 63,* 350–361. https://doi.org/10.1016/j.chb.2016.05.016

Schraagen, J. M., Veld, M. H. I. T., & De Koning, L. (2010). Information sharing during crisis management in hierarchical vs. network teams. *Journal of Contingencies and Crisis Management, 18*(2), 117–127. https://doi.org/10.1111/j.1468-5973.2010.00604.x

Simo, G., & Bies, A. L. (2007). The role of nonprofits in disaster response: An expanded model of cross-sector collaboration. *Public Administration Review, 67*(1), 125–142. https://doi.org/10.1111/j.1540-6210.2007.00821.x

Sonn, C. C., & Fisher, A. T. (1998). Sense of community: Community resilient responses to oppression and change. *Journal of Community Psychology, 26*(5), 457–472. https://doi.org/10.1002/(SICI)1520-6629(199809)26:5<457::AID-JCOP5>3.0.CO;2-O

Springston, J., & Lariscy, R. (2010). The role of public relations in promoting healthy communities. In R. L. Heath (Ed.), *The Sage handbook of public relations* (pp. 547–556). Sage.

Sutton, J., Spiro, E. S., Johnson, B., Fitzhugh, S., Gibson, B., & Butts, C. T. (2014). Warning tweets: Serial transmission of messages during the warning phase of a disaster event. *Information, Communication & Society, 17*(6), 765–787. https://doi.org/10.1080/1369118X.2013.862561

Taylor, M., & Doerfel, M. L. (2003). Building interorganizational relationships that build nations. *Human Communication Research, 29*(2), 153–181. https://doi.org/10.1111/j.1468-2958.2003.tb00835.x

Taylor, M., Wells, G., Howell, G., & Raphael, B. (2012). The role of social media as psychological first aid as a support to community resilience building. *Australian Journal of Emergency Management, 27*(1), 20–26.

van der Meer, T. G., & Jin, Y. (2020). Seeking formula for misinformation treatment in public health crises: The effects of corrective information type and source. *Health Communication, 35*(5), 560–575. https://doi.org/10.1080/10410236.2019.1573295

Waldman, S., Yumagulova, L., Mackwani, Z., Benson, C., & Stone, J. T. (2018). Canadian citizens volunteering in disasters: From emergence to networked governance. *Journal of Contingencies and Crisis Management, 26*(3), 394–402. https://doi.org/10.1111/1468-5973.12206

Wukich, C. (2016). Government social media messages across disaster phases. *Journal of Contingencies and Crisis Management, 24*(4), 230–243. https://doi.org/10.1111/1468-5973.12119

32

THE SOCIAL FUNCTIONS OF IDLE ALERTS

Hamilton Bean and Amy A. Hasinoff

This chapter examines an intersection of two domains of crisis communication and social media research and practice: law enforcement alerts and mobile technology. In what follows, we explore the social significance and implications of what we define as "idle alerts" – messages that ask recipients to increase their alertness or to observe their surroundings. In contrast, crisis communication research has to date mostly focused on improving the effectiveness of what we call "actionable alerts" – messages that typically instruct recipients to perform a specific protective action. We argue that while law enforcement-related idle alerts are intended to improve public safety, they also serve powerful symbolic functions and communicate social values. As such, we urge crisis communication and social media scholars to apply critical-cultural perspectives in studying public alert and warning and to carefully distinguish idle alerts from actionable alerts.

Historically, law enforcement officials have used a variety of media to enlist the public to help solve crimes and capture suspects. One early type of message about crime from law enforcement is the "wanted" poster, which is a form of public notification that asks viewers to be on the lookout for suspects, to report information to police, and in some cases, to collect a reward for it. Crime is also a significant part of fiction and nonfiction popular media, and officials are able to use this interest to their benefit. For example, in 1950, a reporter asked the FBI "for the names and descriptions of the 'toughest guys' the Bureau would like to capture," and the resulting story's considerable publicity led to the creation of the FBI's "Ten Most Wanted Fugitives" program (FBI, 2020, para. 1). The long-running television show *America's Most Wanted* (1988-2012), which vividly depicted criminal acts and invited viewers to report information about

DOI: 10.4324/9781003043409-43

suspects, is credited with leading to the capture of 17 fugitives from the FBI's list (para. 27). In addition to newspapers, radio, and television, officials have used a variety of other media to ask the public for assistance, including publicizing missing children on the backs of milk cartons in the 1980s and 90s and using electronic billboards to display modern-day "wanted" posters. These examples illustrate that law enforcement has long attempted to use new forms of media to deputize the public to help solve crimes and capture suspects.

At an institutional level, beginning in 2003, FEMA began urging state and local governments to integrate human-caused hazards (especially materials accidents and terrorism) into their all-hazard mitigation plans (FEMA, 2003). The all-hazard approach develops broadly applicable mitigation processes across hazards, rather than hazard-specific plans. Laws including the Clery Act (1990), the Prosecutorial Remedies and Other Tools to end the Exploitation of Children Today Act (2003), the Rafael Ramos and Wenjian Liu National Blue Alert Act (2015), and the Ashanti Alert Act (2018) have added a law enforcement dimension to these plans by mandating or encouraging the issuance of alerts (at local, state, or regional levels) related to missing or abducted children and adults, crime, and threats to law enforcement personnel.

Advances in mobile and social media technology have occurred in tandem with these policy developments. In the aftermath of the terrorist attacks of September 11, 2001 and Hurricane Katrina in 2005, President George W. Bush signed Executive Order 13407 in 2006, which mandated that the United States have a comprehensive system to warn the American people in situations of war, terrorist attack, natural disaster, or other hazards to public safety and well-being. This Order spurred the creation of the Integrated Public Alert and Warning System – the federal backbone of multiple alert and warning subsystems, including the Wireless Emergency Alerts (WEA) system, which was launched in 2012. As this volume attests, for nearly two decades, officials have used mobile devices in conjunction with social media platforms to communicate during crisis situations and public safety emergencies. Understanding the role and impact of social media in risk, crisis, and disaster communication is its own established and growing subfield of research: crisis informatics.

However, the conflation over the past decade of planning for natural hazards, human-caused hazards, crime, and threats to public safety – along with the rapid development and deployment of mobile and social media alerting technologies – has generated a fragmented and confusing U.S. public alert and warning system (Bean, 2019; Schatz, 2019; Todd et al., 2019). One Twitter user's response to receiving a Blue Alert illustrates this situation: "Happy 1 am to everyone else in Alabama awake and googling blue alert because our phones just made the tornado noise" (Bridges, 2020). Today, U.S. iPhone users find options in their notification settings to enable or disable "AMBER Alerts," "Emergency Alerts," and "Public Safety Alerts," while Android users find "AMBER Alerts,"

"Extreme Threats," and "Severe Threats" with little indication of what each alert type entails or the possible consequences of disabling it (see Bean, 2019). In addition to these types of WEA messages, officials may also use an array of specialized "built-for-purpose" apps (e.g., FEMA or NOAA) as well as general social media apps (e.g., Facebook or Twitter) to disseminate alerts (Tan et al., 2017). Integration among mass media, social media, and mobile messaging for crisis communication is accelerating. For example, California Highway Patrol's "Active Alerts" Twitter page disseminates alert messages including three subsets of WEA messages: AMBER Alerts (for missing or abducted children), Silver Alerts (for missing adults, especially senior citizens), and Blue Alerts (for crimes against or threats to law enforcement personnel).

Crisis communication scholars have typically focused on the efficacy of mobile and social media alerting, demonstrating concern for message accuracy, (re)transmission, interpretation, and response (Bean et al., 2015; Sutton et al., 2014; van Dijl et al., 2019). Research focused on efficacy is valuable for improving behavioral outcomes in response to hazards, whether they are natural or human-caused. This type of research is well-suited to studying messages that ask recipients to take a specific protective action, in other words, to stop what they are doing and do something else (e.g., "evacuate," "shelter-in-place," "stay home," or "slow down"). We define such messages as "actionable alerts."

However, due to the recent laws, policy changes, and advances in technology mentioned above, an increasing number of alerts do not ask recipients to take a specific protective action. Such messages, which we define as "idle alerts," instead ask recipients to change their cognitive or emotional state, including observing their surroundings more intensely (e.g., "a series of car break-ins have occurred," "monitor media," "report anyone matching the suspect's description"). Officials can issue idle alerts in response to both natural hazards (e.g., "be ready for a sudden drop to zero visibility") and human-caused hazards (e.g., "police are investigating an aggravated assault"), but because idle alerts often do not recommend immediate protective action, the crisis communication literature's message effectiveness paradigm does not well explain their intent, social functions, and potential consequences.

In particular, the message effectiveness paradigm offers little insight into the political and cultural dimensions of recipients' reactions to law enforcement-related idle alerts. For example, people's reactions on Twitter to receiving a Blue Alert range from confusion (e.g., "What is a blue alert?" and "What do police expect us to do?"), to annoyance about being woken up or disturbed, anti-police sentiment, and pro-police responses. Understanding such diverse reactions to idle alerts requires moving beyond a message effectiveness paradigm to ask instead: How do alerts both reflect and reproduce social values and inequalities? Law enforcement-related idle alerts, in particular, describe and enact the social world, which raises questions about how these kinds of alerts construct crime and criminals, whose lives "matter," and how stakeholders balance privacy and security. As we explain in the rest of this chapter, law enforcement-related messages provide a clear illustration of the necessity of critical-cultural perspectives in studying the social functions of idle alerts.

Research on the Social Functions of Idle Alerts

A handful of researchers have begun to explore the social functions of idle alerts (Bean, 2019; Griffin, 2016; Hasinoff & Krueger, 2020; Madden, 2015 Sicafuse & Miller, 2010). These researchers are less concerned with ensuring a given alert's fidelity to an underlying material reality (accuracy) or maximizing its persuasiveness in compelling protective action (efficacy). Instead, these researchers focus more on how such messages collectively function to affirm and perform particular social values, generally viewing alerts as one of many sites of culture in which "reality is produced, maintained, repaired, and transformed" (Carey, 1989, p. 23). This perspective, which is typically informed by theories of social constructionism, maintains that technologies are never neutral but instead "occupy sites of struggle over meanings and power" (Slack & Wise, 2005, p. 2). Applied to idle alerts, the goal is to identify, understand, and critique the ideological work that alerting systems and their messages perform. Research can involve critically analyzing the form and content of alerts, investigating how different groups of people perceive and respond to them, and questioning the ways those alerts reflect and reinforce structures of power and control, including who gets to decide what kinds of alerts people receive in the first place, under what conditions, and why.

One way that researchers have examined the social functions of alerts is by examining them as "crime control theater" (Sicafuse & Miller, 2010). Sicafuse and Miller (2010) introduced this concept to explain why the AMBER Alert system is popular and persists despite its demonstrated ineffectiveness. Griffin (2016) likewise expressed concern that "the AMBER Alert system is part of a larger dysfunction in which … reactionary crime control policies are publicly [given] the benefit of the doubt for no other reason than the emotional language attached to their creation" (p. 43). Bean (2019) similarly analyzed media reports and institutional documents to demonstrate that the WEA system's "Presidential Alert" functionality has more to do with institutional identities and ideology than national protection or public safety.

Studies have also examined the social and cultural dimensions of the issuing and reception of campus crime alerts. Madden (2017) interviewed university officials about the timeliness of campus crime alerts, finding that decision-making concerning the tradeoffs between message urgency and accuracy allowed officials to assert their preferred interpretations of policies and perform their expertise in ways that reinforced their own authority. As one participant stated, "There are no hard and fast rules for this. … I've been in this business 31 years now and when I hear of a crime, I get the call at two in the morning, I know almost immediately whether I'm sending an alert out" (p. 372). Hasinoff and Krueger (2020) surveyed college students, finding that some respondents appeared to overreact to campus crime alerts, which suggests that the Clery Act might actually decrease safety on college campuses. We next apply some of the themes of this "social functions" research to Blue Alerts and further investigate Clery Act notifications.

Applied Examples of Idle Alerts

Since the mid-2010s, there has been a struggle between wireless carriers and various consumer groups who narrowly define smartphones as personal consumer devices and emergency managers and law enforcement officials who position smartphones as critical public safety devices. Here, we discuss two types of law enforcement-related idle alerts: Blue Alerts and Clery Act notifications. Blue Alerts highlight an opportunity to examine the political dimensions of crisis communication, while Clery Act notifications demonstrate how these kinds of messages can have unintended consequences, potentially decreasing public safety. For each alert type, we begin with a brief overview and then assess some of the claims about the rationale, purpose, and effectiveness of these idle alerts that researchers might critically examine.

Blue Alerts

The national Blue Alert system was created in response to the December 20, 2014 killing of New York City police officers Rafael Ramos and Wenjian Liu. The shooter had traveled to New York City from Baltimore, Maryland, specifically to kill police officers in revenge for the deaths of Eric Garner and Michael Brown, two cases in which police officers had killed unarmed black men. Authorities in Baltimore issued a warning that the shooter had threatened law enforcement, but New York City officials received the warning too late to prevent the killings. The Rafael Ramos and Wenjian Liu National Blue Alert Act was passed in 2015, requiring the U.S. Department of Justice (DOJ) to establish a national communications network for planning, facilitating, and issuing Blue Alerts.

Today, most law enforcement agencies can issue a Blue Alert to the public through the WEA system in response to (a) the serious injury or death of a law enforcement officer in the line of duty, (b) an officer who is missing in connection with the officer's official duties, or (c) an imminent and credible threat that an individual intends to cause the serious injury or death of a law enforcement officer. Each state maintains its own Blue Alert Action Plan, and according to the DOJ, as of June 2020, only 11 states did not have a plan in place. The DOJ reported that 44 law enforcement officers were killed in the line of duty in 2019 (COPS, 2020). While the DOJ does not provide information about the number of Blue Alerts issued, media reports indicate that Blue Alerts are rare – perhaps under ten per year nationwide. A Blue Alert issued by the Tennessee Bureau of Investigation in 2018 in response to the shooting death of Sgt. Daniel Baker read, "STEVEN WIGGINS*ARMED AND DANGEROUS W/M BROWN HAIR/EYES**6'1,220 855-ALERTTBI." The suspect later surrendered to the police without incident.

The existence of the Blue Alert system raises obvious, yet under-researched, questions about the social and political functions of this form of crisis communication. We note that alert systems exist for protecting particularly vulnerable people, such as children (AMBER alerts) and elderly people with dementia (Silver Alerts), as well as for people who are trained and (potentially) armed, i.e., Blue Alerts for police officers and new, state-level Camo Alerts for current or former military members. A critical-cultural perspective asks why U.S. alerting systems emphasize threats to law enforcement personnel, rather than to members of other occupations who also risk their lives to protect the public from harm, such as first responders and health professionals, or, for that matter, anyone else. Such a question is particularly salient in light of the large-scale protests of police brutality and racism following the 2020 killing of George Floyd by four members of the Minneapolis Police Department.

Crisis communication's message effectiveness paradigm is insufficient for investigating these issues. A critical-cultural perspective contextualizes Blue Alerts in relation to the Black Lives Matter and Blue Lives Matter movements. Blue Alerts potentially reinforce public perceptions that violence directed at law enforcement originates from political beliefs, whereas law enforcement violence represents (non-political) protection (Turner, 2019). To our knowledge, not one of the 1,099 people killed by police in 2019 in the United States (54 percent of those being people of color) resulted in any WEA messages (Mapping Police Violence, 2019). The difficulty of even *imagining* an alert system designed to warn the public of police violence demonstrates the power of ideological and structural forces that valorize law enforcement. Extending Turner's (2019) analysis of police power, we suggest that Blue Alerts symbolize "unequal representations of death," illustrating how a law enforcement officer's death "is a political act which offers the state a mechanism to (re)emphasize and (re)imagine its own power" (p. 241). Indeed, a DOJ handbook (Office of Community Oriented Policing Services, 2017) claims that the Blue Alert system is necessary because violence against law enforcement officers is "an assault on the American way of life" (p. 19). Crisis communication researchers ought to consider how control over the existence, form, content, and frequency of idle alerts constitutes a way in which the state uses emerging technology to "reanimate itself" (Turner, 2019, p. 241). As U.S. activists and institutions confront the legacy of structural racism, particularly in policing, crisis communication's role in the reproduction of systemic inequalities and the "reanimation" of the state is worthy of critique and transformation.

Clery Act Notifications

The 1990 Jeanne Clery Act mandates that college campuses inform their constituents about certain emergencies and crimes that have occurred. The intent of the legislation is to promote transparency about crime and to increase safety. The Clery Act handbook explains that policies about Timely Warnings and Emergency Notifications are intended to help keep "students and employees informed about threats to their safety and health in a manner that allows them to protect themselves" (U.S. Department of Education, 2016, p. 6-1). One campus police chief explained that the threat of fines may incentivize officials to disseminate messages that are not strictly necessary for safety, which may have unintended consequences. He commented:

> The spirit of the law is good; transparency in police operations is good, … and we provide information that could make people safer if they take it seriously. But I also think there are times when it's just silly and we're worrying people for no reason.
> (quoted in Hasinoff & Krueger, 2020, p. 602)

Clery policies, coupled with advances in mobile and social media technologies, have significantly increased the immediacy and frequency of messages about crime. Mobile technology in particular raises new questions, especially given research establishing that people generally view content on mobile devices as more intimate and potentially with a higher emotional valence than broadcast media (Xie & Newhagen, 2014). Moreover, while the relationship between media depictions of crime and fear of crime is complex, some research suggests that particular kinds of representations are especially fear-inducing. Heath and Gilbert (1996) argue that these qualities include nonfiction depictions, random crimes perpetrated by strangers, crimes that occurred in close proximity to audience members, and depictions of crime that lack a resolution and sense of justice. Notifications about crime on campus are a unique genre of media that often fulfill each of those criteria.

Research on the social implications of the Clery-mandated crime notifications suggests that these policy effects could run counter to their aims of increasing safety. One study explains: "Clery policies may inadvertently decrease safety by desensitizing some audiences while potentially reducing campus participation for those who are particularly fearful" (Hasinoff & Krueger, 2020, p. 603). Questions about the broader effects of emergency alert messages on people's perceptions of risk and safety over time or in a particular location are typically beyond the scope of a study of message effectiveness. This is especially relevant for idle alerts about crimes on college campuses, and there are few studies on the alerts' long-term social costs and benefits. In particular, officials and stakeholders have expressed concern that idle alerts may contribute to over-alerting or alerting fatigue (Bean, 2019). Stakeholders should ask, for example: Do law-enforcement-related idle alerts exacerbate "mean-world syndrome"? (Gerbner et al., 2002). Along these lines, we conclude this chapter with a call for expanding the types of questions and research approaches that crisis communication scholars engage.

Conclusion: Critical-Cultural Research and Idle Alerts

Distinguishing idle alerts from actionable alerts helps clarify that crisis communication can raise questions that a message effectiveness paradigm cannot answer. Officials' expanding use of mobile and social media alerting technologies to issue idle alerts introduces a new set of theoretical, empirical, and political questions that necessitate critical-cultural perspectives. Crisis communication research typically foregrounds issues of organizational effectiveness including planning, response, resilience, and repair. We recommend that researchers complement this effectiveness paradigm with perspectives that pay closer attention to the social functions of crisis communication.

To begin this project, crisis communication researchers might consider paying more attention to one social function in particular: the "enculturating" role of idle alerts. Livingstone (1996) explains that the scope of questions from the enculturation paradigm extends beyond the effects of any individual message on people's actions: "The study of enculturation processes, which work over long time periods, and which are integral to rather than separable from other forms of social determination, would ask not how the media make us act or think, but rather how the media contribute to making us who we are" (p. 320). While Clery-Act-mandated idle alerts may help officials locate suspects and provide an appearance of official action, competence, and attention to risk, we suggest that further research into the enculturating effects of these types of messages is necessary to better understand their implications and unintended consequences. Our discussion of Blue Alerts also suggests that crisis communication researchers might further examine how political values are inscribed not only in the content of alert messages but also in the design and functions of alerting technologies. As Balsamo (2011) argues, "Through the practices of designing, cultural beliefs are materially reproduced, identities are established, and social relations are codified" (p. 3).

Our discussion of the unwanted effects of Clery Act notifications and the political dimensions of Blue Alerts indicates that scholars should critically ask:

Whose "public safety" do these systems prioritize, and why? Crisis communication researchers are well-positioned to address these kinds of questions if they can examine the social functions of alerts and account for the social construction of meaning. We encourage the increased use of critical-cultural perspectives to view such objects of study.

Finally, as this chapter was going to print, we confronted an alerting controversy on our own campus illustrating our claims in this chapter. One afternoon in April 2021, Auraria campus students, staff, and faculty received a text alert stating: "AURARIA CAMPUS lockdown! All entry doors are locked. Increase your awareness. Run, hide, or fight if appropriate. Additional info from police will follow ASAP." This message illustrated that "idle" and "actionable" alerts can be seen as reflecting a spectrum rather than a binary: message recipients were told to increase their "awareness" while also being given the general advice to "run, hide, or fight if appropriate." Although only a few hundred people were working at the Auraria campus at the time due to Covid-19 restrictions, the heart-stopping message left many recipients rattled, especially given that this particular alert was issued just two weeks after the March 22, 2021 mass shooting in nearby Boulder, Colorado that left ten people dead. More than 40 minutes after the initial lockdown message, campus police sent a second message that they had apprehended the suspect in a stabbing incident. The alert was so confusing and unsettling for members of the campus that administrators sent an email the following day to explain why and how the vague-yet-ominous message had been issued:

> The Auraria Campus Police Department sent that alert in compliance with the federal Clery Act that requires such notifications when police believe there's an immediate threat to the health and safety of the campus community. The text was a pre-scripted emergency notification, which is done to get the message out more quickly.

Administrators vowed to investigate and improve emergency alerting processes, "We commit to doing better, and we will." We hope so and believe that a critical-cultural perspective can help.

References

Balsamo, A. M. (2011). *Designing culture: The technological imagination at work*. Duke University Press.

Bean, H. (2019). *Mobile technology and the transformation of public alert and warning*. Praeger Security International.

Bean, H., Sutton, J., Liu, B. F., Madden, S., Wood, M. M., & Mileti, D. S. (2015). The study of mobile public warning messages: A research review and agenda. *Review of Communication*, *15*, 60–80. https://doi.org/10.1080/15358593.2015.1014402

Bridges, B. [@mostlybree]. (2020, February 5). *Happy 1 am to everyone else in Alabama awake and googling blue alert because our phones just made the tornado noise* [Tweet]. Twitter. https://twitter.com/mostlybree/status/1224954575049887746

Carey, J. W. (1989). *Communication as culture: Essays on media and society.* Unwin Hyman.

COPS. (2020). *Law enforcement officers shot in the line of duty – 2019 year-end summary report.* https://cops.usdoj.gov/pdf/Blue-alert/2019_Blue_Alert_Officers_Shot_Year_End_Report.pdf

FBI. (2020). *Ten most wanted fugitives FAQ.* https://www.fbi.gov/wanted/topten/ten-most-wanted-fugitives-faq

FEMA. (2003). *State and local mitigation planning how-to guide: Integrating manmade hazards into mitigation planning.* https://www.fema.gov/media-library/assets/documents/4528

Gerbner, G., Gross, L., Morgan, M., Signorielli, N., & Shanahan, J. (2002). Growing up with television: Cultivation processes. In J. Bryant, & D. Zillmann (Eds.), *Media effects* (pp. 53–78). Routledge.

Griffin, T. (2016). The rhetoric and reality of the AMBER alert: Empirical and public discourse considerations regarding the child abduction phenomenon. In S. Morewit, & C. Sturdy Colls (Eds.), *Handbook of missing persons* (pp. 37–47). Springer.

Hasinoff, A. A., & Krueger, P. M. (2020). Warning: Notifications about crime on campus may have unwanted effects. *International Journal of Communication, 14,* 587–607. https://doi.org/1932–8036/20200005

Heath, L., & Gilbert, K. (1996). Mass media and fear of crime. *American Behavioral Scientist, 39*(4), 379–386. https://doi.org/10.1177/0002764296039004003

Livingstone, S. (1996). On the continuing problems of media effects research. In J. Curran, & M. Gurevitch (Eds.), *Mass media and society* (2nd ed., pp. 305–324). Edward Arnold.

Madden, S. (2015). Alerting a campus community: Emergency notification from a public's perspective. *Journal of Contingencies and Crisis Management, 23*(4), 184–192. https://doi.org/10.1111/1468-5973.12074

Madden, S. (2017). The clock is ticking: Temporal dynamics of campus emergency notifications. *Journal of Contingencies and Crisis Management, 25*(4), 370–375. https://doi.org/10.1111/1468-5973.12162

Mapping Police Violence. (2019). https://mappingpoliceviolence.org/

Office of Community Oriented Policing Services. (2017). *Effective blue alert plans: Guidance and recommendations.* Office of Community Oriented Policing Services.

Schatz, B. (2019, December 10). Schatz legislation to improve emergency alert system included in must-pass bipartisan deal. https://www.schatz.senate.gov/press-releases/schatz-legislation-to-improve-emergency-alert-system-included-in-must pass-bipartisan-deal

Sicafuse, L. L., & Miller, M. K. (2010). Social psychological influences on the popularity of AMBER alerts. *Criminal Justice and Behavior, 37*(11), 1237–1254. https://doi.org/10.1177/0093854810379618

Slack, J. D., & Wise, J. M. (2005). *Culture + technology: A primer.* Peter Lang.

Sutton, J., Spiro, E. S., Johnson, B., Fitzhugh, S., Gibson, B., & Butts, C. T. (2014). Warning tweets: Serial transmission of messages during the warning phase of a disaster event. *Information, Communication & Society, 17*(6), 765–787. https://doi.org/10.1080/1369118X.2013.862561

Tan, M. L., Prasanna, R., Stock, K., Hudson-Doyle, E., Leonard, G., & Johnston, D. (2017). Mobile applications in crisis informatics literature: A systematic review. *International Journal of Disaster Risk Reduction, 24,* 297–311. https://doi.org/10.1016/j.ijdrr.2017.06.009

Todd, Z., Trattner, S., & McMullen, J. (2019, October 25). Ahead of camp fire anniversary, new details emerge of troubled evacuation. *Frontline*. https://www.pbs.org/wgbh/frontline/article/camp-fire-anniversary-new-details-troubled-evacuation/

Turner, J. (2019). "It all started with Eddie": Thanatopolitics, police power, and the murder of Edward Byrne. *Crime, Media, Culture, 15*(2), 239–258. https://doi.org/10.1177/1741659018763898

U.S. Department of Education. (2016). *The handbook for campus safety and security reporting* (2016 ed.). https://www2.ed.gov/admins/lead/safety/handbook.pdf

van Dijl, D. E. M., Zebel, S., & Gutteling, J. M. (2019). Integrating social media features into a cell phone alert system for emergency situations. *Journal of Contingencies and Crisis Management, 27*(3), 214–223. https://doi.org/10.1111/1468-5973.12251

Xie, W., & Newhagen, J. E. (2014). The effects of communication interface proximity on user anxiety for crime alerts received on desktop, laptop, and hand-held devices. *Communication Research, 41*(3), 375–403. https://.doi.org/10.1177/0093650212448670

SECTION V

Emerging Frameworks and Future Directions

33

NEW THEORETICAL DIRECTIONS AND FRAMEWORKS

In Social Media and Crisis Communication Research

Finn Frandsen and Winni Johansen

Introduction

As social media and crisis communication research is developing rapidly, quantitatively (number of publications) as well as qualitatively (advanced concepts, models, and theories), it becomes increasingly relevant to ask questions such as: How far have we come? What are the most significant research trends?

The aim and purpose of this chapter are to provide the reader with a comprehensive overview of the most important and most recent theoretical directions and frameworks elaborated between 2015 and 2020, and to evaluate this research against previous research within this field. To do this, we need to be able to define what we understand by "the joint topic" (Austin & Jin, 2017, p. 1) of social media and crisis communication. Table 33.1 illustrates the complexity and the integrated nature of the field. It consists of four internal and four external parts. Each of the four internal parts contains a key concept: *social*, *media*, *communication*, and *crisis*.

By *social*, we refer to the ability of social media to bring people together and to enable them to share ideas and experiences. However, this does not mean that social media are more social than traditional media. Danish media researcher Klaus Bruhn Jensen explains:

> All media are social, in the sense that they establish and maintain relations between and among humans as individuals and collectives, increasingly across space and time. No medium is more social than any other medium. But each medium is social in distinctive ways. (Jensen, 2015, p. 1)

DOI: 10.4324/9781003043409-45

TABLE 33.1 Key Concepts and Perspectives on Social Media and Crisis Communication (Research)

	Macro level: social theory (1) *Network society* (Castells) *Culture of connectivity* (van Dijk)		
Meso level: theory of organization (2)	**Social**	**Media**	Meso level: theory of technology (3)
Neo-institutional theory	**Crisis**	**Communication**	*Crisis Informatics* (Palen)
	Micro level: theory of social actors (4) *Stakeholders, publics, participants, users, voices*		

By *media,* we understand "a group of Internet-based applications that build on the ideological and technological foundations of Web 2.0, and that allow the creation and exchange of user generated content" (Kaplan & Haenlein, 2010, p. 61). Terms such as online technology and social media platforms are also often used.

By *communication,* we understand several things: the distribution of information; the transmission of a message from a sender to a receiver, or a sense-making process. However, there are alternative versions of crisis management, where we find attempts to make a clear distinction between the two key concepts of information and communication. In the template for general emergency plans, established by the Danish Emergency Management Agency (DEMA), information and communication are defined as two different concepts.

Inspired by American communication theorist Robert T. Craig, we define communication as a *social practice,* that is, a coherent "set of activities that are commonly engaged in, and meaningful in particular ways, among people familiar with a certain culture" (Craig, 2006, p. 38). A practice involves not only engaging in certain activities but also thinking and talking about those activities in particular ways. Practices also have a *conceptual* – sometimes, even, a *theoretical* – aspect.

By *crisis,* we understand small and/or large-scale events and situations that represent a biological and natural, or a social and organizational threat. Thus, crises seem to have what Hacking (2002) would call a rich historical ontology. The concept of crisis is the most important of the four key concepts. Without crisis – social, media, and communication would just be … social, media, and communication.

The four internal parts in Table 33.1 are embedded in four groups of sociocultural perspectives located at three different levels of analysis. At the *macro level,* we find relevant types of social and cultural theory. At the two *meso levels,* the focus is on theories of organization and technology. We need the institutional perspective to explain why private and public organizations adopt social media as a crisis communications tool. Finally, at the *micro level*, we shift to theories of social actors.

The remainder of this chapter is structured in three sections: First, we review a corpus of literature reviews on crisis communication and social media published between 2015 and 2020. Then, we review concepts, models, and theories that represent the first generation of theoretical work *sui generis in* this field. Finally, we present new directions and frameworks, and demonstrate how reframing of the field of crisis management and crisis communication may be studied in relation to crisis communication and social media.

A Review of Literature Reviews

One of the most exciting ways to see how a new field of study, if not a new academic subdiscipline, develops over time, is to follow who, why, how, when, and where the *literature reviews* devoted to this field or discipline by its scholars, emerge (Frandsen & Johansen, 2020b, p. 36).

One of the very first literature reviews on crisis management was published by Pauchant and Douville (1993). It covered 24 researchers' publications from 1986 to 1991. This period corresponds to early crisis management research in the 1980s. One of the most recent literature reviews on crisis management was published by Bundy et al. (2017). It covers the period from 1998 to 2015. Bundy et al. (2017) identified two primary perspectives of the crisis process, including an internal perspective focusing on organizational preparedness, crisis leadership and organizational learning, and an external perspective.

We have examined a large number of literature reviews on social media and crisis communication published between 2015 and 2020 using the same set of analytical categories. Table 33.2 provides an overview of different types of literature reviews and brings answers to questions such as: Who writes literature reviews, why, when, where, and how.

A Review of Concepts, Models, and Theories

Ten years ago, two groups of researchers began investigating how various stakeholder groups increasingly used social media during crisis, and how organizations and their communication professionals have adapted to this new situation (Cheng & Cameron, 2017). In this section, we want to conduct a brief comparative study of the work of these two groups.

The first group consisted mainly of US-based researchers. Among its most prominent members, you find Lucinda Austin, Brooke Fisher Liu, and Yan Jin. From 2010 till today, these researchers have published an important corpus of journal articles and book chapters (e.g., Austin & Jin, 2016; Austin et al., 2012; Jin & Austin, 2020; Jin & Liu, 2010). However, their smost important contribution

TABLE 33.2 Literature Reviews and Meta-Studies on Crisis Communication and Social Media Published in the Period 2015–2020

Who?	Why?	How?	When?	Volume
Ngai et al. (2015)	"to understand how researchers have adapted theories, used research constructs and developed conceptual frameworks" (p. 33)	Systematic and structured literature review	2002–2011	46 peer-reviewed articles
Wang and Dong (2017)	"to provide an over-view of the current paradigm of research on social media and crisis communication" (p. 29)	Systematic review	2009–2017	45 articles 11 journals
Rasmussen and Ihlen (2017)	"The literature on social media use in risk and crisis communication is growing fast, and it is time to take stock before looking forward" (p. 1)	Systematic review, content analysis	2009–2015	200 articles (of which 27 in PRR) 106 journals
Cheng and Cameron (2017)	"to study the social mediated crisis communication (SMCC) research" and "to enrich the theories on crisis communication" (p. 10)	Content analysis	2002–2014	69 articles (of which 38 in PRR) 10 journals
Cheng (2018)	"to study how social media is changing crisis communication strategies" (p. 58)	Content analysis	2002–2014	73 journal articles 11 journals
Eriksson (2018)	"there is still a shortage of systematic reviews that more clearly focus on advice from researchers to crisis communication practitioners" (p. 527)	Systematic content analysis Best practice analysis	2011–2017	104 peer reviewed journal articles and conference papers
Apuke and Tunca (2018)	"the findings of this review confirmed that the growth of social media has transformed crisis communication landscape because it allows interactivity"	–	Collected between 2017 and 2018	60 articles
Bukar et al. (2020)	"to identify the development of theoretical models in the area of social media crisis communication" (p. 185842)	Systematic review	2011–2018	207 theoretical articles

is *Social Media and Crisis Communication* (Austin & Jin, 2017), and their most recent contribution is *Advancing Crisis Communication Effectiveness* (Jin, Reber & Nowak, 20s21).

The second group, on the contrary, consisted mainly of European-based researchers. Among its most prominent members, you find Sonja Utz, Friederike

Schultz, and Sandra Glocka. Like their American colleagues, the European researchers have produced a large number of journal articles (e.g., Schultz et al., 2012; Utz et al., 2013). It is important for us to emphasize that we do not pretend that this overview is exhaustive in any sense. What we claim is only that the researchers introduced in this section are among the most influential.

Crisis Communication and Public Relations

In the United States, there is a long tradition for defining crisis communication as a subdiscipline in public relations. "Currently, crisis communication is more of a subdiscipline in public relations and corporate communication" (Coombs & Holladay, 2010, p. xxvi). It is unnecessary to say that this also applies to the field of social media and crisis communication, see for example, the Social Mediated Crisis Communication (SMCC) research (Liu et al., 2012). Almost ten years later, the same understanding of crisis communication inspired by the excellence theory of crisis public relations is still active (Anderson-Meli & Koshy, 2020; Cheng & Cameron, 2017).

Key Concepts

Concepts are the basic building blocks of human thinking in general and of scientific research in particular. It is from our use of these cognitive entities that we create models and theories (see below). According to many researchers, it is a sign of maturity, if an academic discipline is able to keep the number of concepts as low as possible, and if it is able to provide definitions of these concepts. "Without common and precise theories and definitions, crisis management scholars lose legitimacy and credibility, and they run the risk of poorly discerning what they aim to investigate" (Roux-Dufort, 2007, p. viii).

However, crisis management and crisis communication have not always succeeded in living up to these ideals. First, the concept of crisis has been used in many different disciplines: "'Crisis' is one of these notoriously difficult concepts which abound in the social sciences" (Eastham et al., 1970, p. 463). Second, also inside each of these social science disciplines, there have been disagreements regarding how to define crisis.

British social theorist and philosopher Walter Bryce Gallie (1912–1998) has invented the term *essentially contested concept* that gives a name to a problematic situation that many people recognize: that in certain kinds of talk, there is a variety of meanings employed for key terms in an argument, and there is a feeling that dogmatism ("My answer is right and all others are wrong"), skepticism ("All answers are equally true (or false); everyone has a right to his own truth"), and eclecticism ("Each meaning gives a partial view so the more meanings the better") are none of them the appropriate attitude toward that variety of meanings. Is crisis an essentially contested concept?

Models

Communication research is famous for its many scientific models. What is a theoretical or conceptual model? A model can be defined as a multimodal representation of concepts or ideas. Single and double arrows, small and big squares or circles, the use of bold and plain colors such as black and white are some of the elements used to express implication, causality, and reduction of complexity. Thus, models such as the predominant SMCC model can help us to understand our field of study and how it is structured.

The SMCC model grew out of the so-called blog-mediated communication model (Jin & Liu, 2010). It was developed to describe and explain the flow of information and relationships between different types of media, online and offline communication, organization, and influential publics during crises. Liu et al.'s (2012) version of the SMCC model is divided into the following elements:

- Actors: the organization represents the most important or largest social actor. It is difficult not to interpret this model as an organization-centric model. Among the other actors, we find influential social media creators, social media followers, and social media inactives.
- Both social media and traditional media are represented in the model. However, it is difficult to see whether they are considered a channel or a media organization.
- The concept of publics is also applied, and not the concepts of stakeholders and audiences.
- Finally, information form (on-line, off-line), information source, and the distinction between direct and indirect relationships between the organization and its publics are the last components of the model.

The second tradition and the Networked Crisis Communication (NCC) model was developed because the "classical crisis communication theories neglect the role of the medium and focus mainly on the interplay between crisis type and crisis communication strategy" (Utz et al., 2013, p. 40). Crisis medium includes social media vs. traditional media vs. blogs. The NCC model has a focus on how the reputation of a company is affected by crisis medium, crisis type, and communication strategy, as well as by secondary crisis communication, i.e., information sharing and information forwarding, and secondary crisis reactions such as behavioral intentions (Schultz et al., 2011; Utz et al., 2013).

New Theoretical Directions and Frameworks

In this section, we will take a look at new directions and frameworks, and demonstrate how a new reframing of the field of crisis management and crisis communication into three subfields may be studied in relation to crisis communication and social media.

New Research Trends

It is difficult to provide the reader with a comprehensive and critical overview that can tell us in which direction we have been moving during the past five years. However, we have been able to identify a few important research trends. Please notice that most of these trends have emerged from outside the discipline of public relations.

- *Crisis management (crisis informatics).* The use of social media in managing crisis events has gained increasing interest among researchers. This area is often called crisis informatics. Established by Hagar (2006) and later expanded upon by Palen et al. (2009), crisis informatics has been defined as a "multidisciplinary field combining computing and social science knowledge of disasters; its central tenet is that people use personal information and communication technology to respond to disaster in creative ways to cope with uncertainty" (Palen & Anderson, 2016, p. 224). For examples of research on social media within this field, see Reuter and Kaufhold (2018).
- *Institutionalization.* This research trend investigates how private and/or public organizations adopt social media over time and how this adoption process changes how the organizational members are thinking (Frandsen & Johansen, 2020b). Mergel's (2016) article "Social media institutionalization in the US Federal Government" is an important theoretical contribution illustrating how social media can change the existing organization technology paradigm in public organizations. See also Villodre and Criado (2016).
- *Sense-making.* German researchers Stieglitz and Mirbabaie are authors of several articles on crisis, social media, and sense-making such as "Understanding sense-making in social media during crisis: Categorization of sense-making barriers and strategies" (Stieglitz et al., 2017). See also Stieglitz and Dang-Xuan (2013).
- *Politicization.* Chinese strategic communication scholar Hui Zhao (2020) is one of the scholars that has conducted research within the field of politicization, crisis communication, and social media.
- Finally, *Rhetorical Arena Theory* (RAT). This multivocal approach to crisis communication (Frandsen & Johansen, 2017, 2020a) include sub-arenas and social media. We will take a closer look at this approach below.

Rhetorical Arena Theory and Social Media Sub-Arenas

RAT with its multivocal approach has proven fruitful also as a theoretical framework for the study of social media and crisis communication (Coombs & Holladay, 2012, 2014; Frandsen & Johansen, 2017; Johansen et al., 2016; Palmieri & Musi, 2020; Rodin et al., 2019).

The central idea behind the RAT and its multivocal approach to crisis communication is based on a simple observation: that when a crisis occurs, a social space opens, and multiple voices start communicating *to, with, against, past,* and *about* each other. (Frandsen & Johansen, 2017, 2020a; Johansen & Frandsen, 2007). These multiple voices represent the communicative complexity of crises, and the aim of RAT is to identify, describe and explain patterns of interactions and communicative processes going on in an arena (and in a sub-arena) among various voices during a crisis.

The theory is based on two metaphors: *arena* and *voice*. The concept of *arena*, including sub-arena, is used to emphasize that during a crisis voices that enter the arena may be conflicting, competing, debating, or struggling with each other, and dialogue and consensus may not be achieved or is not the overall goal. The arena is different from the public sphere as it includes private and semi-public spheres (e.g., voices inside the organization hit by a crisis).

The concept of *voice* is used to point to the communicative complexity during a crisis. In contrast to the concept of stakeholder, the concept of voice takes into account both voices that have a stake in the organization hit by a crisis (stakeholders) as well as voices only having a stake in the crisis itself and not in the organization, i.e., using a crisis for their own and specific agenda (e.g., political crisis exploitation, NGO's, or *trolls* stepping into the arena just to create excitement).

Social media form various sub-arenas within the larger arena, i.e., they form social spaces where various voices are communicating around the crisis. These voices are interacting not only with the organization hit by a crisis but also among themselves, contributing to the communicative complexity of the larger arena as well. There are spill-overs and crossovers between sub-arenas, e.g., social media sub-arenas, media sub-arenas, and the larger rhetorical arena (see Rodin et al., 2019).

Although there are similarities with the interactions and communicative complexity of the larger rhetorical arena during a crisis, studies of social media sub-arenas (e.g., Facebook, Twitter, Instagram) have identified specific communicative characteristics and patterns of interaction. For example, we typically find very strong emotional reactions among the voices during a crisis of an organization. Some voices typically act as very angry hateholders attacking a company, and forcing a company to respond in public. Other voices act as faithholders, supporting and defending a company or a brand (see Luoma-aho, 2006). This means that faithholders act as "co-crisis communicators" along with the company, however using the same tone of voice as the hateholders, attacking the hateholders and forcing hateholders to react to their comments in public (see Frandsen & Johansen, 2017; Johansen et al., 2016).

These patterns of interaction emphasize the agonistic aspect of the arena metaphor and highlight the need for studying the specificities of various voices and adding new strategies (attack and support) to the crisis response inventories of image repair theory (Benoit, 2015) and SCCT (Coombs, 2019).

Reframing of Crisis Management and Crisis Communication into Three Subfields

Instead of viewing the field of crisis management and crisis communication as one large monolithic field of study, Frandsen and Johansen (2020c) have proposed a new model that reframes the field into three specific, but closely interrelated subfields: public sector crisis communication, political crisis communication, and corporate crisis communication. By subfield, Frandsen and Johansen understand "a set of institutionalized policies, programs and practices that are connected to a specific sector of society defined as an interinstitutional system" (2020c, p. 61).

So far, social media sub-arenas have primarily been studied, as demonstrated above, through the lenses of corporate crisis communication. However, the rhetorical arena framework can be beneficial to further studies into these three intertwined subfields of crisis management and crisis communication as voices from within all three subfields often appear in one and the same crisis.

Inspired by the new model and the reframing of the field of crisis management and crisis communication of Frandsen and Johansen (2020c), Table 33.3 is an attempt to establish a model that may be applied within the field of crisis communication and social media that takes the three subfields into account as well as their interrelations in the larger rhetorical arena.

Social media plays a role in each subfield. They are in use in emergency situations, in politics, as well as in corporate crises. Voices overlap and interact

TABLE 33.3 Social Media, Subfields within the Rhetorical Arena

CRISIS MANAGEMENT AND CRISIS COMMUNICATION			
Subfields	*Public crisis communication*	*Political crisis communication*	*Corporate crisis communication*
Social media	Voices and patterns of interaction in the emergency field	Voices and patterns of interaction in the political field	Voices and patterns of interaction in the organizational field
	Communication: Crisis and emergency risk communication Information control Closed-loop communication	*Communication:* Crisis exploitation strategies and blame game	*Communication:* Crisis response and strategies, including attacks
Voices and patterns of interactions across the three subfields in *the larger rhetorical arena*			

across all three subfields, both in social media sub-arenas as well as within the larger rhetorical arena. However, each field has its own characteristics as well. The understanding of communication differs. Public sector crisis communication, or emergency communication, has a focus on public safety, and makes use of closed-loop communication and the Crisis Emergency Risk Communication (CERC) model (Seeger et al., 2020). See also Simon et al. (2015). Political crisis communication has a focus on politics and political power. Crises are being politicized, and communication is about blame avoidance, blame game (Hood, 2011), and crisis exploitation strategies (Boin et al., 2009). Finally, corporate crisis communication has a focus on prevention, the reputation of the organization, and crisis response strategies (Benoit, 2015; Coombs, 2019). The COVID-19 epidemic has clearly demonstrated the intertwining of the three subfields.

We need more studies in these fields. It would be very relevant and interesting to examine the social media sub-arenas in order to identify the nature of the voices and their interaction during crisis situations as well as the interrelations between the three subfields within crisis management and crisis communication in the larger rhetorical arena.

With this chapter, we hope to have shown that crisis communication and social media research is indeed a vibrant field, constantly on the move.

References

Anderson-Meli, L., & Koshy, S. (2020). *Public relations crisis communication: A new model.* Routledge Focus.

Apuke, O. D., & Tunca, E. A. (2018). Social media and crisis management: A review and analysis of existing studies. *LAÜ Sosyal Bilimler Dergisi (IX-II) [EUL Journal of Social Sciences]*, December, 199–215.

Austin, L., & Jin, Y. (2016). Social media and crisis communication: Explicating the social-mediated crisis communication model. In A. Dudo, & L. A. Kahlor (Eds.), *Strategic communication: New agendas in communication* (pp. 163–186). Routledge.

Austin, L., & Jin, Y. (Eds.) (2017). *Social media and crisis communication.* Routledge.

Austin, L., Liu, B. F., & Jin, Y. (2012). How audiences seek out crisis information: Exploring the social-meditated crisis communication model. *Journal of Applied Communication Research, 40*(2), 188–207. https://doi.org/10.1080/00909882.2012.654498

Benoit, W. L. (2015). *Accounts, excuses, and apologies: Image repair theory and research* (2nd ed.). State University of New York.

Boin, A., 't Hart, P., & McConnell, A. (2009). Crisis exploitation: Political and policy impacts of framing contests. *Journal of European Public Policy, 16*(1), 81–106. https://doi.org/10.1080/13501760802453221

Bukar, U. A., Jabar, M. A., Sidi, F., Nor, R. N. H. B., Ardullah, S., & Othman, M. (2020). Crisis informatics in the context of social media crisis communication: Theoretical models, taxonomy, and open issues. *IEEE Access*, 185842–185869.

Bundy, J., Pfarrer, M. D., Short, C. E., & Coombs, W. T. (2017). Crisis and crisis management: Integration, interpretation, and research development. *Journal of Management, 43*(6), 1661–1692

Castells, M. (1996). *The rise of the network society, the information age: Economy society, and culture.* Oxford University Press.

Cheng, Y. (2018). How social media is changing crisis communication strategies: Evidence from the updated literature. *Journal of Contingencies and Crisis Management, 26*(1), 58–68. https://doi.org/10.1111/1468-5973.12130

Cheng, Y., & Cameron, G. T. (2017). The status of social-mediated crisis communication (SMCC) research. In L. Austin, & Y. Jin (Eds.), *Social media and crisis communication* (pp. 9–20). Routledge.

Coombs, W. T. (2019). *Ongoing crisis communication: Planning, managing, and responding* (5th ed.). Sage.

Coombs, W. T., & Holladay, S. J. (2010). *The handbook of crisis communication.* Wiley Blackwell.

Coombs, W. T., & Holladay, S. J. (2012). Faith-holders as crisis managers: The costa-Concordia crisis rhetorical arena on Facebook. *Proceedings from EUPRERA 2012 Congress,* Istanbul, September 20–22, 2012.

Coombs, W. T., & Holladay, S. J. (2014). How publics react to crisis communication efforts: Comparing crisis response reactions across sub-arenas. *Journal of Communication Management, 18*(1), 40–57. https://doi.org/10.1108/JCOM-03-2013-0015

Craig, R. T. (2006). A practice. In G. J. Shepherd, J. St. John, & T. Striphas (Eds.), *Communication as … perspectives on theory* (pp. 38–47). Sage.

Eastham, K., Coates, D., & Allodi, F. (1970). The concept of crisis. *The Canadian Journal of Psychiatry, 15*(5), 463–472. https://doi.org/10.1177/070674377001500508

Eriksson, M. (2018). Lessons for crisis communication on social media: A systematic review of what research tells the practice. *International Journal of Strategic Communication, 12*(5), 526–551. https://doi.org/10.1080/1553118X.2018.1510405

Frandsen, F., & Johansen, W. (2017). *Organizational crisis communication: A multivocal approach.* Sage.

Frandsen, F., & Johansen, W. (2020a). Arenas and voices in organizational crisis communication: How far have we come? In F. Frandsen, & W. W. Johansen (Eds.), *Crisis communication. Handbooks of communication science* (pp. 195–212). Mouton de Gruyter.

Frandsen, F., & Johansen, W. (2020b). A brief history of crisis management and crisis communication: From organizational practice to academic discipline. In F. Frandsen, & W. W. Johansen (Eds.), *Crisis communication. Handbooks of communication science* (pp. 17–58). Mouton de Gruyter.

Frandsen, F., & Johansen, W. (2020c). Reframing the field: Public crisis management, political crisis management, and corporate crisis management. In F. Frandsen, & W. W. Johansen (Eds.), *Crisis communication. Handbooks of communication science* (pp. 59 102). Mouton de Gruyter.

Hacking, I. (2002). *Historical ontology.* Harvard University Press.

Hagar, C. (2006). *Using research to aid the design of a crisis information management course.* Presented at the Association of Library and Information.

Hood, C. (2011). *The blame game: Spin, bureaucracy, and self-preservation in government.* Princeton University Press.

Jensen, K. B. (2015). What's social about social media? *Social Media + Society, 1*(1), 1–2. https://doi.org/10.1177/2056305115578874

Jin, Y., & Austin, L. (2020). Crisis communication and social media: Short history of the evolution of social media in crisis communication. In F. Frandsen, & W. Johansen (Eds.), *Crisis communication. Handbooks of communication science* (Vol. 23, pp. 473–488). De Gruyter Mouton.

Jin, Y., & Liu, B. F. (2010). The blog-mediated crisis communication model: Recommendations for responding to influential external blogs. *Journal of Public Relations Research, 22*(4), 429–455. https://doi.org/10.1080/10627261003801420

Jin, Y., Reber, B. H., & Nowak, G. J. (Eds.). (2021). *Advancing crisis communication effectiveness: Integrating public relations scholarship with practice.* Routledge.

Johansen, W., & Frandsen, F. (2007). *Krisekommunikation. Når virksomhedens image og omdømme er truet* [Crisis communication. When the image and reputation of a company is threatened]. Samfundslitteratur.

Johansen, B. F., Johansen, W., & Weckesser, N. (2016). Emotional stakeholders as "crisis communicators" in social media: The case of the Telenor customer complaints crisis. *Corporate Communications: An International Journal, 21*(3), 289–308. https://doi.org/10.1108/CCIJ-05-2015-0026

Kaplan, A. M., & Haenlein, M. (2010). Users of the world, unite! The challenges and opportunities of social media. *Business Horizons, 53*(1), 59–68.

Liu, B. F., Jin, Y., Austin, L. L., & Janoske, M. (2012). The social-mediated crisis communication model: Guidelines for effective crisis management in a changing media landscape. In S. C. Duhé (Ed.), *New media and public relations* (2nd ed., pp. 257–266). Peter Lang.

Luoma-aho, V. (2006). *From stakeholders to faith-holders: reputational advantage of frequent contact and high trust.* http://research.jyu.fi/orgevolution/researchpapers/ luamo-ahoIC-CRIIC06.pdf.

Mergel, I. (2016). Social media institutionalization in the US Federal Government. *Government Information Quarterly, 33*(1), 142–148.

Ngai, E. W. T., Tao, S. S. C., & Moon, K. K. L. (2015). Social media research: Theories, constructs, and conceptual frameworks. *International Journal of Information Management, 35*(1), 33–44. https://doi.org/10.1016/j.ijinfomgt.2014.09.004

Palen, L., & Anderson, K. M. (2016). Crisis informatics. New data for extraordinary times. *Policy Forum, 353*(6296), 224–225. https://doi.org/10.1126/science.aag2579

Palen, L., Vieweg, S., Liu, S. B., & Hughes, S. L. (2009). Crisis in a networked world. Features of computer-mediated communication in the April 16, 2007, Virginia Tech event. *Social Science Computer Review, 27*(4), 467–480. https://doi.org/10.1177/0894439309332302

Palmieri, R., & Musi, E. (2020). Trust-repair strategies in crisis rhetorical (sub-)arenas: An argumentative perspective. *International Journal of Strategic Communication, 14*(4), 272–293. https://doi.org/10.1080/1553118X.2020.1805452

Pauchant, T. C., & Douville, R. (1993). Recent research in crisis management: A study of 24 authors' publications from 1986 to 1991. *Industrial and Environmental Crisis Quarterly, 7*(1), 43–66. https://doi.org/10.1177/108602669300700104

Rasmussen, J., & Ihlen, Ø (2017). Risk, crisis and social media: A systematic review of seven years' research. *Nordicom Review, 38*(2), 1–17. https://dx.doi.org/10.1515/nor-2017-0393

Reuter, C., & Kaufhold, M.-A. (2018). Fifteen years of social media in emergencies: A retrospective review and future directions for crisis informatics. *Journal of Contingencies and Crisis Management, 26*, 41–57. https://doi.org/10.1111/1468-5973.12196

Rodin, P., Ghersetti, M., & Oden, T. (2019). Disentangling rhetorical subarenas of public health crisis communication: A study of the 2014–2015 Ebola outbreak in the news media and social media in Sweden. *Journal of Contingencies and Crisis Management, 27*, 237–246. https://doi.org/10.1111/1468-5973.12196

Roux-Dufort, C. (2007). Is crisis management (only) a management of exceptions? *Journal of Contingencies and Crisis Management, 15*(2), 105–114. https://doi.org/10.1111/j.1468-5973.2007.00507.x

Schultz, F., Utz, S., & Glocka, S. (2012). Crisis communication and social media. On the effects of medium, media credibility, crisis type and emotions. In *Etmaal Conference Leuven*, Belgium.

Schultz, F., Utz, S., & Göritz, A. (2011). Is the medium the message? Perceptions of and reactions to crisis communication via Twitter, blogs and traditional media. *Public Relations Review*, *37*(1), 20–27. https://doi.org/10.1016/j.pubrev.2010.12.001

Seeger, M., Reynolds, B., & Day, A. M. (2020). Crisis and emergency risk communication: Past, present, and future. In F. Frandsen, & W. W. Johansen (Eds.), *Crisis communication. Handbook of communication* (pp. 401–419). Mouton de Gruyter.

Simon, T., Goldberg, A., & Adini, B. (2015). Socializing in emergencies: A review of the use of social media in emergency situations. *International Journal of Information Management*, *35*(5), 609–619. https://doi.org/10.1016/j.ijinfomgt.2015.07.001

Stieglitz, S., & Dang-Xuan, L. (2013). Social media and political communication: A social media analytics framework. *Social Network Analysis and Mining*, *3*(4), 1277–1291. https://doi.org/10.1007/s13278-012-0079-3

Stieglitz, S., Mirbabaie, M., & Fromm, J. (2017). Understanding sense-making on social media during crises: Categorization of sense-making barriers and strategies. *International Journal of Information Systems for Crisis Response and Management*, *9*(4), 49–69. https://doi.org/10.4018/IJISCRAM.2017100103

Utz, S., Schultz, F., & Glocka, S. (2013). Crisis communication online: How medium, crisis type and emotions affected public reactions in the Fukushima Daiichi nuclear disaster. *Public Relations Review*, *39*(1), 40–46. https://doi.org/10.1016/j.pubrev.2012.09.010

van Dijk, J. (2013). *The culture of connectivity: A critical history of social media*. Oxford University Press.

Villodre, J., & Criado, J. I. (2016). Analyzing social media institutionalization in public administration. The role of inhibitors in local governments. *ACM Proceedings* (pp. 31–40). https://doi.org/10.1145/3396956.3396984

Wang, Y., & Dong, C. (2017). Applying social media in crisis communication: A quantitative review of social media-related crisis communication research from 2009 to 2017. *International Journal of Crisis Communication*, *1*, 29–37.

Zhao, H. (2020). *Politicizing crisis communication via social media: A contextual understanding of organizational crises in China* (Doctoral dissertation). Lund University.

34

TOWARD MORE VALID AND TRANSPARENT RESEARCH

A Methodological Review of Social Media and Crisis Communication

Xinyan Zhao

Introduction

In recent decades featuring proliferating communication infrastructures, emerging global networks, and deepening dynamic information environments, there has been rapidly accumulating literature regarding crisis communication on social media (Cheng & Cameron, 2017). Crisis, broadly defined, can be a corporation crisis, natural disaster, man-made accident, or terrorist attack (Coombs, 2018). Social media and crisis communication are growing as an interdisciplinary community with researchers and practitioners from public relations, strategic communication, crisis informatics, and information management.

This chapter reviews the methodological landscape in social media and crisis communication, with an emphasis on emerging measures and methods. It is beyond this short article's capacity to provide a comprehensive review of all existing methods. Rather, this chapter aims to open meaningful discussions regarding a unique opportunity and challenge confronting many researchers and practitioners in crisis communication in the digital era: How can we best use new methods and tools to advance theory building and refine managerial practice for crisis preparedness, response, and recovery?

Therefore, this chapter focuses on three methodological topics that are gaining ground in the area: instrument development, social network approach, and computational methods. I will first discuss the development of theory-based measures, as crafting measurement instruments has been at the heart of the positivist paradigm emphasizing the generalized patterns of communication. Next, I will delve into the social network approach that goes beyond the functional perspective by providing a systemic and relational perspective in understanding

DOI: 10.4324/9781003043409-46

the communication structure (Shumate et al., 2013). I will also discuss computational methods (Shah et al., 2015) that are increasingly applied by researchers and professionals, emphasizing its potential in providing access to a plethora of naturally occurring social data and conducting automated content analysis.

Instrument Development

Communication scholars are naturally interested in abstract concepts for formulating and testing theoretical ideas. These abstract and latent constructs, such as dialogues or frames, cannot be observed directly and thus need to be operationalized for concrete measures. According to Cheng and Cameron (2017), more than half of the social media and crisis communication studies used quantitative methods including content analysis, experiment, and survey. Experiment and survey studies typically demand valid, reliable, and generalizable measures for precise assessment of constructs and valid findings that allow meaningful theory construction. As argued by Brown and Ki (2013), "reliable and valid scales should be adapted or created to measure these constructs as precisely as possible" (p. 2) to understand publics' specific responses to crisis. The following paragraphs summarize important instruments in social media and crisis communication.

Crisis Responsibility

Coombs considered crisis responsibility as "the degree to which stakeholders blame the organization of the crisis event" (Coombs, 2004, p. 268). During a crisis, publics typically hold a party responsible and blame it for the harm. Several crisis communication theories, such as the situational crisis communication theory (SCCT) (Coombs, 2007), stipulate that how publics attribute crisis responsibility associated with an organization determine outcomes of organizational crisis communication. In general, SCCT provides a typology of crisis clusters based on the responsibility attribution and recommends optimal organizational crisis response strategies based on crisis clusters (Coombs, 2007).

Crisis responsibility has different dimensions (Weiner, 1985). To capture the full spectrum of crisis responsibility, Brown and Ki (2013) proposed a theory-based and reliable scale measuring multidimensions of crisis responsibility including intentionally, accountability, and locality. Zhou et al. (2019) also developed a three-dimensional scale of crisis severity by capturing emotion-induced severity, relevance-induced severity, and interest-induced severity.

Renewal Discourse

The discourse of renewal (DOR) theory emphasizes the communication of organizational learning to develop a renewed sense of purpose for crisis communication (Ulmer et al., 2019). DOR argues that organizations should consider crises as opportunities for growth and improvement. To conduct effective crisis communication, organizations should engage in the DOR, which includes organizational learning, ethical communication, prospective vision, and effective organizational rhetoric (Ulmer et al., 2019).

Using the four DOR components, Xu (2018) developed a multidimensional scale to measure organizational DOR in post-crisis communication. The four dimensions include engagement, prospective focus, communication efficiency, and emphasis on organizational culture and value. Focusing on organizational readiness for renewal in the pre-crisis stage, Fuller et al. (2019) identified two factors of organizational renewal preparedness, ethical communication, and effective organizational rhetoric, using cross-national subjects.

Publics' Behaviors and Emotions

From a public-centric perspective, the social-mediated crisis communication (SMCC) model emphasizes publics' communicative behaviors – information seeking and sharing – during a social-mediated crisis. SMCC theorizes various antecedents of communicative behaviors, including information forms (e.g., social media), sources (e.g., the responsible organization), and types of social media publics (i.e., influentials, followers, and inactives) (Austin et al., 2012; Fraustino & Liu, 2017). Based on SMCC, Lee and Jin (2019) proposed two multi-item scales measuring publics' information seeking and sharing behaviors across platforms, channels, and sources in health crises.

Publics' emotional responses are also gaining significance in crisis communication research. The theory of integrated crisis mapping (ICM) (Jin et al., 2007) explains publics' experience of six negative emotions (anger, sadness, fright, anxiety, guilt, shame) as mechanisms of cognitive appraisal in different types of crisis situations. Based on ICM, Jin et al. (2014) developed a scale identifying three dimensions of crisis emotions: attribution-independent (e.g., anxiety), external-attribution dependent (e.g., anger), and internal-attribution dependent (e.g., guilt) emotions.

Furthermore, Zhao et al. (2018a) developed a four-factor model assessing social media influence of organizational and individual actors across crises using large-scale data. These factors include output, reactive outtake (e.g., number of shares), proactive outtake (e.g., positive references), and network positioning (e.g., degree centrality).

Directions

The new measures can be applied to generate theory-informed and reliable findings and serve as the basis for further instrument testing and refining. There are several future directions. First, most scales were only initially tested using data from subjects' recall or imagination of particular crises. Additional efforts are needed to increase these scales' ecological validity and generalizability in terms of crisis cases, subject types, and culture differences. For example, ecological validity can be improved by using "real" crisis data, such as social media texts or naturally occurring field data. Generalizability can be increased by using data from multiple crises.

Second, more research should be conducted to provide evidence supporting higher validity of the instruments. For example, convergent/divergent validity can be measured by comparing a construct measured by the scale with other logically similar/dissimilar constructs of theoretical interest. Considering divergent validity is beneficial because it allows us to differentiate key theoretical constructs, such as engagement and DOR, for more refined theory building. The scale efficiency should also be considered by reducing excessive items while maintaining the validity and stability so that the emerging scales can be more readily applied.

Social Network Perspective

Social network analysis studies the patterns of relationships among nodes. Nodes are actors or symbols, such as individuals, organizations, websites, or symbols such as words. These nodes are connected by ties (aka edges or links). Ties represent specific types of relations, such as friendship, cooperation, hyperlinks, information flow, or symbolic relations such as word co-occurrence. Distinct patterns of ties give rise to a structure, and nodes occupy certain positions in the structure.

While the traditional positivist paradigm focuses on variable-based explanations of communication phenomena (e.g., what affects purchase intentions), the network perspective as a systems paradigm emphasizes the antecedents, processes, and outcomes of structural patterns (e.g., how one's relations with those in a brand community affects purchase intentions). Communication networks, according to Shumate et al. (2013), are "relations among various types of nodes that illustrate the ways in which messages are transmitted or interpreted" (p. 97).

A Social Network Perspective to Social Media and Crisis Communication

There has been thriving scholarly interest in social network analysis in various subfields of communication. In social media and crisis communication, scholars have also begun to apply social network analysis to describe interrelations among actors on a social media platform (Getchell & Sellnow, 2016), to study associations among symbols in people's cognitive space (Podnar et al., 2012), and to investigate the impact of organizational network positioning on the social media mentions (e.g., Yang & Saffer, 2018). A social network perspective promises more "relational, systemic, and contextual explanations" (Shumate et al., 2013, p. 95) of communication phenomena by better capturing the interconnectedness of organizations, messages, and stakeholders (O'Connor & Shumate, 2018).

More researchers are recognizing the importance of social networks for addressing the complexities of crisis communication on social media. There have been network extensions of several social media and crisis communication theories, such as the rhetorical arena theory (RAT; Frandsen & Johansen, 2017). The RAT argues that various organizations and stakeholders rhetorically co-construct the crisis reality in an issue arena. Raupp (2019) proposed a networked perspective of RAT by examining the rhetorical relations of various voices and their power struggles in the media in the Volkswagen emission crisis. Meanwhile, new theories that explicate the network perspective in crisis communication are surfacing, such as the interorganizational frame convergence framework that explicates the formation of semantic ties between organizations facing the opoid crisis (Zhao & Oh, 2021) or how people resort to diverse kinds of networks for reducing uncertainty in disasters (Ford et al., 2016).

Furthermore, researchers have examined a variety of networks in crises and disasters, including information flow networks among social media users (e.g., Hellsten et al., 2019; Saffer et al., 2019; Yang & Saffer, 2018), semantic networks of individual and organizational actors for representing how these actors construct crisis interpretations (Schultz et al., 2012; van der Meer et al., 2014; Yang & Veil, 2017), hyperlink or endorsement networks among organizations online (Getchell & Sellnow, 2016; Lai et al., 2017; Uysal & Yang, 2013), and organizations' resource contacts in disasters (Doerfel et al., 2010; Lai et al., 2019). Together, these studies deepen our understanding of communication structures and dynamics in different stages of crises.

Development: From Description to Prediction

Many have applied the social network analysis to provide descriptive analyses of interactions and relations among nodes during a single crisis, such as a corporation crisis, an epidemic, or a natural disaster. Existing studies typically relied on two kinds of network measures: first, structure measures like density, which is the proportion of all possible ties that are actually present in the network (for more structure measures, see Wasserman & Faust, 1994); second, centrality measures that gauge the influence of a node in the structure, such as degree centrality (a total number of connections a node has) or betweenness centrality ("the property of frequently lying along the shortest paths between pairs of nodes," Borgatti et al., 2009, p. 894). For example, Uysal and Yang (2013) found that a hyperlink network surrounding the non-governmental organizations (NGOs) of WikiLeaks was not cohesive, as it was characterized by some well-connected clusters among a small number of websites.

More recent work has begun to model the antecedents (Lai et al., 2017; Zhao & Oh, 2021), processes (Lai et al., 2019), and outcomes (Saffer et al., 2019) of a crisis network. For example, Saffer et al. (2019) found that NGOs' communicative network positions, including a "star" structure (e.g., brokerage) and a "village" structure (e.g., cliques), impacted the public engagement NGOs received during the global refugee crisis. Lai et al. (2017) examined a variety of interorganizational networks on Twitter and Facebook (e.g., mention network, comment network) before, during, and after a typhoon and found that organizations' positional centrality was stable on social media networks over time.

Directions

Several meaningful directions can be identified to help the community fully benefit from a social network perspective. First, researchers can better leverage the transformative capacity of a network perspective by examining multiple types of ties/relationships in a network (i.e., *multiplexity*; Shumate et al., 2013). According to Shumate and Contractor (2013), there are four types of communication networks based on relation types: affinity (e.g., brand communities, employees), flow (e.g., word of mouth, information dissemination), representational (the communication of the association between two entities to a third party, such as endorsement or hyperlinks), and semantic (shared meanings or used symbols, such as one's cognitive map).

Considering several types of relations simultaneously in one network allows scholars to ask new questions like how routine affinity ties in a brand community affect information ties among members during crises or how organizations' online networks interact with their offline affinity networks (e.g., Lai et al., 2019).

In addition, more theory-based efforts should be promoted to understand the formulation and dynamics of crisis networks, especially semantic networks. As most predictive analyses focused on flow and representational networks on social media networks, researchers should spend more efforts in the theorization of semantic networks (Shumate et al., 2013). It is also crucial to go beyond a single crisis or a single stage of crisis to understand more generalized patterns of interrelations across crises and the dynamics of relational and/or interactional ties in different crisis stages.

Computational Methods

With the rapid accumulation of digitally available data and the rising computation power and tools, a growing number of scholars are using computational methods for analyzing social behaviors. These scholars come from various established subfields of communication such as political communication, as well as emerging areas such as crisis informatics and computational social science. Emerging datasets of communication artifacts such as tweets, hyperlinks, reviews analyzed by enhanced automatic text analysis tools (e.g., topic modeling) or network analysis methods reveal new knowledge in the processes and structures of human communication.

Following Shah et al. (2015), computational methods to communication usually involve (1) large and complex datasets; (2) digital traces and other naturally occurring social data; (3) analyzing the data using algorithmic solutions; and (4) allowing the test and building of communication theories. I echo with several computational social scientists regarding the relationship between computational methods and the existing methods: computational methods complement rather than replace the existing quantitative and qualitative methods (e.g., Atteveldt & Peng, 2018; Shah et al., 2015). Namely, the improved and sharpened methodological toolbox enables scholars to explore new questions in innovative ways.

Like any existing method, computational methods have unique advantages and challenges. Naturally occurring data (e.g., tweets) provide measures of real behaviors in an unobtrusive manner, allowing more precise and unbiased measures of communicative behaviors, especially those with social desirability problems or ecological concerns (e.g., ask subjects to image how they behave in a crisis). During significant events such as crises, social media users' heated discussions usually generate abundant and rich data. The large-scale data are dynamic and tractable in nature, enabling the inquiry of longitudinal trends of crisis communication. Nevertheless, social media data are not representative of populations or even social media users, so the findings should always be generalized with caution (Freelon, 2008). Recently, several computational social scientists have recognized the issue of "privileged access" (Atteveldt & Peng, 2018, p. 85) of big data by a small group of researchers due to the cost and difficulty in data collection and management.

The surge of computational methods creates an unprecedented opportunity and challenge for social media and crisis communication researchers. Automated content analysis is among the most widely applied types of computational methods. Namely, sentiment analysis has been adopted to examine how publics respond to organizational use of social media platforms (e.g., Ji et al., 2019; Zhao et al., 2020). Semantic network analysis (Nerghes et al., 2015; van der Meer et al., 2014), topic modeling (Zhao et al., 2018b), and automated frame analysis (van der Meer, 2018) have also been used to understand how social actors construct and co-construct meanings during crises. Instead of covering a kaleidoscope of tools broadly, I focus on sentiment analysis for a more condensed discussion below.

Sentiment Analysis

Sentiment analysis measures the valence of tone in texts. The valence of a text can be positive, neutral, or negative. Sentiment analysis typically provides scores quantifying how positive/negative the texts are, which have been widely used in marketing for commercial interests (e.g., product reviews). Dictionary-based methods are among the most prevalent approaches to sentiment analysis (Soroka et al., 2015; van der Meer, 2016). A dictionary is a collection of words that define a specific category, and dictionary-based methods automatically measure the sentiments of texts based on the count of words in pre-determined categories for certain research purposes. Generic computerized text analysis tools, such as the Linguistic Inquiry and Word Count (LIWC; Pennebaker et al., 2007) program, can measure sentiments as well as many more psychologically meaningful categories. Specialized tools dedicated to more refined measurement of sentiments and discrete emotions, such as SentiStregnth (Thelwall et al., 2011), NRC (Mohammad & Turney, 2013), VADER (Hutto & Gilbert, 2014), are also emerging in the recent decade.

Several scholars have applied sentiment analysis to analyze social media text by organizations and/or publics. Zhao et al. (2020) used sentiment analysis to measure Twitter users' reactions to organizational crisis responses, namely situational and renewing responses, in different crises with varying responsibility attribution. W. Liu et al. (2020) examined how organizations' different levels of dialogic communication affected public engagement and positive sentiments during a natural disaster. Ji et al. (2019) also looked into how public engagement on Facebook was predicted by two dimensions of sentiments (i.e., valence and strength) in organizational posts.

Directions

As compared to human-based content analysis relying on intensive human coding for satisfactory intercoder reliability, dictionary-based sentiment analysis has perfect reproducibility, reliability, and high efficiency (Riff et al., 2019), yet at the cost of validity and accuracy. The dictionary creators, typically computer scientists and natural language processing scholars, usually validate the sentiment analysis methods by (1) using "ground truth" determined by the majority vote of multiple coders and (2) reporting accuracy of labeling/prediction using the public datasets in their community (Hutto & Gilbert, 2014). Thus, communication scholars should be careful in the direct application of existing dictionaries in new contexts and domains such as crises (e.g., van der Meer, 2016), due to a number of validity concerns (e.g., the connotation of a word in terms of valence may change based on the context). Crisis communication researchers can validate the output of sentiments analysis by comparing computer generated results with hand-coded results.

Further, supervised machine learning (e.g., transformer neural network) as an alternative approach to dictionary-based methods has demonstrated much satisfactory validity in predicting employees' use of tweets (van Zoonen & van der Meer, 2016) despite its high demand for human labor. Using a crowdsourcing approach, Wu et al. (2021) showed that sentiments and certain discrete emotions in the Flint water crisis can be classified with approximately 70% accuracy.

Conclusion

Several recommendations are made to help scholars and practitioners take full advantage of the emerging methods and gain more refined knowledge on crisis copreparedness, response, and recovery in the social media context. First, the burgeoning scholarly attention to the precision of measurement is a beneficial starting point. Scholars should continue the voyage by further testing new instruments with different subjects in different crisis settings to increase the generalizability, validity, and reproducibility of the instruments. Second, we need to be aware that the social network approach and computational methods enrich rather than invalidate the existing quantitative and qualitative methods. The addition of new methods empowers us to adopt a more holistic methodological approach by triangulating different empirical methods for more convincing results that inform the theory. Last, it is crucial to reflect on the resolution for the "privileged access" of large-scale data by a small group of scholars as it engenders problems of transparency, reproducibility, and ethics. The technological, ethical, and social challenges brought about by new data and methods can be alleviated by data sharing among scholars and interdisciplinary collaboration for complex data analysis. As argued by Atteveldt and Peng (2018), "an increased focus on sharing data and tools will also force us to be more rigorous in defining operationalizations and documenting the data and analysis process, furthering transparency and reproducibility of research" (p. 84).

References

Atteveldt, W., & Peng, T. (2018). When communication meets computation: Opportunities, challenges, and pitfalls in computational communication science. *Communication Methods and Measures, 12*, 81–92. https://doi.org/10.1080/19312458.2018.1458084

Austin, L., Liu, B. F., & Jin, Y. (2012). How audiences seek out crisis information: Exploring the social-mediated crisis communication model. *Journal of Applied Communication Research, 40*, 188–207. https://doi.org/10.1080/00909882.2012.654498

Borgatti, S. P., Mehra, A., Brass, D. J., & Labianca, G. (2009). Network analysis in the social sciences. *Science, 323*(5916), 892–895. https://doi.org/10.1126/science.1165821

Brown, K. A., & Ki, E. J. (2013). Developing a valid and reliable measure of organizational crisis responsibility. *Journalism & Mass Communication Quarterly, 90*(2), 363–384. https://doi.org/10.1177/1077699013482911

Cheng, Y., & Cameron, G. (2017). The status of social-mediated crisis communication (SMCC) research. In L. Austin, & Y. Jin (Eds.), *Social media and crisis communication* (pp. 21–37). Routledge.

Coombs, W. T. (2004). Impact of past crises on current crisis communication: Insights from situational crisis communication theory. *The Journal of Business Communication, 41*(3), 265–289. https://doi.org/10.1177/0021943604265607

Coombs, W. T. (2007). Protecting organization reputations during a crisis: The development and application of situational crisis communication theory. *Corporate Reputation Review, 10*(3), 163–176. https://doi.org/10.1057/palgrave.crr.1550049

Coombs, W. T. (2018). *Ongoing crisis communication: Planning, managing, and responding* (5th ed.). Sage Publications.

Doerfel, M. L., Lai, C. H., & Chewning, L.V. (2010). The evolutionary role of interorganizational communication: Modeling social capital in disaster contexts. *Human Communication Research, 36*(2), 125–162. https://doi.org/10.1111/j.1468-2958.2010.01371.x

Ford, J. L., Ford, J. S., Frei, S. S., Pilny, A., & Berkelaar, B. L. (2016). A network under stress: Using embeddedness to understand uncertainty management and resilience in campus emergencies. *Journal of Applied Communication Research, 44*(3), 316–335. https://doi.org/10.1080/00909882.2016.1192288

Frandsen, F., & Johansen, W. (2017). *Organizational crisis communication: A multivocal approach.* Sage.

Fraustino, J. D., & Liu, B. F. (2017). Toward more audience-oriented approaches to crisis communication and social media research. In L. Austin, & Y. Jin (Eds.), *Social media and crisis communication* (pp. 129–140). Routledge.

Freelon, D. (2008). Big data analysis. *The international encyclopedia of communication.* Wiley.

Fuller, R. P., Ulmer, R. R., McNatt, A., & Ruiz, J. B. (2019). Extending discourse of renewal to preparedness: Construct and scale development of readiness for renewal. *Management Communication Quarterly, 33*(2), 272–301. https://doi.org/10.1177/0893318919834333

Getchell, M. C., & Sellnow, T. L. (2016). A network analysis of official Twitter accounts during the West Virginia water crisis. *Computers in Human Behavior, 54*, 597–606. https://doi.org/10.1016/j.chb.2015.06.044

Hellsten, I., Jacobs, S., & Wonneberger, A. (2019). Active and passive stakeholders in issue arenas: A communication network approach to the bird flu debate on Twitter. *Public Relations Review, 45*(1), 35–48. https://doi.org/10.1016/j.pubrev.2018.12.009

Hutto, C. J., & Gilbert, E. (2014, May). VADER: A parsimonious rule-based model for sentiment analysis of social media text. *Presented at* Eighth International AAAI Conference on *Weblogs and Social Media.* Oxford.

Ji, Y. G., Chen, Z. F., Tao, W., & Li, Z. C. (2019). Functional and emotional traits of corporate social media message strategies: Behavioral insights from S&P 500 Facebook data. *Public Relations Review, 45*(1), 88–103. https://doi.org/10.1016/j.pubrev.2018.12.001

Jin, Y., Liu, B. F., Anagondahalli, D., & Austin, L. (2014). Scale development for measuring publics' emotions in organizational crises. *Public Relations Review, 40*(3), 509–518. https://doi.org/10.1016/j.pubrev.2014.04.007

Jin, Y., Pang, A., & Cameron, G. T. (2007). Integrated crisis mapping: Toward a publics-based, emotion-driven conceptualization in crisis communication. *Sphera Publica, 7*, 81–95. https://doi.org/10.1080/1062726X.2012.676747

Lai, C. H., She, B., & Tao, C. C. (2017). Connecting the dots: A longitudinal observation of relief organizations' representational networks on social media. *Computers in Human Behavior, 74*, 224–234. https://doi.org/10.1016/j.chb.2017.04.037

Lai, C. H., She, B., & Ye, X. (2019). Unpacking the network processes and outcomes of online and offline humanitarian collaboration. *Communication Research, 46*(1), 88–116. https://doi.org/10.1177/0093650215616862

Lee, Y., & Jin, Y. (2019). Crisis information seeking and sharing (CISS): Scale development for measuring publics' communicative behavior in social-mediated public health crises. *Journal of International Crisis and Risk Communication Research, 2*(1), 13–38. https://doi.org/10.30658/jicrcr.2.1.2

Liu, W., Xu, W. W., Tsai, J., & Y. J. (2020). Developing a multi-level organization-public dialogic communication framework to assess social media-mediated disaster communication and engagement outcomes. *Public Relations Review, 46*(4), 101949. https://doi.org/10.1016/j.pubrev.2020.101949

Mohammad, S. M. & Turney, P. D. (2013). Crowdsourcing a word–emotion association lexicon. *Computational Intelligence, 29*(3), 436–465. https://doi.org/10.1111/j.1467-8640.2012.00460.x

Nerghes, A., Lee, J. S., Groenewegen, P., & Hellsten, I. (2015). Mapping discursive dynamics of the financial crisis: A structural perspective of concept roles in semantic networks. *Computational Social Networks, 2*(1), 1–29. https://doi.org/10.1186/s40649-015-0021-8

O'Connor, A., & Shumate, M. (2018). A multidimensional network approach to strategic communication. *International Journal of Strategic Communication, 12*(4), 399–416. https://doi.org/10.1080/1553118X.2018.1452242

Pennebaker, J. W., Booth, R. J., & Francis, M. E. (2007). Linguistic inquiry and word count: LIWC [Computer software].

Podnar, K., Tuškej, U., & Golob, U. (2012). Mapping semantic meaning of corporate reputation in global economic crisis context: A Slovenian study. *Public Relations Review, 38*(5), 906–915. https://doi.org/10.1016/j.pubrev.2012.08.003

Raupp, J. (2019). Crisis communication in the rhetorical arena. *Public Relations Review, 45*(4), 101768. https://doi.org/10.1016/j.pubrev.2019.04.002

Riff, D., Lacy, S., Fico, F., & Watson, B. (2019). *Analyzing media messages: Using quantitative content analysis in research* (3rd ed.). Routledge.

Saffer, A. J., Yang, A., Morehouse, J., & Qu, Y. (2019). It takes a village: A social network approach to NGOs' international public engagement. *American Behavioral Scientist, 63*(12), 1708–1727. https://doi.org/10.1177/0002764219835265

Schultz, F., Kleinnijenhuis, J., Oegema, D., Utz, S., & van Atteveldt, W. (2012). Strategic framing in the BP crisis: A semantic network analysis of associative frames. *Public Relations Review, 38*(1), 97–107. https://doi.org/10.1016/j.pubrev.2011.08.003

Shah, D. V., Cappella, J. N., & Neuman, W. R. (2015). Big data, digital media, and computational social science: Possibilities and perils. *The Annals of the American Academy of Political and Social Science, 659*(1), 6–13. https://doi.org/10.1177/0002716215572084

Shumate, M., & Contractor, N. (2013). The emergence of multidimensional social networks. In L. L. Putnam & D. K. Mumby (Eds.), *The SAGE handbook of organizational communication* (3rd ed., pp. 449–474). Sage.

Shumate, M., Pilny, A., Atouba, Y. C., Kim, J., Pena-y-Lillo, M., Cooper, K. R., & Yang, Y. (2013). A taxonomy of communication networks. *Communication Yearbook, 37*, 95–123. https://doi.org/10.1080/23808985.2013.11679147

Soroka, S., Young, L., & Balmas, M. (2015). Bad news or mad news? Sentiment scoring of negativity, fear, and anger in news content. *The Annals of the American Academy of Political and Social Science, 659*(1), 108–121. https://doi.org/10.1177/0002716215569217

Thelwall, M., Buckley, K., Paltoglou, G., Cai, D., & Kappas, A. (2011). Sentiment in short strength detection informal text. *Journal of the American Society for Information Science and Technology, 61*(12), 2544–2558. https://doi.org/10.1002/asi.21475

Ulmer, R. R., Sellnow, T. L., & Seeger, M. W. (2019). *Effective crisis communication: Moving from crisis to opportunity* (4th ed.). Sage Publications.

Uysal, N., & Yang, A. (2013). The power of activist networks in the mass self-communication era: A triangulation study of the impact of WikiLeaks on the stock value of Bank of America. *Public Relations Review, 39*(5), 459–469. https://doi.org/10.1016/j.pubrev.2013.09.007

van der Meer, T. G. (2016). Automated content analysis and crisis communication research. *Public Relations Review, 42*(5), 952–961. https://doi.org/10.1016/j.pubrev.2016.09.001

van der Meer, T. G. (2018). Public frame building: The role of source usage in times of crisis. *Communication Research, 45*(6), 956–981. https://doi.org/10.1177/0093650216644027

van der Meer, T. G., Verhoeven, P., Beentjes, H., & Vliegenthart, R. (2014). When frames align: The interplay between PR, news media, and the public in times of crisis. *Public Relations Review, 40*(5), 751–761. https://doi.org/10.1016/j.pubrev.2014.07.008

van Zoonen, W., & van der Meer, T. G. (2016). Social media research: The application of supervised machine learning in organizational communication research. *Computers in Human Behavior, 63*, 132–141. https://doi.org/10.1016/j.chb.2016.05.028

Wasserman, S., & Faust, K. (1994). *Social network analysis: Methods and applications.* Cambridge University Press.

Weiner, B. (1985). An attributional theory of achievement motivation and emotion. *Psychological Review, 92*(4), 548–573.

Wu, J., Wong, C. W., Zhao, X., & Liu, X. (2021, July). Toward Effective Automated Content Analysis via Crowdsourcing. In *2021 IEEE International Conference on Multimedia and Expo (ICME)* (pp. 1–6). IEEE.

Xu, S. (2018). Discourse of renewal: Developing multiple-item measurement and analyzing effects on relationships. *Public Relations Review, 44*(1), 108–119. https://doi.org/10.1016/j.pubrev.2017.09.005

Yang, A., & Saffer, A. (2018). NGOs' advocacy in the 2015 refugee crisis: A study of agenda building in the digital age. *The American Behavioral Scientist, 62*(4), 421–439. https://doi.org/10.1177/0002764218759578

Yang, A., & Veil, S. R. (2017). Nationalism versus animal rights: A semantic network analysis of value advocacy in corporate crisis. *International Journal of Business Communication, 54*(4), 408–430. https://doi.org/10.1177/2329488415572781

Zhao, X., & Oh, H. J. (2021). What fosters interorganizational frame convergence: Examining a semantic network during the opioid crisis. *Public Relations Review, 47*(3). https://doi.org/10.1016/j.pubrev.2021.102042

Zhao, X., Zhan, M., & Liu, B. F. (2018a). Disentangling social media influence in crises: Testing a four-factor model of social media influence with large data. *Public Relations Review, 44*(4), 549–561. https://doi.org/10.1016/j.pubrev.2018.08.002

Zhao, X., Zhan, M., & Jie, C. (2018b). Examining multiplicity and dynamics of publics' crisis narratives with large-scale Twitter data. *Public Relations Review, 44*(4), 619–632. https://doi.org/10.1016/j.pubrev.2018.07.004

Zhao, X., Zhan, M., & Ma, L. (2020). How publics react to situational and renewing organizational responses across crises: Examining SCCT and DOR in social-mediated crises. *Public Relations Review, 46*(4), 1–10. https://doi.org/10.1016/j.pubrev.2020.101944

Zhou, Z., Ki, E., & Brown, K. A. (2019). A measure of perceived severity in organizational crises: A multidimensional scale development and validation. *Journal of International Crisis and Risk Communication Research, 2*(1), 39–60. https://doi.org/10.30658/jicrcr.2.1.3

INDEX

Note: Page numbers in *italics* represent figures; page numbers in **bold** represent tables.

athletes 320–321; and crisis communication decisions during COVID-19
318–325; NFL 321
Attribution Theory 123
audience engagement, dark social in:
Integrated Relationship Management
(IRM) Framework 196–197, *197*; new
consumer journey 197; online brand
community engagement 197; relationship marketing 194–196, *195*, **196**
augmented reality (AR) 186
Australian Christian Lobby (ACL) 261
authenticity: brand 106; consistency of
response 109–110; defined 106; of
emotions 110–111; evaluation of 107;
importance of 106–107; perceived 106,
218; role of 107; of source 108–109;
spontaneous communication 111–112
authentic talk 106
authorship, SMCC model 9–10, **10**
avatars 188
axial coding 305
Ayres, Yovana Mendoza 89–90
Aziz, Afdhel 73

baseball 314–316
Beckham, David 24, 25
Behavioral Crisis Communication
Theory 23
Benckiser, Reckitt 49
Benoit, William L. 21
Betts, Mookie 315
big data 181; operational efficiency 182;
risk management 182; use cases 182
BIGtoken 183
Black Lives Matter (BLM) movement
65–66, 214
blasting 333
Blue Alert 364–366
Boeing 737 Max jets, crashes of 53
bolstering 125
boundary spanner 60–61, 63–64
boycotts 213
brand advocacy 196, 197
brand advocates 88
brand authenticity 106
brands, SMI as 89–90
Brexit 307
Bush, George W. 361

California Consumer Privacy Act 183
Cambridge Analytica 183

case studies methods, relationship
marketing **198**, 198–200
Catholic Church: sexual abuse crisis
257–259
CEO (chief executive officer): personal
social media messages 108; role in deter-
mining organizations' purpose 81–82
#ChargeGate (Apple iPhone's 2018) 227,
231–235
chatbots 185, 187
Chauvin, Derek 65
Chavez, Cesar 213
Chenault, Ken 211
China: crises 14; Weibo 12–13
Christchurch earthquake (2011) 344
Christian and Missionary Alliance
(C&MA) 260
Cinnamon Toast Crunch's (CTC) sugary
shrimp tails 83
Citizens United (Lau) 211
Claeys, A. 2, 23
Clery Act (1990) 361, 366–367
Coca-Cola 182
Coexistence of Animal Rights on Earth
(CARE) 250–251
collateral damage cluster 122
Commitment-Trust Theory 194
Communications Decency Act, 1996 41
community emergency response team
(CERT) volunteer 162
completely false information 131
computational methods 391–392; sentiment analysis 392–393
confirmatory factor analysis (CFA)
149–150
consumer communication, on social
media platforms 37–39
consumer-organization interactions on
social media 36–37
consumer reviews 39–40
content analysis 8–9, **9**
content moderation 39–40
contextual modifiers 124
Contingency Theory of Strategic
Conflict Management 21–22
Coombs, W. Timothy 22, 23, 52
coping, in response to crisis 335
corporate ability (CA) crisis 50
corporate apology 53
corporate crises: employee positive megaphoning during 218; relationship quality
as foundation for appropriate ECBs 217

Printed in the United States
by Baker & Taylor Publisher Services